FRENCH

for

Oral and Written Review

FRENCH
for
Oral and Written Review

Charles Carlut   *Walter Meiden*

THE OHIO STATE UNIVERSITY

HOLT, RINEHART AND WINSTON
New York   Toronto   London

Preface

This text is designed to review all the common elements of French grammar, both orally and in written form. To that end it provides taped pattern practice, all-French exercises, and English-to-French translations on the various phases of the French language. Ways of expressing certain problem words are studied, and the verb is systematically reviewed. In addition, there are eight twentieth century texts edited for grammatical analysis.

The organization of the chapters

In general, each chapter deals with a specific grammatical topic. The chapters are divided into short sections, each one of which takes up a particular aspect of the subject. At the end of a certain number of sections treating related topics, there are short oral and written exercises which afford practice on the material of the preceding paragraphs. Finally, some three or four problem words are explained, and the chapter ends with a verb review.

This type of organization affords great flexibility: it allows teachers who so desire to assign a limited amount of grammar each day with reading from other texts; it permits those using the book in a pure grammar review course to adjust the number of sections and exercises to the needs of the class; topics can easily be omitted without disturbing the unity of the whole. For those wishing exercises which offer practice on all aspects of a grammatical topic, there are *exercices d'ensemble* at the end of most chapters.

Inductive presentation of grammar

To encourage students to arrive at grammatical generalizations inductively, each section is set up as follows:
  (1) question on grammatical point
  (2) examples to illustrate the point
  (3) answer to the question in form of a generalization

v

It is hoped that this presentation will induce the students to work out the answers to the questions by studying the examples given.

The Pattern Practice

Taped pattern practice exercises complete each group of written exercises except where the topic at hand does not lend itself to oral drill. In the text itself, the existence of these pattern practice exercises is indicated only by a model sentence illustrating the type of responses desired. The entire drill does not appear because of the desirability of having the student prepare the pattern practice orally in the language laboratory without seeing it in print. However, for the use of the teacher and for those classes whose instructor wishes the student to have the script of the taped material for home study, there is a *Pattern Practice Manual* which contains all the sentences which the student may hear in the laboratory. The pattern practice exercises may be handled in various ways, e.g.:

METHOD 1: The students do not see the printed form of the drills, but they listen to them in the language laboratory and then later go over them in the class hour.

METHOD 2: The students first prepare the exercises at home from the *Pattern Practice Manual*, next listen to and repeat them in the language laboratory, and finally practice them during the class hour.

METHOD 3 (where the school has no laboratory facilities): The students prepare the exercises at home from the *Pattern Practice Manual*, then in class they reproduce them orally without reference to the manual.

However the students prepare the pattern practice, it is suggested that a part of each recitation hour be devoted to the laboratory material and that the students be required to repeat the exercises without looking at the printed manual during the class hour. It is important for the teacher to insist on rapid and accurate responses, for in that case the students tend to prepare the lesson in such a way as to make such responses.

The Problem Words

Each chapter treats ways of expressing some three or four English words which habitually cause trouble because usages in the two languages are different. Although these words constitute a vocabulary rather than a syntactical problem, they would seem properly a part of a review of French, for the ability to express them correctly is at least as important in speaking and writing as a knowledge of points of grammar.

The words presented are among those most frequently misused by students in their compositions and French translations. No attempt has been made to give every possible way of expressing such words, but rather to focus the attention of the reader on the commonest difficulties inherent in them. Often there comes into consideration also the fact that the spoken and written language express such words in different ways.

The PROBLEM WORDS are presented at the end of each chapter and in alphabetical order partly so as to be easily available for reference and partly so that where it is found desirable, they may be studied independently of the grammar and could even be used as part of the subject-matter of a separate conversation or composition course.

The Texts

Eight texts from twentieth century French literature afford the students the opportunity to study French grammar as used by contemporary writers. These passages have been edited with comments and questions in order to guide the students in their study. Only a limited number of possible points of grammar are taken up in any one selection, since the authors desire to present different grammatical material in each text wherever possible.

If the detailed study of the texts is begun early in the course, many points of grammar not yet learned through work on the chapters will arise in the texts. But it is sometimes advantageous to meet a new grammatical phenomenon for the first time in a text. To introduce and discuss such a topic before the student has encountered it in his more organized study has the advantage of acquainting him with it in advance and of preparing him to understand it more fully when he meets it in the more formal discussion.

Naturally, instructors so desiring may use the "Textes" for purposes other than grammatical study. They lend themselves to conversation, to literary comment, to a study of style, etc.

Ways in which the book may be adjusted to fit the needs of different types of courses

Where the number of recitations in a course is limited, parts of the book may be omitted without affecting the study of the parts that are assigned, for each chapter is an independent unit. No chapter depends on what has been learned in any preceding chapter. There-fore, the chapters may be studied in any order, and any group of sec-tions which terminates in exercises based on them may be omitted without affecting the rest of the study.

For the shorter grammar course, the PROBLEM WORDS, the "Exer-cices d'ensemble" at the end of the chapters, Chapter 17 dealing with Problem Prepositions, and the "Textes" could be omitted at the dis-cretion of the instructor.

For the course where reading material is considered especially de-sirable, the "Textes" could be given an important role. They could be assigned at every second chapter, if the teacher wished to distribute them equally throughout the course.

For the course where an emphasis on the proper use of words is paramount, the core of the study could be built around the PROBLEM WORDS and, where necessary, certain grammatical sections might be omitted.

ACKNOWLEDGMENTS

We wish to thank the instructors who have taught this book in its mimeographed form and who have aided us with their suggestions as to how specific parts could be improved. We particularly appreciate the help of our colleagues at the Ohio State University, Professor Pierre Astier, Mr. Antoine Spacagna, Miss Nicole Boursier, Mrs. Ariane Foureman, Mrs. Nicole Meier, and Miss Marguerite Rocle.

We are most grateful to Miss Ethel La Velle, formerly of North High School, Columbus, and to Professor Jerry Bidwell of the Mans-field Campus of the Ohio State University for their reading of the proof and for their many helpful suggestions.

Charles Carlut
Walter Meiden

Table of Contents

FRENCH

for

Oral and Written Review

To the Student

Grammar is an organized study of the usages of the various aspects of a language. This study usually consists of a series of principles or rules.

A rule is simply a statement of usage in a generalized form.

To formulate a rule to govern any French grammatical construction, one looks for as many examples as possible of this construction in both written and spoken French, and, after carefully examining how the construction is expressed, one tells how it is expressed in generalized form.

In a small way, you should try to make your own rules by studying the examples of the constructions found in this book.

To that end, each section of a chapter begins with a question on some type of French construction. There follow examples of the construction. Study these examples carefully in light of the question which precedes them. From what you observe, try to derive a generalization which will answer the question and which will then constitute your own rule for that construction. To permit you to check the accuracy of your generalization, the answer to the question follows the examples. This answer is likewise in form of a generalization and constitutes a rule.

It is not necessary to learn these rules verbatim, but it is valuable to understand the principle at hand and to be able to state it accurately and clearly as a generalization.

Naturally, a knowledge of French grammar will not be of much use to you unless you can apply it in speaking and writing. For that reason, each grammatical unit is followed by oral and written exercises which will give you the opportunity to apply what you have learned in the unit. Practice the oral exercises and work out the written exercises as your teacher directs. If you have access to a

1

laboratory, listen carefully to the tapes and repeat with the indicated changes during the intervals of silence until you can say the pattern in question without hesitation. If you do not have a laboratory, go over the exercises in the *Pattern Practice Manual* again and again until you can say them rapidly and without hesitation.

But a knowledge of grammatical principles and the ability to apply them will not alone give you a mastery of French, even if you learn to say the patterns automatically. In addition, you must know how to use the common words of the language properly.

In English and French, there are a certain number of common words and ideas which are expressed in several ways in each language, but their usages do not correspond. Let us consider two examples:

EXAMPLE 1: The French word **temps**

Je n'ai pas beaucoup de **temps**.	*I don't have much* time.
Le **temps** est splendide aujourd'hui.	*The* weather *is marvelous today.*

In each sentence, we find the French word **temps**. But English expresses **temps** of the first sentence by *time*, of the second sentence by *weather*.

EXAMPLE 2: The English word *time*

Je n'ai pas beaucoup de **temps**.	*I don't have much* time.
Je vous ai appelé trois **fois**.	*I called you three* times.
Quelle **heure** est-il?	*What* time *is it?*
Que faites-vous en ce **moment**?	*What are you doing at this* time?
A cette **époque**-là, j'étais très jeune.	*At that* time *I was very young.*
Vous êtes-vous amusé à cette soirée?	Did you have a good time *at that party?*

In each sentence, English has used the same word — *time*. But French has used successively **temps, fois, heure, moment,** and **époque** to express the English word *time*, and in the last sentence it uses the verb **s'amuser** to convey the idea of *having a good time.*

It is very important to know when French uses one word and when another to express a given English word, for often the various French words that express the same English word cannot be interchanged. To teach you how to deal with such words, there is at the end of each lesson a group of some three or four "problem words". Through the examples, explanations, and exercises, familiarize yourself with all aspects of the words given.

A thorough knowledge of the forms of the most used tenses of regular and irregular verbs is essential if you wish to speak and write French correctly. For that reason, two verbs are reviewed at the end of each lesson. On pages 281–283 you are shown how you can organize your knowledge of the verb by deriving its tenses from the five principal parts.

CHAPTER 1

Interrogatives

I. Interrogative Adjectives

An interrogative adjective is one which modifies a noun and asks a question. In English the interrogative adjectives are *which* and *what*.

1. What are the French interrogative adjectives and how are they used before a noun?

Quel livre lisez vous? — Which *book are you reading?*
Quelles leçons préparent-ils? — Which *lessons are they preparing?*
Quel homme! **Quels** beaux enfants! — What *a man!* What *good-looking children!*

The interrogative adjectives are:

	MASCULINE	FEMININE
Singular	quel	quelle
Plural	quels	quelles

Interrogative adjectives precede their noun and its modifiers directly and agree with it in gender and number.

The interrogative **quel** is also used in an exclamation and is then the equivalent of the English *what . . . !* or *what a . . . !*

2. Under what circumstances is the interrogative *quel* used before some form of the verb *être*?

Quelle est la règle la plus difficile? — Which *is the most difficult rule?*
Quels sont ces hommes en noir? — Who *are these men in black?*

4

NOTE: It is also possible to say: «**Qui** sont ces hommes en noir?» But by using **Quels** the nature of the question is changed slightly to mean: *What sort of* . . .

The interrogative adjective is used before a form of the verb **être** to ask which of a number of possible answers is the case and to ask the nature of a person or thing.

A. *Remplacez les tirets par la forme convenable de l'adjectif interrogatif.*

1. _quelle_ est la vraie raison de votre départ? 2. Dans _quelle_ rue habitent vos amis? 3. _Quel_ est votre acteur préféré? 4. _Quels_ pays étrangers avez-vous visités? 5. _Quelles_ sont les plus belles villes des États-Unis? 6. _Quel_ professeur! 7. _Quelle_ heure est-il? 8. _Quelles_ sont les dernières nouvelles?

B. *Traduisez en français.*

1. What dress do you want to put on? 2. Which is the best pupil in[1] the class? 3. What are your favorite[2] songs? 4. What courses interest you the most? 5. What a car! 6. What is this girl's telephone number[3]? 7. What animal do you prefer, the dog or the cat?

---

[1] not **dans** [2] The normal position for descriptive adjectives in French is treated fully on pages 23–25. [3] **numéro de téléphone**

PATTERN PRACTICE: forms of **quel**

Pattern 1

YOU HEAR   Je regarde les photos de notre voyage en Europe.
YOU SAY   Quelles photos regardez-vous?

Pattern 2

YOU HEAR   Paris est la capitale de la France.
YOU SAY   Quelle est la capitale de la France?

II. Interrogative Pronouns

An interrogative pronoun is one that asks a question. In English, the interrogative pronouns are *who? whose? whom? which? what? which one?*

3. What interrogative pronoun is used in French to refer to persons?

Qui a ouvert la porte?	Who *opened the door?*
Qui avez-vous vu?	Whom *did you see?*
Avec **qui** êtes-vous sorti?	*With* whom *did you go out?*

In French, **qui** is the interrogative pronoun which refers to persons.

NOTE: For **qui** as the subject, the longer form **qui est-ce qui** may be used; for **qui** as the object, the longer form **qui est-ce que** may be used. But since the longer forms sometimes entail a change in word order, students are advised to use the shorter forms for the present.

4. When *qui* is the object of the sentence, what word order is used when the subject of the sentence is a pronoun? a noun?

Qui voyez-vous?	Whom *do you see?*
Qui Jacques voit-il?	Whom *does Jack see?*

When **qui** is the direct object of the sentence, note the word order:

Qui + VERB + PRONOUN SUBJECT
Qui + NOUN SUBJECT + VERB + PRONOUN SUBJECT

5. Which interrogative pronouns are used to refer to things in French?

Qu'est-ce qui est sur la table?	What *is on the table?*
Que faites-vous?	What *are you doing?*
Qu'est-ce que vous faites?	
Avec **quoi** avez-vous ouvert la boîte?	*With* what *did you open the box?*

The four French interrogative pronouns referring to things are **qu'est-ce qui**, **que**, **qu'est-ce que** and **quoi**. Their use depends on their function in the sentence.

6. When is *que* and when *qu'est-ce que* used as the object of the sentence to refer to a thing?

Que voyez-vous?	What *do you see?*
Qu'est-ce que vous voyez?	
Que fait Françoise?	What *does Frances do?*
Qu'est-ce que Françoise fait?	

When the direct object is a thing, either **que** or **qu'est-ce que** may be used, but notice the difference in word order:

Que + VERB + SUBJECT	and	**Qu'est-ce que** + SUBJECT + VERB

7. What are the various uses of the word *quoi*?

De **quoi** parlez-vous?	*Of* what *are you speaking?*
—Ah! je vois quelque chose.	*"Oh, I see something."*
—**Quoi?**	"What?"
Je ne sais pas **quoi** faire.	*I don't know* what *to do.*
Quoi! Vous partez?	What! *You're leaving?*

The word **quoi** is used to refer to a thing after a preposition, it is used when asking: "*What?*" alone, it is often used instead of **que** before an infinitive, especially in a negative sentence, and it is used to express the exclamatory *What!*

—Va chercher du vin.	*"Go and get some wine."*
—**Comment?**	"What?"

In English, when we do not hear or do not understand what someone has said, we normally ask: "*What?*" The French normally ask «**Comment?**» rather than «**Quoi?**» under such circumstances. However, «**Quoi?**» is often used by children who have not yet learned the amenities and by certain uneducated people.

8. How can the interrogative pronouns be presented in graphic tabular form?

FUNCTION	PERSONS	THINGS
SUBJECT	qui	qu'est-ce qui
OBJECT	qui	que qu'est-ce que
AFTER PREPOSITION	qui	quoi

C. *Remplacez le mot anglais par son équivalent français.*

1. (*Whom*) avez-vous vu en allant à la bibliothèque?   2. De (*what*) avez-vous parlé pendant mon absence?   3. A (*whom*) donc écrivez-vous, toutes ces lettres?   4. (*What*) doit-on faire dans ce cas? 5. (*What*) vous trouvez de si difficile dans ce devoir?   6. (*Who*) me montrera le chemin?   7. De (*whom*) est le roman que vous avez acheté?   8. (*What*) vous intéresse le plus dans ce livre?   9. (*What*) vous aimeriez faire maintenant?   10. (*What*) est sur votre bureau? 11. Je vais vous faire un petit cadeau. (*What?*)

D. *Traduisez en français.*

1. Who took my fountain pen?   2. There are no more vases. In what do you want me to put these flowers?   3. What makes you laugh? 4. What did you learn in[1] class today?   5. With whom are you going to the movies?   6. What are you going to write?   7. Whom did your friend meet in the station?   8. He seems[2] angry. What did you say to him?   9. Whom will Maurice and Marie see?   10. "I'd like to tell you something." "What?"   11. Who told you that it was a good film?   12. What! You're crying?

---

[1] **en**   [2] Use a form of **avoir l'air.**

PATTERN PRACTICE: **qui** used as the subject

Pattern 3

     YOU HEAR   Jeanne arrive demain.

     YOU SAY   Qui arrive demain?

PATTERN PRACTICE: **qui** used as the object

Pattern 4

     YOU HEAR   J'ai interrogé les élèves après la classe.

     YOU SAY   Qui avez-vous interrogé après la classe?

Pattern 5

     YOU HEAR   Les ouvriers attendent leur patron.

     YOU SAY   Qui les ouvriers attendent-ils?

PATTERN PRACTICE: **qu'est-ce qui**

Pattern 6

     YOU HEAR   Un livre est sur la table.

     YOU SAY   Qu'est-ce qui est sur la table?

PATTERN PRACTICE: **que** used as the object

Pattern 7

> YOU HEAR Marie fait son travail.
> YOU SAY Que fait Marie?

PATTERN PRACTICE: **qu'est-ce que** used as the object

Pattern 8

> YOU HEAR Sylvie a écrit un roman pendant ses vacances.
> YOU SAY Qu'est-ce que Sylvie a écrit pendant ses vacances?

9. When is a form of *lequel* used to ask *which one* in French? What are the forms of *lequel*?

J'ai trois stylos. **Lequel** voulez-vous?   *I have three fountain pens. Which one do you want?*

Laquelle de ces personnes parle français?   *Which one of these persons speaks French?*

The interrogative *which one*, referring to a definite object already mentioned or mentioned immediately after *which one of* is expressed by the following:

	MASCULINE	FEMININE
Singular	lequel	laquelle
Plural	lesquels	lesquelles

These pronouns contract with **à** and **de** forming: **auquel, auxquels, auxquelles; duquel, desquels, desquelles.**

10. When must *qui, que* or *qu'est-ce que* be used to express *which one*?

Que préférez-vous, le français ou l'italien?

Qu'est-ce que vous préférez, le français ou l'italien?

Which one do you prefer, French or Italian?

When asking a question about something which has not yet been mentioned, *which one* must be expressed by **qui . . . ?** (referring to persons), or **que . . . ?** or **qu'est-ce que . . . ?** (referring to things) except that *which one of* + THE OBJECT is expressed by a form of **lequel de** + THE OBJECT.

E. *Remplacez les tirets par la forme convenable de* **lequel.** *Faites les contractions nécessaires.*

1. ____ de vous deux veut bien me prêter sa voiture? 2.—Votre ami est très original. —Duquel parlez-vous? 3. —Voyez-vous ces deux dames? Lesquelles? 4. Laquelle de ses filles va épouser Henri? 5. Tous ces exercices sont bons, mais lesquels sont les plus utiles?

F. *Traduisez en français.*

1. These books are expensive, and I do not know which one to buy.
2. "I have many difficulties." "Which?" 3. Which of the two roads[1] must we take? 4. Which do you prefer, milk or wine? 5. I like Italian films a great deal.[2] Which ones do you prefer? 6. There are several programs. Which one do you wish to see?

_____
[1] **routes** [2] The adverb comes immediately after the verb.

PATTERN PRACTICE: forms of **lequel**

Pattern 9

YOU HEAR   Voici trois stylos. Je veux celui-ci.
YOU SAY   Voici trois stylos. Lequel voulez-vous?

11. When does French use a variation of *quel est* **. . . to express** *what is* **. . . or** *what are* **. . .?**

Quelle est la capitale de la Bel-   What is *the capital of Belgium?*
gique?
Quels sont les produits les plus   What are *the most important products*
importants de ce pays?   *of that country?*

When *what is* . . . or *what are* . . . ask 'which of a number of possibilities,' French uses **quel est** . . . or some variation of it.

12. How does French express *what is* **. . . or** *what are* **. . . when asking a definition?**

Qu'est-ce que la philosophie?   What is *philosophy?*
Qu'est-ce que c'est que le com-   What is *communism?*
munisme?
Qu'est-ce que c'est que les mathé-   What are *mathematics?*
matiques?

When *what is* . . . or *what are* . . . ask for a definition of a word, French uses either **qu'est-ce que** . . . or **qu'est-ce que c'est que** . . . with that word.

G. *Remplacez les tirets par l'équivalent de* what is *ou* what are *selon le cas.*

1. ____ un héros? 2. ____ les présidents des États-Unis les plus connus? 3. ____ la biologie? 4. ____ votre fleur favorite? 5. ____ le meilleur système de gouvernement?

H. *Traduisez en français.*

1. What is the longest river in[1] the United States? 2. What is the Louvre? 3. What are the qualities of a good teacher? 4. What is democracy? 5. What is the aim of your work?

---
[1] Not dans

PATTERN PRACTICE: asking for a definition with **Qu'est-ce que . . .?**

Pattern 10

YOU HEAR le capitalisme
YOU SAY Qu'est-ce que le capitalisme?

PATTERN PRACTICE: asking for a definition with **Qu'est-ce que c'est que . . .?**

Pattern 11

YOU HEAR le capitalisme
YOU SAY Qu'est-ce que c'est que le capitalisme?

EXERCICES D'ENSEMBLE

I. *Remplacez les mots anglais par leur équivalent français.*

1. (*Which*) jeune fille Jacques veut-il épouser? 2. (*Who*) est là? 3. (*Which one*) aimez-vous le mieux, votre oncle ou votre tante? 4. (*What*) nous ferons cet après-midi? 5. Chez (*whom*) passerez-vous le week-end? 6. (*What*) l'empêche de venir? 7. (*What*) dites-vous? 8. (*What*) sont les fruits les plus nourrissants? 9. Avec (*whom*) allez-vous jouer au bridge? 10. (*Who*) est ce monsieur à la barbe blanche? 11. (*What is*) un mythe? 12. (*What*) vous me donnerez en échange? 13. (*What*) regardez-vous? 14. Avec (*what*) a-t-il fait cette réparation? 15. (*Whom*) êtes-vous allé voir? 16. Nous ne savons pas (*what*) faire.

J. *Traduisez en français.*

1. "What is the smallest state in[1] the United States?" "What?"[2]
2. What are you going to do now?   3. What is astrology?   4. Who
has just gone out?   5. To whom shall we give this gift?   6. Which
are the most useful languages?   7. What sort of films do you like to
see?   8. Whom did the policeman arrest?   9. What are you speaking of?   10. What makes you believe that?   11. Who is the author
of this play?   12. What did your friends do last evening?   13. What
is making that noise?   14. To whom did Mary lend her necklace?
15. "What can you say about your trip?" "Which one?"   16. What!
Paul isn't here?

---

[1] Not **dans**   [2] This "What?" indicates that the second speaker did not understand the
question.

Problem Words

1. actually

(**a**) When *actually* = *really*

Avez-vous **réellement** vu l'accident? ⎫
Avez-vous **vraiment** vu l'accident? ⎬ *Did you* actually *see the accident?*

When *actually* means *really*, it may be expressed by **vraiment,
véritablement,** or **réellement,** depending on the sentence.

(**b**) When *actually* = *as a matter of fact*

Il caresse vos chats, mais **en fait** ⎫
   il ne les aime pas beaucoup.   ⎪   *He pets your cats, but* actually *he*
Il caresse vos chats, mais **à vrai dire,** ⎬ *doesn't like them very much.*
   il ne les aime pas beaucoup.   ⎭

When *actually* means *as a matter of fact* and contradicts what seems
to be the case, it may be expressed by **en fait** or **à vrai dire.**

CAUTION: DO NOT use «actuellement» for *actually*. It means *at present.*

2. advice

(**a**) How to say *a piece of advice*

Donnez-moi **un conseil.**   *Give me* a piece of advice.

The singular **un conseil** means *some advice* or *a piece of advice.*

(b) How to say *advice*

J'ai toujours écouté **les conseils** de   *I always listened to* the advice *of my*
  mon vieux maître.   *old teacher.*

The word *advice* is expressed by the plural form, **les conseils**.

CAUTION: The French word **avis** means *opinion*. Do NOT use it for
advice.

3. again

(a) The prefix **re-** + VERB = *again*

Voulez-vous **relire** cette phrase?   *Will you* read *that sentence* again?
Je te **retéléphonerai** tout de suite.   *I'll* telephone *you* again *right away.*

If it is possible to express *again* by **re** + VERB, French often prefers
this method to any other.

(b) **encore, encore une fois, de nouveau** and **à nouveau** = *again*

Mon avocat m'a parlé **de nouveau**   *My lawyer talked to me on that matter*
  à ce sujet.   *again.*
Écoutons **encore** ce disque.   *Let's listen to that record* again.
Faites cela **encore une fois**.   *Do that* again.

In affirmative sentences, *again* is expressed by **encore, encore une
fois, de nouveau** and occasionally by **à nouveau**.

(c) In negative sentences **ne . . . plus** = *again*

Je **ne** le ferai **plus**.   *I will* not *do it* again.

In negative sentences, *not . . . again* is often expressed by **ne . . .
plus,** but it may also be expressed by **ne . . . re-** + VERB.

4. agree

(a) When *agree to* = *consent to*

Monsieur Pommier **a consenti à** ⎫
  venir parler devant notre groupe. ⎪ *Mr. Pommier* has agreed to *come and*
Monsieur Pommier **a accepté de** ⎬   *speak to our group.*
  venir parler devant notre groupe. ⎭

When *agree to* means *consent to*, it may be expressed by **consentir à**
or by **accepter de**.

(b) When *agree = be in agreement*

Ma femme et moi **sommes d'accord**   *My wife and I* agree *on the bringing-up*
sur l'éducation de nos enfants.   *of our children.*

When *agree* means *be in agreement*, it may be expressed by **être
d'accord.**

(c) When *agreed = OK*

—Voulez-vous venir à six heures?   *"Do you want to come at six o'clock?"*
—**C'est entendu.**   "Agreed."

The English *agreed*, indicating assent, may be rendered by: **c'est
entendu** or by: **entendu,** or: **d'accord.**

(d) When *agree* is a grammatical term

L'adjectif **s'accorde** avec le nom   *The adjective* agrees *with the noun it*
qu'il modifie.   *modifies.*

Grammatical agreement is expressed by forms of the verb **s'accorder.**

CAUTION: Do NOT use «agréer» for *agree*. French use **agréer** only
in special situations, and it normally means *accept*.

K. *Remplacez les mots anglais par leur équivalent français.*

1. Jacques est (*again*) en retard.   2. Est-ce que le participe passé
(*agrees*) avec le sujet?   3. Vos (*advice*) sont toujours très utiles.   4. Il
paraît que Marcel est (*actually*) très malade.   5. Le patron (*agreed
to*) vous voir ce soir après cinq heures.   6. Je vous répète (*again*) que
vous regretterez cette action.   7. (*Actually*), j'aimerais mieux ne pas
aller voir cet opéra.   8. (*Advice*) ne servent à rien à la plupart des
gens.   9. Il faut (*begin the lesson again*).   10. —Voulez-vous venir me
chercher à midi? —(*Agreed*).   11. Je (*agree*) avec vous sur la politique actuelle.

L. *Traduisez en français. Attention aux mots en italique.*

1. Copy that letter *again*.   2. He *agreed* to write a letter of recommendation for me.   3. Do you want me to give you a piece of good
advice?   4. John says he works hard, but *actually* he wastes a great
deal of time.   5. You should follow my *advice*.   6. Jack told me that

he would not smoke *again*. 7. We all *agree* that you must leave immediately. 8. Did you *actually* go to the movies yesterday evening? 9. Tell me *again* what you want. 10. Does the present participle *agree* with the noun it modifies? 11. I heard that noise *again* last night. 12. You don't see them? Look *again*.

Verb Review

Review the verbs **parler** and **finir** according to the outline on page 283.

CHAPTER 2

Adjectives

An adjective is a word that modifies a noun or pronoun. Ex.: the *green* house; the *tall* tree; the *interesting* letter. The house is *green*. The trees were *tall*. The letter will be *interesting*.

I. The Formation of Adjectives

In English, adjectives have one form only. In French, they usually have four forms: masculine singular, feminine singular, masculine plural, feminine plural.

PLURAL OF ADJECTIVES

1. How do most French adjectives form their masculine plural?

petit   petits

Most French adjectives form their masculine plural by adding **-s** to the masculine singular.

2. What about the masculine plural of adjectives whose masculine singular ends in -s, -x or -z?

gris   gris
heureux   heureux

Adjectives whose masculine singular ends in **-s, -x** or **-z** do not change in the plural.

3. What about the masculine plural of adjectives whose masculine singular ends in -eau?

nouveau   nouveaux

Adjectives whose masculine singular ends in **-eau** add **-x** to form the masculine plural.

16

4. What about the masculine plural of adjectives whose masculine singular ends in *-al?*

national   nationaux

Most adjectives whose masculine singular ends in **-al** change the **-al** to **-aux** in the masculine plural.

5. How is the feminine plural of adjectives formed?

petite	petites
grise	grises
nouvelle	nouvelles
nationale	nationales

Feminine adjectives normally form their plural by adding **-s** to the feminine singular form.

A. *Écrivez le pluriel de l'adjectif indiqué.*

1. des chats (gris)   2. de (nouveau) livres   3. de (grand) événe-ments   4. des enfants très (gentil)   5. deux (gros) garçons   6. des docteurs (distingué)   7. de (riche) touristes   8. de (mauvais) livres   9. des hôtels (élégant)   10. de (vieux) amis   11. des amis (loyal)   12. de (beau) musées

FEMININE OF ADJECTIVES

English adjectives have no feminine form. French adjectives have a special feminine form. The forms of the examples that follow are given in this order:

masculine singular; feminine singular;
masculine plural; feminine plural.

6. How do most adjectives form their feminine singular and plural?

| petit | petite | petits | petites |
| fermé | fermée | fermés | fermées |

Most adjectives form their feminine singular by adding **-e** to the masculine singular form.

7. What about adjectives whose masculine form ends in unaccented -e?

| difficile | difficile | difficiles | difficiles |

Adjectives whose masculine form ends in unaccented **-e** do not change in the feminine.

8. What about certain adjectives whose masculine form ends in -e-+ consonant?

premier	première	premiers	premières
étranger	étrangère	étrangers	étrangères
complet	complète	complets	complètes

Certain adjectives whose masculine form ends in **-e-** + CONSONANT place a grave accent (ˋ) over this **-e-** as well as adding the regular **-e** to form the feminine.

9. What about adjectives whose masculine form ends in -f?

| actif | active | actifs | actives |
| neuf | neuve | neufs | neuves |

Adjectives whose masculine form ends in **-f** change the **-f** to **-ve** in the feminine.

10. What about adjectives whose masculine form ends in -x?

| nombreux | nombreuse | nombreux | nombreuses |
| heureux | heureuse | heureux | heureuses |

Adjectives whose masculine form ends in **-x** change the **-x** to **-se** in the feminine.

11. What about adjectives whose masculine form ends in -el, -eil, -ien, -as, and -os?

quel	quelle	quels	quelles
pareil	pareille	pareils	pareilles
ancien	ancienne	anciens	anciennes
bas	basse	bas	basses
gros	grosse	gros	grosses

Adjectives whose masculine form ends in **-el, -eil, -ien, -as** and **-os** double the final consonant before adding **-e**.

12. What are the irregular feminine forms of the adjectives blanc, bon, doux, épais, faux, frais, gentil, grec, long, public, and sec?

blanc	blanche	blancs	blanches	white
bon	bonne	bons	bonnes	good
doux	douce	doux	douces	soft, sweet
épais	épaisse	épais	épaisses	thick
faux	fausse	faux	fausses	false
frais	fraîche	frais	fraîches	fresh
gentil	gentille	gentils	gentilles	nice
grec	grecque	grecs	grecques	Greek
long	longue	longs	longues	long
public	publique	publics	publiques	public
sec	sèche	secs	sèches	dry

B. *Écrivez la forme féminine de l'adjectif indiqué.*

1. une leçon (difficile) 2. des femmes (actif) 3. la semaine (dernier) 4. deux robes (pareil) 5. une (long) histoire 6. les familles (nombreux) 7. des souliers (usé) 8. la maison (blanc) 9. des chansons (italien) 10. les populations (natif) 11. des années (heureux) 12. une armoire (massif) 13. une nuit (frais) 14. des jeunes filles (sérieux)

PATTERN PRACTICE: the feminine of adjectives

Pattern 1

YOU HEAR   Le bureau est grand. Et la lampe?
YOU SAY   La lampe est grande aussi.

13. What are the masculine and feminine singular and plural forms of the adjectives beau, fou, mou, nouveau and vieux, and when is the second masculine form used?

| MASCULINE | | Singular | | Plural | | |
(before consonant)	(before vowel)	FEMININE	MASCULINE	FEMININE		
beau	bel	belle	beaux	belles	beautiful
fou	fol	folle	fous	folles	foolish
mou	mol	molle	mous	molles	soft
nouveau	nouvel	nouvelle	nouveaux	nouvelles	new
vieux	vieil	vieille	vieux	vieilles	old

Some adjectives have two masculine singular forms, one of which is used when the word it directly precedes begins with a consonant, the other when the word it directly precedes begins with a vowel or a mute **h**. In the plural, they have only one form for the masculine and one for the feminine.

C. *Écrivez la forme convenable de l'adjectif indiqué.*

1. de (vieux) rues   2. la (nouveau) mode   3. un très (beau) homme
4. le (nouveau) an   5. une vitesse (fou)   6. une personne un peu
(mou)   7. de (vieux) souvenirs   8. les (beau) quartiers   9. un
(vieux) oncle   10. de (vieux) dames   11. un (beau) arbre

PATTERN PRACTICE: **beau, nouveau** and **vieux**

Pattern 2

> YOU HEAR   J'ai visité une ville.
> YOU SAY   J'ai visité une belle ville.

Pattern 3

> YOU HEAR   J'ai acheté un costume.
> YOU SAY   J'ai acheté un nouveau costume.

Pattern 4

> YOU HEAR   Nous avons vu cette ville.
> YOU SAY   Nous avons vu cette vieille ville.

II. Comparison of Adjectives

In English, adjectives are compared with *more* or *less* (comparative degree) and *most* and *least* (superlative degree) if they have more than two syllables.

POSITIVE	COMPARATIVE	SUPERLATIVE
beautiful	*more* beautiful	*most* beautiful
interesting	*less* interesting	*least* interesting

French adjectives are compared in somewhat the same way.

14. How are French adjectives compared?

POSITIVE	COMPARATIVE	SUPERLATIVE
cher	**plus** cher	**le plus** cher
difficile	**moins** difficile	**le moins** difficile

The comparative form of the French adjective is formed by placing **plus** (*more*) or **moins** (*less*) before the positive form. The superlative form is reached by placing the definite article (**le, la, les**) before the comparative form.

15. How are the adjectives *bon*, *mauvais*, and *petit* compared?

POSITIVE	COMPARATIVE	SUPERLATIVE
bon	meilleur	le meilleur
mauvais	{ plus mauvais { pire	{ le plus mauvais { le pire
petit	{ plus petit { moindre	{ le plus petit { le moindre

The adjective **bon** is always compared irregularly, the adjectives **mauvais** and **petit** have a regular and irregular comparative form. The form **moindre** is ordinarily used in the superlative and means *slightest*.

16. How is *than* expressed in French?

> Les hivers sont plus froids **que** les étés.

After a comparative, *than* is expressed by **que**.

BUT

> Nous avons **plus de vingt** pages à lire.
> Vous avez **moins de dix** minutes pour y arriver.

After **plus** and **moins** before a numeral *than* is expressed by **de**.

17. When the superlative form of an adjective follows its noun, what is the sign of the superlative?

> Le russe est la langue **la plus difficile** à apprendre.

When the superlative form of an adjective follows its noun, the definite article must always directly precede **plus** or **moins**.

18. What preposition regularly follows the French superlative?

La France et la Russie sont les pays les plus grands **d**'Europe. *France and Russia are the largest countries in Europe.*

Quel est le meilleur élève **de** la classe? *Who is the best pupil in the class?*

In English, the superlative is usually followed by *in*. But in French, **de** is regularly used after the superlative.

19. How is the *as* **. . .** *as* **comparative expressed in French?**

Jacques est **aussi** consciencieux **que**   *Jacques is* as *conscientious* as *Paul.*
Paul.

Le français n'est **pas aussi** difficile   *French is* not as *hard* as *Latin.*
que le latin.

The comparison with *as* . . . *as* is called the comparative of equality. In French this comparative is formed with **aussi . . . que**. In present day French, the negative is expressed by **pas aussi . . . que**.

D. *Remplacez les adjectifs indiqués entre parenthèses par le comparatif ou le superlatif de l'adjectif, selon le cas.*

1. Robert est l'élève (vif) de la classe. 2. Est-ce que les hommes sont (curieux) que les femmes? 3. La campagne de Normandie est (vert) que celle de Provence. 4. L'étoile du Berger est (brillant) des étoiles. 5. Les automobiles françaises sont (petit) que les américaines. 6. Quels sont les livres (intéressants) de votre bibliothèque? 7. Prenez ce fauteuil. Il est (confortable) que celui-là. 8. Je trouve les poires (savoureux) que les pommes. 9. Mon chien est mon (bon) ami. 10. Le tennis est bien (fatigant) que le ping-pong. 11. Les (beau) années sont souvent celles de la jeunesse. 12. Il travaille plus et pourtant ses résultats sont (mauvais) que l'année dernière.

E. *Remplacez les mots anglais par leur équivalent français.*

1. Voici les meilleurs élèves (*in*) la classe. 2. Il habite la plus belle maison (*in*) la ville. 3. Je vais vous montrer le timbre le plus rare (*in*) ma collection. 4. Nous avons moins (*than*) cent dollars pour faire le voyage. 5. Qui est plus occupé (*than*) le président? 6. Ce chien est (*as*) méchant (*as*) un loup. 7. Les routes sont (*as*) bonnes en France (*as*) en Angleterre. 8. Les prix des repas ne sont pas (*as*) élevés en Espagne (*as*) en Italie.

F. *Traduisez en français.*

1. What is the largest city in Canada? 2. He refuses to read even the most interesting books. 3. I have never more than five dollars with[1] me. 4. Le Mont Blanc is the highest mountain in Europe. 5. He has nothing, but he is as happy as a king. 6. His closest friends do not understand his attitude. 7. A conversation[2] class is too large if there are more than twelve students. 8. Bridge requires

---

[1] sur   [2] **classe de conversation**

more attention than poker.   9. It is easier to preach than to put into practice what one preaches.   10. I waited for you more than half an hour.   11. Motorcycles are more dangerous than cars.   12. The richest people have not all gone to the university.   13. He allows[3] himself to be stopped by the slightest difficulty.   14. The poorest[4] man in the world can be as able as the richest.

---

[3] Use a form of **se laisser arrêter.**   [4] Place after noun.

PATTERN PRACTICE: various aspects of the comparison of adjectives

Pattern 5

YOU HEAR   L'anglais est facile. Et l'histoire?

YOU SAY   L'histoire est plus facile que l'anglais.

Pattern 6

YOU HEAR   Shakespeare est un grand écrivain de la littérature anglaise.

YOU SAY   Shakespeare est le plus grand écrivain de la littérature anglaise.

Pattern 7

YOU HEAR   Madame Aubert a vingt chapeaux.

YOU SAY   Madame Aubert a plus de vingt chapeaux.

Pattern 8

YOU HEAR   Ce fauteuil est confortable. Et cette chaise?

YOU SAY   Cette chaise est aussi confortable que ce fauteuil.

III. Position of Adjectives

In English, adjectives precede their nouns. Ex.: *bad* weather, *disagreeable* work.

20. What is the normal position of a descriptive adjective in French?

Il m'a fait une proposition **intéressante.**
C'est une maison **blanche.**
Quelles sont les couleurs du drapeau **français?**
Voulez-vous du pain **grillé?**

In French, descriptive adjectives normally follow their nouns. They distinguish the object under consideration from others of its kind. Adjectives of color, nationality, religion, and past participles almost always follow their noun.

21. Why are descriptive adjectives sometimes placed before their noun?

Il a été victime d'un **terrible** accident.
M. Garet est un **excellent** professeur.
Chenonceaux est un **magnifique château** de la Renaissance.
Elle oubliait la **triste soirée** de la veille.

Many descriptive adjectives may precede their noun for stylistic effect. In such cases, the adjective, which usually indicates a quality inherent in the noun, adorns its noun rather than distinguishing it from other objects of its kind.

22. When is a descriptive adjective placed before and when after its noun?

une **porte étroite**	une **mer profonde**
une **étroite amitié**	un **profond sentiment**
une **boisson amère**	un **chat maigre**
un **amer reproche**	un **maigre salaire**

Certain adjectives are sometimes placed before and sometimes after their noun. They have a literal meaning when they follow their noun and take on a figurative meaning when they precede the noun.

23. What is the meaning of the following adjectives when they precede and when they follow their noun?

MEANING WHEN PRECEDING NOUN	ADJECTIVE	MEANING WHEN FOLLOWING NOUN
former	**ancien**	*old, ancient*
fine, good (referring to a person)	**brave**	*brave* (but usually the word **courageux** is used instead)
certain (*one of many*)	**certain**	*certain* (*sure*)
dear, beloved	**cher**	*dear, expensive*
last (*of a series*)	**dernier**	*last* (used with time element to indicate the one just passed)
different, various	**différent**	*different* (*unlike*)
same	**même**	*very*
many different kinds	**nombreux**	*many of the same kind*
poor (*unfortunate*)	**pauvre**	*poor* (*not rich*) (ordinarily used with **très**)
next (*in a series*)	**prochain**	*next* (used with time element to indicate one about to come)
own	**propre**	*clean*
darned, confounded	**sacré**	*sacred*

ugly, bad	**sale**	*dirty*
only	**seul**	*alone*
mere	**simple**	*simple in character*
real	**vrai**	*true*

24. What is the position of limiting adjectives in French?

deux leçons	**ces** journaux	**son** père
quelles difficultés	**plusieurs** personnes	**quelques** amis

Numerals, both cardinal and ordinal, and demonstrative, interrogative, possessive and indefinite adjectives regularly precede their noun. These are called LIMITING ADJECTIVES, for they limit the meaning of the noun.

25. What about the position of the short, common descriptive adjectives?

une **autre** femme	un **beau** rêve	une **bonne** solution
une **grande** ville	un **jeune** enfant	une **jolie** maison
une **longue** histoire	un **mauvais** tour	une **petite** bouche

A number of commonly used short adjectives regularly precede their noun. The most common of these are: **autre, bon, gentil, grand, gros, haut, jeune, joli, long, mauvais, méchant, meilleur, moindre, nouveau, petit, vieux,** and **vilain.**

G. *Mettez l'adjectif à la position convenable, en faisant l'accord de l'adjectif.*

1. (rouge) une fleur   2. (inestimable) des trésors   3. (difficile) une leçon   4. (mauvais) une route   5. (anglican) l'église   6. (gentil) un garçon   7. (social) les conflits   8. (bruyant) une salle   9. (insupportable) des enfants   10. (noir) le drapeau   11. (usé) des souliers   12. (profond) un puits   13. (absolu) un monarque   14. (réussi) un spectacle   15. (vert) des volets   16. (secondaire) les écoles   17. (indien) des étoffes

H. *Traduisez en français. Faites attention à l'accord et à la position de l'adjectif.*

1. Send him some[1] flowers.   2. There was[2] a TERRIBLE[3] accident.   3. There are American soldiers in every country in[4] the world.

---

[1] Use a form of **quelque**.   [2] Use the compound past.   [3] Adjectives used to adorn their nouns for stylistic effect, as described in §21, are capitalized in this exercise.

4. There is a real hero. 5. There are still certain difficulties. 6. We want a free country. 7. Those fine people don't have any luck. 8. It was a somber story. 9. High[5] mountains separate those two countries. 10. You always make the same mistakes. 11. There is a slight difference between those two words. 12. Take a course with that EXCELLENT[3] professor. 13. He has a bad cold. 14. A hostile crowd was in[6] the square. 15. I like illustrated magazines. 16. Have you seen those ELEGANT[3] models? 17. Numerous foreigners study here. 18. I should like a good warm meal. 19. That book made a deep impression on the students. 20. Next week you will write your last résumé.

---

[4] *in the* = **du**   [5] Use a form of **haut**.   [6] **sur**

PATTERN PRACTICE: the position of adjectives

Pattern 9

> YOU HEAR   Cet homme est intelligent.
> YOU SAY   C'est un homme intelligent.

EXERCICE D'ENSEMBLE

I. *Traduisez en français. Attention aux adjectifs.*

1. I should like to thank you for your MARVELOUS[1] gift. 2. I find her much prettier than her sister. 3. Will you finish your studies next month? 4. I do not know how he can live in this ugly[2] room. 5. Have you noticed the deep-seated uneasiness which exists[3] in this country? 6. The most expensive products are not always the best. 7. The young people were exchanging tender smiles and ardent glances. 8. You sent me some beautiful carnations. 9. This INTER-ESTING[1] hypothesis has been condemned by experience. 10. Public opinion favors that change. 11. We made the trip more than ten years ago. 12. Certain[4] pupils do not work enough. 13. I like your nice apartment. 14. I am your HUMBLE[1] servant. 15. The Italians are one of the most musical peoples in the world. 16. They are richer than we, but are they happier? 17. Tomorrow we will discuss this GRAVE affair. 18. Do you write to your former teacher from time to time? 19. My examinations are harder than yours. 20. They served us a meager meal.

---

[1] Consider adjectives which are capitalized as being used to adorn their noun for stylistic effect.   [2] Use a form of **vilain**.   [3] Use a form of **régner**.   [4] Do not use the partitive or any substitute for it here.

Problem Words

5. become

(a) When *become* is followed by a NOUN

Jacques **est devenu** <u>officier</u>.   *Jack* became an <u>officer</u>.

The verb *become* is **devenir,** and when a noun follows *become,* the French usually employ a form of **devenir.**

(b) When *become* is followed by an ADJECTIVE

Ne **vous fâchez** pas si je vous dis cela.	*Don't* become angry *if I tell you that.*
Le patron **s'est impatienté** en vous attendant.	*The boss* became impatient *while waiting for you.*

French often uses the reflexive form of a verb where English uses *become* + ADJECTIVE.

(c) How to express *became* in certain idiomatic expressions

Tout à coup **il a fait** très **chaud.**	*Suddenly it* became *very* warm.
Vers onze heures **j'ai eu** très **sommeil.**	*About eleven o'clock* I became *very* sleepy.

The English *became* + ADJECTIVE is often expressed in French by using the simple past or the compound past of the verb. This is especially true in the case of idiomatic expressions with **avoir** and **faire.**

CAUTION: Avoid using **devenir** + ADJECTIVE. To express *become* + ADJECTIVE, French occasionally does use **devenir** + ADJECTIVE, but far more often it uses a reflexive verb or a past tense of **avoir** or **être.**

6. better

(a) When *better* is an adjective

Je cherche une **meilleure** solution.   *I am looking for a* better *solution.*

As an adjective, *better* is normally expressed by **meilleur.**

Ces peintures sont **mieux** que les *These paintings are* better *than the* autres. *others.*

However, when the adjective *better* is used after a form of **être,** French sometimes uses **mieux.** In such cases, a form of **meilleur** could also be used.

(**b**) When *better* is an adverb

Jacques lit **mieux** que Jean.   *Jack reads* better *than John.*

The adverb *better* is expressed by **mieux.**

(**c**) How to say *much better*

Le livre est **bien meilleur** que le ⎫
film.   ⎬ *The book is* much better *than the film.*
Le livre est **beaucoup mieux** que le ⎭
film.

After forms of **être,** *much better* may be expressed by **bien meilleur, bien mieux** or **beaucoup mieux.** But the French do not say «beaucoup meilleur».

Cet élève comprend ⎰ **bien**   *This pupil understands algebra* much
                   ⎱ **beaucoup**   better *now.*
mieux l'algèbre maintenant.

As an adverb, *much better* is either **beaucoup mieux** or **bien mieux.**

CAUTION: When expressing *better* in French, determine whether it is used as an adjective or an adverb. Do NOT use «meilleur» as an adverb.

CAUTION: Do NOT use «beaucoup meilleur» for *much better.* This combination does not exist in French.

7. bring

(**a**) How to say *bring a thing*

Apportez-moi ce livre.   *Bring me that book.*

When it is a question of *bringing a thing*, French usually employs a form of **apporter.**

(**b**) How to say *bring a person*

Est-ce que je pourrais **amener** mon   *Could I* bring *my husband?*
   mari?

   When it is a question of *bringing a person*, a form of **amener** is used.
But **amener** is also used for taking a person somewhere.

   CAUTION: Do NOT use «apporter» when it is a question of bringing
a *person*.

8. can

(**a**) When *can* = *be able*

Vous ne **pouvez** pas porter cela tout   *You* can*not carry that all alone. Let me*
   seul. Laissez-moi vous aider.   *help you.*

   The English *can* (= *be able*) is ordinarily expressed by **pouvoir.**

(**b**) When *can* = *may*

Vous **pouvez** partir si vous voulez.   *You* $\left\{ \begin{array}{l} can \\ may \end{array} \right.$ *leave if you wish.*

   Careful speakers of English distinguish between *can* and *may*. In
French, the verb **pouvoir** is used for both ideas.

(**c**) When to use **je peux** and when **je puis**

Je peux vous accompagner demain.   I can *go with you tomorrow.*
Puis-je vous voir à huit heures?   Can I *see you at eight o'clock?*

   The **je** form of the present tense of **pouvoir** is both **peux** and **puis.**
In non-interrogative sentences **je peux** is normally used. When an
interrogative sentence has inverted word order, **puis-je** is used, but
this form is mainly literary.

(**d**) When *can* = *know how to*

Est-ce que Thérèse **sait** conduire?   Can *Theresa drive?*

   When *can* = *know how to*, French often uses a form of **savoir** rather
than of **pouvoir.**

J. *Remplacez les mots anglais par leur équivalent français.*

1. Il a fallu à Georges plusieurs années d'études pour (*become*) pharmacien.   2. N'hésitez pas à (*bring*) votre frère; nous serons très heureux de faire sa connaissance.   3. La représentation des *Femmes savantes* était bien, mais celle du *Misanthrope* était (*better*).   4. Les programmes du dimanche sont (*much better*) que ceux de la semaine. 5. (*Can*) -vous me dire l'heure?   6. Quand la lumière s'est éteinte, tout le monde (*became frightened*[1]).   7. Les résultats de cet étudiant sont (*better*) ce trimestre.   8. Finis tes études avant de te marier, ce serait (*much better*).   9. (*Can*) -on traverser l'Atlantique en moins de six heures?   10. Prenez plutôt cette route; elle est (*better*) que l'autre. 11. On (*becomes tired*) à faire toujours la même chose.   12. Claude nous (*brings*) toujours des chocolats quand il vient nous voir. 13. François a beaucoup souffert ces derniers jours, mais maintenant il se sent (*better*).   14. Les repas dans ce petit bistrot sont (*much better*) que dans les autres restaurants du quartier.

---

[1] Use a form of **avoir peur**.

K. *Traduisez en français. Attention aux mots en italique.*

1. The climate of the Riviera would be *much better* for you.   2. *Could* you explain this problem to me?   3. Henry *became* interested in that writer after hearing your lecture.   4. If these stamps interest you, I'll *bring* you my collection next week.   5. The day was warm, but it *became* cold as soon as the sun set. 6. *Can* your fiancée play the piano? 7. It is in Paris that you will find the *best* perfumes.   8. Mr. Borel *became* one of the directors of the company[1].   9. *Can* I *bring* my friend André to the next meeting of our club?   10. Pierrette finally *brought* us the snapshots of her family.   11. *Bring* me what you have just written.   12. *Can* you speak French fluently?

---

[1] **société**

Verb Review

Review the verbs **dormir** and **perdre** according to the outline on page 283.

CHAPTER 3

Adverbs

An adverb is a word that modifies a verb, an adjective or another adverb. Ex.: He writes *clearly*. They have a *very* difficult lesson. He speaks *somewhat* slowly.

I. Formation of Adverbs

1. How are adverbs usually formed from adjectives?

rapide	rapide**ment**	sérieux	sérieuse**ment**
vrai	vrai**ment**	naturel	naturelle**ment**

In French, adverbs are usually formed by adding **-ment** to the masculine form of adjectives ending in a vowel and to the feminine form of adjectives ending in a consonant.

NOTE: A certain number of adverbs have an **-é-** before **-ment**. The most common of these are: **aveuglément, commodément, conformément, énormément, obscurément, précisément, profondément.**

To the adjective **gentil** corresponds the adverb **gentiment**, to **bref** the adverb **brièvement**. The adjective **bon** has not only the very common adverb **bien** (meaning *well*) but also **bonnement** (*simply*).

A certain number of adjectives do not have a corresponding adverbial form. Such adjectives may be used adverbially in a phrase. For instance, **charmant** and **amusant** have no adverbial form. But one can say: Elle a agi **d'une façon charmante**. Il a parlé **d'une façon amusante**.

2. How are adverbs formed from adjectives ending in -*ant* and -*ent*?

suffisant	suffis**amment**	récent	réc**emment**

Adjectives in **-ant** and **-ent** usually have adverbial forms in **-amment** and **-emment**. These suffixes are both pronounced [amã].

But the adjective **lent** has the corresponding adverb **lentement**.

31

3. Which adjectives have irregular adverbial forms?

| bon | **bien** | meilleur | **mieux** | petit | **peu** |
| vite | **vite** | | | mauvais | **mal** |

A. *Écrivez les adverbes qui correspondent aux adjectifs suivants.*

1. clair   2. heureux   3. rare   4. évident   5. faux   6. constant
7. discrètement 8. patient   9. profond   10. ardent   11. bruyant
12. mauvais   13. triste   14. bon   15. sage   16. savant 17. tendre
18. violent   19. élégant

PATTERN PRACTICE: formation of adverbs

Pattern 1

YOU HEAR   Il est poli. Il répond . . .
YOU SAY   Il est poli. Il répond poliment.

II. Position of Adverbs

4. What is the usual position of the adverb in a sentence with a simple verb?

Jean sait **aussi** le français.   *John* also *knows French.*

The adverb usually follows a simple verb directly.

5. What is the position of most common adverbs in sentences with compound tenses?

Nous avons **beaucoup** travaillé.   *We worked* a great deal.
Il a **bien** compris la phrase.   *He understood the sentence* well.
Vous n'avez pas **encore** remis votre devoir.   *You have not* yet *handed in your exercise.*

In sentences with compound tenses, most common adverbs not ending in **-ment** are placed between the auxiliary verb and the past participle and after **pas**. But sometimes the position of these adverbs is changed because the speaker wishes to stress a certain word. Also, see §7.

6. Where are adverbs in *-ment* placed?

Nous avons soulevé ce poids **facilement.**	*We lifted this weight* easily.
Il a **complètement** oublié mon nom.	*He* completely *forgot my name.*
Vous avez **probablement** envoyé cette lettre.	*You* probably *sent this letter.*
Nous avons marché **lentement** jusqu'à la poste.	*We walked* slowly *up to the post office.*

Some adverbs in **-ment** come between the auxiliary verb and the past participle, some follow the past participle directly and some follow the noun object of the sentence. The length of the adverb in **-ment** does not determine its position in sentences with compound tenses.

7. What is the position of adverbs of place and time?

Jean est venu me voir **hier.**	*John came to see me* yesterday.
Aujourd'hui, nous avons parlé avec votre mère.	Today *we spoke with your mother.*
M. Dupont est arrivé **ici** après un long voyage.	*Mr. Dupont arrived* here *after a long trip.*

The adverbs of time and place **aujourd'hui, hier, demain, autrefois, tôt, tard, ici, là, ailleurs** and **partout** never come between the auxiliary verb and the past participle. They normally follow the past participle, but not always directly. The adverbs of time **aujourd'hui, hier, demain,** and **autrefois** often begin the sentence.

8. When a sentence begins with *peut-être, aussi* (therefore), or *à peine,* what word order follows?

Peut-être est-il déjà parti. **Peut-être** qu'il est déjà parti. }	Perhaps *he has already left.*
Aussi a-t-il perdu ses amis.	Therefore *he lost his friends.*
A peine est-il parti que les autres ont commencé à parler.	Scarcely *did he leave when the others began to speak.*

After **peut-être** and **à peine** when placed at the beginning of the sentence, the subject and the verb are inverted. After **peut-être** this construction is normally found only in written literary style. In conversational French, the usual word order is **peut-être que** + sub-

JECT + VERB. When **aussi** has the meaning of *therefore*, it must come first in its clause, and it is usually followed by inverted word order. For that reason, **aussi** meaning *also* must NEVER come first in a sentence.

B. *Introduisez les adverbes indiqués pour qu'ils modifient le verbe en italique.*

MODEL: (vite) Il *a fermé* la porte. **Il a vite fermé la porte.**

1. (trop) Il *travaille;* il se rendra malade.   2. (toujours) Le vice *est* puni et la vertu aussi.   3. (attentivement) *Avez*-vous *lu* cette page? 4. (immédiatement) Pourquoi *est*-il *parti* après la conférence? 5. (peut-être) Vous *devriez* voir un docteur.   6. (déjà) Il *a raconté* cette histoire aux enfants.   7. (ardemment) Elle l'*a aimé* dans sa jeunesse.   8. (continuellement) Le pauvre *se plaint* de ses douleurs. 9. (à peine) Je dois m'en aller; j'*ai* le temps de manger.   10. (lentement) Ils *se sont promenés* le long de la rivière.   11. (demain) Je vous *enverrai* la lettre.   12. (tôt) Marie *est arrivée* à la maison.   13. (enfin) Il *s'est arrêté* de parler.

C. *Traduisez en français.*

1. He would have liked to see me at[1] length tomorrow.   2. You received him well at your house.   3. Have you read a good book recently?   5. I often wonder what John was writing.   4. What did you do yesterday?   6. He spoke brilliantly.   7. You have scarcely arrived and you already wish to leave.   8. It rained so much[2] that I could not come.   9. Man always seeks happiness.   10. So he often finds what he wants.   11. We haven't received any[3] news from him; perhaps he is dead.

---

[1] **longuement**   [2] **tellement**   [3] any news from him = **de ses nouvelles**

PATTERN PRACTICE: the position of adverbs

Pattern 2

YOU HEAR   Nous comprenons le professeur. (bien)
YOU SAY   Nous comprenons bien le professeur.

Pattern 3

YOU HEAR   Ce matin j'ai travaillé. (beaucoup)
YOU SAY   Ce matin j'ai beaucoup travaillé.

III. Negative Adverbs

9. What is the normal position of the *ne . . . pas* **in an affirmative sentence with a simple verb?**

Je **ne** parle **pas** allemand.   Ce jeune homme **ne** me salue **pas.**
Il **ne** me donnera **pas** ce livre.   Paul **ne** le lui montrera **pas.**

The word order is:

$$\text{SUBJECT}^* + \textbf{ne} + \substack{\text{PRONOUN} \\ \text{OBJECT}^{**}} + \text{VERB} + \textbf{pas}$$

10. What is the position of *ne . . . pas* **in interrogative sentences with a simple verb?**

Ne parle-t-il **pas** allemand?   Paul **ne** le lui montrera-t-il **pas?**
Ne me donnera-t-il **pas** ce livre?   Ce jeune homme **ne** vous salue-t-il **pas?**

In sentences with a pronoun-subject, negative interrogative order is:

$$\textbf{Ne} + \substack{\text{PRONOUN} \\ \text{OBJECT}^{**}} + \text{VERB} + \substack{\text{PRONOUN} \\ \text{SUBJECT}} + \textbf{pas} + \text{following words}$$

In questions with a noun-subject, negative interrogative word order is:

$$\substack{\text{NOUN} \\ \text{SUBJECT}^*} + \textbf{ne} + \substack{\text{PRONOUN} \\ \text{OBJECT}^{**}} + \text{VERB} + \substack{\text{PRONOUN} \\ \text{SUBJECT}} + \textbf{pas} + \text{following words}$$

---

* that is, the subject with all its modifiers
** The pronoun-object comes here if there is one. Many sentences do not have a pronoun-object.

11. What is the position of *ne . . . pas* in sentences with compound verbs?

Je **n'**ai **pas** parlé allemand.   **N'**avez-vous **pas** parlé allemand?
Il **ne** m'a **pas** donné ce livre.   Paul **ne** le lui a-t-il **pas** montré?

In sentences with verbs in compound tenses, the auxiliary verb only is regarded as the verb as far as the position of negative words is concerned. In other words, the word order in §§9–10 is followed, but **pas** comes directly after the auxiliary verb.

D. *Écrivez les phrases suivantes au négatif.*

1. Je partirai avant son retour.   2. Il lui a donné beaucoup d'argent. 3. Êtes-vous allé en Europe l'année dernière?   4. Pourquoi venez-vous me voir?   5. Je suis sûr que tout s'arrangera.   6. Il a cru ce que vous avez dit.   7. Se décidera-t-il à venir?   8. Les questions de grammaire m'intéressent.   9. Aimeriez-vous faire une promenade avec Lucie?

E. *Traduisez en français.*

1. This news[1] did not surprise me a great deal.   2. Isn't it difficult to learn Russian?   3. He doesn't go to[2] Florida[3] every winter.   4. These events do not worry me.   5. Didn't this painter make your portrait? 6. He didn't continue his work.   7. Doesn't the Rhone[3] cross Lyons[3]? 8. Didn't you buy that car last year?   9. Didn't Denis get up at six o'clock?

---

[1] Use the singular to indicate *piece of news*.   [2] **en**   [3] The French spelling is slightly different.

PATTERN PRACTICE: the position of **pas** in compound tenses

Pattern 4

> YOU HEAR   Avez-vous vu le film?
> YOU SAY   Non, je n'ai pas vu le film.

12. What other negative combinations are there?

ne . . . aucun	*no, not any*		ne . . . plus	*no longer, no more*
ne . . . guère	*scarcely*		ne . . . point	*not at all*
ne . . . jamais	*never*		ne . . . que	*only*
ne . . . ni . . . ni	*neither . . . nor*		ne . . . rien	*nothing*
ne . . . personne	*no one*			

In addition to **ne . . . pas** these are the negative combinations often used in French.

13. What word order is used with these combinations?

Je **ne** le vois **jamais**.   N'avez-vous **jamais** visité la Suisse?
Il **ne** vient **plus** ici.   Paul n'a-t-il **jamais** vu son oncle?

In all negative sentences, **ne** comes exactly where it would if used with **pas**. (See §§9–11)

The negatives **guère, jamais, plus,** and **point** follow the same rules for position as **pas**. (See §§9–11)

In sentences with simple tenses, **personne** and **rien** come where they would in the corresponding English sentence.

Je n'ai vu **personne**.   Il n'a **rien** compris.

In compound tenses, **personne** follows the past participle, whereas **rien** comes between the auxiliary and the past participle.

Il n'a vu **que** trois élèves.   Nous n'avons écrit **que** dix pages.

The **que** of the **ne . . . que** combination follows the entire verb.

Aucun étudiant **ne** travaille.   Nous n'avons trouvé **aucune** trace
                                                    de lui.

The negative **aucun** is an adjective and comes directly before its noun.

Nous n'avons trouvé **ni** livres **ni** papier.

The negative adverbs **ni . . . ni,** precede their noun immediately. If these nouns are indefinite, they follow **ni . . . ni** without any article. (See page 177, §9)

14. When negative words are used in a sentence without a verb, what happens to *ne*?

—Qui a-t-il trouvé?   —Quand le ferez-vous?
—**Personne**.   —**Jamais**.

—Puis-je boire du café,   —Combien de fautes avez-vous trou-
docteur?   vées?
—Non, **plus** de café.   —**Aucune**.

When negative words are used in a sentence without a verb, the **ne** disappears.

F. *Traduisez en français.*

1. I like the movies very much, but I no longer have the time to[1] go there.   2. He has neither money nor friends.   3. Who knocked at the door? No one.   4. In any case, I didn't hear anything.   5. I know no one who can[2] do what you ask.   6. No gift gave[3] me so much pleasure.   7. He asked me for some stamps, but I didn't have any at all.   8. When will I be able to see[4] you again? Never.   9. She saw no one in the corridor.   10. I looked for[5] a long time, but I found nothing.   11. No one has ever done anything for him.   12. There are only twelve pupils in the class.   13. Neither you nor I know[6] anything about it[7].   14. We read only half of the book last week.

---

[1] **d'**   [2] The subjunctive is required. See p. 150, §10.   [3] Use a form of **faire**.   [4] Use a form of **revoir**. Whenever possible, French expresses *again* by using the prefix **re-** + the verb.   [5] Included in the verb.   [6] This verb must be in the first person plural.   [7] **en**

PATTERN PRACTICE: negative combinations

Pattern 5

| YOU HEAR | Est-ce que Marie est allée en France? |
| YOU SAY | Non, Marie n'est jamais allée en France. |

Pattern 6

| YOU HEAR | Qui parle anglais en classe? |
| YOU SAY | Personne ne parle anglais en classe. |

Pattern 7

| YOU HEAR | Qui avez-vous cherché cet après-midi? |
| YOU SAY | Je n'ai cherché personne cet après-midi. |

Pattern 8

| YOU HEAR | J'ai trouvé votre stylo. |
| YOU SAY | Je n'ai rien trouvé. |

Problem Words

9. change

(a) How to say *a change*

| Avez-vous remarqué **un change-ment** en entrant? | *Did you notice* a change *when you came in?* |

Ces dernières années il y a eu de | *In these last few years there have been*
grands **changements** dans le | *great* changes *in the world.*
monde.

The ordinary French word for *change* is **le changement.**

CAUTION: Do NOT use «le change» for *change.* The French **le change**
is used for financial transactions, in expressions such as **le cours du**
change (*the rate of exchange*), **l'office des changes** (*office dealing with*
foreign exchange), **agent de change** (*stock broker*), etc.

(**b**) How to say *small change*

Je n'aime pas avoir toute cette **mon-** | *I don't like to have all this* change *in*
naie dans ma poche. | *my pocket.*

When *change* = *small change*, French uses **la monnaie.**

(**c**) How to say that *something changes*

Cécile **a** beaucoup **changé** depuis | *Cecilia* has changed *a great deal since*
l'année dernière. | *last year.*

The English *to change* is expressed by **changer.**

(**d**) When **changer** has a direct object

J'ai **changé mes projets de voyage** | *I* changed my travel plans *the last*
au dernier moment. | *minute.*

The verb **changer** + OBJECT means *to alter something.*

(**e**) When **changer de** is used

Tous les combien **change-t-on de** | *How often do they* change towels *in this*
serviettes dans cet hôtel? | *hotel?*

The expression **changer de quelque chose** means *to replace things*
of the same kind.

(**f**) When **se changer** is used

Vous êtes tout mouillé; allez vite | *You're all wet; quick, go and* change
vous changer. | your clothes.

The reflexive **se changer** = *change one's clothes.*

(g) When to use **échanger**

Je voudrais **échanger** ma moto contre une voiture. *I'd like* to exchange *my motorcycle for a car.*

The verb **échanger** means *exchange*, and *to exchange one thing for another* is **échanger une chose contre une autre.**

10. character

(a) How to say a *character* (in a literary work)

Combien de **personnages** y a-t-il dans cette pièce? *How many* characters *are there in that play?*

A *character* in a literary work is **un personnage.**

(b) How to speak of *a person's character*

Georges est intelligent, mais je n'aime pas beaucoup son **caractère.** *George is intelligent, but I don't care much for his* character.

One's personal attributes or one's *character* is **le caractère.**

CAUTION: Do NOT use «le caractère» to indicate *a character* in a novel or a play.

11. day (morning, evening)

(a) The ordinary way of saying *day*

Nous avons passé trois **jours** à Rome. *We spent three* days *in Rome.*

The common word for *day* is **jour,** for *morning* is **matin,** for *evening* is **soir.**

(b) When the **-ée** forms are used

Toute la **journée** nous avons visité des églises et des musées. *The whole* day *we visited churches and museums.*

But **la journée** is used to indicate *day* when the speaker wishes to emphasize the duration of the time during the day and what happened during that time. The same distinction applies to **la matinée** and **la soirée,** but **la soirée** has the additional meaning of *evening gathering* or *evening party.*

(c) When **tous les jours** and when **toute la journée** is used

Note the following:

toute la journée = *the whole day*	**tous les jours** = *every day*
toute la matinée = *the whole morning*	**tous les matins** = *every morning*
toute la soirée = *the whole evening*	**tous les soirs** = *every evening*

G. *Remplacez les mots anglais par leur équivalent français.*

1. Pierre a cessé de fumer, mais cela influe sur son (*character*). 2. Il faut comprendre que les gens (*change*). 3. J'ai peu dormi cette nuit et j'ai eu sommeil (*the whole day*). 4. Avec quelques (*changes*), notre salle de séjour serait beaucoup mieux. 5. Pour réussir, une pièce ne doit pas avoir trop de (*characters*). 6. C'est ennuyeux de (*change clothes*) juste pour leur dire bonjour et au revoir. 7. En hiver il fait sombre à six heures (*in*[1] *the evening*). 8. Il serait bon de (*exchange*) nos vues sur la question. 9. J'ai toujours (*change*) sur moi quand je prends l'autobus. 10. J'ai passé (*the whole evening*) à rédiger cette composition. 11. Suzanne a la manie de tout (*change*) au dernier moment. 12. Jean a si mauvais (*character*) qu'on ne peut rien lui dire sans qu'il se fâche. 13. La traversée en bateau a duré cinq (*days*). 14. Qu'est-ce qui a pu (*change*) Paul comme cela? 15. A midi je prends mon repas au restaurant, (*in*[2] *the evening*) je dîne chez moi. 16. Va (*change*) souliers si tu veux aller à la pêche. 17. Roland organise (*an evening party*) la semaine prochaine.

---

[1] How is *in* expressed after the time of day? See pages 242–243.   [2] How is *in* expressed with units of time? See pages 242–243.

H. *Traduisez en français. Attention aux mots en italique.*

1. I spoke of it to Daniel two *days* ago. 2. That author had to make many *changes* in his book in order to have[1] it published. 3. At Christmas everyone *exchanges* gifts. 4. Who are the main *characters* in[2] *The Cid?* 5. Where did you spend the *day?* 6. Do you have any *change* to buy a newspaper? 7. Which *characters* of Molière have become

---

[1] le faire publier   [2] *in the* = du

most famous?   8. The Carrels[3] will come to play bridge tomorrow *evening*.   9. Mrs. Clair has *changed* chauffeurs[4] again.   10. How can a person *change* in that way?   11. I must *change clothes* in order to go out this *evening*.

---

[3] In French, proper names do not take an -s in the plural.   [4] Use the singular form.

Verb Review

Review the verbs **recevoir** and **avoir** according to the outline on page 283.

CHAPTER 4

Personal Pronouns

A pronoun is a word that takes the place of a noun. The subject pronouns are: *I, you, he, she, it, we,* the object pronouns are: *me, you, him,* etc.

I. Object Pronouns and Their Uses

1. What are the direct object pronouns?

Jean **me** voit.
Jacques **la** vend.
Je l'achète.

Louise **nous** appelle.
Mes amis **vous** connaissent.
Nous **les** trouverons.

The direct object pronouns are:

me	*me*		**nous**	*us*
te	*you*		**vous**	*you*
le	*him, it*		**les**	*them*
la	*her, it*			

NOTE: When the forms **me, te, se, le** or **la** precede a verb beginning with a vowel or a mute **h**, they elide, becoming **m', t', s',** or **l'**.

2. What are the indirect object pronouns?

Gilbert **me** montre sa voiture.
Anne **lui** explique la leçon.
Jacques **te** parlera demain.

Brigitte **nous** téléphonera.
Gérard **vous** indiquera la route.
Vous **leur** obéirez.

The indirect object pronouns are:

me	*to me*		**nous**	*to us*
te	*to you*		**vous**	*to you*
lui	*to him* / *to her*		**leur**	*to them*

The reflexive pronoun **se** may be either a direct or indirect object and means: (*to*) *himself, herself, itself, themselves, oneself.* As a reciprocal pronoun **se** means (*to*) *each other.*

A. *Remplacez les tirets par le pronom qui convient au sens.*

1. Qu'est-ce que Paul vous a fait? Cessez de ____ tourmenter.
2. Quand il arrivera, dites ____ de venir ____ voir. 3. Jean est heureux que vous ____ ayez promis ce voyage. 4. Entrez donc, je suis seul et vous ne ____ dérangez pas. 5. Regardez bien ces gens, car vous ne ____ reverrez plus. 6. Ils sont partis avant que j'aie pu ____ parler. 7. J'aurais voulu ____ demander où ils allaient.

B. *Traduisez en français.*

1. Do you like spring? Yes, I prefer it to the other seasons. 2. The boys have arrived. I will ask them if they know my cousins and if they saw them on the way. 3. We'll tell them to write him at once. 4. I will give you that magazine.

PATTERN PRACTICE: single pronoun objects

Pattern 1

> YOU HEAR Est-ce que Robert lit le livre?
> YOU SAY Oui, il le lit.

Pattern 2

> YOU HEAR Jacques écrira à Roger.
> YOU SAY Jacques écrira à Roger et il nous écrira aussi.

Pattern 3

> YOU HEAR Est-ce que vous parlerez à Jacques?
> YOU SAY Oui, je lui parlerai.

Pattern 4

> YOU HEAR Avez-vous mis le livre sur le bureau?
> YOU SAY Oui, je l'ai mis sur le bureau.

Pattern 5

> YOU HEAR Est-ce que vous me voyez?
> YOU SAY Oui, je vous vois.

3. When is *y* used as the place pronoun *there*, and when is the adverb *là* used?

> —Allez-vous à Paris? —J'**y** vais demain.
> —Je vais en classe. —**Y** serez-vous à neuf heures?
> —Où est Georges? —Il est **là,** derrière vous.

The pronoun **y** is used to express *there* when the place has been previously mentioned. The adverb **là** points out, usually when the place has not been previously mentioned.

4. When is en used as a pronoun object instead of le, la and les?

Il voit **sa sœur** souvent.   *He sees* his sister *often.*
Il **la** voit souvent.   *He sees* her *often.*

Il achète **des fleurs** dans la rue.   *He buys some* flowers *in the street.*
Il **en** achète dans la rue.   *He buys* some *in the street.*

Il a trouvé **trois amis** au café.   *He found* three friends *in the café.*
Il **en** a trouvé trois au café.   *He found three* of them *in the café.*

The pronoun **en** replaces a noun object when that object is indefinite in nature. A noun object is indefinite when it is modified by a partitive construction, by a numeral, by adverbs of quantity, etc.

For practical purposes, one can say that **en** is used whenever in the English sentence the pronoun object is rendered by *some* or by *of them*.

C. *Remplacez les tirets par* **le, la, les ə, y** *ou* **en,** *selon le cas.*

1. —Comment trouvez-vous sa maison? —Je ____ trouve superbe.
2. —Voyez-vous des taxis dans la rue? —Oui, nous ____ voyons.
3. —Combien d'enfants ont-ils? —Ils ____ ont cinq. 4. —Il est parti pour Bordeaux. —Qu'est-ce qu'il va ____ faire? 5. —Combien de courses avez-vous à faire? —Nous ____ avons beaucoup.
6. —Avez-vous un but dans la vie? —Oui, je ____ ai plusieurs.
7. —Vous me dites que vous allez en France. ____ allez-vous bientôt? 8. —Connaissez-vous cette femme? —Oui, et je ____ plains.

D. *Traduisez en français.*

1. I have many friends and I see them every week. 2. I should like to spend a few days in the country. Do you want to go there with me? 3. Do you want some tea? Yes, I'll take some. 4. When will he arrive in Paris? He has already arrived there. 5. How many brothers do you have? I have two[1]. 6. Are there many students in that class? Yes, there are many[2]. 7. The telephone book is there, under the desk.

---

[1] In French, one must say *two of them*.   [2] In French, one must say *many of them*.

PATTERN PRACTICE: **y, en** and **le, la, les.**

Pattern 6

     YOU HEAR   Allez-vous en classe?
     YOU SAY   Oui, j'y vais.

Pattern 7

YOU HEAR Est-ce que Robert a beaucoup d'argent?
YOU SAY Oui, il en a beaucoup.

Pattern 8

YOU HEAR Est-ce que Suzanne a trouvé ses affaires?
YOU SAY Oui, elle les a trouvées.

Pattern 9

YOU HEAR Est-ce que vous avez trouvé des amis?
YOU SAY Oui, j'en ai trouvé.

II. Position of Object Pronouns

5. Where do object pronouns come in relation to the verb?

Je **le** donne à Jean.   Je ne **la** vois pas.   Donnez-**le** à Marc.
Il **en** a trouvé.   Ne **me le** dites pas.   Allez-**y.**

Pronoun objects come immediately before the verb except in the affirmative imperative, in which case they follow the verb and are appended to it by a hyphen.

6. Where do object pronouns come when the sentence contains an auxiliary verb followed by an infinitive?

Jacques veut **vous** voir.   Qui peut **me le** dire?
Vous devez **en** chercher.   Nous commencerons à **le** faire.
Qui a refusé de **lui** parler?   Ils vont **y** aller.

When there is a pronoun object in a sentence which has a verb followed by an infinitive, the pronoun object normally precedes the infinitive. This is because in most cases, it is the infinitive which governs the pronoun object.

NOTE: When the main verb governs the object, then the object precedes it. Ex.: Je l'ai laissé partir.

7. Where do y and en come in relation to other pronoun objects?

Je **lui en** ai donné.   Donnez-**lui-en.**   Il **y en** a dans le couloir.
Il **vous en** a montré.   Montrez-**m'en** trois.   Donnez-**leur-en.**

The pronouns **y** and **en** follow all other object pronouns and in that order.

8. What is the order of pronoun objects other than y and en?

Georges **me le** montre. Montrez-**le-moi.**
Ils **nous les** expliquent. Expliquez-**les-nous.**

When there are two object pronouns other than **y** or **en,** the *l*-form comes nearest the verb.

Je **le lui** indique. Indiquez-**la-leur.**

When there are two *l*-forms, they come in alphabetical order, that is, **le, la** and **les** always precede **lui** and **leur.**

E. *Remplacez les expressions en italique par des pronoms compléments.*

1. —Expliquera-t-il aux élèves la théorie de la relativité? —Non, il n'expliquera pas *aux élèves la théorie de la relativité.* 2. —Portez ce paquet à mon cousin. —Je porterai *ce paquet à votre cousin* quand j'aurai le temps. 3. —Êtes-vous allé voir ce film? —Oui, je suis allé voir *ce film.* 4. —Voulez-vous montrer vos tableaux à notre ami? —Oui, je veux bien montrer *mes tableaux à notre ami.* 5. —Prêtez-moi les notes de votre cours. —Je vous rendrai *les notes* la semaine prochaine. 6. —Donnez ce rapport au directeur. —Je donnerai *ce rapport au directeur.* 7. —Est-ce qu'il a annoncé son mariage à ses parents? —Oui, il a annoncé *son mariage à ses parents.* 8. —Puis-je demander des renseignements à cet agent? —Oui, vous pouvez demander *des renseignements à cet agent.* 9. —Ne voulez-vous pas raconter votre accident à ces journalistes? —Non, je ne veux pas raconter *cet accident aux journalistes.* 10. —Voulez-vous m'acheter un journal? —Oui, je vous achèterai un *journal.* 11. Les enfants aiment les jouets à Noël, mais il ne faut pas donner *aux enfants* trop *de jouets.*

F. *Traduisez en français.*

1. Here are some oranges. If you see your brother, give him some. 2. Your first French[1] class must[2] have been interesting. Describe it to us. 3. I have seven books. I will bring them to you tomorrow. 4. Where are your magazines? Show them to him at once. 5. Did you hear the news[3]? Do not tell it to them. 6. She spoke of it to him. 7. Those rules are not difficult. The teacher will explain them to you tomorrow. 8. You have eggs? Send me some this afternoon. 9. Do

---

[1] **classe de français** [2] **a dû être** [3] Use the singular form.

you have that article? Do you want to read it to me? 10. Give it to us tomorrow. 11. Do you know[4] any interesting stories? Tell us some.

---

[4] Use a form of **connaître**.

PATTERN PRACTICE: the position and order of object pronouns

Pattern 10

YOU HEAR   Je vais acheter cette voiture.
YOU SAY   Je vais l'acheter.

Pattern 11

YOU HEAR   Ouvrez la porte.
YOU SAY   Ouvrez-la.

Pattern 12

YOU HEAR   N'ouvrez pas la fenêtre.
YOU SAY   Ne l'ouvrez pas.

Pattern 13

YOU HEAR   Est-ce que Jean donne le livre à Robert?
YOU SAY   Oui, il le lui donne.

Pattern 14

YOU HEAR   Est-ce que Roger vous donnera le livre?
YOU SAY   Oui, il me le donnera.

Pattern 15

YOU HEAR   Donnez le livre à Marie.
YOU SAY   Donnez-le-lui.

Pattern 16

YOU HEAR   Ne montrez pas ce journal à Louise.
YOU SAY   Ne le lui montrez pas.

Pattern 17

YOU HEAR   Donnez-moi le couteau.
YOU SAY   Donnez-le-moi.

Pattern 18

YOU HEAR   Ne me donnez pas cette assiette.
YOU SAY   Ne me la donnez pas.

III. Disjunctive Pronouns

9. What are the disjunctive pronouns?

moi	*me*		**nous**	*us*
toi	*you*		**vous**	*you*
lui	*him*		**eux**	*them*, (*m.*)
elle	*her*		**elles**	*them*, (*f.*)
		soi *oneself*		

10. What are the seven commonest uses of the disjunctive pronouns?

The disjunctive pronoun is always used in an emphatic position.

    (a) Nous sommes allés en France avec **eux.**

The disjunctive pronoun is used after prepositions.

    (b) Jean et **lui** sont partis ce matin.
         Eux et **moi** avons l'intention de la voir.
         Avez-vous vu Maurice et **lui?**

The disjunctive pronoun is used as a part of a compound subject or object.

    (c) **Moi,** je vais y aller.
         Lui, il n'en sait rien.
         Eux seuls peuvent le faire.

The disjunctive pronoun is used to emphasize the subject of the sentence or when the subject is separated from the verb.

    (d) Mes frères sont plus grands que **moi.**   Je suis aussi intelligent qu'**eux.**
         Vous parlez mieux que **lui.**   Vous êtes aussi riche qu'**elle.**

The disjunctive pronoun is used after **que** meaning *as* or *than* in comparisons.

    (e) C'est **moi.**   C'est **lui.**   Ce sont **eux.**

The disjunctive is used after **ce** + a form of the verb **être.**

(f) —Qui est là? —**Lui.**   —Qui partira le premier? —**Toi.**

The disjunctive is used alone, in answer to questions.

(g) **moi**-même   **lui**-même   **eux**-mêmes   **soi**-même

The disjunctive is used when compounded with **-même** (*self*).

11. When is *soi* ordinarily used as a disjunctive?

Là, on ne pense qu'à **soi.**
Chacun travaille pour **soi.**
La télévision en **soi** n'est pas mauvaise.

The disjunctive **soi** is most often used in a sentence where an indefinite subject such as **on** or **chacun** is its antecedent and in the fixed expressions **en soi** and **de soi.**

G. *Remplacez le mot anglais par le pronom disjoint convenable.*

1. Je crois qu'ils finiront par se marier, (*she*) et Pierre.   2. Regardez ce que cet enfant a fabriqué (*himself*).   3. Pierre va aller avec (*me*) au bureau.   4. (*As for me*), maintenant, je m'en moque[1].   5. Ah! qu'on est bien chez (*oneself*[2]).   6.—Les voilà. —Qui? —(*They*). 7. Tu es ingrat après tout ce qu'ils ont fait pour (*you*).   8. Chacun parle de (*himself*).   9. (*You*), tu as toujours eu de la chance!   10. Vous pouvez continuer sans (*me*).   11. C'est (*he*) qui m'a raconté votre aventure.   12. Qui a cassé le vase? —Ce n'est pas (*I*).   13. Est-ce qu'elle est aussi amusante que (*he*)?   14. Dans un moment de danger, pense-t-on à (*himself*)?

---

[1] In this sense, the expression means: *I don't care.*   [2] French tends not to use the **—même** form unless it is absolutely needed for clarity.

H. *Traduisez en français.*

1. Would you like to work for him?   2. His friend and he can go to the movies this evening.   3. I found out[1] this news[2] through them. 4. You must do your exercises yourself.   5. They[3] are the ones who are happy[4] at his return.   6. You have a better car than he.   7. Who will go to that meeting? She and I.   8. He is much more patient than they.

---

[1] Use a form of **apprendre.**   [2] Use the singular noun.   [3] lit.: *It is they*   [4] **contents de**

PATTERN PRACTICE: disjunctive pronouns

Pattern 19

YOU HEAR   Marie et Jean-Jacques suivent le même cours.
YOU SAY   Marie et lui suivent le même cours.

Pattern 20

YOU HEAR   Nous partons avec Suzanne.
YOU SAY   Nous partons avec elle.

12. What pronoun construction replaces *de* + noun?

(a) noun-person

Je parle **de ma sœur.**	Je parle **d'elle.**
Il se souvient **de son frère.**	Il se souvient **de lui.**
J'ai besoin **d'amis.**	J'**en** ai besoin.

In general, one may say that **de** + NOUN (person) is replaced by **de** + DISJUNCTIVE PRONOUN. However, **en** sometimes replaces this construction, especially when the person in question is indefinite.

(b) noun-thing

Je parle **de mon travail.**	J'**en** parle.
Il se souvient **de ses voyages.**	Il s'**en** souvient.
Ils ont besoin **d'argent.**	Ils **en** ont besoin.

But **de** + NOUN (thing) is regularly replaced by **en.**

13. What pronoun construction replaces *à* + noun?

(a) noun-person after verbs which take an indirect object

Jacques a raconté son aventure **à l'agent.**	Jacques **lui** a raconté son aventure.
Vous ressemblez **à vos frères.**	Vous **leur** ressemblez.
Ils obéissent **à leur mère.**	Ils **lui** obéissent.

When **à** + NOUN (person) follows a non-reflexive verb which takes an indirect object, the construction is replaced by the indirect object pronouns. In French, in addition to the common verbs such as **dire, raconter, demander,** etc., a number of other verbs such as **obéir à, ressembler à** and **plaire à** take an indirect object.

(b) noun-person after reflexive verbs and after certain non-reflexive verbs which are followed by **à** but which do not take an indirect object

Je m'intéresse **à cet enfant.**   Je m'intéresse **à lui.**
Nous pensons **à Marie.**   Nous pensons **à elle.**
Faites attention **à l'agent.**   Faites attention **à lui.**

When **à** + NOUN (person) follows any reflexive verb and certain other verbs, the most common of which are **penser à** and **faire attention à,** the construction is replaced by **à** + DISJUNCTIVE PRONOUN.

(c) noun-things

Je réponds **à la lettre.**   J'**y** réponds.
Nous pensons **à nos études.**   Nous **y** pensons.
Qui s'intéresse **aux langues?**   Qui s'**y** intéresse?

When **à** + NOUN (thing) follows a verb, it is generally replaced by **y.**

I. *Remplacez l'expression en italique par le pronom convenable.*

1. La police s'est emparée *de ces criminels.*   2. Nous ressemblons *à nos parents.*   3. Je me chargerai *de ce problème.*   4. Croyez-vous *à cette histoire?*   5. Essayez de ne plus penser *à ces imbéciles.*   6. Je m'intéresse beaucoup *à la politique.*   7. A-t-on besoin *d'argent* pour s'amuser?   8. Ne vous adressez pas *à cet homme.*   9. Il a dit *à sa mère* ce qu'il voulait.   10. Obéissez *aux agents.*   11. Nous avons parlé *des Français.*   12. Vous souvenez-vous *de ce monsieur?*   13. Je me souviens bien *de sa voiture.*   14. Croyez-vous *aux protestations de cet individu?*   15. Faites attention *au signal.*   16. Faites attention *à ces gens.*

J. *Traduisez en français.*

1. Why don't you ever speak of him?   2. She is rather strange, but you will get accustomed to her.   3. You are very kind to take an interest in us.   4. I received the letter and I answered it.   5. When the teacher asked me a question yesterday, I answered him.   6. His father is easy-going; it is easy to obey him.   7. Unfortunately, I have a lot of work, but I wasn't thinking of it.   8. It's Maurice. Were you thinking of him?

PATTERN PRACTICE: replacing **à** and **de** + NOUN (person and thing)

Pattern 21

    YOU HEAR   Je pense à mon frère.

    YOU SAY   Je pense à lui.

EXERCICE D'ENSEMBLE

K. *Traduisez en français.*

1. These books are too heavy. Don't take[1] them to them. 2. Tell them what happened to you. 3. Who will get[2] the first prize? I. 4. Do you like tea? Yes, I prefer it to coffee. 5. You have only one car; we have two. 6. Can you do this problem yourself? 7. Helen is my best friend. I speak of her with pleasure. 8. They[3] are the ones who gave us this picture. 9. Are there many pupils in this class? Yes, there are many. 10. Do you remember them? 11. They too[4] can leave now. 12. His brother is not as ambitious as he. 13. Do you want to go to Europe with me? 14. Since they are late, let's leave without them. 15. Are you going to France, or are you coming back from there? 16. You and I agree on this point. 17. You like exotic countries, but do you go there from time to time? 18. They want to know the truth; tell it to them. 19. They should[5] be there, but I do not see them. 20. *He* can do that, not I.

---

[1] Use a form of **apporter.**   [2] Use a form of **avoir.**   [3] lit.: *It is they*   [4] Put *too* in this place in the sentence.   [5] Use a form of **devoir.**

Problem Words

12. early

(a) When *early* means *early in a certain period of time*

Est-ce que vous vous couchez **tôt?**   ⎫
Est-ce que vous vous couchez **de** ⎬ *Do you go to bed* early?
bonne heure?   ⎭
Ne venez pas trop **tôt.**   *Don't come too* early.

Both **tôt** and **de bonne heure** mean *early* in a given period of time.

(b) When *early = ahead of time*

Il y aura beaucoup de monde; il   *There will be a lot of people there; it is*
vaut mieux arriver **en avance.**   *better to arrive* early.

But *early*, meaning *ahead of time*, is expressed by **en avance,** which
is the opposite of **en retard.**

Sometimes **d'avance** and **à l'avance** are also used to express
early = ahead of time, but it is rather difficult to indicate just when
one of these expressions is used rather than the other.

13. end

(a) When *end* is the opposite of *beginning*

C'est **la fin** de la leçon.   *It is* the end *of the lesson.*

The word **la fin** means *end* when it implies the opposite of *beginning*.

(b) When *end* means *tip* or *extremity*

Ne touchez pas **le bout** de ce fil.   *Don't touch* the end *of this wire.*
Il y a un cinéma au **bout** de la rue.   *There is a movie at* the end *of the street.*

The French uses **le bout** to express *end* meaning *tip or extremity*.

(c) How to say *at the end of* + PERIOD OF TIME

A la fin du mois il ne me reste jamais   At the end of *the month I don't ever*
rien.   *have anything left.*
Au bout de trois mois M. Roux a   At the end of three *months,* Mr. Roux
donné sa démission.   *resigned.*
Au bout de quelques semaines j'en   At the end of some *weeks I had enough*
ai eu assez.   *(of it).*

French expresses *at the end of the* + PERIOD OF TIME by **à la fin de** +
DEFINITE ARTICLE + PERIOD OF TIME. On the other hand, when the
period of time is accompanied by a numeral or by some other adjective indicating quantity, **au bout de . . .** is used.

14. escape

(a) When *escape* means *avoid*

Le criminel a réussi à **échapper** à la   *The criminal succeeded in* escaping *the*
police.   *police.*

The non-reflexive form **échapper à** is used to indicate that one has avoided or escaped someone or something that one has not yet confronted.

(b) When *escape* means *get out of*

C'est la troisième fois que ce criminel **s'est échappé de** prison.	*It's the third time that this criminal has escaped from prison.*

The reflexive form **s'échapper de** is used to indicate that one has succeeded in getting away from a person or thing that one has confronted.

In the first example, the thief evaded the police, therefore, never came in contact with them, whereas in the second he was in prison and got out of it.

15. every

(a) How to express *every* by **chaque**

Chaque fois que je vois Paul, il me parle de ses ennuis.	*Every time I see Paul, he talks to me of his troubles.*

The adjective **chaque** means *every* or *each*.

(b) How to express *every* by **tous les . . .**

Tous les matins nous sortons de bonne heure et **tous les soirs** nous rentrons tard.	*Every morning we leave early and every evening we return home late.*

The English *every* is frequently expressed by **tous les** + UNIT OF TIME (**toutes les** + UNIT OF TIME). This formula is more common with units of time than **chaque,** although **chaque** is not incorrect.

(c) How to say *everyone*

Tout le monde est parti.	*Everyone has left.*

The pronoun *everyone* is expressed by **tout le monde,** which is singular and which must be followed by a singular verb.

CAUTION: Do NOT use a plural verb after **tout le monde.**

(d) How to say *everything*

Tout est perdu.	*Everything is lost.*
J'ai **tout** oublié.	*I've forgotten everything.*

The pronoun *everything* is expressed by **tout.** In the compound tenses, **tout** comes between the auxiliary and the past participle.

(e) How to say *everything that*

Tout ce qui est sur la table est à Jean.	Everything that *is on the table is John's.*
Donnez-moi **tout ce que** vous pouvez.	*Give me* everything that *you can.*

In French, *everything* used as the subject of its clause = **tout ce qui;** *everything* used as the object of its clause = **tout ce que.**

CAUTION: The indefinite **ce** must come between **tout** and the relative pronoun. Do NOT write «tout qui» or «tout que».

L. *Remplacez les mots anglais par leur équivalent français.*

1. Sauve qui peut! Un lion (*has escaped from*) sa cage. 2. Il me reste tant de travail à faire que je n'en vois pas (*the end*). 3. Je préfère travailler le soir; je n'aime pas me lever (*early*). 4. Voilà le menu; commande (*everything that*) tu veux. 5. (*Everyone laughed*) quand Pierre a raconté ses aventures. 6. (*At the end*) du deuxième acte, la situation semblait inextricable. 7. Jacques fait une période militaire (*every summer*). 8. Nous avons eu de la chance de (*escape*) cette épidémie. 9. (*Everything that*) vous dites est très juste. 10. Vous arrivez trop (*early*), Jacques n'est pas encore rentré. 11. —Où se trouve le bureau de tabac? —(*At the end*) de la rue, à droite. 12. Il y aura un cadeau pour (*every*) invité. 13. Saluez (*everyone*) de ma part. 14. Il vaudrait mieux arriver (*early*) au théâtre; sinon, nous ne trouverons plus de places. 15. Leurs enfants aiment (*everything that*) fait du bruit.

M. *Traduisez en français. Attention aux mots en italique.*

1. Nicole likes *everything that* is beautiful. 2. The airplane will not wait for us; it is better to arrive *early* than[1] to be late. 3. At the *end* of the book I finally understood what the author meant. 4. *Every* time that he gets angry, he regrets it. 5. We are invited for seven o'clock; we must not arrive too *early*. 6. If I am caught[2], I'll do *everything* to[3] *escape*. 7. At the *end* of two weeks at the university, Jack dropped his courses. 8. Paul and Anne-Marie see each other *every* day. 9. She is hurt[4] because they put her at the *end* of the table.

---

[1] than to be = **que d'être** [2] **pris** [3] **pour** [4] **vexée**

10. *Everyone* knows that.   11. That teacher is remarkable; he knows absolutely *everything*.   12. Is *everyone* there?   13. I don't know how you can *escape* his anger.   14. I heard *everything*.

Verb Review

Review the verbs **être** and **aller** according to the outline on page 283.

CHAPTER 5

Participles

A participle has properties of both a verb and an adjective. English and French have a present and a past participle.

Verb	Present Participle	Past Participle
(*speak*) parler	(*speaking*) **parlant**	(*spoken*) **parlé**
(*finish*) finir	(*finishing*) **finissant**	(*finished*) **fini**
(*lose*) perdre	(*losing*) **perdant**	(*lost*) **perdu**
(*drink*) boire	(*drinking*) **buvant**	(*drunk*) **bu**

Syntactically, the past participle offers almost no problems in spoken French and only the problem of agreement in written French.

The present participle is somewhat more complex, since French often expresses an English present participle by some construction other than the French present participle.

I. The Past Participle

1. With what auxiliaries are French verbs conjugated in the compound tenses?

Nous **avons donné** un livre à l'élève.
Robert **a vu** un film intéressant.
Les étudiants **avaient beaucoup** travaillé.

Vous **êtes venu** trop tard.
Nous **sommes arrivés** vers trois heures.
J'**étais parti** quand mon ami est arrivé chez moi.

La voiture **s'est arrêtée** devant notre porte.
Nous **nous sommes échappés** par la fenêtre.
Je ne **m'étais** pas **rasé** ce matin-là.

Most verbs are conjugated with the auxiliary **avoir**. Ordinarily, intransitive verbs of motion are conjugated with **être**. All reflexive verbs are conjugated with **être**.

58

A. *Remplacez les tirets par l'auxiliaire convenable pour former le passé composé.*

1. Qui __a__ ouvert la porte pour laisser rentrer le chat? 2. Pourquoi vous __êtes__ -vous caché quand je __suis__ arrivé? 3. Le président __a__ reçu le nouvel ambassadeur aujourd'hui. 4. Cette pièce était ennuyeuse; je __suis__ parti après le premier acte. 5. Le chauffeur s'__est__ arrêté brusquement pour éviter un accident. 6. __Êtes__ -vous monté sur la Tour Eiffel? 7. A Paris nous nous __sommes__ promenés le long de la Seine. 8. Il était trois heures du matin quand Jacques __est__ rentré. 9. Ils ont une belle pelouse et ils __ont__ interdit aux enfants de jouer dessus.

B. *Traduisez en français en faisant bien attention à l'auxiliaire des verbes au passé composé.*

1. I recommend this hotel to you — we stayed there a month. 2. I was so tired that I did not wake up early enough to go to[1] class. 3. I have finished my exercises and now I can go out. 4. You'll be sick; you were warm, and you drank some ice water. 5. Henry did not remember[2] his date with Pierrette. 6. After his retirement, he went back to[3] his little village. 7. What have you learned up to now[4]? 8. Many children were[5] born during the last war. 9. The little boys sat down in[6] the first row at the movies.

---

[1] **en** [2] Use a form of **se souvenir de.** [3] **dans** [4] **ici** [5] What tense will this verb be in? What will be the tense of the auxiliary? [6] *in the* = **au**

PATTERN PRACTICE: the use of auxiliaries in compound tenses

Pattern 1

YOU HEAR   Je vais en France.
YOU SAY   Je suis allé en France.

2. When and how does the past participle of a verb conjugated with *avoir* agree?

Le père a **mené** ses enfants au cirque.	(No agreement. Why?)
Il **les** a **menés** au cirque.	(Agreement. Why?)
Les enfants qu'il a **menés** au cirque sont les siens.	(Agreement. Why?)
Quels enfants a-t-il **menés** au cirque?	(Agreement. Why?)

The past participle of a verb conjugated with **avoir** is invariable unless a direct object precedes the verb. The past participle of a verb conjugated with **avoir** agrees with the preceding direct object in gender and number.

3. Does the past participle of a verb conjugated with *avoir* agree with a preceding *en?*

Nous avons **mené** des enfants au cirque.   (No agreement. Why)?
Nous **en** avons **mené** au cirque.   (No agreement. Why?)

The past participle of a verb conjugated with **avoir** does not ordinarily agree with a preceding **en.**

C. *Remplacez l'infinitif par la forme convenable du participe passé.*

1. Où sont ces belles photos que vous avez (prendre)?   2. Nous avons (entendre) une bonne chanteuse.   3. —Avez-vous (voir) ma femme? —Oui, je l'ai (voir) il y a un instant.   4. Qui est la personne que vous avez (saluer)?   5. Quelles fleurs avez-vous (choisir)? 6. —Où sont les gâteaux? En avez-vous (acheter)?   7. —Je n'en ai pas (voir) dans la cuisine.

D. *Traduisez en français.*

1. You have told me an interesting story.   2. Where is the person that you introduced to me?   3. What beautiful gifts you bought! 4. I didn't receive your letter. When did you send it?   5. I like his book. Has he written others[1]?   6. You wish some stamps? I bought some yesterday.

---

[1] d'autres

PATTERN PRACTICE: the agreement of the past participle

Pattern 2

 YOU HEAR   J'ai peint la maison.
 YOU SAY   Je l'ai peinte.

Pattern 3

 YOU HEAR   Quel tableau avez-vous peint?   (Quelle chambre . . .)
 YOU SAY   Quelle chambre avez-vous peinte?

Pattern 4

 YOU HEAR   L'édifice qu'il a construit est superbe.   (La maison . . .)
 YOU SAY   La maison qu'il a construite est superbe.

4. When and how does the past participle of a verb of motion conjugated with *être* agree?

Jacqueline était déjà **revenue** quand nous   (Agreement. Why?)
   sommes partis.
Mes camarades sont **morts** pendant la guerre.   (Agreement. Why?)
Ils sont **allés** à Paris avant votre arrivée.   (Agreement. Why?)

The past participle of a verb of motion conjugated with **être** always agrees with the subject of the sentence in gender and number.

5. In matters of agreement, is the pronoun *vous* considered singular or plural?

Vous êtes **tombé**(e)(s), n'est-ce pas?   (Agreement. Why?)

The pronoun **vous** may be singular or plural, masculine or feminine. The past participle of a verb agrees according to whether **vous** refers to one or more than one person, and whether these persons are masculine or feminine. When **vous** refers to both masculine and feminine nouns the masculine plural agreement is used.

E. *Remplacez l'infinitif par la forme convenable du participe passé.*

1. Les élèves étaient déjà (sortir) quand leur professeur est (arriver).
2. Marie est (partir) sans se retourner.   3. Nous sommes (tomber) dans un piège.   4. Mes chers amis, vous êtes (arriver) trop tôt.
5. Pourquoi ne sont-ils pas (venir)?   6. Êtes-vous déjà (monter) sur la Tour Eiffel, Jacqueline?

F. *Traduisez en français.*

1. He had said that he would come back, and he came back.   2. Did you come[1] back home to[2] rest?   3. Our friends became important men.   4. Those who stayed all[3] died.   5. When did your sisters arrive?

---

[1] *come back home* = **rentrer**   [2] either **pour** or no preposition at all   [3] Put this word between the auxiliary and the past participle.

6. When and how does the past participle of a reflexive or reciprocal verb agree?

A reflexive verb is one in which the reflexive object refers back to the subject of the sentence. Ex.: *I* see *myself* in the mirror. *She* washes *herself*.

A reciprocal verb is one whose reciprocal object has the connotation of *each other*. Ex.: *They* see *each other* every week. *We* spoke to *each other* yesterday.

In French, reflexive and reciprocal verbs have the same pronominal forms and follow the same rules for agreement.

French reflexive objects may be

(**a**) direct objects

Elle **s'**est coupée.	*She cut* herself.
Ils **se** sont lavés.	*They washed* themselves.

(**b**) indirect objects

Elles **se** sont parlé.	*They spoke* to each other.
Elle **s'**est coupé le doigt.	*She cut her finger* (lit.: *She cut the finger to herself*).

(**c**) inherent objects

Some reflexive pronouns are neither direct nor indirect in function but simply an integral part of the verb. We may call the verbs with which they are used INHERENTLY REFLEXIVE VERBS.

Elle **s'**est souvenue de son rendez-vous.	*She remembered her appointment.*
Nous **nous** sommes échappés.	*We escaped.*
Elles **se** sont doutées de ce qui se passait.	*They suspected what was happening.*

Let us now examine the agreement of such verbs.

Madame Dupont et Madame Durand **se sont vues** hier.	(Agreement. Why?)
Nous **nous sommes levés** à dix heures.	(Agreement. Why?)
Janine **s'est souvenue** de mon adresse.	(Agreement. Why?)
Nos amis **se sont parlé** longtemps.	(No agreement. Why?)
Les enfants **se sont lavé** les mains.	(No agreement. Why?)

The past participle of a reflexive or reciprocal verb agrees with the reflexive object unless it is an indirect object. In that case, the past participle remains invariable. (In other words, the past participle of a reflexive verb agrees with the reflexive object when it is direct or inherent but not when it is indirect.)

G. *Écrivez la forme convenable du participe passé.*

1. Nous nous sommes (lever) à six heures, nous avons déjeuné, et puis nous nous sommes (dire) au revoir. 2. Lucile s'est (habiller) et puis elle s'est (brosser) les dents. 3. Ces enfants se sont-ils (laver) les oreilles comme il faut? 4. Ils se sont (raconter) leurs souvenirs pendant des heures. 5. Elle s'est beaucoup (amuser) à ce bal. 6. Nous nous sommes (apercevoir) qu'il était tard. 7. Sylvie s'est (marier) il y a deux mois. 8. Vous[1] êtes-vous (rendre) compte de votre erreur, Charlotte? 9. Comment vous êtes-vous (faire) mal, vous deux? 10. Nous nous sommes (revoir) avec plaisir.

---

[1] lit.: *Did you render account to yourself of your error?* What is the function of the reflexive pronoun in this sentence?

H. *Traduisez en français.*

1. We met each other on[1] the street and then we spoke to each other. 2. They rushed into the store. 3. Why didn't they speak to each other? 4. She cut her finger yesterday. 5. Finally we all[2] found[3] each other again. 6. We were mistaken. 7. They blamed each other for the accident. 8. They related their adventures to each other. 9. You made fun of me, both[4] of you.

---

[1] **dans** [2] Place directly after the auxiliary. [3] *find again* = **retrouver** [4] **vous deux**

II. The Present Participle

7. How is the present participle formed?

First Person Plural Present	PRESENT PARTICIPLE	First Person Plural Present	PRESENT PARTICIPLE
donn**ons**	donn**ant**	dorm**ons**	dorm**ant**
finiss**ons**	finiss**ant**	lis**ons**	lis**ant**
perd**ons**	perd**ant**	pren**ons**	pren**ant**
buv**ons**	buv**ant**	voy**ons**	voy**ant**

The present participle is formed by adding **-ant** to the stem of the verb which is derived by taking away the **-ons** from the first person plural present.

8. What three verbs have irregular present participles?

être   **étant**   avoir   **ayant**   savoir   **sachant**

Être, avoir and **savoir** have irregular present participles.

9. What is the nature of the present participle?

Voyant la porte ouverte, je suis   Seeing *the open door, I entered.*
entré.

Beaucoup de gens, **profitant** de leur   *Many people were at the beach,* taking
week-end, étaient à la plage.   advantage *of their weekend.*

The present participle is a verbal adjective, that is, it partakes both of the nature of an adjective and of a verb. As an adjective, it modifies some noun or pronoun in the sentence; as a verb, it indicates action or mode of being and may be followed by whatever types of constructions other forms of the same verb are followed.

10. When and with what does the present participle agree?

Les Michaud ont de la chance   *The Michauds are lucky to have such*
d'avoir des enfants si **obéissants.**   obedient *children.*

When the **-ant** form of the verb is used entirely as an adjective, it agrees in gender and number with the noun it modifies.

In that case, it has none of the functions of a verb, that is, it does not indicate action or mode of being, and it cannot govern an object or be followed by constructions which could follow it when used as a verb.

Les enfants, **obéissant** à leurs pa-   *The children,* obeying *their parents,*
rents, sont allés se coucher.   *went to bed.*

When the **-ant** word is used as a present participle, it is invariable.

As a present participle, the **-ant** word is an adjective in that it is identified with some noun or pronoun in the sentence, and it is a verb in that it indicates action or mode of being and may be followed by whatever types of constructions other forms of the same verb are followed.

11. The present participle is sometimes used without *en*, at other times with *en* or *tout en*. To what does it refer when used without *en*? when used with *en*?

J'ai vu **Marie sortant*** de la biblio-   *I saw* Marie leaving *the library.*
thèque.

---

* More common than **sortant** in this sentence would be **qui sortait**; also possible is **sortir** but with a slight change in meaning.

J'ai vu Marie **en sortant** de la　　I *saw Marie* on leaving *the library*.
bibliothèque.

When the present participle is used without **en,** it generally refers to the nearest preceding noun or pronoun. When it is used with **en** or with **tout en,** its action regularly refers to the subject of the sentence.

12. How does the use of *en* or *tout en* with the present participle influence its relation to the action of the main verb in respect to time?

Disant ces mots, le pasteur **s'est**　Saying *these words, the pastor* arose.
levé.

En sortant de la poste, notre facteur　On leaving *the post office, our mailman*
est tombé sur le verglas.　　　　　fell *on the ice.*

Tout en parlant, le docteur **a remis**　While he was talking, *the doctor* put on
son manteau.　　　　　　　　　　　*his overcoat.*

Tout en étant sévère, le professeur　Although he was *strict, the teacher* was
aimait beaucoup ses élèves.　　　*very* fond *of his pupils.*

When the present participle is used without **en,** its action is usually followed by another action. When it is used with **en,** the two actions are somewhat more simultaneous, and when it is used with **tout en,** the simultaneous nature of the action is emphasized still more.

Notice that **en** + PRESENT PARTICIPLE is expressed in English by *in, on, by,* and *while* + PRESENT PARTICIPLE and sometimes by *while, when* or *as* + CLAUSE. The expression **tout en** + PRESENT PARTICIPLE is expressed in a variety of ways in English: *all the while* or *still* + PRESENT PARTICIPLE, *while* + CLAUSE, *even though* + CLAUSE, etc.

I. *Dans le devoir suivant, le mot entre parenthèses se termine en **-ant.** Il peut être un adjectif pur ou un participe présent. Faites l'accord du mot entre parenthèses où il y a lieu.*

1. Cécile est revenue, (rassurant) toute la famille.　2. Vos remarques ne sont pas très (rassurant).　3. Nous avons passé une journée (fatigant) à l'exposition.　4. (Fatigant) tout le monde, Jeanne a recommencé son histoire.　5. On ne sait pas ce que sont les soucoupes (volant).　6. Avez-vous vu ces gros oiseaux (volant) au-dessus de notre maison?　7. Il y a dans la pièce des scènes (étonnant).　8. (Étonnant) ses amies, Madame Delom a déchiré toutes les lettres.　9. Nous avons trouvé les pauvres enfants (tremblant) de peur.

10. Le malade mangeait encore avec peine, la main (tremblant).
11. Nicole, (courant) vers la porte, a renversé la lampe. 12. Les
Bérard ont l'eau (courant) dans leur ferme.

J. *Traduisez en français les phrases suivantes. La traduction française de
chaque phrase comporte un participe présent — seul, avec* **en** *ou avec* **tout en.**

1. Closing her[1] eyes, Genevieve listened attentively to the music.
2. The painter hurt himself by falling from the ladder. 3. Even
though he was sick, George used to read a great deal. 4. Opening
the door with care[2], Bernard looked into the room. 5. On seeing
that Mr. Lambert was busy, we left at once. 6. I saw Frederick
while coming back from the office. 7. All the while that I was listening to her, I was thinking of something else. 8. You do me
wrong[3] in saying that. 9. Even though he knew of[4] my difficulties,
the boss hired me. 10. On arriving in Paris, go to see the Jamois.

---

[1] Not the possessive adjective in French.   [2] **prudence**   [3] **du tort**   [4] *know of* = **connaître**

PATTERN PRACTICE: using the present participle with **en**

Pattern 5

> YOU HEAR   Pendant que j'attendais l'autobus, je faisais des mots croisés.
> YOU SAY   En attendant l'autobus, je faisais des mots croisés.

13. When is the English present participle expressed by à + infinitive in French?

Nous avons passé trois heures **à**   *We spent three hours* playing *cards.*
   jouer aux cartes.
Paul est resté au moins dix minutes   *Paul stood at least ten minutes* reading
   à lire l'affiche.   *the announcement.*
L'enfant s'est amusé **à découper** des   *The child amused himself* cutting out
   images.   *pictures.*

The English present participle is not always expressed by a French
present participle. (English present participles and gerunds are expressed in a variety of ways in French. We give only two of the most
common of these.)

When the English present participle expresses manner of passing
time, French often uses **à** + INFINITIVE.

After forms of the verb **passer** (*to spend time*), this construction
must be used rather than a present participle.

14. How does French express the English present participle when it stresses the idea of *in the act of*?

Marc était **en train de lire** le jour- nal.	*Mark* was reading (was in the act of reading) *the newspaper.*

When the English present participle stresses the idea of *in the act of*, French often uses **en train de** + INFINITIVE. This may also be expressed in English by *be busy doing something.*

K. *Traduisez en français.*

1. We spent two hours looking at television.   2. I found Philip looking for his new tie.   3. Lucienne stayed in the store for an hour trying on dresses.   4. John was busy writing a letter when I entered. 5. Will you spend the evening playing cards?   6. Don't bother me now — I'm busy working.   7. Don't spend so much time reading detective stories.   8. We amused ourselves doing crossword puzzles.

PATTERN PRACTICE: the use of the passing time construction

Pattern 6

YOU HEAR   J'ai lu la leçon en une heure.
YOU SAY   J'ai passé une heure à lire la leçon.

Pattern 7

YOU HEAR   Maurice réparait sa moto quand je suis arrivé.
YOU SAY   Maurice était en train de réparer sa moto quand je suis arrivé.

Problem Words

16. expect

(a) How to say *expect a person or a material thing*

J'**attends** ma femme demain.	*I* expect *my wife tomorrow.*
Nous **attendons** une augmentation le mois prochain.	*We* expect *a raise next month.*

The non-reflexive **attendre** may mean *expect* when it is followed by a direct object which is either *a person* or *a material thing.*

(**b**) How to say *expect an event or some other immaterial thing*

Nous nous attendons à une belle   We are expecting *a great surprise.*
  surprise.

The reflexive **s'attendre à** is often the equivalent of *to expect* followed by an event or some other immaterial thing.

(**c**) How to say *expect that* + CLAUSE

Jacques **s'attend à ce que nous**   *Jack* expects us to come.
  venions.

The expression **s'attendre à ce que** + SUBJUNCTIVE is the equivalent of *expect that* + CLAUSE.

(**d**) When *expect to* = *intend to*

Nous **comptons** le voir cet après-   *We* expect to *see him this afternoon.*
  midi.
J'**ai l'intention de** lire cet article.   *I* expect to *read that article.*

When *expect to* = *intend to*, French may express it by **compter** + INFINITIVE or **avoir l'intention de** + INFINITIVE.

(**e**) How to say: *What do you expect? What do you expect me to . . . .?*

Que voulez-vous, il est si jeune!   What do you expect, *he is so young!*
Où veut-il que j'aille?   Where does he expect *me to go?*

When *expect* is used to ask a question with a shrug of the shoulders and implies inevitability, the French often use a form of **vouloir** as in the above examples.

17. fail

(**a**) How to say *to fail to do something*

Il **ne s'est pas arrêté** au feu rouge.   *He* failed to stop *at the red light.*

The French have no special way of expressing *to fail to do something.* They simply use the negative form of the main verb.

(b) How to say *not to fail to do something*

Ne manquez pas de nous **écrire** à   Don't fail to write *us when you arrive.*
votre arrivée.

To express *not to fail to do something*, use the negative of **manquer de** + INFINITIVE.

Notice that the affirmative of **manquer de** has another meaning, as for example: **J'ai manqué de tomber** = *I almost fell.*

(c) How to say *fail an examination or a course*

Jean-Pierre **a échoué à** son examen
  de biologie.
Jean-Pierre **n'a pas réussi à** son   *Jean-Pierre* failed *his biology test.*
  examen de biologie.

The English *to fail an examination* is **échouer à un examen** and *fail a course* is **échouer à un cours.** But one can also say **ne pas réussir** or **ne pas être reçu à un examen.**

(d) How to say *to fail someone in a course*

Ce professeur **colle** rarement **ses**   *That teacher rarely* fails his pupils.
 élèves.

To express the English *to fail someone*, the expression **coller quelqu'un** is used colloquially. More formal but not so common are: **ne pas recevoir quelqu'un** and **faire échouer quelqu'un.**

CAUTION: Do NOT say «échouer quelqu'un». Say either **faire échouer quelqu'un** or **coller quelqu'un.**

18. feel

(a) When to use **sentir que**

Georges **a senti qu**'il valait mieux   *George* felt that *it was better to leave.*
partir.

The English *to feel that* + CLAUSE = **sentir que** + CLAUSE.

(b) When to use **se sentir**

Je **me sens** vraiment mal.	*I really* feel *bad.*
Vous sentez-vous un peu mieux?	Do *you* feel *a little better?*
Je **me sens** bien.	*I feel well.*

Forms of **se sentir** are used to express *feel* when it refers to the state of one's health; this verb is used with the adverbs **bien, mal, mieux,** etc.

CAUTION: The verb **sentir** sometimes means *to smell.* Do not confuse: **Il se sent bien.** (*He feels good.*) with: **Ça sent bon.** (*That smells good.*)

(c) How to express: *How do you feel?*

Comment **allez**-vous?	*How* are *you? How* do *you* feel?
Je **vais** bien, merci.	*I'm well, thank you.*

To ask a person how he feels in English, we normally say: *How are you?* although we sometimes say: *How do you feel?* To ask how a person is, French normally uses the verb **aller.**

19. get

(a) When *get = obtain*

J'ai pu **obtenir** un exemplaire de ce livre.	*I was able to* get *a copy of that book.*
Où est-ce que je peux **me procurer** une machine à écrire?	*Where can I* get *a typewriter?*
Avez-vous **reçu** une lettre ce matin?	Did *you* get *a letter this morning?*

When *get = obtain,* it may be expressed by **obtenir, se procurer** and **recevoir,** but these verbs are not always interchangeable.

(b) When *got = received*

Louis **a eu** une augmentation de salaire.	*Louis* got *a raise in pay.*
Philippe **a eu** une bonne note.	*Philip* got *a good grade.*

The compound past and simple past of **avoir** are often used in the sense of *got.*

(c) When *get = go and get*

Veux-tu **chercher** le journal?   *Will you* get *the paper?*
Allez **chercher** le courrier.   Get *the mail.*

When *get = go and get*, it may be expressed by **chercher** or **aller chercher.**

(d) When *get = catch* (a disease)

Jean a dû **attraper** la rougeole à   *John must have* gotten *the measles at*
l'école.   *school.*

(e) When *get = become*

Anne **se fatigue** facilement.   *Anne* gets tired *easily.*
Cette année je **me suis intéressé** au   *This year I* got interested *in judo.*
judo.

Some reflexive verbs carry with them the sense of *get* + ADJECTIVE in all tenses, some only in the past tenses.

Tout à coup **il a fait** très **froid.**   *Suddenly* it got *very* cold.
J'ai eu très **sommeil** après le dîner.   *I* got *very* sleepy *after dinner.*

The compound past and the simple past of idiomatic expressions with **avoir** and **faire** are often used to express *get.*

L. *Remplacez les mots anglais par leur équivalent français.*

1. Arrêtez-vous de tourner en rond, je vais (*feel*) mal. 2. Comment fait-on pour (*get*) un passeport? 3. Que (*do you expect*) qu'il fasse contre tous ces gens? 4. Je (*won't fail*) lui transmettre votre message. 5. On (*gets*) facilement des rhumes dans l'autobus. 6. Georges a l'air très fatigué; est-ce qu'il (*feels*) bien? 7. Je ne sais pas pourquoi il (*failed to come*). 8. Je (*expected*) un mot d'excuse de sa part. 9. Monsieur Bayard (*got pale*) en entendant cela. 10. Dans ce milieu mondain Jules (*feels*) mal à l'aise. 11. Si Jean-Paul (*fails*) son examen, il sera obligé de suivre des cours de vacances. 12. Je (*expect*) faire le voyage de Paris à Marseille en dix heures. 13. Eric était sûr de lui, mais les examinateurs le (*failed*). 14. Ma femme voudrait bien (*get*) cette recette. 15. Voudriez-vous (*get*) cette revue pour moi à la bibliothèque? 16. J'ai un peu froid; veux-tu (*get*) mon écharpe? 17. Ma propriétaire (*is getting*) complètement sourde.

M. *Traduisez en français. Attention aux mots en italique.*

1. I *got* good results with that machine. 2. Do you want me to open the window? You'll *feel* better. 3. Don't *fail* to telephone me tomorrow before noon. 4. What do you *expect* her to do for him now? 5. The most intelligent pupils can *fail* an examination. 6. I *got* a strange reply to my letter. 7. If Monique *feels* tired, she should go to see the doctor. 8. Alain *failed* to hand in his work. 9. I did not *expect* to go to Brussels before next week. 10. George, I left my purse in the car. Will you *get* it for me? 11. Frances *expects* a letter from Paul. 12. I did not *expect* to be invited to the Dubois. 13. If one doesn't *expect* anything, one doesn't have any disillusions. 14. What did you *get* for Christmas? 15. Odette *gets* angry when people don't do everything she wishes. 16. It *got* so warm that we were able to go out without a coat.

Verb Review

Review the verbs **boire** and **connaître** according to the outline on page 283.

CHAPTER 6

Possessives

A possessive is a word which shows possession. English has possessive adjectives: *my, your, his, her, its, our, their,* and possessive pronouns: *mine, yours, his, hers, its, ours,* and *theirs.*

I. Possessive Adjectives

1. What are the French possessive adjectives?

Singular Masculine	Feminine	Plural		Singular Maculine	Feminine	Plural	
mon	ma	mes	*my*	notre	notre	nos	*our*
ton	ta	tes	*your*	votre	votre	vos	*your*
son	sa	ses	*his, her, its*	leur	leur	leurs	*their*

2. How and with what do the French possessive adjectives agree?

J'ai perdu **mon** portefeuille et **ma** montre. — *I've lost* my *billfold and* my *watch.*

Jacques est allé voir **son** cousin chez **sa** tante. — *Jack went to see* his *cousin at* his *aunt's.*

Elle a mis **son** courrier et **sa** revue sur la table. — *She put* her *mail and* her *magazine on the table.*

The French possessive adjectives agree in gender and number with the thing possessed. They do not agree with the possessor.

In English, the possessive adjectives agree with the possessor, not with the thing possessed.

73

3. When are mon, ton, and son used for ma, ta, and sa?

Son auto est belle.   His *car is beautiful.*
Mon ancienne maison était plus   My *former house was more convenient*
commode que celle-ci.   *than this one.*

The forms **mon, ton,** and **son** are used to modify feminine singular nouns when the word immediately following these forms, whether a noun or an adjective, begins with a vowel sound.

4. How is the French usage in respect to the possessive adjective different from the English in a sentence such as the following:

Son père et sa mère sont partis ce   Her father and mother *left this morn-*
matin.   *ing.*

In English, the same possessive adjective may refer to two or more connected nouns, whereas in French, the proper possessive adjective must be used before each noun.

A. *Remplacez les mots anglais par l'adjectif français convenable.*

1. (*My*) parents et (*my*) oncle sont partis pour le Canada.   2. (*His*) livre est en bien mauvais état.   3. Je n'ai pas beaucoup aimé (*their*) remarque à (*your*) sujet.   4. As-tu passé (*your*) examen?   5. Que pensez-vous de (*my*) tableaux?   6. (*Our*) existence est ce que nous la faisons.   7. (*Your*) références sont bonnes, mais (*your*) expérience est insuffisante.   8. Avez-vous vu (*their*) nouveaux chapeaux?   9. Il veut me vendre (*his*) voiture, mais elle marche mal.   10. Elle m'a montré (*her*) maison et (*her*) jardin.   11. (*Her*) adresse est inconnue.

B. *Traduisez en français.*

1. My parents would like to invite you to our party[1].   2. Do we take my car or your motorcycle?   3. Do you know whether her brother and sister speak German?   4. His voice is not as beautiful as formerly.   5. Would you do everything for your country?   6. My grandchildren are my greatest joy.   7. I hope that her son and daughter will have her good looks and intelligence.

---
[1] soirée

Pattern Practice: possessive adjectives

Pattern 1

YOU HEAR   J'ai pris ma voiture. Les voisins ont pris . . .
YOU SAY   J'ai pris ma voiture. Les voisins ont pris leur voiture.

II. Possessive Adjectives with Nouns

(parts of the body)

5. How, in general, does French express possession with nouns denoting parts of the body?

Marie a baissé **les** yeux.   *Marie lowered* her *eyes.*
Nous avons mal à **la** gorge.   Our *throats are sore.*
Il dort toujours **la** bouche ouverte.   *He always sleeps with* his *mouth open.*

In French, the definite article is often used with nouns denoting parts of the body, where English would use the possessive adjective. However, French normally employs the possessive adjective with parts of the body: (a) if ambiguity would result from the use of the article; (b) usually if the part of the body is modified; (c) if the part of the body is the subject of the sentence.

The exact usage of the article with parts of the body is so complicated that at this stage we shall present only a few of the most frequently used constructions. (§§6–10)

6. How is possession indicated in French when the subject of the sentence performs an action with a part of his body?

Marie lève **la** main.   *Marie raises* her *hand.*
Jean tourne **la** tête.   *John turns* his *head.*

When the subject of the sentence performs an action with a part of his body, in French that part of the body is modified by the definite article where English would use the possessive adjective.

$$\text{SUBJECT} + \text{VERB} + \genfrac{}{}{0pt}{}{\text{DEFINITE}}{\text{ARTICLE}} + \text{NOUN (part of body)}$$

C. *Traduisez en français.*

1. Raise your hand.   2. Jack closed his eyes.   3. Louise moved her foot.   4. She opened her mouth but didn't say anything.   5. The teacher shrugged his shoulders.

PATTERN PRACTICE: the subject of the sentence performs an action
with a part of his body

Pattern 2

  YOU HEAR   Nous levons la main. (le bras)
  YOU SAY   Nous levons le bras.

Pattern 3

  YOU HEAR   J'ai levé la main et les autres élèves aussi . . .
  YOU SAY   J'ai levé la main et les autres élèves aussi ont levé la main.

**7. How is possession indicated in French when the subject of the sentence performs
an action <u>on</u> some part of his body?**

Marie se lave la figure.   *Marie washes* her *face.*
Je me suis cassé la jambe.   *I broke* my *leg.*
Jean, tu t'es brossé les dents ce   *John, did you brush* your *teeth this*
matin?   *morning?*

When an action is performed <u>on</u> some part of the subject's body,
in French that part of the body is modified by the definite article
where English would use the possessive adjective, and the reflexive
pronoun is used with the verb.

SUBJECT + REFLEXIVE PRONOUN + VERB + DEFINITE ARTICLE + NOUN (part of body)

NOTE: This reflexive pronoun is the indirect object.

D. *Traduisez en français.*

1. I rub my back every morning. 2. John broke his arm. 3. They
brushed their hair. 4. I cut my finger yesterday. 5. Wash your
face.

PATTERN PRACTICE: sentences where an action is performed on a
part of the subject's body

Pattern 4

  YOU HEAR   Marie se lave les mains. (Je)
  YOU SAY   Je me lave les mains.

Pattern 5

  YOU HEAR   Jacques se lave les oreilles. (la figure)
  YOU SAY   Jacques se lave la figure.

8. How is possession expressed in French when the subject of the sentence performs an action on <u>a part of someone else's body</u>?

Marie **lui** lave **la** figure.   *Marie washes* his *face.*
L'infirmière **me** frotte **le** dos tous les   *The nurse rubs* my *back every morning.*
matins.

When the subject of the sentence performs an action on <u>someone else's</u> body, that part of the body is modified by the definite article where English would use a possessive adjective, and an indirect object pronoun is used with the verb.

$$\text{SUBJECT} + \begin{matrix} \text{INDIRECT} \\ \text{OBJECT} \\ \text{PRONOUN} \end{matrix} + \text{VERB} + \begin{matrix} \text{DEFINITE} \\ \text{ARTICLE} \end{matrix} + \text{NOUN (part of body)}$$

NOTE: Compare the above with what happens when a noun showing possession modifies the part of the body in the English sentence:

Marie lave **la figure <u>de Jean</u>.**   *Marie washes* <u>John's</u> face.
Le médecin frotte **le dos <u>du malade</u>.**   *The doctor rubs* <u>the patient's</u> back.

E. *Traduisez en français.*

1. I rub his back every morning.   2. Michael twisted her arm.
3. Wash her face.   4. He shook my hand.   5. We cut their hair.

PATTERN PRACTICE: action performed by the subject on a part of someone else's body

Pattern 6

    YOU HEAR   Marie lave la figure du malade.
    YOU SAY   Marie lui lave la figure.

9. When a part of the body is the subject of the English sentence, how does French express possession?

Elle **a de** jolis **yeux.**   Her *eyes are pretty.*
Il **a les cheveux** bruns.   His *hair is dark.*
J'**ai** mal à **la gorge.**   My *throat is sore.*

Whenever possible, the French avoid having a part of the body as the subject of the sentence. Generally, they use the verb **avoir** with the part of the body as the object of the sentence. The part of the body is often modified by the definite article.

F. *Traduisez en français.*

1. Your eyes are blue.   2. Her skin is soft.   3. My head aches.
4. My feet are sore.   5. Do your eyes hurt?   6. His finger hurts.

PATTERN PRACTICE: **avoir** + ARTICLE + NOUN (part of body)

Pattern 7

    YOU HEAR   J'ai mal aux yeux. (pieds)
    YOU SAY   J'ai mal aux pieds.

10. How does French express attitude or manner of being of a part of the body?

Il est entré **la tête baissée.**   *He entered* with his head down.
Jacques dort toujours **la bouche**   *Jack always sleeps* with his mouth
   ouverte.   open.

French expresses attitude or manner of a part of the body simply
by modifying the part of the body by the definite article. English
often uses the preposition *with* in such cases.

G. *Traduisez en français.*

1. He eats with his elbows on the table.   2. He likes to read with his
feet up[1] on the desk.   3. The little boy stood in front of the teacher
with his hands in his[2] pockets.   4. Marie refuses to speak, with her
lips pressed together.   5. Her husband, with his hand in[3] the air,
tried to stop a taxi.   6. Micheline was watching[4] me with her eyes
almost closed.   7. The poor old lady was in front of me with her
hand stretched out.

---

[1] Omit in translation.   [2] Use the article. French sometimes but not always uses the article
with a piece of clothing where English uses the possessive adjective.   [3] **en l'air**   [4] Use a
form of **observer.**

III. Possessive Pronouns

11. What are the French possessive pronouns?

SINGULAR		PLURAL		
Masculine	*Feminine*	*Masculine*	*Feminine*	
le mien	la mienne	les miens	les miennes	*mine*
le tien	la tienne	les tiens	les tiennes	*yours*
le sien	la sienne	les siens	les siennes	*his, hers*
le nôtre	la nôtre	les nôtres	les nôtres	*ours*
le vôtre	la vôtre	les vôtres	les vôtres	*yours*
le leur	la leur	les leurs	les leurs	*theirs*

12. How do the possessive pronouns agree? How are they used?

Vos leçons sont faciles; **les miennes** sont plus difficiles.

Your lessons are easy; mine *are more difficult.*

Elle expliquera cela à son père; je l'expliquerai **au mien.**

She will explain it to her father; I will explain it to mine.

Possessive pronouns, like possessive adjectives, agree in gender and number with the object possessed rather than the possessor. Possessive pronouns regularly take the place of nouns modified by a possessive adjective. Notice that the possessive pronouns contract with **à** and **de**.

H. *Remplacez les pronoms possessifs anglais par l'équivalent français[1].*

1. Il aime sa maison; j'aime (*mine*). 2. Je me souviens de mon premier bal; elles se souviennent de (*theirs*, s.). 3. Quelles aventures! Je ris encore quand je pense à (*his*, p.). 4. Je m'occupe de mes affaires, occupe-toi de (*yours*). 5. J'aime bien son jardin, mais je préfère (*ours*, s.). 6. Est-ce votre chien? Non, c'est (*his*). 7. Sa robe est beaucoup moins jolie que (*yours*, s.). 8. Si vous trouvez nos enfants mal élevés, vous devriez voir (*theirs*, p.). 9. Ma voiture ne marche pas; nous prendrons (*theirs*, s.).

---

[1] In this exercise, s = singular, p = plural.

PATTERN PRACTICE: possessive pronouns

Pattern 8

YOU HEAR   Jean a fini ses devoirs. Avez-vous fini . . .
YOU SAY   Jean a fini ses devoirs. Avez-vous fini les vôtres?

13. What are three ways of showing possession in a sentence of the following type?

Ce livre **est à moi.**
Ce livre **m'appartient.**   *This book* is mine.
Ce livre **est le mien.**

The most common way of expressing possession after **être** is by **à +** DISJUNCTIVE PRONOUN. When the possessive pronoun is used instead, the idea of the possessor is stressed. Possession is also often expressed by using an indirect object with a form of the verb **appartenir.**

PATTERN PRACTICE: ways of showing possession

Pattern 9

YOU HEAR   Cette voiture est à moi.
YOU SAY   Cette voiture est la mienne.

Pattern 10

YOU HEAR   Ces crayons sont les leurs.
YOU SAY   Ces crayons sont à eux.

(In this pattern practice drill, forms of **le leur** should be replaced by the masculine form of the disjunctive pronoun simply to duplicate the reply made on the tape.)

EXERCICES D'ENSEMBLE

I. *Traduisez en français.*

1. Do your duty, and I'll do mine.   2. Why are you shrugging your shoulders?   3. When will they finish their exercises?   4. All the pupils raised their hands[1] to answer the question.   5. Give him your arm; that will please him[2].   6. She always has a headache. 7. If that coat is yours, leave it here.   8. He broke his arm. 9. Listen

---

[1] French uses the singular here.   [2] Use a form of **faire plaisir à.**

to him talk about his trip. 10. If your feet hurt, rest. 11. I remember your sister and his. 12. I have something for you; close your eyes. 13. She broke her leg for the third time. 14. I do not want to see your snapshots of³ France. 15. Is this fine car yours? 16. This dictionary is mine; I need it. 17. You are going to hurt him if you twist his arm. 18. It is perhaps your opinion, but not mine. 19. Put down your hand. 20. It is his wife who cuts his hair. 21. What is there in this desk? I don't know; the desk isn't mine. 22. Go wash your face right away. 23. I have never seen a³ diamond as beautiful as yours. 24. The hairdresser will wash her hair tomorrow. 25. If you haven't any fountain pen, use⁴ mine. 26. Do you have a sore throat?

---

³ **de**   ⁴ Use the proper form of **se servir de.**

Problem Words

20. go

(a) How to say *I'm going, I went*, etc.

—Il paraît qu'il y a un bon film au   *"It seems that there's a good film at the*
  Rex. **Tu y es allé?**   Rex. Did you go?"
—Oui, **j'y suis allé** hier soir.   *"Yes,* I went *last night."*
—Moi, **j'irai** demain.   "I'll go *tomorrow."*

In English, we often say: "Are you going?" "Yes, I'm going." French rarely uses the verb **aller** without indicating a place to which, and if the place has already been mentioned, they then use the adverb **y** to refer to it.

But **y** is not used with the forms of the future and conditional of **aller,** because then two *i*-sounds would come together.

CAUTION: In French sentences such as the English "I'm going," and "Did you go?", do not use the verb **aller** without indicating the place to which or without using the adverb **y.**

(b) How to express certain combinations of *go* + PREPOSITION and *go* + ADVERB

go back	retourner	*go out*	sortir
go back home	rentrer	*go through*	traverser
go by	passer	*go toward*	se diriger vers
go down	descendre	*go up*	monter
go in	entrer	*go with*	accompagner

The English verb *go* is used with certain prepositions and adverbs in special ways, and such combinations are expressed by separate verbs in French.

(c) When *go to* = *attend*

Avez-vous **assisté à la** conférence?	*Did you* go to the *lecture?*
Non, j'**ai assisté au** match de basket-ball.	*No, I* went to the *basketball game.*
En France il n'est pas obligatoire d'**assister aux** cours de la faculté tous les jours.	*In France you don't have to* go to *university classes every day.*

The verb **assister** means *go to* when *go to* is equivalent to *be present at* or *attend*. However, **assister à** may be used only with certain places and specific occasions and not with all places. For instance, the verb **assister** could not be used to render the sentence: *I go to the university* in French. Therefore, be careful when using **assister à**. In general, one can safely use **aller à** to express the idea of *being present at*.

21. happen

(a) When to use **se passer**

Qu'est-ce qui **s'est passé?**	*What* happened?
Il **s'est passé** beaucoup de choses.	*Many things* happened.
Dites-moi ce qui **s'est passé** chez les Monnier.	*Tell me what* happened *at the Monniers.*

When *happen* = *take place*, when there is no personal indirect object, and when the subject is impersonal and somewhat indefinite, **se passer** may be used to express *to happen*.

CAUTION: When something *happens to someone*, do NOT use «se passer» for *happen*.

CAUTION: When there is a definite subject, avoid using «se passer» for *happen*.

(b) When to use **arriver**

Qu'est-ce qui **est arrivé?**	*What* happened?
Dites-moi ce qui **est arrivé** chez vous.	*Tell me what* happened *at your home.*
Qu'est-ce qui **est arrivé à Simone?**	*What* happened to Simone?
Quand est-ce que **cet accident est arrivé?**	*When* did that accident happen?

Whenever *happen* may be expressed by **se passer,** it may also be expressed by **arriver.** But in addition, **arriver** may be used when there is a personal indirect object (something *happens to someone*) and when the subject is neither impersonal nor indefinite.

(c) How to say that someone *happened to do something*

J'**étais** là **par hasard.**	*I* happened to be *there.*
Nous **avons rencontré** Jean dans la rue **tout à fait par hasard.**	*We* happened to meet *John on the street.*

When *happen to* + VERB means *by chance,* French often uses **par hasard** or **tout à fait par hasard** with the verb.

(d) When *happen = it happens that . . .* (or *someone happens to . . .*)

Il se trouvait que j'habitais dans le même immeuble que Monsieur Martin.	I happened to *live in the same building as Mr. Martin.*
Il se trouve justement que Monsieur et Madame Drouet doivent venir ce soir.	It (just) happens that *Mr. and Mrs. Drouet are to come over this evening.*

When a sentence with *happen* can be begun: *It happens that . . .,* the French often express this idea by placing the proper tense of: **Il se trouve que . . .** or: **Il se trouve justement que . . .** before the main part of the sentence.

(e) How to say: *How does it happen that . . .*

Comment se fait-il que vous $\begin{cases} \text{avez} \\ \text{ayez} \end{cases}$ acheté une nouvelle voiture?	How does it happen that *you bought a new car?*

Comment se fait-il que Marc$\begin{cases} \text{est} \\ \text{soit} \end{cases}$ How does it happen that *Mark is*
absent?   *absent?*

How does it happen that . . .? is expressed by **Comment se fait-il que . . .,** which is sometimes followed by the indicative, sometimes by the subjunctive.

22. hear

(a) How to say *to hear* (someone or something)

J'ai entendu un bruit en bas.   *I heard a noise downstairs.*

To hear (someone or something) is expressed by the verb **entendre·** Here there is no problem, for English and French usage are the same·

(b) How to say *to hear of* (someone or something)

Avez-vous **entendu parler de** cette   *Have* you *heard of* that invention?
invention?

In French *to hear of* must be expressed by **entendre parler de.**

(c) How to say *to hear that . . .*

Nous **avons entendu dire que** le   *We* heard that *the prime minister is*
premier ministre va démissionner.   *going to resign.*

In French *to hear that* must be expressed by **entendre dire que.**

CAUTION: Do NOT use «entendre de» for to *hear of* nor «entendre que» for *to hear that.*

J. *Remplacez les mots anglais par leur équivalent français.*

1. Je (*heard*) de cette affaire, mais il y a déjà longtemps.   2. Je me demande ce qui (*happened*) pendant mon absence.   3. Georgette refuse absolument de (*go*) à un match de boxe.   4. Est-ce que ce sont les cloches de la cathédrale que nous (*hear*)?   5. La chose (*happened*) comme je l'avais prévu.   6. J'aime bien (*hear*) tomber la pluie. 7. Vous les (*hear*) rire?   8. Je voudrais bien savoir ce qui (*is happening*).   9. C'est ennuyeux de (*hear*) la radio du voisin tous les soirs. 10. Il (*are happening*) des choses bizarres dans la maison d'en face. 11. Je (*hear*) sortir les employés. Est-ce qu'il est déjà cinq heures?

K. *Traduisez en français. Attention aux mots en italique.*

1. Did you *hear* that we will have a meeting Thursday?   2. There will be a football game Saturday. Do you want to *go?*   3. How does it *happen* that you left[1] New York?   4. To what lycée *did* you *go?*   5. Did you *hear* of Raoul's marriage?   6. Bernard broke his leg. How *did* that *happen?*   7. If you don't *go* to the concert, I won't *go* either.   8. We *heard* that you *were going* to Greece this summer.   9. I *happened* to see the Benoîts[2] at the florist's.   10. It was raining, but I *went* all the same.   11. Come[3] to dinner; we *happen* to have a nice[4] roast duck.   12. If you *happen* to receive a letter from Nicolas, telephone me right away.   13. How does it *happen* that the children are not in[5] school today?   14. There will be a parade tomorrow. Can you *go?*

---

[1] Use a form of **quitter.**   [2] French family names do not take -s in the plural.   [3] French says: *come to dine.*   [4] **beau**   [5] *in school* = **à l'école**

Verb Review

Review the verbs **courir** and **craindre** according to the outline on page 283.

CHAPTER 7

The Use of Past Tenses in Narration

1. What sort of actions are expressed by the verbs in boldface type in the following passage? What is the normal function of the compound past?

Il **s'est** alors **levé** après avoir bu un verre de vin. Il **a repoussé** les assiettes et le peu de boudin[1] froid que nous avions laissé. Il **a** soigneusement **essuyé** la toile cirée de la table. Il **a pris** dans un tiroir de sa table de nuit une feuille de papier[2] quadrillé, une enveloppe jaune, un petit porte-plume de bois rouge et un encrier carré d'encre violette. Quand il **m'a dit** le nom de la femme, j'**ai vu** que c'était une Mauresque[3]. J'**ai fait** la lettre. Je l'**ai écrite** un peu au hasard, mais je **me suis appliqué** à contenter Raymond parce que je n'avais pas de raison de ne pas le contenter. Puis j'**ai lu** la lettre à haute voix. Il **m'a écouté** en fumant et en hochant la tête, puis il **m'a demandé** de la relire. Il **a été** tout à fait content.

Camus: *L'Étranger*

---

[1] black pudding   [2] paper ruled in squares   [3] Moorish woman

The COMPOUND PAST expresses a series of successive actions in conversation or in an informal narrative. Each successive action serves to forward the plot of the narrative.

The COMPOUND PAST also expresses a change of mental state. Thus, the last sentence in the above passage: **Il a été tout à fait content** means: *He was* (in the sense of *became*) *quite satisfied*.

2. What sort of actions are expressed by the italicized verbs in the following passage? What are the various functions of the imperfect?

. . . Il m'a dit: «Je *savais* bien que tu *connaissais* la vie». Je ne me suis pas aperçu d'abord qu'il me *tutoyait*. C'est seulement quand il m'a déclaré: «Maintenant, tu es un vrai copain», que cela m'a frappé. Il a répété sa phrase et j'ai dit: «Oui». Cela m'*était* égal d'être son copain et il *avait* vraiment l'air d'en avoir envie. Il a cacheté la lettre et nous avons fini le vin.

Puis nous sommes restés un moment à fumer sans rien dire. Au dehors, tout *était* calme, et nous avons entendu le glissement d'une auto qui *passait*. J'ai dit: «Il est tard». Raymond le *pensait* aussi. Il a remarqué que le temps *passait* vite, et, dans un sens, c'*était* vrai. J'*avais* sommeil, mais j'*avais* de la
10 peine à me lever.

Camus: L'Étranger

The IMPERFECT describes a state or action which was going on when some other action took place. The imperfect often sets a background for the principal actions. Actions in the imperfect do not take place successively; they have no beginning or end in reference to the time of the main action. They simply go on.

Let us consider the various types of imperfects in the above passage.

(a) Cela m'*était* égal d'être son copain et il *avait* vraiment l'air d'en avoir envie . . . Au dehors, tout *était* calme . . . C'*était* vrai. J'*avais* sommeil, mais j'*avais* de la peine à me lever.

The IMPERFECT is used in past descriptions. Each of these verbs describes a state of being in the past. Note that these states have neither beginning nor end, nor are they successive actions which forward a narrative.

(b) Je ne **me suis** pas **aperçu** d'abord qu'il me *tutoyait* . . . Nous **avons entendu** le glissement d'une auto qui *passait* . . . Il **a remarqué** que le temps *passait* vite.

The IMPERFECT often describes what was going on when it was interrupted by some other action.

As a rule of thumb, we can say that most past actions in which the verb has an *-ing* ending in English are expressed by the imperfect in French.

The action of each of the italicized verbs in the above passage was going on when it was interrupted by the action of the verbs in bold-face type.

(c) «Je *savais* bien que tu *connaissais* la vie». . . . Raymond le *pensait* aussi.

The IMPERFECT is used to indicate a mental state in the past, for there is no beginning nor end to this state as far as the immediate actions are concerned.

Each of the above italicized verbs expresses a mental state.

3. The imperfect has still another important common function. What is the function of the imperfects in italics in the following passage?

A huit heures la cloche *annonçait* le souper. Après le souper, dans les beaux jours, on *s'asseyait* sur le perron. Mon père, armé de son fusil, *tirait* les chouettes[1] qui *sortaient* des crénaux[2] à l'entrée de la nuit. Ma mère, Lucile et moi, nous *regardions* le ciel, les bois, les derniers rayons du soleil, les premières étoiles. A dix heures, on *rentrait* et l'on *se couchait*.   5

Les soirées d'automne et d'hiver *étaient* d'une autre nature. Le souper fini et les quatre convives revenus de la table à la cheminée, ma mère *se jetait*, en soupirant, sur un vieux lit de jour de siamoise[3] flambée; on *mettait* devant elle un guéridon[4] avec une bougie[5]. Je *m'asseyais* auprès du feu avec Lucile; les domestiques *enlevaient* le couvert et *se retiraient*. Mon père *commençait* alors   10 une promenade qui ne *cessait* qu'à l'heure de son coucher . . . Sa tête, demi-chauve, était couverte d'un grand bonnet blanc qui *se tenait* tout droit.

Chateaubriand: Mémoires d'outre-tombe

---

[1] owls   [2] indentures in the wall   [3] bright colored siamese cotton   [4] round table   [5] candle

Habitual or repeated past actions are expressed by the IMPERFECT. In English, such actions are usually expressed by $\left.\begin{array}{l} used\ to \\ would \end{array}\right\}$ + VERB.

4. How can an English-speaking person avoid overusing the French imperfect?

English-speaking students tend to use the French imperfect where the French would use the compound past (**passé composé**). Before expressing an action or state in the imperfect, ask yourself some questions to test whether this is the proper tense.

Use of the COMPOUND PAST (passé composé)

(a) Does the action advance the narrative even in the slightest degree? In that case, use the compound past rather than the imperfect.

(b) Is the action limited in time in any way? In that case, use the compound past rather than the imperfect. Even if the action takes place over twenty years or twenty centuries, if the time is limited, do not use the imperfect.

(c) Does the action state a past fact, one which does not set a background? Then use the compound past rather than the imperfect.

NOTE: The fact that the action is continued has nothing to do with whether it is imperfect or **passé composé**. All actions continue for some time — some much longer than others — but the mere fact that they continue is no criterion for the choice of tense.

Use of the IMPERFECT

(a) Does the action merely form a background for the plot by describing a state? Then use the imperfect.

(b) Is it a question of a continuing action which is interrupted by another action? In this case, put the continuing action in the imperfect.

(c) Is it a question of a past action expressed in English by $\left. \begin{array}{l} was \\ were \end{array} \right\}$ + the *-ing* form of the verb? Then use the imperfect.

(d) Is it a customary action, repeated regularly, which would be expressed in English by $\left. \begin{array}{l} would \\ used\ to \end{array} \right\}$ + verb? Then use the imperfect.

(e) Is it a question of a state of mind rather than a change of state of mind? Then use the imperfect.

There are a few other less common uses of the imperfect, but these are the principal ones.

A. *Remplacez l'infinitif par la forme convenable du passé composé ou de l'imparfait, selon le cas. Expliquez oralement chaque emploi de l'imparfait.*

Il (faire) froid hier et nous n'(avoir) rien de spécial à faire. Je (vouloir) rester chez moi, mais Pierre (préférer) aller voir un de nos amis. Donc, nous y (aller). Nous (quitter) la maison à sept heures du soir et quand nous (arriver) dans la rue, il (faire) déjà sombre et il (neiger).

5 Nous (prendre) ma voiture, et nous (rouler) pendant une demi-heure. Quand notre ami nous (ouvrir) la porte de son appartement, nous (entendre) des voix au salon. Nous ne (savoir) pas qui (être) là, et nous ne (vouloir) pas déranger notre ami Jacques, mais il nous (dire) d'entrer.

10 Pierre (s'excuser) de ne pas lui avoir téléphoné d'abord. Nous (enlever) nos manteaux et nous (entrer) au salon. Il y (avoir) là plusieurs personnes que nous (connaître) et qui (parler) de musique.

Nous (être) en pleine conversation quand la sœur de mon ami (proposer) de nous montrer des photographies qu'elle avait prises en
Europe. Il (falloir) les regarder. Ensuite, on nous (servir) à boire et 15
à manger. Nous y (rester) une heure et demie. Il y (avoir) des jeunes
filles qui (vouloir) danser ensuite, mais il (être) trop tard. Nous les
(inviter) à venir chez nous le lendemain soir. A dix heures, nous
(rentrer) chez nous.

B. *Traduisez en français en employant le passé composé et l'imparfait. Expliquez oralement chaque emploi de l'imparfait.*

A curious thing happened[1] to me the other day. I was[2] taking a walk
in the country with my dog. I was[3] walking along a road when I saw
a man who wore an old coat. He was about[4] forty years old. When
he caught[5] sight of me, he became afraid and began to run. That
surprised me, and I decided to follow him. We walked rapidly[6] for[7]   5
five minutes. Finally, he slowed[8] down and I overtook him. I asked
him why he was acting like that. He told me that I resembled a policeman[9] he knew and said: "I was afraid[10] when I saw you." The man
spoke with an accent. I learned that he was a foreigner. He didn't
know English well, but he was able to tell me that he had become   10
frightened[11] on seeing my dog. He told me that he often used[2] to go
walking in the country, where he would pick up fruit[12] and would
eat at the farmers'[13]. We chatted a bit, and I tried to reassure him.
Finally, we shook hands, and then we continued[14] on our way.

---

[1] Use a form of **arriver.**   [2] Use a form of **se promener.**   [3] Use a form of **marcher.**   [4] en-
viron   [5] Use a form of **apercevoir.**   [6] **à grand pas**   [7] **pendant**   [8] *slow down* = **ralentir**
[9] **un policier**   [10] This means that he became frightened. Use a form of **avoir peur.**   [11] Use
a form of **s'effrayer.**   [12] **des fruits**   [13] *farmer* = **le fermier**   [14] Use a form of **continuer
notre route.**

PATTERN PRACTICE: certain uses of the imperfect and compound past

Pattern 1

YOU HEAR   Que faisiez-vous quand le téléphone a sonné? (lire votre
lettre)

YOU SAY   Je lisais votre lettre quand le téléphone a sonné.

Pattern 2

YOU HEAR   Qu'est-ce que vous avez fait quand le professeur est arrivé? (se lever)

YOU SAY   Nous nous sommes levés quand le professeur est arrivé.

Pattern 3

YOU HEAR   Qu'est-ce que Suzanne a fait pendant que Jacques se reposait? (préparer le dîner)

YOU SAY   Suzanne a préparé le dîner pendant que Jacques se reposait.

Pattern 4

YOU HEAR   Maintenant je ne joue plus au bridge.

YOU SAY   Autrefois je jouais souvent au bridge.

Pattern 5

YOU HEAR   Quand j'étais jeune, je faisais la cour à Marie.

YOU SAY   Pendant deux ans, j'ai fait la cour à Marie.

5. When is the simple past used?

Le Tigre

Une femme *lavait* son linge dans une fontaine, à cent pas de la maison; elle *avait* avec elle un enfant de quatorze à quinze mois.

Elle **manqua** de savon, **retourna** chez elle pour en chercher, et, jugeant inutile d'emmener son enfant, le **laissa** jouer sur le gazon, près de la fontaine.

5 Pendant qu'elle *cherchait* son savon, elle **jeta** par la fenêtre ouverte les yeux sur la fontaine pour s'assurer si l'enfant ne *s'aventurait* pas au bord de l'eau; mais sa terreur **fut** grande lorsqu'elle **vit** un tigre sortir de la forêt, traverser le chemin, aller droit à l'enfant et poser sur lui sa large patte.

10 Elle **resta** immobile, haletante, pâle, presque morte.

Mais sans doute l'enfant **prit** l'animal féroce pour un gros chien; il lui **empoigna** les oreilles avec ses petites mains et **commença** de[1] jouer avec lui.

Le tigre ne **fut** pas en[2] reste; c'*était* un tigre d'un caractère jovial, il **joua** lui-même avec l'enfant.

15 Ce jeu effroyable **dura** dix minutes, puis le tigre, laissant l'enfant, **retraversa** la route et **rentra** dans le bois.

La mère **s'élança, courut** tout éperdue à l'enfant, et le **trouva** riant et sans une égratignure.

Alexandre Dumas: *Le Caucase*

---

[1] Most often one finds **commencer à** + INFINITIVE, but sometimes **commencer de** + INFINITIVE is found in literary style.   [2] backward, reticent

The SIMPLE PAST is normally used in written French to express a series of successive actions in a literary narrative. It also sometimes states a past fact.

The SIMPLE PAST is a written tense, not used in speaking except in very formal lectures or orations. It is used in formal literary writing rather than in letters.

The SIMPLE PAST has the advantage over the COMPOUND PAST of being a single form and thus producing a less jerky effect.

Notice the exact use of the simple past (**passé simple**) in the following sentences taken from the above passage:

> Elle **manqua** de savon.
> Mais sa terreur **fut** grande lorsqu'elle **vit** un tigre sortir de la forêt.
> Elle **resta** immobile, haletante, pâle, presque morte.
> Le tigre ne **fut** pas en reste; c'était un tigre d'un caractère jovial.
> Ce jeu effroyable **dura** dix minutes.

The uses of the imperfect are the same, whether the passage is written in the **passé simple** or the **passé composé**.

C. *Remplacez les infinitifs entre parenthèses par la forme convenable du passé composé ou de l'imparfait.*

(Use the compound past for successive actions unless your instructor tells you to use the simple past for such actions.)

Monsieur Grinci (être) [*était*] toujours de mauvaise humeur. Pour un rien il (crier) [*criait*], il (gronder) [*grondait*] et il (faire) [*faisait*] peur à tous ceux qui l'(approcher) [*approchait*]. Il (avoir) [*avait*] un domestique, Jean, qui (être) [*était*] bien malheureux. Mais Jean (être) [*était*] aussi intelligent et (savoir) [*savait*] bien qu'il (falloir) [*fallait*] obéir à son maître s'il (vouloir) [*voulait*] garder sa place. 5

Un jour, Monsieur Grinci (rentrer) [*est rentré*] chez lui en colère et (se préparer) [*s'est*] à dîner. La table (être) [*était*] mise près d'une fenêtre qui (donner) [*donnait*] sur la cour. Tout (être) [*était*] joliment arrangé et il y (avoir) [*avait*] même un vase de fleurs au milieu.

Pendant que Jean (être) [*était*] à la cuisine, Monsieur Grinci (goûter) [*a goûté*] la 10 soupe et la (trouver) [*a trouvée*] trop chaude. Il (se mettre) [*s'est mis*] encore plus en colère et la (jeter) dans la cour par la fenêtre ouverte.

Ce jour-là, Jean (être) [*était*] plus calme qu'à l'ordinaire. Quand il (voir) [*a vu*] cela, il (penser) [*a pensé*] que son maître (mériter) [*méritait*] une leçon. Il (aller) [*est allé*] vers la table, (prendre) [*a pris*] l'assiette de son maître et la (jeter) [*a jetée*] dans la cour. 15 Puis, il (prendre) [*a pris*] les services, les verres et les fleurs et (jeter) le tout par la fenêtre.

Cela (mettre) [*a mis*] monsieur Grinci hors de lui et il (ordonner) [*a ordonné*] à Jean de lui dire ce qu'il (faire) [*faisait*].

20   Jean lui (répondre) tranquillement: «Monsieur, quand je vous (voir) jeter la soupe par la fenêtre, je (penser) que vous (vouloir) dîner dans la cour et c'est pour cela que je (jeter) tout le reste».

Monsieur Grinci (comprendre) cette leçon. Il (sourire) quand même et, depuis ce jour, s'il ne (changer) pas de caractère, du moins 25 il (maîtriser) ses colères.

D. *Traduisez en français, en employant le passé composé et l'imparfait où il y a lieu.*

(Use the compound past for successive actions unless your instructor tells you to use formal literary style. In that case, use the simple past for such actions.)

Balzac, the great French writer of the nineteenth century, had the habit of working late into the night. Most of the time he did not take the trouble to lock the door of his house.

5   One night as Balzac was sleeping, a thief entered the house and opened the door of the room of the writer. The latter seemed to be sleeping soundly. The thief, reassured, went to Balzac's desk and began to rummage around in the drawers. Suddenly, he heard[1] a loud laugh. He turned around[2] and caught[3] sight of the writer, who was laughing heartily. The thief became frightened[4], but he was not 10 able to keep from asking Balzac what was making him laugh. The latter answered him that it[5] amused him a great deal to see that a thief was coming in the night without light to look in a desk for money which he[6] had never been able to find even in[7] plain daylight.

---

[1] Use a form of **entendre rire très fort.** [2] Use a form of **se retourner.** [3] Use a form of **apercevoir.** [4] Use a form of **s'effrayer.** [5] **ça** [6] **lui** [7] **en plein jour**

Problem Words

23. intend

The word *intend* may be expressed in several ways. Often, but not always, these expressions may be used synonymously.

Jacques **pense** partir demain matin.   *Jack* intends to *leave tomorrow morning.*
J'ai **l'intention de** lire l'article du   *I* intend to *read Professor Dugard's* professeur Dugard.   *article.*

| La secrétaire **compte** prendre ses vacances en juillet. | *The secretary* intends *to take her vacation in July.* |

The word *intend* may be expressed by **penser** + INFINITIVE, **compter** + INFINITIVE and **avoir l'intention de** + INFINITIVE.

24. introduce

How to say *introduce someone to someone*

Voulez-vous me **présenter** à Madame Leduc?	*Will you* introduce *me to Mrs. Leduc?*
Marthe m'**a présenté** à Hélène.	*Martha introduced me to Helen.*
Qui vous **a présenté** à Michel?	*Who introduced you to Michael?*

The English *introduce a person* is expressed in French by **présenter**.

CAUTION: Do NOT use the French verb «introduire» with the meaning of *introduce a person*. The verb **introduire** sometimes expresses the English *introduce* in less common connotations and also it often means *insert*.

25. a knock

How to say *a knock at the door*

| **On a frappé** à la porte. | There was a knock *at the door.* |
| **Avez-vous entendu frapper** à la porte? | Did you hear a knock *at the door?* |

French has no expression which corresponds to the English *a knock at the door*. Instead, it uses the verbal expression **frapper à la porte,** and *to hear a knock at the door* is **entendre frapper à la porte.**

CAUTION: Do NOT try to use a French noun to express the English noun *knock*.

26. know

(a) When *know = be acquainted with*

| —**Connaissez**-vous Geneviève Leroy? | *"Do you* know *Genevieve Leroy?"* |
| —Oui, je la **connais** depuis longtemps. | *"Yes, I* have known *her for a long time."* |

The verb **connaître** is always used to indicate *knowing a person*.

(**b**) When *know* = *be familiar with something*

Les jeunes **connaissent** bien les œuvres de Camus.	*Young people* know (are well acquainted with) *the works of Camus.*
Je **connais** Paris, mais je ne **connais** pas Marseille.	*I* know *Paris, but I don't* know *Marseilles.*

The verb **connaître** is used to indicate familiarity with works, places, etc.

(**c**) When *know* = *meet, get acquainted with*

Où avez-vous **connu** votre mari?	*Where did you* meet *your husband?* *Where did you* get acquainted with *your husband?* *Where did you* get to know *your husband?*

In the compound past and simple past, **connaître** sometimes means *to meet* in the sense of *to get to know* or *to get acquainted with.*

(**d**) When *know* = *know from memory*

Savez-vous les mois de l'année en français?	*Do you* know *the months of the year in French?*

Use **savoir** when *know* = *know from memory.*

(**e**) When *know* = *know from study*

Cet élève **sait** toujours sa leçon.	*That pupil always* knows *his lesson.*

Use **savoir** when *know* = *know from study.*

(**f**) When *know* = *be aware of*

Je **sais** où Pierre a mis son portefeuille.	*I* know *where Peter put his billfold.*

Use **savoir** when *know* = *be aware of.*

(**g**) How to say *to know how to*

Est-ce que Suzanne **sait** faire la cuisine?	*Does Suzanne* know how to *cook?*

The verb **savoir** + INFINITIVE often means *to know how to.*

E. *Remplacez les mots entre parenthèses par leur équivalent français.*

1. Les Beaulieu (*intend to*) faire construire une nouvelle maison de campagne.   2. Tout le monde (*knows*) l'histoire de la femme du docteur.   3. (*Introduce*)-moi à la jeune fille qui est assise là-bas.   4. Je (*don't know how to*) jouer d'un instrument, mais j'aime beaucoup la musique.   5. Je (*know*) parfaitement bien tout ce que vous avez dit.   6. J'habite ici depuis très longtemps; je (*know*) les plus petites rues de la ville.   7. Il (*intended to*) partir hier, mais il a manqué l'avion.   8. Vous (*know*) le russe; pouvez-vous m'aider à faire cette traduction?   9. (*Do you know how to*) conduire une auto sans transmission automatique?

F. *Traduisez en français. Attention aux mots en italique.*

1. There was a *knock* at the door about midnight.   2. Raymond *knows* a great many very important people.   3. What do you *intend* to do during the weekend?   4. Someone already *introduced* me to that person, but she probably doesn't remember me.   5. What!¹ You don't *know how to* swim?   6. I doubt that Paul *intends* to spend his vacation with us.   7. Do you *know* what happened to Francis? 8. Do you really *intend* to marry Blanche?   9. Where *did* you *get* to *know* that artist?

---

¹ Comment

Verb Review

Review the verbs **croire** and **devoir** according to the outline on page 283.

CHAPTER 8

Demonstratives

A demonstrative is a word that points out. The English demonstratives are *this*, *that*, *these*, and *those*.

A demonstrative may modify a noun; in that case, it is a demonstrative adjective. Ex.: *this* book, *that* table, *those* people.

A demonstrative may take the place of a noun; in that case, it is a demonstrative pronoun. Ex.: This book is red, *that one* is green. Don't do *that*.

In French, it is important to know whether the DEMONSTRATIVE is an ADJECTIVE or a PRONOUN. If it is a pronoun, it is necessary to know which type of demonstrative pronoun it is since there are three types of demonstrative pronouns.

I. The Demonstrative Adjective

1. What are the demonstrative adjectives and how do they agree?

MASCULINE

Ce livre est bleu.
Ces livres sont bleus.

Cet arbre est vieux.
Ces arbres sont vieux.

FEMININE

Cette ville est grande.
Ces villes sont grandes.

The demonstrative adjectives are:

	Singular		Plural
MASCULINE	ce	used before masculine noun or adjective beginning with a consonant*	ces
	cet	used before masculine noun or adjective beginning with vowel sound	ces
FEMININE	cette	used before all feminine nouns and adjectives	ces

* That is, all consonants except mute **h.**

2. When and how do the French distinguish between *this* and *that*?

Ce professeur est excellent.	That *teacher is excellent.*
Ce professeur-**ci** est plus âgé que **ce** professeur-**là.**	This *teacher is older than* that *teacher.*
A **ce** moment-**là** il n'y avait pas beaucoup de travail.	*At* that *time there was not much work.*

In French there is one demonstrative adjective with several forms (**ce, cette,** etc.), in English there are two demonstrative adjectives (*this, that*).

French does not usually distinguish between *this* and *that* unless a contrast is desired. In other words, **ce** points out more definitely than **le,** but it does not make a contrast between *this* and *that*.

When two objects are mentioned and a contrast is desired, each of the nouns contrasted is preceded by a form of the demonstrative adjective, and the first noun is followed by **-ci** (to indicate *this*), the second noun is followed by **-là** (to indicate *that*). A hyphen connects **-ci** and **-là** to their nouns.

In certain time expressions referring to the past, **-là** is regularly appended to the noun modified by the demonstrative without there being any corresponding expression with **-ci.**

A. *Remplacez les tirets par un adjectif démonstratif, en mettant* **-ci** *ou* **-là** *après le nom où*[1] *il y a lieu.*

1. Que pensez-vous de _____ nouvelle élève?   2. J'aime bien voir _____ comédiens à la télévision.   3. _____ arbre a plus de deux cents

_____
[1] where it is necessary.

ans.   4. Prenez ____ verre; ____ verre est pour moi.   5. A ____ époque il n'y avait pas d'automobiles.   6. Ne prenez pas ____ lettre; elle est très importante.   7. Combien coûtent ____ roses rouges? 8. ____ journaux de sport ne sont pas très intéressants.   9. ____ oiseau semble triste dans sa cage.   10. Je dois partir ____ soir pour Paris.   11. ____ élèves font trop de bruit.   12. Avez-vous besoin de ____ dictionnaire aujourd'hui?   13. Vous ferez ____ exercices mais pas ____ exercices.   14. D'où vient ____ lumière?

B. *Traduisez en français. Soulignez les démonstratifs.*

1. Who is that gentleman?   2. Do you like that music?   3. At that time[1] I was only four years old.   4. When did you do these exercises? 5. This car is really better than that car.   6. At that time[2] there was no one in the streets.   7. Have you read those short stories?   8. That child is a real prodigy.   9. At that time[3] I was doing the housework. 10. Do you know if that hotel is comfortable?   11. Give me this book and I'll give you that book.

---

[1] époque   [2] heure   [3] moment

PATTERN PRACTICE: demonstrative adjectives

Pattern 1

> YOU HEAR   Le livre n'est pas bon.
> YOU SAY   Ce livre n'est pas bon.

II. The Indefinite Demonstrative Pronouns

3. What are the indefinite demonstrative pronouns? When are they used? When is ça used for cela?

Lisez **ceci**, ne lisez pas **cela**.	*Read* this, *don't read* that.
Avez-vous vu **cela**?	*Did you see* that?
Ne fais pas **ça**.	*Don't do* that.

The indefinite demonstrative pronouns are **ceci, cela,** and **ça.** They refer to something without gender or number, such as an idea, or they point out something indefinite. The pronoun **ça** is a shortened and familiar form of **cela,** common in spoken style but to be avoided in elegant written style.

The indefinite demonstrative pronouns are not normally used in good French before a form of **être**. Before a form of **être,** the demonstrative pronoun **ce** is used instead of **ça.** For example, not «Ça sera facile», but rather **Ce sera facile.**

PATTERN PRACTICE: the indefinite demonstrative pronouns

Pattern 2

    YOU HEAR   Lisez cette chose.

    YOU SAY   Lisez cela.

Pattern 3

    YOU HEAR   Cette chose prend beaucoup de temps.

    YOU SAY   Ça prend beaucoup de temps.

III. The Definite Demonstrative Pronouns

4. What are the definite demonstrative pronouns?

The definite demonstrative pronouns are:

	Singular	*Plural*
MASCULINE	celui	ceux
FEMININE	celle	celles

5. How are the definite demonstrative pronouns used?

Ces livres-ci sont meilleurs que **ceux-là.**   *These books are better than* those.

The definite demonstrative pronouns often refer to something already mentioned which has number and gender. They then agree with this antecedent in gender and number.

Celui qui travaille gagne de l'argent.   He (The one) *who works earns money.*
Ceux qui veulent peuvent partir.   Those (The ones) *who wish can leave.*

The definite demonstrative pronouns + **qui** are also used to express the English *he who, she who, the one who,* etc. In this case, the gender and number of the definite demonstrative depends on its meaning.

6. By what must the definite demonstrative pronouns be followed?

Ceux qui sont en retard sont obligés de rester après la classe.	Those who *are late are obliged to stay after class.*
J'aime mieux mes chiens que **ceux du** voisin.	*I like my dogs better than* the neighbor's (*those of my neighbor*).
Choisissez les fleurs que vous préférez. **Celles-ci** sont plus fraîches que **celles-là.**	*Choose the flowers you prefer.* These *are fresher than* those.

The definite demonstrative pronouns are always followed by **-ci, -là,** by a relative pronoun or by a preposition. They cannot be followed by **-ci** or **-là** if they are followed by either a relative pronoun or a preposition.

7. How are *the former* **and** *the latter* **expressed in French?**

Connaissez-vous ces deux dames? **Celle-ci** est anglaise; **celle-là** est polonaise.	*Do you know these two ladies?* The former *is Polish,* the latter *English.*
Je cherche des renseignements sur Jean Dubois et Pierre Petit. **Ce dernier** habite à Chartres.	*I am looking for information concerning John Dubois and Peter Petit.* The latter *lives in Chartres.*

The English *the former* and *the latter* are expressed in French by the definite demonstrative pronouns. In French *the latter* (**celui-ci,** etc.) precedes *the former* (**celui-là,** etc.). French also expresses *the latter* by a form of **ce dernier.**

C. *Remplacez les mots entre parenthèses par le pronom démonstratif convenable. Mettez* **-ci** *ou* **-là** *s'il y a lieu.*

1. (*This*) doit rester strictement entre nous. 2. Vous avez une belle maison, mais connaissez-vous (*that*) des Delanoy? 3. Si je découvre (*the one*) qui a fait cela, je le punirai. 4. Je l'avais dit, (*that*) devait arriver. 5. Le Rhône et la Garonne prennent leur source hors de France; (*the latter*) se jette dans l'Atlantique, (*the former*) dans la Méditerranée. 6. Ils sont partis; (*that*) me fait beaucoup de peine. 7. —Quelles sont vos fleurs préférées? —(*Those*) que vous m'avez données. 8. Savez-vous ce que veut dire (*this*)? 9. J'envie (*those*) qui peuvent aller passer l'été en France. 10. Si votre voiture ne marche pas, pourquoi ne prenez-vous pas (*your brother's*)? 11. Il y a beaucoup de robes dans le magasin, mais il faut te décider. Veux-tu (*these*) ou (*those*)? 12. —Laquelle de ces dames est Madame Delatour? —(*The one*) qui porte une robe bleue.

D. *Traduisez en français. Soulignez les démonstratifs.*

1. That belongs to me; don't take it.   2. If you don't like that, leave it.   3. This gift is not the one you promised me.   4. This interests me a great deal.   5. There are the good[1] and the bad. The former[2] will be rewarded, the latter will be punished.   6. Those who are not satisfied can leave.   7. I know those girls. Go out with this one but not with that one.   8. My ideas are sometimes different from my mother-in-law's.   9. Don't think of that any more.   10. I like these two photos, this one especially.   11. Those whom you encourage make progress.

---

[1] **les bons**   [2] In French, *the latter* precedes *the former*.

PATTERN PRACTICE: the definite demonstrative pronouns

Pattern 4

> YOU HEAR   Avez-vous le dictionnaire de Jacques?
> YOU SAY   Oui, j'ai celui de Jacques.

Pattern 5

> YOU HEAR   J'ai le stylo que vous cherchez.
> YOU SAY   J'ai celui que vous cherchez.

Pattern 6

> YOU HEAR   Ces enfants-ci sont plus gentils que ces enfants-là.
> YOU SAY   Ces enfants-ci sont plus gentils que ceux-là.

Pattern 7

> YOU HEAR   L'homme qui travaille gagne de l'argent.
> YOU SAY   Celui qui travaille gagne de l'argent.

IV. The Demonstrative Pronoun *ce*

When used as a demonstrative pronoun, **ce** is invariable and is usually the subject of some form of the verb **être**. It has several distinct uses. In one of its functions, we call it the *indefinite* **ce,** in another the *introductory* **ce.**

NOTE: A third function, sometimes called the *pleonastic* **ce,** will not be taken up here. Ex.: La guerre, **c**'est la ruine. Ce que Roger fait, **c**'est son affaire.

THE INDEFINITE ce

8. How is the English *it* expressed in French when it refers back to an idea without gender or number?

Elle nage bien. C'est difficile.	*She swims well.* It's *difficult.*
—Venez avec moi. — C'est impossible.	*"Come with me."* "It's *impossible."*
Il lit vite. C'est facile à voir.	*He reads rapidly.* It's *easy to see.*
Ils vont partir. C'est bon à savoir.	*They are going to leave.* It's *good to know.*

The *indefinite* **ce** refers back to an aforementioned idea. Since an idea has neither gender nor number, the indefinite and neuter **ce** is used to refer to such an idea. English uses *it* to refer back to an idea.

When the indefinite **ce** + a form of **être** has its meaning completed by an infinitive, the preposition **à** normally connects the infinitive to what precedes.

$$\text{idea} \rightarrow \textbf{ce} + \begin{array}{c}\text{form} \\ \text{of} \\ \textbf{être}\end{array} + \text{ADJECTIVE} + \textbf{à} + \text{INFINITIVE}$$

9. When, on the other hand, is the English *it* expressed by the impersonal *il*?

Il est difficile de bien chanter.	It *is difficult to sing well.*
Il est impossible de partir avec vous.	It *is impossible to leave with you.*
Il est facile de lire vite.	It *is easy to read rapidly.*

When one would begin an English sentence with an *it* which does not refer to any previous idea, in French such a sentence is often introduced by the impersonal **il** followed by a form of **être** and an adjective. This construction is usually followed by **de** + INFINITIVE.

$$\textbf{Il} + \begin{array}{c}\text{form} \\ \text{of} \\ \textbf{être}\end{array} + \text{ADJECTIVE} + \textbf{de} + \text{INFINITIVE}$$

In conversational style, the French often replace the impersonal **il** by **ce**, so that **Il est difficile de bien chanter** often becomes **C'est difficile de bien chanter.** The latter is, however, less elegant.

E. *Remplacez les tirets par* **ce** *ou* **il.**

1. Jean n'est pas encore arrivé. _____ est ennuyeux. 2. Où tout cela nous mène-t-il? _____ est triste à penser. 3. _____ est impossible de retourner chez elle maintenant. 4. Voilà ce que je vous ai promis. _____ est joli, n'est-ce pas? 5. _____ est plus facile de critiquer que de créer. 6. Aimez-vous nager? _____ est tellement agréable.

F. *Traduisez en français.*

1. Is your father angry? It's evident. 2. It is easy to make mistakes. 3. What you write surprises me, but it's interesting. 4. It is pleasant to travel. 5. It is interesting to learn a foreign language. 6. He knows what he is doing. It's true. 7. John won't come back any more. It is difficult to believe.

PATTERN PRACTICE: the indefinite **ce**

Pattern 8

> YOU HEAR   (facile) J'apprends à nager.
> YOU SAY   J'apprends à nager. C'est facile.

Pattern 9

> YOU HEAR   Apprendre une langue étrangère est difficile.
> YOU SAY   Il est difficile d'apprendre une langue étrangère.

THE INTRODUCTORY **ce**

10. When is the introductory ce used?

Qui est ce garçon? **C'**est **mon fils.**   *Who is that boy? He's* my son.
Qui est là? **C'**est **lui.**   *Who is there? It's* he.
Qui sont ces personnes? **Ce** sont **mes cousines.**   *Who are those people?* They *are* my cousins.
C'est **Pasteur** qui a découvert un vaccin contre la rage.   *It is* Pasteur *who discovered a vaccine for rabies.*

The *introductory* **ce** is used before a form of the verb **être** when what follows **être** could be the subject of the sentence. After **être** normally a pronoun, a proper name, or a modified noun could be the subject of the sentence.

In such cases, the introductory **ce** is expressed in English sometimes by *it,* sometimes by *he, she,* or *they.*

NOTE: In sentences like **C'est le plus beau des mois,** the introductory **ce** is also used when a superlative form of the adjective follows a form of **être.**

11. When, on the other hand, are the subject pronouns *il, elle, ils,* **and** *elles* **used as the subject of the verb** *être***?**

Où est <u>Marie</u>? **Elle** est en classe.	*Where is <u>Marie</u>? She is in class.*
Voyez-vous souvent <u>Gilbert</u>? **Il** est très intelligent.	*Do you often see <u>Gilbert</u>? He is very intelligent.*
Nous parlons de <u>vos enfants</u>. Sont-**ils** là?	*We are speaking of <u>your children</u>. Are they there?*

Whenever what follows a form of the verb **être** could not be the subject of the sentence, a third person subject pronoun must be used instead of the introductory **ce.** That is, whenever an adverb, an adjective, or a phrase follows **être,** it is NOT possible to use the introductory **ce.**

12. When is the personal pronoun and when is the introductory ce used with names of professions, nationalities, religions, etc., when they follow a form of *être***?**

Il est <u>médecin</u>.	**C**'est <u>un médecin</u>.
Elle est <u>protestante</u>.	**C**'est <u>une protestante très fervente</u>.
Ils sont <u>français</u>.	**Ce** sont <u>des Français distingués</u>.

When the <u>unmodified</u> name of a profession, nationality, religion or any like noun is used after the verb **être,** it is considered an adjective rather than a noun. In such cases, **il, elle, ils** or **elles** are used before the form of **être.** But if such a noun is modified, it is then considered as a noun, and since it can thus be the subject of the sentence, the form of the verb **être** is preceded by the introductory **ce.**

G. *Remplacez les tirets par l'équivalent français du mot indiqué en anglais.*

1. —Où est Jacques? —(*He*) est en France. 2. Voilà Solange. (*She*) est professeur. 3. Connaissez-vous M. Dupont? (*He*) est un célèbre écrivain. 4. Est- (*she*) catholique ou protestante? 5. Ne demandez pas cela à Jacques. (*He*) n'est pas riche. 6. —Que fait son père? —(*He*) est médecin. 7. Où est votre frère maintenant? —(*He*) est à l'armée. 8. (*It*) sont eux qui m'ont ramené à la maison. 9. —De quelle nationalité sont ces gens? —(*They*) sont allemands. 10. (*They*) sont des célibataires endurcis, mais (*they*) sont contents de leur sort.

H. *Traduisez en français.*

1. Who is this man? He is Mr. Lefranc.   2. I like this snapshot a great deal. It is very beautiful.   3. Look at these children; they are so cute.   4. Who took his dictionary? It wasn't[1] I.   5. I remember him; he is a teacher, isn't he?   6. Is he French or American?   7. Who is this girl? She is my sister.   8. Do you know Madame Dumont? She is the mother of that lawyer.

---

[1] Use présent in French.

PATTERN PRACTICE: the INTRODUCTORY **ce**

Pattern 10

    YOU HEAR   Qui est le jeune homme qui nous salue? (mon ami)
    YOU SAY   C'est mon ami qui nous salue.

Pattern 11

    YOU HEAR   Avez-vous vu Jean Perrot? (médecin)
    YOU SAY   Il est médecin.

I. *Remplacez les mots anglais par l'équivalent français. Choisissez un des mots:* **ce, il, elle, ils, elles.**

1. Voyez-vous cette femme au chapeau rouge? (*She*) est la sœur d'Henri.   2. Je connais Pierre et sa femme; (*they*) sont des catholiques pratiquants.   3. J'aime beaucoup cet élève. (*He*) est mon préféré.   4. Qui est là? (*It*) est moi, Françoise.   5. Je n'ai pas fait ce que j'aurais dû, (*it*) est vrai.   6. Parlez plus fort, s'il vous plaît; voilà, (*it*) est mieux.   7. Je voudrais voir votre professeur. Est- (*he*) ici?   8. Qui a dit ces mensonges sur moi? Est- (*it*) Brigitte?   9. Venez tout de suite, (*it*) est très important.   10. Voyez-vous ce monsieur? Qui est- (*he*)[1]?

---

[1] Since **qui** is a pronoun, how must *he* be expressed here?

EXERCICES D'ENSEMBLE

J. *Remplacez les mots anglais par l'équivalent français.*

1. Pardonnez-nous comme nous pardonnons à (*those*) qui nous ont offensés.   2. (*It*) est un petit arbre qui a donné tous (*those*) beaux fruits.   3. Je vous présenterai mon ami. (*He*) est ingénieur.   4. Ne recommencez pas à m'ennuyer avec (*that*).   5. (*He*) est un ancien

prince russe. 6. (*This*) homme de science dit qu'il pourrait créer un être humain. (*It*) est extraordinaire. 7. Je me suis trompé de route. (*It*) est évident. 8. Connaissez-vous (*those*) jeunes gens? (*They*) sont très amusants. 9. Quant à Florence, (*she*) est fâchée de n'avoir pas été invitée. 10. Je connais plusieurs Belges. (*They*) sont tous catholiques. 11. (*It*) est une triste histoire. 12. Je retrouverai (*the one*) qui m'a joué (*that*) tour. 13. (*She*) est polonaise. 14. (*The one*) que j'aime est (*the one*) auquel tu penses.

K. *Traduisez en français.*

1. It is important to do that work. 2. I know him; he is a former classmate. 3. I like that song a great deal. 4. She was sick, but she is[1] better. 5. The one who told you that doesn't know what he is talking about. 6. You do not need two fountain pens; lend me that one. 7. I want to see those who didn't do these exercises. 8. I have already seen this man somewhere. 9. Go[2] and see my friends; they are very nice. 10. It is hard to understand what he is explaining. 11. Look at those birds; they are the most beautiful in[3] the store. 12. Do you have a good doctor? Yes, he is an excellent doctor. 13. Take[4] her those flowers. 14. The one[5] I prefer is red. 15. Where is my briefcase? It is there, on the table. 16. It is clear that you are right. 17. Will he come with his radio? It's probable. 18. Don't say that. 19. It's an excellent idea. 20. It's good to see you again. 21. He is a rich South American.

---

[1] not a form of **être** [2] **Allez voir** [3] What preposition is used after a superlative? [4] Use a form of **apporter**. [5] referring to flowers

Problem Words

27. lack

(**a**) How *to lack* may be expressed by **manquer de**

Cet agent **manque de** tact.   *That policeman lacks tact.*

One of the commonest ways of expressing *to lack* is: SUBJECT + **manquer de** + *what is lacking. What is lacking* is an indefinite noun, and it therefore follows **de** without a definite article.

(b) How *lack* may be expressed by the impersonal **il manque . . .**

Il lui manque de la farine pour   She lacks *flour to make her cake.*
faire son gâteau.

When using the impersonal **Il manque . . .** to begin the sentence, *what is lacking* is a partitive and the person who *lacks* is the indirect object.

(c) How **manquer** is used when *what is lacking* is the SUBJECT

La volonté lui manque pour réussir.   He lacks the will *to succeed.*

When *what is lacking* is the SUBJECT of the sentence, it is modified by the definite article and the person who lacks is the indirect object.

28. last night

(a) When *last night* = *last evening*

Hier soir nous sommes allés au   Last night *we went to the theater.*
théâtre.

When *last night* = *last evening*, the French say **hier soir.**

(b) When *last night* is *late in the night*

Il a fait très chaud **cette nuit.**   *It was very hot* last night.
Cette nuit je n'ai pas pu dormir.   Last night *I couldn't sleep.*
On a volé la banque **la nuit der-**   *The bank was robbed* last night.
nière.

When *last night* refers to something that happened later than the preceding evening, the French use the expression **cette nuit.** Also possible, but less common, is **la nuit dernière.**

29. late

(a) When *late* = *not early*

Il est **tard;** il faut partir.   *It is* late; *we must leave.*

When *late* means *not early*, use **tard.**

(**b**) When *late = not on time*

Il vaut mieux être en avance qu'**en**　　　*It is better to be early than* late.
　retard.

When *late* means *not on time*, use **en retard.**

30. leave

(**a**) How to say *to leave someone or something somewhere* (always with a direct object)

Nous **avons laissé Jean à la biblio-**　　*We* left John at the library.
　thèque.
Où avez-vous **laissé** votre **serviette?**　Where did *you* leave *your* briefcase?

　The verb **laisser** is used when it is a question of *leaving someone or something somewhere.*

(**b**) How to say *to leave someone or something* (always with a direct object)

J'ai quitté mes amis à deux heures.　　*I* left my friends *at two o'clock.*
Nous **avons quitté la maison** de　　*We* left the house *early.*
　bonne heure.

　The verb **quitter** is used when it is a question of *leaving someone or something.*

(**c**) How to say *to leave* (never followed by a place)

Je **m'en vais.**　　　　　　　　　*I'*m leaving.
Marianne **s'en ira** demain.　　　　*Marianne* will leave *tomorrow.*

　The verb **s'en aller** means *leave* in the sense of *go away, go off.* It is not usually followed by a place.

(**d**) How to say *to leave* (for more than just a moment)

Nous **sommes partis** hier soir.　　　*We* left *last night.*

　The verb **partir** is sometimes used to mean *leave* or *go away without indicating a place.*

Quand **partirez-**vous **de New York?**　*When* will *you* leave New York?

　When **partir** indicates *leaving a place*, it must be followed by **de.**

Jacques **est parti en Espagne.**	*Jack* left for Spain.
Michel **est parti pour la Grèce.**	*Michael* left for Greece.

The idea of *leaving for* + PLACE (proper noun) is expressed by **partir pour** or **partir** + PREPOSITION OF PLACE required by the proper noun. Purists prefer **partir pour.**

In general, **partir** means *to leave* in the sense of leaving for a trip or leaving a place for a certain length of time.

(e) When *leave* = *go out*

Sortez par la porte de derrière.	Leave (go out) *by the back door.*
Le patron vient de **sortir.** Revenez dans une heure.	*The boss has just* left. *Come back in an hour.*

The verb **sortir** means *leave* in the sense of *go out.* It often implies leaving for a short time as contrasted with **partir,** which implies leaving for a somewhat longer time and not merely temporarily.

Qui **est sorti du bureau** tout à l'heure?	*Who* left the office *just now?*
Les gens **sont sortis du restaurant** en riant.	*The people* left the restaurant *laughing.*
Rentrez tout de suite **en sortant du cinéma.**	*Come back home right away* after (leaving) the movies.

To indicate *leaving a place*, use **sortir de** + *place.*

(f) Other uses of **sortir** = *go out*

Êtes-vous **sorti** ce matin?	Did *you* go out *this morning?*

When **sortir** is used with no indication of from what place or with whom, it often means *going out of the place* where one habitually is at a given time.

Marc **sort avec** Françoise.	*Mark* is going out with *Frances.*

To indicate *going out with* in the sense of "keeping company with," use **sortir avec.**

L. *Remplacez les mots anglais par leur équivalent français.*

1. Bernard a une décapotable et toutes les jeunes filles veulent (*go out*) avec lui. 2. Avez-vous vu ce clair de lune sur le lac (*last night*)?

3. Je regrette d'être (*late*); j'ai été pris dans un embouteillage. 4. Par ce temps, je refuse de (*leave*) la maison. 5. Excusez-moi de vous presser, mais je ne voudrais pas que vous soyez (*late*). 6. Si les Couve ne sont pas là, nous (*will leave*) notre carte de visite. 7. Il y a eu un formidable incendie (*last night*) vers deux heures du matin. 8. Il est (*late*); rentrons. 9. Les oiseaux (*are leaving*); c'est la fin de la belle saison. 10. Les chiens n'ont pas arrêté d'aboyer (*last night*). 11. Si vous (*leave*), plusieurs de nos collègues (*will leave*) aussi. 12. Comment vous arrangez-vous pour être toujours (*late*)? 13. (*Let's leave*) nos manteaux aù vestiaire; nous serons plus à l'aise. 14. Avant de (*leave*) le bureau, fermez bien la porte et les fenêtres.

M. *Traduisez en français. Attention aux mots en italique.*

1. Did you take the book that I *had left* on the table? 2. The men didn't *lack* courage, but they were not able to gain ground. 3. There was a good film on[1] television at nine *last* night. 4. If you arrive too *late*, we won't be able to have dinner together. 5. Why didn't you come *last* night, Colette? 6. Your plants *lack* sunlight. 7. I *left* the children at the movies. 8. Gilbert *left* last night at eight o'clock. 9. Roger always goes to bed *late*. 10. Oliver doesn't *lack* ideas. 11. Don't *leave* without saying goodbye. 12. Don't fail to *leave* your address on my desk. 13. The travelers *left* at dawn. 14. Even if you arrive *late*, the bus *will leave* at noon.

---

[1] à la

Verb Review

Review the verbs **dire** and **écrire** according to the outline on page 283.

CHAPTER 9

Use of Tenses in General

I. The Present

1. What use of the simple present tense is exactly the same in French and English?

Jean **travaille** beaucoup.

Hélène **lit** un peu tous les jours.

John works *a great deal.*

Helen reads *a little every day.*

In both French and English, the SIMPLE PRESENT tense is used to state a general truth.

2. How does French express the English progressive present, that is, the present in -ing?

Jean **travaille** maintenant.

Hélène **lit** le journal en ce moment.

Je **suis en train de corriger** mes fautes.

John is working *now.*

Helen is reading *the newspaper right now.*

I am correcting *my mistakes.*

In general, French expresses the English progressive present by a simple present. But if French wishes to insist on the progressive nature of an action, it then uses a form of **être en train de** + INFINITIVE.

3. When may the French present tense express a future idea?

Demain nous **partons** pour Paris.

Tomorrow *we* leave *for Paris.*

The present is occasionally used to express an action in the immediate future when some other word in the sentence indicates futurity.

NOTE: The student should recognize this use of the present for the future but use it very sparingly, for it can be used only in certain cases.

112

4. When is the present tense used in French to express an action which would be expressed in the present perfect in English?

Nous **apprenons** le français **depuis deux ans.**	*We* have been learning *French* for *two years.*
Il y a trois jours **qu'il pleut.**	It has been raining for *three days.*
Voilà un an **que** Marc **habite** ici.	*Mark* has been living *here* for *a year.*

When an action which began in the past is still continuing in the present, French uses the present tense with **depuis, il y a . . . que, voici . . . que,** and **voilà . . . que.** English generally uses the progressive form of the present perfect with *for* to express the same concept.

In this type of sentence, **Il y a . . . que, Voici . . . que,** and **Voilà . . . que** normally come at the beginning of the sentence, whereas **depuis** + TIME EXPRESSION usually comes at the end of the sentence.

A. *Traduisez en français.*

1. Peter drives very well. 2. He has been going out with her for[1] a long time. 3. Lucie is talking on[2] the telephone. 4. Next week I will give[3] them my resignation. 5. Leave me alone[4]; I'm working. 6. Albert has had this letter in his pocket for[5] five days. 7. We have been waiting for her for[6] an hour. 8. This evening I'll prepare[3] my lesson. 9. He has refused to see me for[7] two days. 10. Tomorrow we'll go[3] to the movies.

---

[1] Use **depuis.** [2] *on the* = **au** [3] Express this action by the present. [4] **tranquille** [5] Use **il y a . . . que.** [6] Use **voilà . . . que.** [7] Use **voici . . . que.**

PATTERN PRACTICE: **être en train de**

Pattern 1

YOU HEAR   Nos amis parlent de leur voyage.
YOU SAY   Nos amis sont en train de parler de leur voyage.

PATTERN PRACTICE: actions beginning in the past and continuing in the present

Pattern 2

YOU HEAR   Depuis quand les élèves sont-ils en classe? (une heure)
YOU SAY   Ils sont en classe depuis une heure.

Pattern 3

YOU HEAR   Jacques attend son frère depuis une heure.
YOU SAY   Il y a une heure que Jacques attend son frère.

II. The Future

5. In what two ways does French usually express the future?

Un de ces jours j'**achèterai** un chien.   *One of these days* I'll buy *a dog.*
Bientôt je **vais partir** pour la plage.   *Soon I'll* leave *for the beach.*

French usually expresses the future with the FUTURE TENSE or with the present of **aller** + THE INFINITIVE. This normally parallels English usage, but in certain cases of an immediate future, French tends to use **aller** + THE INFINITIVE where English might use the future.

6. When do the French use the future tense where the present would be used in English?

Quand vous **saurez** le français, nous irons en France ensemble.   When *you* know *French, we'll go to France together.*

Dès que je **recevrai** sa lettre, je vous l'enverrai.   As soon as *I* receive *his letter, I'll send it to you.*

Tant que vous **parlerez** ainsi, vous aurez des ennuis.   As long as *you* speak *this way, you'll have trouble.*

In French, the future is used after **quand, lorsque, dès que, aussitôt que,** and **tant que** if the action will take place at some future time. English uses the present in such constructions.

B. *Traduisez en français.*

1. I'll[1] inquire about that immediately.   2. We'll[2] inquire about the cost[3] of the trip next week.   3. When you go to Paris, send me a postcard.   4. As soon as his father gives his permission, you can[4] leave.   5. When it is warm, we will go bathing.   6. As soon as you arrive, telephone me.   7. As long as there are men, there will be problems.   8. When I see you, I'll tell you what I think of it.

---

[1] Because it is an immediate future, French uses **aller** + INFINITIVE here.   [2] Because this is not an immediate future, French does NOT use **aller** + INFINITIVE here.   [3] **le prix**   [4] Note that this is a future action.

Pattern Practice: **quand** and **dès que** with the future

Pattern 4

   you hear   J'ai téléphoné à mon frère quand je suis arrivé à Paris.
   you say   Je téléphonerai à mon frère quand j'arriverai à Paris.

III. The Conditional

7. When is the conditional used to indicate a future action?

Richard croyait que Marc le **ferait.**   *Richard thought that Mark* would do *it.*

Je lui ai demandé s'il **partirait** bientôt.   *I asked him if he* would leave *soon.*

When the main clause of a sentence is in a past tense, the CONDITIONAL is often used in the dependent clause to indicate a future action.

NOTE: English uses the same sort of construction. Compare:

He says he <u>will</u> leave.   *He said he* <u>would</u> leave.
I think it <u>will</u> rain.   *I thought it* <u>would</u> rain.

8. How is the conditional used in polite requests or questions?

Je **voudrais** un verre d'eau.   *I should like a glass of water.*
Aimeriez-vous sortir avec moi?   *Would you like to go out with me?*

The conditional is sometimes used to soften a statement or a question which would be somewhat direct and blunt if stated in the present tense.

NOTE: Compare the politeness of the above examples to the bluntness of the same sentences stated in the present, e.g.: *I want a glass of water. Do you want to go out with me?*

C. *Traduisez en français.*

1. I should prefer to leave at once.　2. Her parents told me that she would come today.　3. Our friends thought that we would spend the

day at their place.   4. I heard[1] that the airplane would be[2] late.
5. Claude asked me if Martha would be in class the next day.
6. Would you like to go to France?

---

[1] *to hear that* = **entendre dire que**   [2] *to be late* = **avoir du retard**

PATTERN PRACTICE: the conditional as the past of the future

Pattern 5

> YOU HEAR   Jacques partira samedi.
> YOU SAY   Roland a dit que Jacques partirait samedi.

IV. The Pluperfect, the Past Anterior, the *Passé Surcomposé*

9. What is the basic use of the pluperfect?

J'**avais fini** mon travail quand Pierre est arrivé.

I had finished my work when Peter arrived.

Colette **était** déjà **sortie** quand il a commencé à pleuvoir.

Colette had already left when it began to rain.

The PLUPERFECT indicates a past action which took place before the beginning of another past action.

PATTERN PRACTICE: the pluperfect

Pattern 6

> YOU HEAR   Nous avons déjà entendu la nouvelle. Hélène nous a téléphoné.
> YOU SAY   Nous avions déjà entendu la nouvelle quand Hélène nous a téléphoné.

10. What tense does French use in cases when an action begins at a certain time in the past and continues until another time in the past?

Monsieur Lenoir **travaillait depuis dix ans** quand il a découvert ce nouveau procédé.

Mr. Lenoir had been working for ten years when he discovered that new process.

Il y avait un an qu'il apprenait le français quand il est parti pour l'Afrique.   He had been learning *French* for one year *when he left for Africa.*

When an action which begins in the past and continues up to a certain point in the past is interrupted by another action, stated or implied, the French express the first action by the IMPERFECT with **depuis** or **il y avait . . . que.** In such cases, English uses the pluperfect and usually the progressive form of the pluperfect.

PATTERN PRACTICE: the imperfect with **depuis**

Pattern 7

    YOU HEAR   J'ai écrit pendant dix minutes. Mon père est rentré.
    YOU SAY   J'écrivais depuis dix minutes quand mon père est rentré.

11. When can the French pluperfect not be used to indicate a past action which took place before another past action?

(a) Literary Style   (b) Conversational Style

Quand j'**eus fini** mon travail, je sortis.	**Quand** j'**ai eu fini** mon travail, je suis sorti.	When *I* had finished *my work, I went out.*
Dès que Louis **eut écrit** la lettre, il la mit à la poste.	**Dès que** Louis **a eu écrit** la lettre, il l'a mise à la poste.	As soon as *Louis* had written *the letter, he mailed it.*

(a) Literary Style

When a past action introduced by **quand, lorsque, dès que, aussitôt que,** or **après que** immediately precedes a second past action which is in the simple past, the first action must be in the PAST ANTERIOR (**passé antérieur**). It cannot be in the pluperfect.

(b) Conversational Style

When a past action introduced by **quand, lorsque, dès que, aussitôt que,** or **après que** immediately precedes a second past action which is in the compound past, the first action must be in the **passé surcomposé** or in the compound past. It cannot be in the pluperfect. (In these constructions, the **passé composé** may be used instead of the **passé surcomposé,** but it is less exact.)

NOTE: The **passé antérieur** and the **passé surcomposé** are relatively infrequent. They are formed as follows:

> **passé antérieur** = simple past of auxiliary + past participle

> **passé surcomposé** = compound past of auxiliary + past participle

EXAMPLES: j'**eus parlé**, je **fus sorti**
j'**ai eu parlé**, j'**ai été sorti**

PATTERN PRACTICE: the use of the **passé surcomposé**

Pattern 8

YOU HEAR   J'ai déjeuné et puis Jacques est venu me voir.
YOU SAY   Quand j'ai eu déjeuné, Jacques est venu me voir.

D. *Remplacez les mots anglais entre parenthèses par l'équivalent français.*

1. Quand nous avons voulu l'acheter, nos voisins (*had sold*) leur auto. 2. (*He had been trying[1] for a year*) à s'évader quand l'occasion s'est enfin présentée. 3. Dès que (*I had finished*) mon travail, je suis allé au cinéma. 4. Le général (*had won[2]*) une grande victoire quand il a été tué. 5. Jacques et Paulette (*had been going out together for three weeks*) quand ils ont décidé de se marier. 6. Dès qu'il (*had made*) sa conférence, il est reparti. 7. Le suspect (*had closed*) la porte quand l'agent est arrivé. 8. Il (*had been calling me for a long time*) quand je l'ai enfin entendu. 9. Quand Michel (*had seen*) l'accident, il est parti tout de suite.   10. Nous (*had left*) quand le téléphone a sonné.

----
[1] Use a form of **chercher.**   [2] Use a form of **remporter.**

E. *Traduisez en français.*

1. Did he ask you where you had found the billfold?   2. I had been reading for some time when there was a knock[1] at the door. 3. As soon as he had opened the door, the stranger entered the room. 4. We had been looking for the dog for an hour when we heard him bark in[2] the distance. 5. He had already spoken when we arrived.

----
[1] There is no noun in French for *knock*. See page 94.   [2] **au loin**

6. When I had finished the letter, Mark mailed it. 7. Had you left the store when it began to snow? 8. As soon as we had eaten, we washed the dishes. 9. They had been there for half an hour when her friend came to get[3] her.

---

[3] Use a form of **chercher.**

V. The Future Perfect

12. **What French use of the future perfect corresponds to the English use?**

J'**aurai vu** ton professeur quand tu *I will have seen your teacher when you*
rentreras.   *get back.*

In French, as in English, the FUTURE PERFECT describes an action which will have taken place before another future action.

NOTE: The FUTURE PERFECT (**futur antérieur**) is made up of the future of the AUXILIARY + THE PAST PARTICIPLE of the verb. Ex.: j'**aurai parlé**, je **serai sorti.**

13. **When is the future perfect used in French where the English might use the present perfect?**

Quand Albert **aura écrit** la lettre, When *Albert* has written *the letter,*
je vous la montrerai.   *I'll show it to you.*

The FUTURE PERFECT is used in French with adverbial conjunctions of time such as **quand, lorsque, dès que, aussitôt que,** and **après que** to express an action which will have taken place before another future action. English generally uses the present perfect in such cases.

F. *Traduisez en français.*

1. That family will have already left when you arrive in Tours. 2. When you have finished that, come and[1] see me. 3. When we have bought our new car, we'll telephone you. 4. As soon as they have arrived, we'll go for a walk. 5. Jack will learn to play[2] the violin after his brother has learned to play[2] the piano. 6. When I

---

[1] Translate: *Come to see me.* [2] Omit *to play* in translation.

have finished my studies, we'll leave for France.   7. Come back as
soon as you get out of the movies.   8. I will have made the acquaintance of the director by[3] the time that I see you again[4].

---

[3] Express *by the time that* with **quand**.   [4] Express *see again* by a form of **revoir**.

PATTERN PRACTICE: the future perfect

Pattern 9

> YOU HEAR   Jean écrira la lettre et puis il vous la montrera.
> YOU SAY   Quand Jean aura écrit la lettre, il vous la montrera.

VI. Conditional Sentences

14. What are the most common types of French conditional sentences?

(a) Si nous **travaillons,** nous **gagne-**   *If we* work, *we* will earn *some money.*
    rons de l'argent.

(b) Si nous **étions** riches, nous **irions**   *If we* were *rich, we* would go *to*
    en France.   *France.*

(c) Si vous **aviez parlé** français,   *If you* had spoken *French, Marie-*
    Marie-Claire vous **aurait com-**   *Claire* would have understood *you.*
    pris.

The three most common tense sequences in conditional sentences
are:

si-(*if*)-CLAUSE	CONCLUSION
present	future
imperfect	conditional
pluperfect	past conditional

G. *Remplacez les infinitifs par la forme convenable du verbe.*

1. Si Philippe partait, il (falloir) lui demander pourquoi.   2. Si vous
me (poser) la question, je vous aurais répondu.   3. S'il le faut, nous
(se battre).   4. Je (être) très content si mon frère réussissait.   5. Si
je (savoir) cela, je n'y serais pas allé.   6. Je (partir) si vous continuez

à me regarder comme cela. 7. Si l'auto ne marche pas, nous (prendre) l'autobus. 8. S'il avait fait beau, nous (aller) vous voir. 9. Si Olga (parler) français, vous n'auriez pas besoin d'un interprète.

H. *Traduisez en français.*

1. If you do what I tell you, you will not regret it. 2. I should be very happy if I could go there with you. 3. If I were free, I would do a great many things. 4. If he would speak louder, one would hear what he says. 5. You would have seen my sister if you had come sooner. 6. If I had brothers, I would[1] have a better time. 7. If I go to Paris, I will not come back before next year. 8. I would have answered him if I had heard him call. 9. If Fredrick had not been sick, he would have come.

_____
[1] Use a form of **s'amuser mieux.**

PATTERN PRACTICE: conditional sentences

{lorsque {quand {dès que {aussitôt que

Pattern 10

YOU HEAR   Quand nous aurons assez d'argent, nous irons en Angleterre.

YOU SAY   Si nous avons assez d'argent, nous irons en Angleterre.

Pattern 11

YOU HEAR   Je ne suis pas riche. Je n'achète pas beaucoup de disques.

YOU SAY   Si j'étais riche, j'achèterais beaucoup de disques.

Pattern 12

YOU HEAR   Je n'ai pas appris le français. Je n'ai pas compris Monsieur Alain.

YOU SAY   Si j'avais appris le français, j'aurais compris Monsieur Alain.

15. What other tense sequences exist in conditional sentences?

PLUPERFECT + CONDITIONAL

Si vous **aviez fait** votre travail, vous **pourriez** venir avec nous aujourd'hui.   *If you had done your work, you could come with us today.*

PRESENT + PRESENT

S'il **pleut,** je **reste** à la maison.   *If it rains, I stay home.*

PLUPERFECT + CONDITIONAL

Si nous **avions pris** des précautions,   *If* we had taken *precautions, we*
nous n'**aurions** pas ces ennuis   wouldn't have *this trouble now.*
maintenant.

PASSÉ COMPOSÉ + FUTURE

S'ils **ont pris** l'avion, ils **seront**   *If they* have taken *the airplane, they*
bientôt ici.   will *soon* be *here.*

Almost any tense sequence which is possible in English conditional
sentences is also possible in French conditional sentences. However:

Si vous **faites** votre travail, vous   *If you* will do *your work, you* will earn
gagnerez beaucoup d'argent.   *a lot of money.*
Si elle **écoutait** ses parents, elle ne   *If she* would obey *her parents, she*
sortirait jamais.   would *never* go out.

In French, neither the future nor the conditional can ever be used
after **si** when **si** means *if.*

Je ne sais pas **si** Jean **viendra.**   *I don't know* whether *John will come.*

When **si** means *whether*, the French future and conditional may
follow it.

I. *Traduisez en français.*

1. If you had left earlier, you would already be in Cannes. 2. If the
children have gone to bed, they must be sleeping now. 3. If the
students spent a lot of money, they always worked to earn more.
4. If you will listen attentively, you will be able to follow his thought.
5. If we would paint our car, we could keep it another year. 6. If
you like football, come to see the game[1] with me. 7. You mustn't
hesitate to tell me if you are bored. 8. If he has found[2] that out, he
must be furious.

[1]**le match** [2]*find out* = **apprendre**

EXERCICES D'ENSEMBLE

J. *Remplacez l'infinitif par la forme convenable du verbe.*

1. Quand ils ne (être) plus là, je ne sais pas ce que je ferai. 2. Voilà
un mois que vous (avoir) mon livre. Pouvez-vous me le rendre?

3. Nous n'avons pas pu sortir, il (pleuvoir) depuis ce matin. 4. Ils (préparer) un excellent dîner quand les invités ont téléphoné qu'ils ne pouvaient pas venir. 5. Il (aller) obtenir son diplôme quand il est tombé malade. 6. Je garderai cette grammaire quand je (finir) mon cours. 7. Si tu veux épouser cette jeune fille, tes parents (être) très heureux. 8. J'ai toujours pensé que cela (finir) mal. 9. Je lirai ce roman quand je (avoir) le temps. 10. Il a cru qu'il (pouvoir) me tromper facilement. 11. Dès que je (apprendre) cela, je suis parti. 12. Donnez-moi la main si vous (avoir) peur. 13. Encore un mot et je (s'en aller). 14. Quand vous lui (écrire), dites-lui mes amitiés. 15. Nous (faire) nos adieux quand il est arrivé. 16. Je (s'endormir) dejà quand ses cris m'ont réveillé. 17. Elle s'est trouvée mieux dès qu'elle (prendre) ce remède. 18. Quand ils (partir), je vous montrerai quelque chose d'intéressant. 19. Si vous (écouter) ses conseils, vous n'en seriez pas là. 20. Si j'avais su, évidemment, je (agir) tout autrement.

K. *Traduisez en français. Indiquez oralement la raison de chaque temps.*

1. I must hurry; I am leaving this evening. 2. I wrote them that we would go to see them Sunday. 3. They had already left when it began to rain. 4. Tell me what she says to you as soon as you have seen her. 5. If you wished to see him, he would be very happy. 6. When I came into the living room, everyone had left. 7. He has been studying Russian for two years, but he does not know it very well. 8. I will be pleased when I know what has happened. 9. If you have done your exercises with care[1], you don't need to worry. 10. As soon as she had won the prize, she changed. 11. Did you tell him that we would not be home tomorrow? 12. I'll speak to him of that affair as soon as I see him. 13. We had finished our meal when we heard the news. 14. I will travel when I have earned enough money. 15. If it is good weather, I always take a walk. 16. What are you doing tomorrow? 17. When you speak to him, be very polite. 18. I was finishing my exercises when she came to ask me to help her. 19. When he heard my reasons, he changed his mind. 20. I'll leave only if you come with me. 21. If she had understood me, things[2] would have been very different.

---

[1] Use no article.   [2] Use the definite article.

Problem Words

31. little

(a) When to use **peu**

Jeannot lit **peu,** il préfère s'amuser.   *Johnnie reads* little, *he prefers to have a good time.*

When **peu,** unaccompanied by the indefinite article, modifies a verb, it means *little, only a little, not very much.*

(b) When to use **un peu**

Si tu as **un peu** d'argent, mets-le de   *If you have* a little *money, save it.*
côté.

But **un peu** means *a little* or *some.*

32. live

(a) When to use **habiter**

Nos amis **habitent**$\begin{cases} \text{à Genève.} \\ \text{Genève.} \end{cases}$ *Our friends* live *in Geneva.*

To indicate where one lives, the French commonly use the verb **habiter,** which may be followed either directly by the place or by the French equivalent of *in* + *place*. It is somewhat synonymous with the English *inhabit*, but it is much more common.

The verb **demeurer,** formerly very frequently used for *live* in the above sense, has now been almost entirely replaced by **habiter.**

(b) When to use **vivre**

Monsieur Seydoux **vit** de ses revenus.   *Mr. Seydoux lives from his income.*
Il est mort comme il **a vécu.**   *He died as he* lived.
Monsieur Rochebois **vivait** entière-   *Mr. Rochebois* lived *entirely for his*
ment pour sa famille.   *family.*

The verb **vivre** means *live* in a larger and more general sense and is sometimes synonymous with *exist*. It is occasionally used in the sense of **habiter,** but the learner should avoid using it in this sense.

33. long

(a) How to say *as long as*

Tant que je serai là, il n'y aura rien à craindre.	As long as I am *there, there will be nothing to fear.*

The time expression *as long as* is rendered in French by **tant que** and is followed by the FUTURE whenever futurity is implied.

(b) How to say *how long*

Combien de temps avez-vous travaillé pour lui?	How long *have you worked for him?*
Pendant combien de temps êtes-vous resté en France?	How long *did you stay in France?*

The English *how long*, meaning *how much time*, may be expressed in French by **combien de temps** or **pendant combien de temps**.

Depuis quand êtes-vous ici?	How long *have you been here?*
Depuis combien de temps attends-tu?	How long *have you been waiting?*

The expressions **depuis quand** and **depuis combien de temps** are often used with the PRESENT where English uses *how long* + PRESENT PERFECT PROGRESSIVE to express the same idea.

(c) How to say *for a long time*

Nous avons parlé **longtemps** de ton avenir.	*We spoke about your future* for a long time.
Il y a **longtemps** que je connais les Jourdan.	*I have known the Jourdans* for a long time.

The English *a long time* is expressed in French by the adverb **longtemps.**

(d) How to say *at length*

Nous avons parlé **longuement** de ton avenir.	*We spoke* at length *of your future.*

The English *at length* is expressed in French by the adverb **longuement,** when *at length* = *in detail*.

34. make

How to say *make someone* + ADJECTIVE

Vous **me rendez très heureux** en disant cela. | *You* make me very happy *in saying that.*

The French equivalent of *to make someone* + ADJECTIVE is **rendre quelqu'un** + ADJECTIVE.

CAUTION: Do NOT use the construction «faire quelqu'un» + adjective. French uses **rendre** in such situations.

L. *Remplacez les mots anglais par leur équivalent français.*

1. Je ne conduis pas depuis (*a long time*), mais je suis très prudente.
2. Inutile de se faire trop de soucis; il faut (*live*) au jour le jour.
3. Henriette écrit (*little*), mais elle nous téléphone souvent. 4. Votre présence (*made*) la soirée très agréable. 5. J'ai (*at length*) réfléchi à ce que vous m'avez dit. 6. Monsieur et Madame Renaud ont une belle auto, mais ils (*live*) dans une très vieille maison. 7. Il faut faire (*a little*) de gymnastique tous les matins. 8. J'observe vos progrès depuis (*a long time*) sans rien dire.

M. *Traduisez en français. Attention aux mots en italique.*

1. I know your friend Daniel *a little*. 2. I *lived* in a large city for twenty years. 3. If you remain here too *long*, you will forget your native language. 4. Don't smoke so much, it[1] will *make* you sick. 5. You really give me *little* time to[2] do that. 6. People *live* a great deal *longer* today than formerly. 7. The mayor spoke *at length* on the problems of the city. 8. Mr. Mollet no longer reads the newspaper; it[1] *makes* him nervous. 9. Those young people went out for[3] *a long time* together before getting married. 10. Wait *a little*.

---

[1] **ça** [2] **pour** [3] Omit in translation.

Verb Review

Review the verbs **envoyer** and **faire** according to the outline on page 283.

CHAPTER 10

Relatives

A relative pronoun is one which connects a dependent to an independent clause. The relative pronoun is part of the dependent clause, performs a function in that clause and usually begins the dependent clause. The English relative pronouns are *who, whom, whose, which, that,* and *what.* Ex.: The student *who* wrote that essay is a genius.

The relative pronoun normally refers back to some noun in the independent clause. This noun is called the antecedent of the pronoun. In the above example, the antecedent of *who* is "student."

Sometimes, however, the relative pronoun is indefinite. In that case, there is no antecedent in the English sentence. Ex.: My father does not know *what* I am doing.

1. What relative pronoun is used as the subject of its clause?

C'est le professeur **qui** parle.　　　　*It is the teacher* who *is talking.*
C'est une voiture **qui** coûte très cher.　*It is a car* which *costs a great deal.*

The relative pronoun **qui** is used as the subject of its clause, whether it refers to a person or a thing.

PATTERN PRACTICE: the use of **qui**

Pattern 1

　　YOU HEAR　Voilà une belle jeune fille. Elle va se marier.
　　YOU SAY　Voilà une belle jeune fille qui va se marier.

127

2. What relative pronoun is used as the object of its clause?

Je voudrais voir les malades **que**   *I should like to see the sick persons* whom
vous soignez.   *you are taking care of.*
Montrez-moi la voiture **que** vous   *Show me the car* that *you want.*
voulez.

The relative pronoun **que** is used as the object of its clause, whether it refers to a person or a thing.

The object relative pronoun may be omitted in English but not in French. Ex.: *Is the book you bought interesting?* Est-ce que le livre **que** vous avez acheté est intéressant?

PATTERN PRACTICE: the use of **que**

Pattern 2

    YOU HEAR   Voilà un beau tableau. Je vais l'acheter.
    YOU SAY   Voilà un beau tableau que je vais acheter.

3. Which two relative pronouns are used after prepositions?

Où habitent les amis avec$\begin{cases} \textbf{qui} \\ \textbf{lesquels} \end{cases}$ *Where do the friends with* whom *you speak French live?*
vous parlez français?

Montrez-moi la clé avec **laquelle**   *Show me the key with* which *you opened*
vous avez ouvert la porte.   *the door.*

After a preposition, either **qui** or a form of **lequel** may be used to refer to persons; a form of **lequel** is used to refer to things.

The forms of **lequel** are: **lequel, laquelle, lesquels, lesquelles.**

PATTERN PRACTICE: preposition + relative

Pattern 3

    YOU HEAR   Voilà le professeur. Je lui ai donné mon livre ce matin.
    YOU SAY   Voilà le professeur à qui j'ai donné mon livre ce matin.

(In this exercise, the antecedent is always a person, therefore, either **qui** or a form of **lequel** could be used. However, use **qui,** which is simpler and more common.)

Pattern 4

YOU HEAR   Voilà ma machine à écrire. J'ai écrit cette lettre avec cette machine à écrire.

YOU SAY   Voilà la machine à écrire avec laquelle j'ai écrit cette lettre.

4. How is the relative pronoun *what* **expressed in French? And how is** *everything that* **expressed?**

(a) SUBJECT

Ce qui est sur la table est à moi.	What *is on the table is mine.*
Il ne faut pas faire **ce qui** est défendu.	*You mustn't do* what *is forbidden.*
Avez-vous lu **tout ce qui** est dans la bibliothèque?	*Have you read* everything that *is in the library?*

(b) OBJECT

Ce que vous lisez est intéressant.	What *you are reading is interesting.*
Savez-vous **ce que** Jean a dit?	*Do you know* what *John said?*
Dites-moi **tout ce que** vous faites.	*Tell me* everything that *you are doing.*

(c) AFTER A PREPOSITION

Ce à quoi je pense est un secret.	What *I am thinking* about *is a secret.*
Je ne comprends pas **de quoi** vous parlez.	*I don't understand* what *you are talking about.*
Maurice a fini ses devoirs, **après quoi** il est sorti.	*Maurice finished his exercises,* after which *he went out.*

The English *what* is expressed in French by

   (a) **ce qui** when it is the subject of its clause;

   (b) **ce que** when it is the object of its clause;

   (c) PREPOSITION + **quoi** or **ce** + PREPOSITION + **quoi** when it is used with a preposition.

In these combinations, **ce** constitutes the antecedent of **qui** and **que.**

The relative **quoi** is sometimes an indefinite which is expressed in English by *which.*

The English *everything that* is expressed in French by

   (a) **tout ce qui** when it is the subject of its clause;

   (b) **tout ce que** when it is the object of its clause.

PATTERN PRACTICE: **ce qui** and **ce que**

Pattern 5

YOU HEAR   Montrez-moi la lettre qui est sur la table.
YOU SAY   Montrez-moi ce qui est sur la table.

Pattern 6

YOU HEAR   J'ai corrigé l'exercice que Jean a écrit.
YOU SAY   J'ai corrigé ce que Jean a écrit.

5. How can the relative pronouns be presented in graphic tabular form?

FUNCTION	PERSONS	THINGS	*what*
SUBJECT	qui	qui	ce qui
OBJECT	que	que	ce que
after preposition	qui lequel*	lequel*	quoi

A. *Remplacez le mot anglais par le mot français.*

1. (*What*) vous dites est vrai.   2. Les conseils (*that*) vous m'avez donnés sont excellents.   3. Les choses (*which*) semblent compliquées sont souvent bien simples.   4. L'acte dans (*which*) elle était le mieux était le dernier.   5. Il voudrait savoir à (*what*) vous vous intéressez. 6. (*What*) se passe aujourd'hui est terrible!   7. Le professeur (*who*) va parler vient de France.   8. L'ami sur (*whom*) je comptais n'est pas venu.   9. L'homme (*whom*) la police vient d'arrêter est un espion. 10. C'est Jeanne avec (*whom*) je suis sorti dimanche.   11. (*What*) je vais chanter maintenant est très connu.   12. Moi (*who*) vous parle, j'ai passé par là.   13. La rose (*which*) vous m'avez donnée est superbe.

---

* i.e., **lequel, laquelle, lesquels,** or **lesquelles,** according to the gender of the antecedent. Sometimes **ce** + preposition + **quoi** is required.

B. *Traduisez en français.*

1. The dress[1] you are wearing is very pretty.   2. The doctor to whom I spoke is very nice.   3. My father, who is a businessman, will come to see you.   4. What we are studying is very useful.   5. The friend whom you invited is charming.   6. I do not understand what you are speaking of.   7. The road by which he came is very bad.   8. Show me everything that you have in your drawer.   9. Tell me of what you are thinking[2].   10. He shut the door, after which we left. 11. What is on the table is yours, but everything that is on the desk is mine.

---

[1] The relative pronoun is missing in English but must be expressed in French. See page 128, §2.   [2] Not **de.**

PATTERN PRACTICE: various relatives

Pattern 7

> YOU HEAR   Vous avez écrit un conte qui est intéressant.
>
> YOU SAY   Le conte que vous avez écrit est intéressant.

Pattern 8

(This exercise contains various types of relatives. You are to choose the proper one.)

> YOU HEAR   Voilà une belle voiture. J'aimerais l'acheter.
>
> YOU SAY   Voilà une belle voiture que j'aimerais acheter.

6. How is de + relative normally expressed in French?

Le livre **dont** vous parlez est connu.   *The book* of which *you are speaking is well known.*

The form **dont** normally replaces **de** + RELATIVE.

NOTE: When a preposition or a prepositional phrase comes between the antecedent and the relative, then **de** + RELATIVE are used instead of **dont.** The relative **dont** must follow its antecedent immediately and therefore must stand first in its clause. Ex.: C'est un livre au milieu **duquel** il y a de jolies illustrations.

Also, *from which* (meaning *whence*) is usually expressed by **d'où** rather than **dont.** Ex.: Je n'ai jamais visité la ville **d'où** il vient.

PATTERN PRACTICE: the use of **dont**

Pattern 9

YOU HEAR   Marie est une jeune fille. Vous m'avez souvent parlé d'elle.
YOU SAY   Marie est une jeune fille dont vous m'avez souvent parlé.

7. Sentences with the French word *dont* present certain problems of word order. What is a practical way of determining the word order of such sentences?

Voici le docteur Galand   *Here is Dr. Galand*
  dont le fils est mon meilleur ami. $\begin{cases}\text{whose } son \text{ } is \text{ } my \text{ } best \text{ } friend.\\ \text{of whom } the \text{ } son \text{ } is \text{ } my \text{ } best \text{ } friend.\end{cases}$

Note that in French, when **dont** is identified with the subject of its clause, the subject is modified by the definite article.

Montrez-moi le livre   *Show me the book*
  dont vous connaissez l'auteur. $\begin{cases}\text{whose } author \text{ } you \text{ } know.\\ \text{of which } you \text{ } know \text{ } the \text{ } author.\end{cases}$

Note that when **dont** is identified with the object of its clause, that object is in quite a different position than it is in the corresponding English clause.

The word order of a French clause introduced by **dont** is:

> **dont** + SUBJECT + VERB + rest of sentence

In order to arrive at the French word order in **dont**-clauses, instead of using *whose* in the English sentence, substitute *of whom* or *of which*. The rest of the English sentence will then fall into exactly the same word order that the French clause normally has.

PATTERN PRACTICE: **dont** modifying the subject and the object of its
                     clause

Pattern 10

YOU HEAR   Voilà une pauvre femme. Son fils travaille chez nous.
YOU SAY   Voilà une pauvre femme dont le fils travaille chez nous.

Pattern 11

YOU HEAR   Paris est une ville. Nous connaissons ses divers quartiers.
YOU SAY   Paris est une ville dont nous connaissons les divers quar-
             tiers.

C. *Traduisez en français.*

1. There is an insult of which you will repent. 2. Jack is a young man whose problems are serious. 3. We know the lady whose husband you saw in Paris. 4. I brought[1] you the book the title of which I had forgotten. 5. Where is the doctor whose office is on the first[2] floor? 6. It[3] is my youthful[4] years that I remember[5] the best. 7. The family whose address you gave me will not come back. 8. That actress, whose talent I admired so much, left yesterday. 9. The friend whose children George adopted died ten years ago. 10. He doesn't like neighbors whose dogs bark so much.

---

[1] Use a form of **apporter.** [2] Not **premier étage** [3] **Ce sont** [4] **années de jeunesse**
[5] Use a form of **se souvenir de.**

8. How is the relative *when* expressed in French?

Au moment **où** nous sommes arrivés ils étaient tous à table.	*At the time when we arrived, they were all at the table.*
Je vous dirai cela le jour **où** vous vous marierez.	*I'll tell you that the day when you get married.*

The ordinary French word for *when* is **quand.** But when the English word *when* modifies a preceding noun — usually a time expression —, it is normally expressed by **où** in French.

The relative **où** also means *where* and indicates place, but this **où** constitutes no problem to the English-speaking student. Ex.: J'ai visité la ville **où** le poète a vécu.

D. *Traduisez en français.*

1. Show me the house where Balzac was born. 2. Do you remember the day when we saw each other for the first time? 3. At the moment when he arrives[1], I'll leave. 4. I did not feel well the evening when you came to see me. 5. Have you forgotten the winter when it was so cold? 6. I prefer the months when there is sun.

---

[1] What tense? See page 114, §6.

PATTERN PRACTICE: the relative **où**

Pattern 12

YOU HEAR J'ai rencontré Jean cette année-là. Il était à Paris.
YOU SAY J'ai rencontré Jean l'année où il était à Paris.

Pattern 13

YOU HEAR   Nous avons parlé des vacances quand nous nous sommes
           rencontrés dans la rue. (le jour)
YOU SAY   Nous avons parlé des vacances le jour où nous nous
           sommes rencontrés dans la rue.

EXERCICES D'ENSEMBLE

E. *Remplacez le mot anglais par son équivalent français.*

1. Pouvez-vous me prêter les livres (*which I need*)? 2. Connaissez-vous la femme (*who*) vient de passer? 3. Il est parti; c'est le mois (*when*) il prend ses vacances. 4. Où est la montre (*which*) je vous ai achetée? 5. Racontez-nous seulement (*what*) est important. 6. Je me demande avec (*what*) ils ont pu faire cela. 7. Les élèves (*of which*) vous vous plaignez ne travaillent pas assez. 8. La sonnerie (*that*) vous entendez marque la fin de la classe. 9. Il fait (*everything that*) il veut. 10. Je vous prêterai ma voiture le jour (*when*) vous aurez du travail. 11. Elle vous promettra tout (*that*) vous voulez. 12. L'homme (*who*) doit venir me voir ce matin est russe. 13. C'est un ami pour (*whom*) je ferais n'importe quoi. 14. Puisque vous le pouvez, prenez donc (*what*) est devant vous. 15. Je ne sais pas exactement à (*what*) il pense. 16. Le train dans (*which*) je me trouvais a eu un accident.

F. *Traduisez en français.*

1. The person you are making fun of is one of my friends. 2. I remember the year when we went to Europe. 3. The man for whom I work is very nice. 4. What you say concerning[1] them does not surprise me. 5. You must ask him what he is suffering from. 6. I cannot read what you are writing. 7. The pupils who work succeed without difficulty. 8. Speak to me of the young man whose father is so rich. 9. The chair on which he sat down was broken. 10. What is happening in those countries is dangerous. 11. I should like to know what you are thinking of[2] now. 12. She left the[3] moment I entered. 13. The dress with which she had so much success came from Paris. 14. I cannot stand the noise the neighbors are making. 15. I like people who are a bit optimistic. 16. Tell me what makes[4] you so sad. 17. Where is the book whose title you just mentioned?

---

[1] à leur sujet   [2] Not de   [3] The French say the equivalent of the English *at the moment when*.
[4] Use a form of **rendre**.

Problem Words

35. marry

(a) How to say *to get married*

Michelle **s'est mariée** au mois de   *Michelle got married in the month of*
juin.   *June.*

French expresses *to get married* by **se marier.**

(b) How to say *to marry someone*

Robert **s'est marié avec la fille du**   *Robert married the boss's daughter.*
patron.
Isabelle devrait **épouser un homme**   *Isabelle should marry a rich man.*
riche.

French expresses *to marry someone* by either **se marier avec quelqu'un** or **épouser quelqu'un.**

(c) How to say *to marry someone to someone*

Les Moreau **vont marier leur fille**   *The Moreaux are going to marry their*
à l'aîné des Duparc.   *daughter to the oldest Duparc boy.*

French expresses *to marry someone to someone* by **marier quelqu'un à
quelqu'un.**

36. miss

(a) When *miss = feel the absence of*

Nous **regrettons** notre ancienne   *We miss our former house.*
maison.

The verb **regretter** may be used in the sense of *miss;* in that case,
the subject of the English and French sentences is the same.

Ma voiture **me manque** beaucoup   *I miss my car a great deal here.*
ici.

The verb **manquer** may also be used in the sense of *miss,* but in
that case, the object missed becomes the subject of the French sentence.

(b) When *miss = fail to reach*

Gérard **a manqué** l'autobus; il va encore être en retard.	*Gerard* missed *the bus; he is going to be late again.*
Pourquoi **avez**-vous **manqué** la classe?	*Why did you* miss *class?*

French uses the verb **manquer** to express the idea of missing a means of transportation or of missing a gathering of some kind. With this sense, the subject of **manquer** is the person and the object of the sentence is the thing missed. Note that **manquer la classe** means *to cut class.*

37. more

(a) How to say *more and more*

Je m'intéresse **de plus en plus** à la politique.	*I am becoming* more and more *interested in politics.*
Je suis **de plus en plus** étonné.	*I am* more and more *surprised.*

The English *more and more* + ADJECTIVE is expressed by **de plus en plus** modifying an adjective, an adverb or a verb.

NOTE: The formula *more and more* is really an intensive comparative, so that it also includes the English comparatives in *-er:*

Georges devient **de plus en plus** grand.	*George is getting* taller and taller.

(b) How to say *the more . . . the more . . .*

Plus je connais Marianne, **plus** j'apprécie ses qualités.	The more *I know Marianne,* the more *I appreciate her good qualities.*
Plus Georges est riche, **plus** il veut d'argent.	The richer *George is,* the more *money he wants.*

CAUTION: Do NOT express *the more . . . the more* by «le plus . . . le plus». The correct formula is **plus . . ., plus . . . .**

French expresses *the more . . . the more* by **plus** + CLAUSE, followed by **plus** + CLAUSE.

NOTE: The formula *the more . . . the more* is a type of comparative, so that it also includes the English comparatives in *-er*, as in the sentence:

Plus on est riche, **plus** on est heureux.	The richer *one is,* the happier *one is.*

38. next

(a) When *next* is expressed by **prochain**

Nous irons voir vos amis en France   *We'll go to see your friends in France*
l'été **prochain**.   *next summer.*
Est-ce que Toulon est le **prochain** *Is Toulon the* next *stop?*
arrêt?

The ordinary French word for *next* is **prochain**. In general, it can be used except when one could substitute *following* for *next* in the English sentence without changing the meaning of the sentence.

(b) When *next* is expressed by **suivant**

J'ai expliqué à Robert pourquoi   *I explained to Robert why we had re-*
nous étions retournés en Suisse   *turned to Switzerland the* next (= fol-
l'été **suivant**.   *lowing) summer.*
Regardez la page **suivante**.   *Look at the* next (= following) *page.*

Whenever *next* = *following* and when *following* can be substituted for *next* without changing the meaning of the sentence, French uses **suivant**.

CAUTION: Do NOT use «prochain» for *next* when *next* = *following*. This is a very common error.

(c) How to say *the next day*

Le **lendemain** ⎫
Le **jour suivant** ⎬ nos invités sont partis.   The next day *our guests left.*
Le **jour après** ⎭

The next day may be expressed by **le lendemain, le jour suivant** or **le jour après**.

CAUTION: Do NOT say «le jour prochain» for *the next day*.

(d) How to say *the next morning (afternoon, evening,* etc.)

Le **lendemain matin** ⎫
Le **matin suivant**   ⎬ il a plu sans arrêt.   The next morning *it rained*
Le **matin après**   ⎭   *continually.*

The adverb **lendemain** is used with times of day to express the English *next*.

G. *Remplacez les mots anglais par leur équivalent français.*

1. On ne demande plus beaucoup aujourd'hui l'avis de ses parents pour (*get married*). 2. Allons bon! nous (*missed*) le train de sept heures quarante-cinq. 3. (*The more*) ça change, (*the more*) c'est la même chose. 4. Je serai à New York mercredi, et je m'envolerai (*the next day*) pour Paris. 5. On dit que cet acteur va (*marry*) une ancienne camarade d'enfance. 6. Quand je voyage, je (*miss*) le confort de ma maison. 7. Je suis (*more and more*) étonné par ton indifférence. 8. Madame Drouet passera (*next week*) chez nous, et elle ira chez vous (*the next week*). 9. Paul (*got married*) beaucoup trop jeune. 10. J'ai passé mon baccalauréat et (*the next year*) j'ai fait mon service militaire. 11. Suivez mon conseil: (*marry*) une jeune fille de votre condition.

H. *Traduisez en français. Attention aux mots en italique.*

1. Why don't you *marry* Albertine? 2. Robert will spend *next* year in Italy. 3. *The more* I know Paris, *the more* I like it. 4. Do the children *miss* the television set? 5. Mr. Martel would like to *marry* his daughter to a doctor. 6. If you *miss* your bus[1], you will have to wait until tomorrow morning. 7. That child is becoming *more and more* unbearable. 8. Edmond went to bed late and the *next* morning, he didn't hear his alarm clock. 9. I *miss* you a great deal these days. 10. If they arrive at midnight, they will certainly not leave[2] again the *next* day. 11. Michael and Colette met at Nice and will *get married* in Paris. 12. I arrived in London on[3] June 7 and the *next* week I went to Brussels.

---

[1] In French, a city bus is **un autobus,** whereas an interurban bus is **un autocar.**   [2] *leave again* = **repartir**   [3] For how to express French dates, see page 161.

Verb Review

Review the verbs **falloir** and **lire** according to the outline on page 283.

CHAPTER 11

The Subjunctive

In connection with the subjunctive, we must consider four important questions:

(a) What is the basic function of the subjunctive as compared with that of the indicative?

(b) Under what specific circumstances is the subjunctive used in French, and how do those uses fit into the basic concept of the function of the subjunctive?

(c) When is the present subjunctive used and when the past subjunctive, in other words, what is the concept of time in the subjunctive tenses?

(d) When must the infinitive be used instead of the subjunctive, even though the nature of the main clause seems to indicate a subjunctive in the subordinate clause?

1. What is the essential difference between the indicative and the subjunctive mode?

INDICATIVE	SUBJUNCTIVE
Jean **est** à la maison.	**Nous sommes contents** que Jean **soit** à la maison.
John is *at home*.	We are glad *that John* is *at home*.
Marie ne **sait** pas la leçon.	**Je regrette** que Marie ne **sache** pas la leçon.
Marie does *not* know *the lesson*.	I regret *that Marie* does *not* know *the lesson*.
Les enfants **ont perdu** leur ballon.	**C'est dommage** que les enfants **aient perdu** leur ballon.
The children lost *their ball*.	It is too bad *that the children* lost *their ball*.

The INDICATIVE states an objective fact. It is concerned with the fact as a fact.

The SUBJUNCTIVE sometimes deals with facts, but in such cases it deals with them not objectively but from the point of view of the speaker of the main clause. It indicates the subjective attitude of the speaker in the main clause toward the action in the subordinate clause.

2. What other type of state or action does the subjunctive deal with? (Compare it with the indicative in this respect.)

INDICATIVE	SUBJUNCTIVE
Vous **faites** votre travail.	**Je voudrais** que vous **fassiez** votre travail.
You do *your work*.	I wish *that you* would do *your work*.
Monsieur Texier **viendra** demain.	**Il est possible** que Monsieur Texier **vienne** demain.
Mr. Texier will come *tomorrow*.	It is possible *that Mr. Texier* will come *tomorrow*.
Nous n'**arriverons** pas à l'heure.	**Roger a peur** que nous n'**arrivions** pas à l'heure.
We'll *not* arrive *on time*.	Roger is afraid *that we*'ll *not* arrive *on time*.

The INDICATIVE states an objective fact, whether in the present, past or future.

The SUBJUNCTIVE often deals with hypothetical actions, that is, actions which have not occurred and may never occur. It often states the attitude of the subject in the main clause toward such hypothetical actions.

3. Which types of verbs in the main clause are followed by the subjunctive in the subordinate clause, and why?

Il veut que nous l'**aidions**.	He wishes *us* to help *him*.
Je doute qu'il **puisse** le faire.	I doubt *that he* can *do it*.
Nous craignons qu'il **pleuve**.	We fear *that it* will rain.

Verbs of wishing, verbs of doubting, and verbs and expressions of emotion, such as fearing, being glad, being sorry, etc., all of which indicate the attitude of the subject of the main clause toward either a fact or a hypothetical action, are followed by the subjunctive in the subordinate clause, that is, in the clause introduced by **que**.

4. When is the present subjunctive used in French? When the past subjunctive? What is the concept of time in the subjunctive?

Je suis content que Maurice **puisse** le faire maintenant.	*I am glad that Maurice* can *do it now.*
Je suis content que Maurice **puisse** le faire demain.	*I am glad that Maurice* will be able *to do it tomorrow.*
Je suis content que Maurice **ait pu** le faire hier.	*I am glad that Maurice* could *do it yesterday.*

The only two tenses of the subjunctive used in conversational French are the present and the past. The PRESENT SUBJUNCTIVE is used if the action of the subordinate clause takes place <u>at the same time</u> as the action of the main clause or <u>after</u> the action of the main clause. The PAST SUBJUNCTIVE is used if the action of the subordinate clause took place <u>before</u> the action of the main clause. In other words, time in the subjunctive is relative to time in the main clause.

The past subjunctive (**passé du subjonctif**) is a compound tense corresponding to the compound past in the indicative. Ex.: que j'**aie vu**, que tu **aies parlé**, qu'il **soit parti**, etc.

5. When must the infinitive be used instead of a *que*-clause with the subjunctive even after constructions which seem to require a subjunctive?

SUBJUNCTIVE	INFINITIVE
Je suis content **que vous soyez ici.**	**Je** suis content **d'être ici.**
I am glad that *you* are *here.*	*I am glad* that *I* am *here.*
Avez-**vous** peur **que Marcel fasse cela?**	Avez-**vous** peur **de faire cela?**
Are you *afraid* that Marcel will do *it?*	*Are* you *afraid* that you will do it?
Anne-Marie veut **que vous le sachiez.**	**Anne-Marie** veut **le savoir.**
Anne-Marie *wants* you to know it.	Anne-Marie *wishes* that she might know it.

When the subject of a subordinate clause requiring the subjunctive would be the same as the subject of the main clause, the INFINITIVE is normally required instead of **que** with the SUBJUNCTIVE.

NOTE: In a few cases, such as in sentences with **bien que, quoique, pourvu que,** and **jusqu'à ce que,** it is impossible to replace a clause in the subjunctive by an infinitive construction even when the subject of the main clause and that of the dependent **que**-clause would be the same, since there is no prepositional construction which corresponds to the subordinate conjunctions. In these few special cases only, the subjunctive may be used even when the subject of the main clause and that of the dependent clause are the same. Ex.: Nous viendrons **bien que nous soyons** fatigués. Jean-Paul le fera pourvu **qu'il soit** libre.

Verbs of wishing are followed directly by the infinitive without a preposition; verbs of emotion require **de** before an infinitive.

A. *Remplacez les infinitifs entre parenthèses par la forme convenable du verbe.*

(These verbs must be either in the present or past subjunctive or in some tense of the indicative. Often the sentence will give some indication in its wording of the tense required.)

1. Je veux que tu me (dire) où tu iras ce soir.   2. Nous craignons qu'il (perdre) tout son argent l'année dernière.   3. Georges dit que vous (pouvoir) partir tout de suite.   4. Je doute que les élèves (savoir) leur leçon aujourd'hui.   5. Nous savons que vous (aimer) aller en France.   6. Désirez-vous que nous (allumer) la lampe?   7. Vous

devez être content que votre fils (réussir) si bien. 8. Je vois que vous
(se moquer) de nous. 9. Êtes-vous heureux que vos amis (arriver)
hier soir? 10. Elle a toujours peur que son mari (être) en retard.
11. Je m'étonne que nous n'(avoir) pas de ses nouvelles hier soir.
12. Votre père dit que vous ne (savoir) pas ce que vous voulez.
13. Vous savez que Pierre (finir) son travail le mois prochain.
14. Nous regrettons que vous ne (pouvoir) pas venir avec nous demain. 15. Je remarque que vous (aller) souvent au cinéma ces
jours-ci. 16. Je doute que votre idée (valoir) grand-chose.

B. *Traduisez en français.*

(The verbs in the subordinate clauses of the sentences of this exercise are in
the present or past subjunctive or in some tense of the indicative, or, the
infinitive must be used instead of a **que**-clause.)

1. I am afraid that you do not understand me. 2. You know that
she will not come this morning. 3. He says that it will rain tomorrow.
4. I doubt that he has done his work. 5. We are glad that you have
a new car. 6. I wish[1] that I were rich enough to travel every summer.
7. We are sorry that your friend is not here. 8. Do you want us to
speak French with him? 9. Are you glad that you will go to France
next year? 10. I am surprised that he is absent. 11. I see that you
are wearing a new dress. 12. We are surprised that he spoke Italian
with his parents. 13. When he is elsewhere, he wishes[1] that he were
here. 14. I doubt that you will be able to see him. 15. We are
glad that we were able to go out. 16. What do you expect him to
do all alone? 17. They are sorry that they cannot[2] stay longer.
18. I see that you are alone today. 19. We doubt that we can go to
the fair with you. 20. I am afraid that I do not[2] know what you
want. 21. I am afraid that I lost my billfold in the street. 22. I am
sorry that I arrived too late.

---

[1] Use the conditional of **vouloir** to express *wish*. [2] Both parts of the negative precede a
simple infinitive. Ex.: **Il est impossible de ne pas le faire.**

PATTERN PRACTICE: various types and tenses of the subjunctive, the
use of the infinitive for the subjunctive

Pattern 1

    YOU HEAR   Georges apprend le français.
    YOU SAY   Je veux que Georges apprenne le français.

Pattern 2

YOU HEAR   Mon fils suit vos conseils. J'en suis heureux.

YOU SAY   Je suis heureux que mon fils suive vos conseils.

Pattern 3

YOU HEAR   Je regrette que tu ne puisses pas venir.

YOU SAY   Je regrette que tu n'aies pas pu venir hier.

Pattern 4

YOU HEAR   Sylvie est heureuse que nous connaissions des artistes.

YOU SAY   Sylvie est heureuse de connaître des artistes.

Pattern 5

YOU HEAR   Je regrette d'avoir tellement à faire.

YOU SAY   Je regrette que vous ayez tellement à faire.

6. When is the indicative and when the subjunctive used after impersonal expressions?

INDICATIVE	SUBJUNCTIVE
Il **est certain** que Louis <u>est</u> intelligent.	Il **est possible** que Louis <u>soit</u> intelligent.
It is certain *that Louis* is intelligent.	It is possible *that Louis* is *intelligent*.
Il **est évident** que vous <u>savez</u> votre leçon.	Il **est important** que vous <u>sachiez</u> votre leçon.
It is obvious *that you* know *your lesson*.	It is important *that you* know *your lesson*.
Il **est exact** que Monsieur et Madame Minard <u>vont</u> en France cet été.	Il **est naturel** que Monsieur et Madame Minard <u>aillent</u> en France cet été.
It is true *that Mr. and Mrs. Minard* are going *to France this summer*.	It is natural *that Mr. and Mrs. Minard* should go *to France this summer*.

Impersonal expressions which insist on a fact or on the certainty of a fact are followed by the INDICATIVE.

Impersonal expressions where not the fact but the attitude or opinion of the speaker toward a hypothetical state or action is given are followed by the SUBJUNCTIVE.

Among the impersonal expressions followed by the INDICATIVE are:	Among the impersonal expressions followed by the SUBJUNCTIVE are:	
Il est certain	Il est bien	Il est possible
Il est clair	Il est bon	Il est préférable
Il est évident	Il est douteux	Il est peu probable
Il est exact	Il est étonnant	Il est rare
Il est probable	Il est étrange	Il est temps
Il est sûr	Il est important	Il faut
Il est vrai	Il est impossible	Il importe
	Il est juste	Il se peut
	Il est naturel	Il suffit
	Il est nécessaire	Il vaut mieux

C. *Dans le devoir suivant, mettez les infinitifs indiqués entre parenthèses soit au présent soit au passé du subjonctif ou au temps convenable de l'indicatif. Justifiez oralement votre choix du temps et du mode.*

1. Il est évident que vous (avoir) besoin de leçons. 2. Il est étrange que Jacqueline ne nous (écrire) pas depuis son départ. 3. Docteur, vaut-il mieux que je lui (dire) la vérité? 4. Il est possible que M. Bigot (acheter) cette maison l'année dernière. 5. Il est certain que l'étude (être) le meilleur moyen pour réussir. 6. —Madame, vous paraissez si jeune! Il est impossible que vous (être) sa mère. 7. Il est étrange que ces ouvriers (perdre) leur place vendredi dernier. 8. Il serait bon que vous (se reposer) un peu. 9. Il est possible que vous (connaître) cette affaire mieux que moi. 10. Il est vrai que nous (avoir) peur de lui. 11. —Mon garçon, il est grand temps que tu (prendre) tes responsabilités. 12. Il suffit que mon fils me (dire) la vérité pour être pardonné. 13. Il vaut mieux que vous ne la (revoir) pas pendant quelque temps. 14. Il est sûr qu'ils ne (revenir) pas la semaine prochaine.

D. *Traduisez en français. Justifiez oralement l'emploi du temps et du mode.*

1. It is rare that your wife comes to see us. 2. It is clear that you are mistaken. 3. It is important for you not to speak of this story[1]. 4. It is doubtful that the teacher will punish those pupils. 5. It is good that you have already finished your work. 6. It is surprising

that he is so hateful². 7. It is necessary for¹ me to think³ before answering you. 8. It is time that the president act energetically. 9. It is doubtful that they have found the money. 10. It is natural that you should wish to have a good time. 11. It is remarkable that man can go to⁴ the moon. 12. It is correct that he has never read a single book. 13. I am surprised, but it is possible that I said that. 14. It is evident that you do not work too much.

---

¹ Rearrange the wording before translating. ² **méchant** ³ Use a form of **réfléchir**.
⁴ **dans** or **sur**

PATTERN PRACTICE: impersonal expressions followed by a clause

Pattern 6

YOU HEAR   Il est certain que vous savez son adresse. (Il est possible . . .)
YOU SAY   Il est possible que vous sachiez son adresse.

Pattern 7

YOU HEAR   Il est indispensable que vous réussissiez à votre examen.
           (Il est certain . . .)
YOU SAY   Il est certain que vous réussirez à votre examen.

7. What mode follows verbs of 'thinking' and 'believing' in French?

AFFIRMATIVE	NEGATIVE AND INTERROGATIVE
Je **crois** que vous **êtes** malade.	Je **ne crois pas** que vous $\begin{cases}\textbf{êtes}\\\textbf{soyez}\end{cases}$ malade.
Il **pense** que sa femme **partira**.	Il **ne pense pas** que sa femme $\begin{cases}\textbf{partira.}\\\textbf{parte.}\end{cases}$
Nous **croyons** que Paul **a lu** cela.	**Croyez-vous** que Paul $\begin{cases}\textbf{a lu} \text{ cela?}\\\textbf{ait lu} \text{ cela?}\end{cases}$
Moi, je **trouve** qu'il **a bien fait**.	**Trouvez-vous** qu'il $\begin{cases}\textbf{a bien fait?}\\\textbf{ait bien fait?}\end{cases}$

Affirmative forms of verbs of thinking and believing are ALWAYS followed by the indicative — NEVER by the subjunctive.

Negative and interrogative forms of verbs of thinking and believing may be followed by the subjunctive when there is considerable doubt on the part of the speaker and when the speaker is a person who is grammatically precise in his use of the subjunctive. When the element of doubt is minor and especially when the idea in the subordinate clause is of a future nature, the indicative is normally used.

E. *Mettez les infinitifs à la forme convenable et expliquez oralement le temps et le mode que vous aurez choisis.*

1. Je trouve que cette robe vous (aller) très bien.   2. Il trouve que vous ne lui (donner) pas assez d'argent.   3. Je ne pense pas que nous (pouvoir) nous revoir.   4. Ils croient que leur fils (être) toujours un enfant.   5. Ne croyez-vous pas que vos amis (savoir) cela?   6. Je ne crois pas que Jean (venir) demain.   7. Je trouve qu'il (conduire) bien.   8. Je ne crois pas que cet homme (connaître) bien son métier. 9. Nous ne croyons pas que Philippe (venir) hier soir.

F. *Traduisez en français.*

1. He thinks we are foolish.   2. Do you think that he will do that? 3. I do not believe that he can tell it to us.   4. He believes that they are going to Paris.   5. Do you believe that they will invite us?   6. I don't think that you understand the problem.

Pattern Practice: affirmative verbs of 'believing' and 'thinking'

Pattern 8

YOU HEAR   Vous pouvez partir demain.
YOU SAY   Je crois que vous pouvez partir demain.

8. What are the subordinate conjunctions which are always followed by the subjunctive in French, and what in the nature of their meaning causes them to be followed by a subjunctive rather than an indicative?

afin que \ **pour que** ∫ *in order that*	**à moins que** *unless*
bien que \ **quoique** ∫ *although*	**sans que** *without*
	avant que *before*
pourvu que \ **à condition que** ∫ *provided that*	**jusqu'à ce que** *until*

Each of these expressions embodies a concept which is concerned either with a hypothetical action or with an attitude toward a real action:

(a) **afin que** and **pour que** indicate purpose, and the intended purpose is hypothetical, not yet real.

(b) **bien que** and **quoique** indicate concession on the part of the speaker toward what is either a reality or something which could be so and is therefore hypothetical.

(c) **pourvu que** and **à condition que** indicate a restrictive condition which is not a reality.

(d) **à moins que** and **sans que** also indicate a restrictive condition which is not a reality.

(e) **avant que** and **jusqu'à ce que** are conjunctions concerned with actions to take place at some time after the action of the main clause and which, in the mind of the speaker, depend on some other action taking place. Thus they are restrictive to a certain extent.

9. Under what conditions are these conjunctions replaced by a corresponding preposition which is followed by an infinitive?

Je lui écrirai **pour qu'il sache** cela.
I *will write him* so that he may know *that.*

Je lui écrirai **pour savoir** cela.
I *will write him* so that I may know *that.*

Je conduirai vite **afin que vous arriviez** à l'heure.
I'*ll drive fast* so that you arrive *on time.*

Je conduirai vite **afin d'arriver** à l'heure.
I'*ll drive fast* $\begin{cases} \text{to arrive } \textit{on time.} \\ \text{so that I may arrive} \\ \quad \textit{on time.} \end{cases}$

Je viendrai **à moins que** Marc soit malade.
I'*ll come* unless Mark is sick.

Je viendrai **à moins d'être malade**·
I'*ll come* unless I am sick.

Je partirai **avant que** Georges apprenne les résultats.
I'*ll leave* before George learns *the results.*

Je partirai **avant d'apprendre** les résultats.
I'*ll leave* before learning *the results.*

Je ferai cette affaire <u>sans que</u> **vous**
    perdiez un sou.
  I *will carry this thing out* without
    your losing *a penny*.

Je ferai cette affaire <u>sans</u> **perdre** un
    sou.
  I'*ll carry this thing out* without losing
    a penny.

When the subject of the subordinate clause introduced by conjunctions requiring the subjunctive in French would be the same as the subject of the main clause, French normally uses a preposition with an infinitive if such a construction exists.

NOTE: However, in the case of **à moins que,** one finds both **à moins que** + the subject of the main clause and **à moins de** + the infinitive.

G. *Traduisez en français les phrases suivantes. Attention au temps et au mode.*

1. I'll go with you although that will be difficult. 2. Read this letter quickly before my father comes back. 3. Do something so that they will go away sooner. 4. Do what you please, provided that you do not make any noise. 5. He will always be poor unless his uncle should die. 6. I'll arrive at his house before I know his answer. 7. She refuses to speak, although she knows the whole story. 8. I'll do that provided that you don't speak of it to anyone. 9. She truly loves me although she doesn't tell me so[1]. 10. He left without having done half[2] the work. 11. You will not see[3] Martine again unless she comes this evening. 12. How[4] can we leave without their being angry? 13. I wrote this letter today so that I might have a reply tomorrow. 14. I'll wear a white dress so that you may recognize me. 15. Have a good time before it is too late. 16. They did everything so that their children might be happy. 17. He works a great deal although he is very rich. 18. I'll work until I understand these rules.

---

[1] **le** [2] *half the* = **la moitié de** + DEFINITE ARTICLE [3] *not see again* = **ne plus revoir**
[4] *How can we leave* = **Comment partir** . . .

PATTERN PRACTICE: adverbial conjunctions followed by the subjunctive

Pattern 9
YOU HEAR Je travaillerai. Vous me téléphonerez. (jusqu'à ce que)
YOU SAY Je travaillerai jusqu'à ce que vous me téléphoniez.

Pattern 10
YOU HEAR Je resterai avec vous pour que vous écriviez cette lettre.
YOU SAY Je resterai avec vous pour écrire cette lettre.

10. Why do the sentences on the left use the indicative in the subordinate clause while those on the right use the subjunctive?

INDICATIVE	SUBJUNCTIVE
J'ai un domestique **qui sait** tout faire.	**Je cherche** un domestique **qui sache** tout faire.
Il y a beaucoup de gens **qui veulent** aider ce malheureux.	**Il y a très peu** de gens **qui veuillent** aider ce malheureux.
Je connais quelqu'un **qui peut** vous accompagner.	**Je ne connais personne** qui **puisse** vous accompagner.
Vous avez un collègue **qui est** très au courant de ces choses.	**Avez-vous** un collègue **qui soit** très au courant de ces choses?

The INDICATIVE is normally used in dependent relative clauses, since relative clauses normally state a fact.

The SUBJUNCTIVE is often used in relative clauses where there is some doubt or denial of the existence or attainability of the antecedent, but certain tenses of the indicative are also found in such clauses.

H. *Remplacez l'infinitif entre parenthèses par le temps convenable de l'indicatif ou du subjonctif, selon le cas.*

1. Avez-vous une amie qui (pouvoir) venir avec nous dimanche?
2. Il y a à la porte un homme qui (vouloir) vous voir. 3. Pouvez-vous m'indiquer un film qui (plaire) à tout le monde? 4. Il cherche quelqu'un qui (vouloir) bien acheter sa vieille maison. 5. Y a-t-il ici un étudiant qui (savoir) parler chinois? 6. Connaissez-vous une seule personne qui (être) capable de se sacrifier pour cela? 7. Nous cherchons un cadeau qui lui (faire) plaisir. 8. Je vous apporte un livre qui vous (intéresser). 9. Y a-t-il quelque chose que je (pouvoir) faire pour vous?

I. *Traduisez en français.*

1. We do not know anyone who has been able to solve your problem.
2. He is looking for someone who can help him. 3. I know a girl who drives well. 4. Can you tell me the name of a student who goes to class every day? 5. Is there a restaurant near here which is not too expensive? 6. You have a hat which looks well on[1] you. 7. Do you really have a dog who knows how to count? 8. Bring me a book

---

[1] Use the indirect object form of the pronoun to express *on you*.

which is not too long.   9. We are looking for a little house which is peaceful.   10. I see no one whom I know.   11. There are people who know how to speak several languages.   12. There is nothing that can save him.

PATTERN PRACTICE: clauses with a special antecedent

Pattern 11

    YOU HEAR   Nous avons une chambre qui est très fraîche en été.

    YOU SAY   Nous cherchons une chambre qui soit très fraîche en été.

Pattern 12

    YOU HEAR   Je connais un homme qui sait le russe.

    YOU SAY   Je ne connais personne qui sache le russe.

11. When and why is the subjunctive used in the following examples?

C'est **le plus beau musée** que je **connaisse.**	*It is* the most beautiful museum *that I* know.
Quel est **le plus grand** édifice qu'on **ait** (**a**) construit à Paris?	*What is* the largest building *that they* have built *in Paris?*
C'est **le seul** homme qui **puisse** (**peut**) faire cela.	*He is* the only man *who* can *do that.*
C'est **le plus long voyage** que nous **avons** (**ayons**) jamais fait.	*It is* the longest trip *that we* have *ever* taken.

In clauses whose antecedent is modified by a superlative or by adjectives such as **premier, dernier,** and **seul,** the INDICATIVE is used when the speaker wishes to state an objective fact. When there is an element of doubt or personal opinion or of subjective feeling, the SUBJUNCTIVE may be used.

J. *Traduisez en français.*

1. Who[1] is the most interesting author that you have read?   2. It is the first thing that he must do.   3. Here are the only friends that I was able to find.   4. Is France the only country where one is really free?   5. Is the Louvre the only museum you saw on[2] your trip?   6. They are the only persons who are nice to[3] us.   7. It's the last book that I am obliged to read for this class.   8. What is the most

---

[1] **Quel**   [2] **pendant**   [3] **avec**

beautiful song that you ever heard?   9. Here is the only person who
saw the accident.   10. Who is the best teacher you have had?
11. Your advice is the only advice[4] which is useful.

---

[4] Omit in translation.

12. What is the basic idea of the subjunctive in the sentences below?

Qui que ce soit, il n'a pas le droit   *Whoever he* $\begin{cases} is \\ may\ be, \end{cases}$ *he does not have*
de fumer.   *the right to smoke.*

Quel que soit son métier, il faut   *Whatever his trade* $\begin{cases} is \\ may\ be, \end{cases}$ *he must*
qu'il fasse son service militaire.   *do his military service.*

Quoi qu'il en soit, vous devez reve-   *However that may be, you must come*
nir.   *back.*

Où que nous soyons, nous n'oublie-   *Wherever we* $\begin{cases} are \\ may\ be, \end{cases}$ *we will not for-*
rons pas nos parents.   *get our parents.*

Si riches qu'ils soient, ils ne sont pas   *However rich they* $\begin{cases} are \\ may\ be, \end{cases}$ *they are*
heureux.   *not happy.*

Quelles que soient vos objections,   *Whatever your objections* $\begin{cases} are \\ may\ be, \end{cases}$ *he*
il s'en ira.   *will go away.*

When a construction combines with **que** to form an indefinite
which introduces a relative clause (**qui que, quel que, quoi que,
si** + ADJECTIVE + **que**, etc.), the verb of that clause is in the subjunctive. Such clauses introduced by indefinites imply a type of concession
in which the hypothetical rather than the factual nature of the action
of the verb is stressed.

K. *Traduisez en français.*

1. Whoever[1] he is, tell him to come to see me at once.   2. Whatever[2]
your religion may be, you must help your neighbor[3].   3. Whatever[2]

---

[1] Either **Qui que ce soit** or **Quel qu'il soit.**   [2] In such constructions, the **Quel** must
agree with the noun that follows.   [3] **prochain**

your ideas are, keep them to[4] yourself.   4. Whatever he does, he will not be able to change the situation.   5. However[5] lazy they may be, they are obliged to work in order to live.   6. However that may be, you must come to class every day.   7. Wherever he goes, he finds friends quickly.   8. Whatever he does, fate is against him.   9. However[5] good[6] they may be, their mother is never satisfied[7].

---

[4] *to yourself* = **pour vous**   [5] Use **si** + ADJECTIVE.   [6] **sages**   [7] **contente**

Exercices d'ensemble

L. *Remplacez les infinitifs entre parenthèses par la forme convenable de l'indicatif ou du subjonctif, ou bien gardez l'infinitif où il le faut.*

1. Il est certain que ces gens ne (savoir) pas ce qu'ils font.   2. Nous cherchons une maison qui (être) climatisée et qui (avoir) un grand jardin.   3. Je pense que vous (travailler) mieux la semaine prochaine.   4. Claire craint de (se trouver) seule pour rentrer chez elle.   5. Monsieur Dutour regrette beaucoup que vous (refuser) son offre hier matin.   6. Je vous prêterai cet argent pourvu que vous me (promettre) d'être raisonnable.   7. Où que vous (aller), je vous suivrai.   8. Nous nous étonnons de (voir) que le gouvernement ne fait rien pour ces gens.   9. Demande l'auto à ton père avant qu'il (aller) se coucher.   10. Anne-Lise a peur que son père la (mettre) en pension.   11. Je sais que vous (plaisanter) sur tout, mais ce n'est pas le moment.   12. Réfléchissez donc avant de (répondre) n'importe quoi.   13. C'est le plus grand acteur que nous (avoir) jamais vu.   14. Il est naturel que les étudiants (vouloir) faire connaître leur point de vue.   15. Nos parents sont désolés que vous (décider) de ne plus venir à nos réunions.   16. Qui que vous (être), vous avez les mêmes droits que les autres.   17. Il est possible que vous (avoir) une allergie quelconque.   18. Georges et Michel recommencent à faire des farces bien qu'on les (prévenir).   19. Il faut être bien naïf pour (croire) tout ce qu'il raconte.   20. Il faut que nous (prendre) une décision une fois pour toutes.

M. *Traduisez en français.*

1. It is true that we are sometimes too demanding toward others[1].
2. Do you know someone who can repair my television right away?
3. Madame Lesage is glad that you promised to come to her evening

---

[1] **les autres**

party. 4. I don't find that you are making a great deal of progress.
5. They questioned the suspect until he admitted his crime. 6. I
believe that this new novel will interest you, but I do not believe that
you can read it in[2] two hours. 7. The boss wants everyone to be at
the office at eight o'clock. 8. However busy you may be, give[3] some
time to your family. 9. The children are sorry that they were so
silly this afternoon. 10. His uncle will take him to Paris on the condition that he passes his examination. 11. Is he the only man who
can really save the country? 12. It is important for you not to say
a word about[4] that affair. 13. Whatever your reasons are, I advise[5]
you against this course. 14. Are you looking for the boys who broke
your window with their football? 15. I'll go to see him next week
unless he writes me not to come. 16. I believe that it will be necessary to buy a new car. 17. I am giving you this ring so that you will
remember me. 18. It is probable that we will not come back before
Christmas.

---

[2] en   [3] Use a form of **consacrer.**   [4] **sur**   [5] *advise against* = **déconseiller**

Problem Words

39. notice

(a) When *to notice* is expressed by **remarquer**

Avez-vous **remarqué** ces deux per-sonnes au premier rang?	*Did you* notice *those two people in the first row?*
J'ai remarqué tout de suite que tu n'avais pas reconnu Monsieur Lévêque.	*I* noticed *right away that you had not recognized Mr. Lévêque.*

The verb **remarquer** may be used for *notice* in almost any circumstances.

(b) When *to notice* is expressed by **apercevoir**

J'ai aperçu Elizabeth dans un taxi.	*I* noticed *Elizabeth in a taxi.*

The verb **apercevoir** means *notice* in the sense of *catch sight of.*

(c) When *notice* is expressed by **s'apercevoir**

Le conférencier ne **s'aperçoit** pas   *The lecturer doesn't* notice (= realize)
qu'on ne l'écoute plus.   *that people are no longer listening to*
                                           him.
Je **me suis aperçu** de son inquiétude.   *I* noticed (= realized) *his uneasiness.*

The verb **s'apercevoir** may be followed by **que** or by **de**. It is synonymous with *realize* or *be aware of*. When **s'apercevoir** is followed by **de,** the object of **de** is something intangible.

40. opportunity

(a) When *opportunity* = **l'occasion**

J'espère que nous aurons souvent   *I hope that we will often have* the oppor-
l'occasion de nous revoir.   tunity *to see each other.*

When *opportunity* means a favorable conjunction of circumstances, it is expressed by **l'occasion.**

(b) When *opportunity* = **la possibilité**

Ces étudiants n'ont pas encore eu **la**   *Those students haven't yet had* the op-
possibilité d'aller en France.   portunity *to go to France.*

The English *opportunity* is expressed by **la possibilité** when *opportunity* means *possibility*.

CAUTION: Do NOT use the word «opportunité» for *opportunity*. The word **opportunité** means *opportuneness* and is relatively uncommon.

41. paper

(a) When *paper* = *a piece of paper*

Jacques dit qu'il ne peut pas finir   *John says that he can't finish his home-*
son devoir parce qu'il n'a plus   *work because he doesn't have any more*
de **papier.**   paper.
Votre livre est imprimé sur un beau   *Your book is printed on very good* paper.
papier.

When *paper* means *material to write on* it is expressed by **le papier.**

(b) When *paper* = *newspaper*

Avez-vous lu **le journal** ce matin?   *Did you read* the paper *this morning?*

When *paper* is used in the sense of *newspaper*, it is **le journal**.
CAUTION: Do NOT use «papier» for *newspaper*.

(c) When *paper* is *a classroom exercise*

Remettez vos **copies** à la fin de   *Hand in your* papers *at the end of the*
l'heure.   *hour.*

For *papers* to be handed in to the teacher one can say **les copies, les devoirs** or **les exercices.** The classroom expression: *Hand in your papers* is: **Remettez vos copies** or **Donnez-moi vos copies.**

CAUTION: Do NOT use «papier» for *classroom exercise*, and do not say «Passez les papiers» for: *Hand in your papers.* The classroom exercise is **la copie;** say: **Remettez les copies** for: *Hand in your papers.**

(d) When *paper* is *a classroom report*

J'ai **un travail** à préparer.   *I have* a paper *to prepare.*

In French, there are various names for *classroom report*, such as **un travail, un compte-rendu, une composition, une dissertation** or **une étude** — but NOT «un papier».

42. people

(a) When *people* is expressed by **personnes**

Ses idées ont offensé plusieurs **per-**   *His ideas offended several* people.
sonnes.

When *people* means *a few persons*, French uses **personnes.**

(b) When *people* is expressed by **gens**

Il y a trop de **gens** sur la Côte d'Azur   *There are too many* people *on the French*
en été.   *Riviera in summer.*

When *people* means *a considerable number of persons*, French often uses **les gens.**

---

* Either the definite article or the possessive adjective may be used in this sentence.

(c) When *people* is expressed by **monde**

Il y avait beaucoup de **monde** au concert.   *There were many* people *at the concert.*

To state that there were *many people* at some function, French often uses **monde.**

(d) When *people* is expressed by **peuple**

Les Italiens sont **un peuple** très musicien.   *The Italians are* a *very musical* people.

The English *a people* in the sense of *a nation* is expressed by **le peuple.** Note that **le peuple** also sometimes means *the masses.*

CAUTION: Do NOT use «peuple» to express *people* except when it means *nation* or *the masses.*

(e) When *people* is expressed by **on**

Qu'est-ce qu'**on** dirait si on savait cela?   *What would* people *say if they knew that?*

When *people* has the very indefinite sense of *people in general*, French uses the indefinite pronoun **on.**

N. *Remplacez les mots anglais par leur équivalent français.*

1. (*Notice*) que nous sommes presque du même avis.   2. (*People*) n'aime pas conduire quand il neige.   3. Venez me voir à la première (*opportunity*).   4. Étienne corrige des (*papers*) pour le professeur Grémillot.   5. Les Hongrois sont un (*people*) très artiste.   6. Nous (*noticed*) un renard au bord de la route cette nuit.   7. Deux (*people*) sont venues pendant que vous étiez absent.   8. Ce (*paper*)-là a des tendances libérales.   9. J'aimerais vivre dans ce pays, mais je n'aurais pas la (*opportunity*) d'y travailler.   10. D'où vient tout ce (*people*)?   11. Ce (*paper*) n'est pas assez bon pour taper une thèse.   12. Tous ces (*people*) attendent[1] la sortie des artistes.   13. Il lui a fallu long-temps pour (*notice*) qu'on le volait.   14. (*People*) aime bien prendre des vacances l'été.

---

[1] are waiting for the artists to come out

O. *Traduisez en français. Attention aux mots en italique.*

1. Anne always writes on purple *paper*.   2. Several *people* came to see
me this morning.   3. Irene *noticed* the new painting as soon as she
entered the house.   4. A *people* should know its history.   5. I have
never had the *opportunity* to visit Sweden.   6. I *noticed* too late that I
had left my briefcase in the taxi.   7. One mustn't believe everything
one sees in the *paper*.   8. I saw many *people* that I didn't know.   9. I
noticed Guy at the theater last evening.   10. Would there be an *opportunity* to see the director?   11. Were there many *people* at the reception?   12. Don't forget to hand in your *papers*.   13. The teacher
didn't *notice* that I was finishing my exercises in class.   14. Don't
believe everything that *people* tell you.

Verb Review

Review the verbs **mettre** and **mourir** according to the outline on
page 283.

CHAPTER 12

The Article

1. What are the forms of the definite and indefinite articles?

	DEFINITE		INDEFINITE	
	Singular	*Plural*	*Singular*	*Plural*
MASCULINE	le	les	un	des
FEMININE	la	les	une	des

Before any singular noun or adjective beginning with a vowel or a mute **h**, **le** and **la** elide, that is, they become **l'**.

This elision must be made before a noun or adjective beginning with a vowel or mute **h**.

2. What is the commonest use of the definite article in both French and English?

Les pommes sont dans **le** frigidaire.   The *apples are in* the *refrigerator*.
Le papier et **les** crayons sont sur **la**   The *paper and pencils are on* the *table*.
  table.

The definite article is used to indicate a particular noun.

When there is more than one noun used with the definite article, the article must be repeated before each noun. English often uses the article before the first noun only.

159

3. How do English and French differ in their treatment of nouns used in a general sense?

Les pommes sont bonnes pour la santé.

Apples *are good for the health.*

J'aime beaucoup **les pommes.**

I like apples *a great deal.*

La justice est une chose bien relative.

Justice *is a very relative thing.*

Le travail éloigne de nous trois grands maux: **l'ennui, le vice** et **le besoin.** (Voltaire)

Work *protects us from three great evils:* boredom, vice, *and* need.

In French the definite article is placed before nouns used in a general sense. This is not the case in English.

A great many nouns used in a general sense are abstract.

PATTERN PRACTICE: nouns used in a general sense

Pattern 1

> YOU HEAR   champagne
>
> YOU SAY   Le champagne coûte plus cher que l'année dernière.

Pattern 2

> YOU HEAR   peinture
>
> YOU SAY   J'aime beaucoup la peinture.

Pattern 3

> YOU HEAR   Voulez-vous de la glace?
>
> YOU SAY   Oui, j'aime beaucoup la glace.

4. In French, how is the definite article used with the days of the week?

Lundi nous aurons un examen.

Monday *we'll have a test.*

Nous avons toujours un examen **le lundi.**

We always have a test Mondays.

Days of the week are used without the article when they refer to an occurrence which takes place once on a given day. The definite article is used with the singular form of the day of the week when the occurrence takes place regularly every week on a given day.

PATTERN PRACTICE: the article with days of the week

Pattern 4

YOU HEAR   J'irai à l'église dimanche.
YOU SAY   Je vais toujours à l'église le dimanche.

5. How is the article used with dates?

le lundi 30 avril   Monday, *April 30*

When both the day of the week and the date are given, the definite article is normally placed before the day of the week but not before the day of the month. No comma separates the day of the week from the day of the month. Also found is **lundi,** 30 avril. In this case, a comma separates the day of the week from the day of the month.

le 30 avril 1970   *April 30, 1970*

When the date alone is given, the article normally precedes the day of the month. No commas are used.

6. When is the article used with the seasons?

Le printemps est très beau.   Spring *is very beautiful.*
Nous en parlerons **l'été** prochain. *We'll speak of it next* summer.
Au printemps nous avons beaucoup   In the spring *we have a great deal to*
  à faire.   *do.*
Où irez-vous **en hiver?**   *Where will you go* in winter?

The article is used with names of seasons, except when they are preceded by **en**. Note the expressions **au printemps, en été, en automne, en hiver.**

PATTERN PRACTICE: the article with seasons

Pattern 5

YOU HEAR   Je fais du bateau en été.
YOU SAY   L'été est une bonne saison pour faire du bateau.

7. When is the article used with names of languages?

Le français est une langue facile.	French *is an easy language.*
Comprenez-vous **l'allemand?**	*Do you understand* German?
Je ne parle pas **anglais.**	*I do not speak* English.
Marie parle bien **(le) russe.**	*Marie speaks* Russian *well.*
En italien on prononce toutes les lettres.	In Italian *all the letters are pronounced.*

The article is used with names of languages except when the language is preceded by **en** or when it follows a form of the verb **parler.**

When the language does not follow a form of the verb **parler** immediately, sometimes the article is used with the language, sometimes not.

All names of languages are masculine.

PATTERN PRACTICE: the use of the article with languages

Pattern 6

YOU HEAR   On parle chinois à Hong-kong.
YOU SAY   Le chinois est une langue très répandue.

Pattern 7

YOU HEAR   Le portugais est une langue romane.
YOU SAY   Comment dit-on «bonjour» en portugais?

A. *Traduisez en français.*

(All exercises in this lesson are English-to-French. In each sentence there is some word with which the definite article must be either used or omitted. Identify this word and connect it with one of the rules in the preceding sections. Explain orally why you use or omit the definite article.)

1. Summer is a very beautiful season.   2. It is necessary to be patient with women.   3. The last war began on December 7, 1941.   4. The flowers that I prefer are roses.   5. We celebrate our anniversary Tuesday, March 8.   6. I like to hear my friend Sergio Tonelli speak Italian.   7. He adores children.   8. In spring all nature awakens. 9. It is difficult to know German well[1].   10. In English they use the word "sorry" a great deal.   11. Men are truly curious.   12. Do you like French coffee?   13. Are you free Saturday afternoon?   14. Many Frenchmen speak Spanish.   15. Sundays I always go to church.

---

[1] Place this adverb before *know.*

16. There are interesting concerts in winter.   17. French is a beautiful language.   18. We never have any class on Saturday.   19. Large countries are the most powerful.

8. When is the article used with nouns in apposition?

Pasteur, **le grand savant français,** mourut en 1895.

Pasteur, the great French scientist, *died in 1895.*

Philippe, **le fils de notre voisin,** est parti à l'armée.

Philip, our neighbor's son, *has left for the army.*

Pierre Dupont, **étudiant en médecine,** habite à Paris.

Pierre Dupont, a medical student, *lives in Paris.*

Yvetot, **petite ville de Normandie,** se trouve entre Le Havre et Rouen.

Yvetot, a little Norman town, *lies between Le Havre and Rouen.*

In French, the definite article is normally used with nouns in apposition where it would be in English, to state what the speaker considers a well-known fact.

But in French, the indefinite article is not often used with nouns in apposition. Wherever the noun in apposition furnishes additional and presumably unknown information, the noun in apposition tends to be used without any article.

9. What about the use of the article with a noun following the preposition *en*?

Jacques est un étudiant **en droit.**

Jack is a law *student.*

L'Europe est divisée **en pays.**

Europe is divided into countries.

Normally, no article follows the preposition **en.**

L'Arc de Triomphe fut construit **en l'honneur** des armées de Napoléon.

The Arc de Triomphe was constructed in honor *of Napoleon's armies.*

L'agent a tiré **en l'air.**

The policeman fired a shot into the air.

En l'absence du professeur les élèves ont fait beaucoup de bruit.

In the absence *of the teacher the pupils made a lot of noise.*

In certain set expressions, the commonest of which are **en l'honneur, en l'air** and **en l'absence,** the article is used after **en.**

10. Is the article used with given (first) names?

Marie est partie hier avec **le petit Claude** et son frère Henri.

Mary left yesterday with little Claude *and her brother Henry.*

The article is not normally used with given names. But it is used with first names modified by an adjective.

11. When speaking of someone, how is the article used with titles?

Hier, j'ai vu **le docteur Lemaître.**

Yesterday, I saw Dr. Lemaître.

Le capitaine Lebeau arrivera demain.

Captain Lebeau *will arrive tomorrow.*

Connaissez-vous **le professeur Dupré?**

Do you know Professor Dupré?

Le président Wilson est allé en Europe en 1919.

President Wilson *went to Europe in 1919.*

When speaking of a person, the definite article is used before titles indicating a profession.

Monsieur Lebrun habite 30, rue de Vaugirard.

Mr. Lebrun *lives at 30 Vaugirard Street.*

Où est **Madame Rivière?**

Where is Mrs. Rivière?

Jacques sort souvent avec **Mademoiselle Moreau.**

Jack often goes out with Miss Moreau.

But no article is used before **monsieur, madame,** or **mademoiselle** when speaking of a person.

monsieur = **M.**   madame = **Mme** or **Mme**   mademoiselle = **Mlle** or **Mlle**

A period is used after the abbreviation for **monsieur** but no period is used after the abbreviations for **madame** and **mademoiselle.**

12. How is the article used with titles when addressing a person?

Docteur, je ne me sens pas bien du tout.

Doctor, *I don't feel well at all.*

J'ai suivi vos conseils, **Dr. Perret.**

I followed your advice, Dr. Perret.

In addressing a doctor, no article is used either with or without the name of the doctor.

—Bonjour, **mon capitaine.**	*"Good morning,* captain."
—Je suis à vos ordres, **mon général.**	*"I am at your orders,* general."

In the military, when a soldier of lower rank or an officer speaks to an officer of higher rank, the possessive adjective is used before the title.

Je n'ai pas encore lu ce livre, **mon-sieur.**	*I haven't yet read that book,* Professor Lemercier.

In addressing teachers in France, especially professors, neither the title nor the name is used, but simply **monsieur, madame,** or **mademoiselle.**

Bonsoir, **Monsieur.**	*Good evening,* Mr. Jones.
Bonjour, **Madame.**	*Good morning,* Mrs. Leroque.
Mademoiselle, j'espère que nous nous reverrons.	Miss Smith, *I hope that we'll see each other again.*

In French, a person is normally addressed as **Monsieur, Madame** or **Mademoiselle,** and no last name is normally used when addressing a person, although the last name is sometimes heard.

Monsieur le Président, vous avez toujours raison.	Mr. President, *you are always right.*
Monsieur le professeur, voulez-vous nous donner votre opinion?	Professor Bruce, *will you give us your opinion?*

With certain titles, the formula **Monsieur le . . .** is sometimes used in address.

B. *Traduisez en français.*

1. He was speaking of Mr. Leduc, a publisher from Strasbourg.
2. There will be a big dinner in honor of Senator Amieux.   3. Have you invited the beautiful Sylvia to the dance?   4. She knows Prince Louis very well.   5. General Lacaze will inspect the troops tomorrow morning.   6. Pasteur, the great French scientist[1], was a very generous man.   7. They spent the night in prison.   8. In the absence of the teacher, you will teach the lesson to the class.   9. Doctor, I don't know what[2] is the matter with me.   10. I'll do what you wish, colonel.

---

[1] Not **scientiste.**   [2] This is an idiom.

11. Mr. Duneau, a mathematics professor at the university, died yesterday. 12. We'll go to France by[3] plane. 13. She loves Roger and would like to marry him. 14. The best specialist in that field[4] is Dr. Petit. 15. I'll follow you everywhere, lieutenant.

---

[3] en or par   [4] domaine

13. When is the article used before names of countries and continents?

La France est un grand pays.	France *is a large country.*
Je suis allé en Angleterre.	*I went* to England.
Il vient de Grèce.	*He comes* from Greece.
Nous sommes arrivés au Portugal.	*We arrived* in Portugal.
Il vient du Danemark.	*He comes* from Denmark.

The article is normally used before names of countries and continents.

But the article is not used after **en** (which expresses *in* or *to* with feminine countries) nor after **de** (meaning *from*) when it precedes a feminine country.

PATTERN PRACTICE: the use of the article with countries

Pattern 8

YOU HEAR   Mes amis sont en France.
YOU SAY   Ils visitent la France tous les ans.

14. Is the article used with names of cities?

Il va à Paris.	*He is going to* Paris.
Avez-vous vu Londres?	*Have you seen* London?
La Nouvelle-Orléans est en Louisiane, Le Havre en France.	New Orleans *is in Louisiana,* Le Havre *in France.*

The article is not usually found with names of cities. However, a few cities, such as **La Haye** (*The Hague*), **La Nouvelle Orléans, Le Havre, La Rochelle,** etc., have the article as part of the name.

15. When is the article used before names of streets and avenues?

Dites-moi où est la rue Racine.	*Tell me where* Racine Street *is.*
Le Boulevard Saint-Germain est très pittoresque.	Boulevard Saint-Germain *is very picturesque.*

| Connaissez-vous **l'avenue** **des** | *Do you know* Champs-Elysées Ave- |
| **Champs-Élysées?** | nue? |

The article is normally used before names of streets and avenues.

Nous sommes arrivés **Boulevard**	*We arrived at* St. Michel Boulevard.
Saint-Michel.	
On me trouvera **rue Royale.**	*They'll find me on* Royal Street.

When the prepositions *in* or *on* precede the street name in English, the French tend to omit the preposition and article. However, the preposition and the article may be used.

The French say:

dans la rue	*on the street*
dans⎱**l'avenue**	*on the avenue*
sur ⎰	
sur la place	*in the square*
sur le boulevard	*on the boulevard*

16. How is the English word *per* **expressed in French with various types of units of measure?**

(a) speed per hour

| Le train roulait à cent soixante | *The train was going at a hundred miles* |
| kilomètres **à l'heure.** | *per hour.* |

With expressions of *time indicating speed*, **à** + ARTICLE is used, and this is especially common with **à l'heure.**

(b) money per hour

| Marie gagne trois dollars **de l'heure.** | *Mary earns three dollars* per hour. |

Money per hour is expressed by **de l'heure.**

(c) something accomplished per unit of time

Dans ce pays on travaille huit	*In this country they work eight hours* a
heures **par jour** et quarante	day *and forty hours* per week.
heures **par semaine.**	

Jacques gagne neuf cent dollars **par**   *Jack earns nine hundred dollars* per
mois.   month.

In general, French expresses *per* + *unit of time* by **par** + *unit of time:*
par jour, par semaine, par mois, par an. No article is used after
par.

(**d**) expressions of dry measure, weight, etc.

Les pommes de terre coûtent cinq   *Potatoes cost five francs* per pound.
francs **la livre.**
Le sucre coûte deux francs **le kilo.**   *Sugar costs two francs* per kilogram.

French expresses *per* with expressions of *dry measure, weight,* and so
on, by placing the definite article before the expression.

**17. What prepositions are used with expressions of means of locomotion, and
when is the article used?**

Nous sommes venus <u>dans</u> le train,   *We came* <u>in</u> *the train,* <u>in</u> *a car,* <u>in</u> *an*
<u>en</u> voiture, <u>en</u> avion (or **par**   *airplane,* <u>on</u> *foot,* <u>on</u> *a bicycle.*
avion), <u>à</u> pied, <u>à</u> bicyclette.

The prepositions used with means of locomotion must often be
learned. In general **dans** or **en** is used if one can enter the vehicle,
à if one is on the vehicle. However for *on a motorcycle* the French say
en moto.

**18. What about the use of the article in stating the profession, nationality, or
religion of the subject of the sentence?**

M. Delong est **avocat.**   *Mr. Delong is* a lawyer.
M. Bajard est **un excellent profes-**   *Mr. Bajard is* an excellent teacher.
seur.

After forms of the verb **être,** French designates profession, religion,
nationality, etc., by an unmodified noun. English uses the noun
modified by an indefinite article.

In French, if the name of the profession, position, or religion is
modified, the indefinite article is used as in English.

C. *Traduisez en français.*

1. Mrs. Dallier is a milliner.   2. Did they arrive by train or on[1] a
motorcycle?   3. Products imported from Japan are cheap.   4. In

---
[1] **en**

the United States people[2] work a great deal and rapidly.   5. Mr.
Perrier is Catholic.   6. First we arrived at Peace Street, where we
found some very elegant stores.   7. In summer there are sometimes
several storms per day.   8. It is dangerous to go[3] faster than fifty
kilometers per hour.   9. *They* left on foot, *we* in a car.   10. His father
is a good doctor.   11. These toys come from Germany.   12. I like to
go[4] horseback riding in[5] the woods.   13. Formerly there was a prison
in the Place de la Bastille.   14. There are many lakes in Canada.
14. I caught a fish which I'll sell at a dollar a pound,   16. Some
tourists who come back from Poland say that they prefer America.
17. She gets[6] five dollars an hour, which[7] seems expensive.   18. My
mother-in-law comes to see us twice a year.   19. I should like to go
to Italy.   20. They left[8] for Portugal yesterday.   21. In Paris life
has a special charm.   22. He earns $300 a week, but that will not
last, for he gets[9] very tired.

[2] **on**   [3] Use a form of **rouler à plus de.**   [4] *go horseback riding* = **faire une promenade à
cheval**   [5] **dans les**   [6] Use a form of **prendre.**   [7] **ce qui**   [8] Use a form of **partir.**
[9] *get very tired* = **se fatiguer beaucoup**

PATTERN PRACTICE: the article before names of professions, etc.

Pattern 9

   YOU HEAR   Monsieur Monod est un excellent pasteur.
   YOU SAY   Monsieur Monod est pasteur.

Pattern 10

   YOU HEAR   Monsieur Lalou est ingénieur.
   YOU SAY   Monsieur Lalou est un ingénieur très connu.

Problem Words

43. piece

(a) How to say *piece* in general

Aimez-vous ce **morceau** de musique?   *Do you like this* piece *of music?*

The general word for *piece* is **le morceau.**

(b) Ways of saying *a piece of paper*

Donnez-moi **un bout de papier.** ⎫

Donnez-moi **un morceau de papier.** ⎬ *Give me* a piece of paper.

Donnez-moi **une feuille de papier.** ⎭

The word *piece* in *piece of paper* may be expressed by **morceau** or **feuille** (*sheet*) or **bout** (somewhat familiar).

CAUTION: Do NOT use «la pièce» for *piece;* **la pièce** means *play* (to be acted) or *room*.

44. place

(a) When *place* is expressed by **endroit**

Le guide nous fera voir les **endroits** les plus curieux.	*The guide will show us the most curious places.*
Il y a bien des **endroits** où la vie est plus facile qu'ici.	*There are many* places *where life is easier than here.*

The common word for *place* is **l'endroit** (*m.*).

(b) When *place* is expressed by **lieu**

Il paraît qu'on revient toujours au **lieu** de son crime.	*It seems that one always returns to the* place *of his crime.*

The word **le lieu** means *place* in the sense of *spot*. It is literary and not very common, but it is used specifically in certain instances and also in some compound expressions such as **le chef-lieu** (county seat). It is also used in the idiomatic expression **avoir lieu.** It is best to avoid using **lieu** in other cases.

(c) When *place* means *space*

Avez-vous **de la place** pour ma voiture dans votre garage?	*Do you have* a place *for my car in your garage?*

When *place* means *space*, French uses **la place.**

(d) When *place* means *a seat*

Montez vite dans le train si vous voulez **une place** près de la fenêtre.	*Get on the train right away if you want* a place *near the window.*

When *place* means *a seat*, often a paid accommodation, *place* is expressed by **la place.**

(**e**) When *place* means *a job*

Jean-Paul a une bonne $\begin{cases} \textbf{situation.} \\ \textbf{position.} \\ \textbf{place.} \end{cases}$ *Jean-Paul has a good* place (= job).

When the English word *place* means *job*, it may be expressed by **la situation, la position** or **la place.**

CAUTION: Do NOT use «place» to express *place in general*. The ordinary word for *place* is **endroit.**

45. rather

(**a**) How to say *rather than*

Je voudrais une revue **plutôt qu'**un   *I would like a magazine* rather than *a*
  journal.   *newspaper.*
Allez vous promener **plutôt que de**   *Go and take a walk* rather than *staying*
  rester ici par ce beau temps.   *here in this nice weather.*

The expression *rather than* is often rendered in French by **plutôt que** and when it precedes an infinitive, it may be rendered by **plutôt que de.**

(**b**) How to say *rather* + ADJECTIVE or ADVERB

Je suis **assez fatigué** ce soir après   *I am* rather tired *this evening after this*
  cette longue journée.   *long day.*
Après un an d'étude vous parlerez   *After a year of study you will speak*
  assez couramment.   rather fluently.

When the adverb *rather* modifies an adjective or another adverb, French uses **assez.**

(**c**) How to say *I would rather* . . .

Nous **aimerions mieux** rester à la
  maison ce soir. $\left.\begin{array}{l} \\ \\ \\ \\ \end{array}\right\}$ *We* would rather *stay home this evening.*
Nous **préférerions** rester à la maison
  ce soir.

J'aimerais **mieux** jouer au bridge
qu'au poker.

Je **préférerais** jouer au bridge
plutôt qu'au poker.

I would rather *play bridge than poker.*

The English *would rather* + VERB may be expressed in French by
the conditional of **aimer mieux** + INFINITIVE or of **préférer** + IN-
FINITIVE.

46. reason

(**a**) How to say *the reason for*

Quelle est **la raison de** votre refus? *What is* the reason for *your refusal?*

French expresses *the reason for* by **la raison de.**

(**b**) How to say *the reason that*

Philippe m'a expliqué **la raison pour
laquelle** il n'a pas pu venir.

Philippe m'a expliqué **pour quelle
raison** il n'a pas pu venir.

Philippe m'a expliqué **pourquoi** il
n'a pas pu venir.

Philip explained to me the reason that
he could not come.

French expresses *the reason that* (colloquially *the reason why*) by **la
raison pour laquelle** or **pour quelle raison** or simply by **pourquoi.**

CAUTION: Do NOT say «la raison pourquoi», which is incorrect
even colloquially.

D. *Remplacez les mots anglais par leur équivalent français.*

1. Je ne peux pas être dans deux (*places*) à la fois. 2. Béatrice est
(*rather*) découragée par tout ce qui s'est passé. 3. Je voudrais savoir
(*the reason*) Monsieur Béraud a changé d'avis. 4. Allez en avant et
gardez-nous une (*place*). 5. Il me faut un petit (*piece*) de ficelle.
6. Les enfants (*would rather*) passer leurs vacances à la mer qu'à la
montagne. 7. Il n'y a pas assez de (*place*) pour deux dans ce bureau.
8. Le beau vase chinois s'est cassé en mille (*pieces*). 9. Juliette a
laissé une lettre pour expliquer (*the reason for*) son départ. 10. On
ira voir (*the place*) de l'accident. 11. Faisons quelque chose chez
nous (*rather than*) d'aller au restaurant ce soir.

E. *Traduisez en français. Attention aux mots en italique.*

1. I know a *place* where we can work in peace. 2. Lucien works *rather* well, but he could do better. 3. Now you know the *reason* I came back. 4. The children don't have enough *place* to play. 5. What are those *pieces* of paper on the floor? 6. Johnnie, give your *place* to that lady. 7. I would *rather* leave this evening than tomorrow morning. 8. What is the *reason* for his absence? 9. Do you take one *piece* of sugar or two? 10. I decided that Jack should do that work *rather* than George.

Verb Review

Review the verbs **ouvrir** and **pouvoir** according to the outline on page 283.

CHAPTER 13

Indefinite Nouns

1. A noun may be definite, general, or indefinite. How is an indefinite noun expressed in English and in French?

Il y a **du papier** sur mon bureau.   *There is* (some) paper *on my desk.*
Vous trouverez **des cartes postales**   *You will find* (some) postcards *in the*
   dans le tiroir.   *drawer.*
Avez-vous **des enfants?**   *Have you* any children?

In English, a noun is made indefinite either by the use of the noun alone or by the use of *some* or *any* with the noun.

In French, a noun is usually made indefinite by the partitive construction.

NOTE: In both French and English, a noun modified by the indefinite article is also indefinite. Ex.: **un livre** (*a book*), **une pomme** (*an apple*).

2. What are the partitive articles?

	Singular	*Plural*
MASCULINE	**du**	**des**
FEMININE	**de la**	**des**
MASCULINE or FEMININE	**de l'**	**des**

If the word following the partitive singular begins with a vowel or a mute **h,** the form **de l'** must be used.

The partitive construction is, in effect, **de** + DEFINITE ARTICLE, but as a partitive it has lost its original meaning of *of the.*

174

3. What is the partitive construction?

Le laitier vend **du beurre** et **de la**   *The milk dealer sells* butter *and* cream.
crème.
Y a-t-il **des chevaux** dans la ferme?   *Are there* any horses *on the farm?*

The partitive construction indicates that an indefinite quantity of a given noun (part of all there is) exists in the sentence at hand.

In French, a noun is made indefinite by the partitive construction except in certain cases, when <u>the noun alone</u> indicates indefiniteness. It is the fact that there are times when <u>the noun alone</u> rather than the partitive is used that complicates the problem.

4. When an indefinite noun is modified by a preceding adjective, what happens to the partitive construction?

(**a**) when the noun is singular

Nous avons entendu **de la belle**   *We heard* some beautiful music.
musique.
Avez-vous **du bon vin?**   *Do you have* any good wine?

When an adjective precedes an indefinite singular noun, the partitive construction normally is used.

(**b**) when the noun is plural

Nous avons vu **de jolies fleurs** dans   *We saw* some pretty flowers *in the*
le bois.   *woods.*
Il y a **de magnifiques châteaux**   *There are* some magnificent castles *in*
dans ce pays.   *that country.*

When a preceding adjective modifies a plural indefinite noun, **de** takes the place of the partitive construction. One normally finds **de** + ADJECTIVE + PLURAL NOUN.

5. When does one find des + adjective + plural noun?

Ils ont vu **des jeunes gens** sur le   *They saw* some young men *on the*
boulevard.   *boulevard.*
Y a-t-il **des jeunes filles** dans cette   *Are there* any girls *in that boarding*
pension?   *house?*
Voulez-vous **des petits pois?**   *Do you want* any peas?

When ADJECTIVE + NOUN constitute a unit, so that the adjective has lost its identity as an adjective, the construction is treated like a single word, and as a single word it is modified by the partitive article **des** with the plural noun.

A. *Remplacez les tirets par l'article partitif ou par* **de.** *Expliquez oralement votre choix.*

1. Il y a ＿＿ arbres tout le long de la Seine. 2. Les étudiants viennent dans le jardin passer ＿＿ bons moments avec leurs camarades. 3. Avez-vous entendu ＿＿ belle musique hier soir? 4. Les femmes aiment acheter ＿＿ nouvelles robes. 5. Avez-vous trouvé ＿＿ petits pois dans ce magasin? 6. Il y a ＿＿ excellents romans dans votre bibliothèque. 7. Ce fermier vient nous vendre ＿＿ pommes de terre et ＿＿ maïs. 8. Il n'est pas très intelligent, mais il a ＿＿ bonne volonté.

B. *Traduisez en français. Expliquez oralement chaque article partitif et chaque* **de.**

1. I saw some cats and dogs in your garden. 2. We found some girls in the group who did not know how to speak French. 3. They sell good milk in Denmark. 4. Is there any ice in the frigidaire? 5. We drank some good cider in Normandy. 6. Were there any young men[1] on your boat? 7. There were numerous students on the beach. 8. They spent long hours in the library.

---

[1] The plural of **jeune homme** is NOT «jeunes hommes».

PATTERN PRACTICE : partitives

Pattern 1

> YOU HEAR   Catherine aime beaucoup les fleurs.
> YOU SAY   Donnez-lui des fleurs.

6. Is an indefinite noun always modified by a partitive article?

J'ai **faim.**	*I'm* hungry. (lit. *I have* hunger.)
Jacques a travaillé avec **soin.**	*Jack worked with* care (*carefully*).
Nous sommes arrivés sans **argent.**	*We arrived without* money.
La maison est pleine de **poussière.**	*The house is full of* dust.

There are several cases in which an indefinite noun is not modified by a partitive but rather in which the noun stands alone. We shall now examine each of these cases — and their exceptions.

7. When is the noun alone used in idiomatic sentences with avoir?

Marie **a soif.**	*Mary* is thirsty. (lit. *Mary* has thirst.)
J'**ai mal** à la gorge.	*I* have a sore throat. (lit. *I have* hurt *in the throat.*)

Certain set expressions made up of a form of **avoir** + the noun alone came into the language before there was any partitive article. Many of these expressions still exist.

8. When is the preposition avec used with the noun alone?

Pierre a parlé avec **hésitation.**	*Peter spoke with* hesitation (i.e., hesitatingly, *in a hesitating manner.*).
Sa femme l'a reçu avec **joie.**	*His wife received him with* joy (joyfully).

The preposition **avec** is used with abstract nouns alone when the resulting prepositional phrase indicates manner. Often this phrase can be expressed by an adverb in English.

9. When is the noun alone used with sans and ni . . . ni . . .?

Paul est parti sans **livres.**	*Paul left without* books.
Nous n'avons ni **crayons** ni **papier.**	*We have neither* pencils *nor* paper.

The noun alone follows **sans** and **ni . . . ni . . .** when it is an indefinite noun.

PATTERN PRACTICE: the indefinite noun after **sans** and **ni . . . ni . . .**

Pattern 2

YOU HEAR   Michel est venu chez nous avec des disques.
YOU SAY   Michel est venu chez nous sans disques.

Pattern 3

YOU HEAR   Monsieur Simon vend des cigares et des cigarettes.
YOU SAY   Monsieur Simon ne vend ni cigares ni cigarettes.

C. *Traduisez en français. Expliquez oralement chaque omission de l'article partitif devant un nom indéfini.*

1. The poor woman is cold. 2. Without friends life is not pleasant.
3. They fought with courage, but they lost. 4. Was he able to do it
without tools? 5. What are we going to do? There are neither chairs
nor tables. 6. They claim that they have a headache. 7. We left
their house without regret. 8. You are afraid of your teacher,
aren't you? 9. You are right, but I am not wrong. 10. We need
your dictionary. 11. That lady has neither beauty nor charm.
12. Are you sleepy? You are yawning all[1] the time. 13. Will you
help me move? With pleasure. 14. They are ashamed of their mistakes. 15. He is a lawyer; he speaks with ease. 16. I have a cold
and[2] a sore throat. 17. Madame Belleau went out without gloves.

---

[1] Use **sans** with the noun **arrêt** (m.).   [2] In French, repeat *I have* here.

10. How is an indefinite noun expressed when it is immediately preceded by the preposition *de*?

J'ai beaucoup **de travail.**	*I have a lot* of work.
Jacques n'a pas **de chance.**	*Jack doesn't have* any luck.
Ne me privez pas **de cigarettes.**	*Don't deprive me* of cigarettes.
Elle porte une robe **de soie.**	*She is wearing a* silk dress.

Whenever the preposition **de** precedes an indefinite noun for any
reason whatever, the noun follows **de** immediately, without any
partitive article.

We will now examine the cases in which **de** most often precedes an
indefinite noun.

11. What construction follows adverbs of quantity?

Nous avons **beaucoup de livres.**	*We have* many books.
Avez-vous **assez d'argent?**	*Have you* enough money?
Il y a **trop de voitures** dans la rue.	*There are* too many cars *in the street.*

Adverbs of quantity are followed by **de** because of the nature of
their meaning (*much of, enough of, too much of, more of,* etc.). The noun
alone follows **de.**

NOTE: However, the adverb of quantity **bien** (meaning *many*) is followed by the partitive **des** before an indefinite noun. Ex.: Il a **bien des** ennuis. (He has *many* troubles.) **Bien des** fois nous restons à la maison. (*Many* times we stay home.)

La plupart des (*the majority of the*) is followed by a definite noun and a plural verb.

The only singular construction with **la plupart** is **la plupart du temps**. Otherwise, say: **la plus grande partie**. Ex.: **la plus grande partie de l'été**, etc.

12. By what construction is the negative *pas* followed when it indicates negative quantity?

Je n'ai **pas de** <u>temps</u> à perdre.	*I don't have* any time *to lose.*
Nous ne voyons **pas de** <u>maisons</u>.	*We see* no houses.

When **pas** indicates negative quantity, it is followed by **de** as are other adverbs of quantity. Then **pas** is translated into English as *not . . . any* or *no*.

NOTE: By analogy, **de** also follows other negatives used quantitatively. Ex.: **Il n'a jamais d'argent.** (*He never has any money*).

13. What construction follows *pas* when it indicates a type?

Ce n'est **pas** <u>du beurre</u>.	*That isn't* butter.
Ce ne sont **pas** <u>des soldats</u>.	*Those aren't* soldiers.

When **pas** is used as an absolute negative and indicates type or quality, **pas** is followed by <u>the partitive article before the noun</u>, and in that case it is translated into English as *not*. This construction is most often found in sentences such as: **Ce n'est pas . . .** and **Ce ne sont pas . . . .**

14. How is the indefinite noun expressed after verbs and adjectives regularly followed by *de*?

Les enfants seront **privés de** <u>dessert</u>.	*The children will be* deprived of des- sert.
La maison est **entourée d'**<u>agents</u>.	*The house is* surrounded by police- men.
Il y a encore trop de gens qui **man- quent de** <u>pain</u>.	*There are still too many people who* lack bread.

Le pays **manque de** <u>ressources</u>.	*The country* lacks resources.
Il **a rempli** le sac **de** <u>billets</u> **de** banque.	*He* filled *the bag* with bank notes.
J'ai besoin de <u>timbres</u>.	*I* need stamps.

Whenever a verb, adjective, or special construction is followed by **de,** <u>the</u> indefinite <u>noun alone</u> follows **de.**

15. How are English adjectives or phrases indicating material expressed in French?

une maison **de** <u>bois</u>	*a* wooden *house*
un chapeau **de** <u>paille</u>	*a* straw *hat*

Where English uses an adjective or a phrase of 'material', French uses an adjectival phrase consisting of **de** + NOUN.

NOTE: Sometimes **en** is used to indicate material. One can say: **une maison de pierre** or **une maison en pierre.** But distinguish between **un sac d'argent** (*a bag of money*, or, *a bag of silver*) and **un sac en argent** (*a silver bag*, i.e., a bag made of silver).

D. *Remplacez les tirets par l'article partitif ou par* **de.** *Expliquez oralement votre choix.*

1. J'aimerais avoir un bon pull-over _____ laine.   2. Ces arbres ne sont pas _____ orangers, ce sont des pommiers.   3. Bien _____ étrangers viennent visiter l'Amérique.   4. Ses parents lui laissent trop _____ liberté pour son âge.   5. Donnez-moi une tasse _____ thé avec _____ citron, s'il vous plaît.   6. Ils ont plus _____ ressources que vous. 7. Nous ne mangeons pas _____ viande le soir.   8 Nous avons tous besoin _____ affection pour vivre.   9. Il y a bien _____ gens qui seraient heureux d'aller en France avec vous.   10. Cet arbre est plein _____ oiseaux tous les soirs.   11. Ce sont des taudis, ce ne sont pas _____ maisons.   12. Je me passerai _____ café, parce qu'il m'empêche de dormir.

E. *Traduisez en français. Expliquez oralement chaque emploi de l'article partitif ou du* **de.**

1. Women always like to get[1] silk stockings.   2. These people aren't men.   3. Many[2] times I regretted my indifference.   4. They are students, but they read few books.   5. The room was full of people.

---

[1] Use a form of **recevoir.**   [2] Use **bien.**

6. He bought a new nylon shirt to go to Florida.   7. Those aren't mountains.   8. That house is very quiet; one doesn't hear any noise there.   9. Many students do not work enough.   10. They always look at television and do not read any books.   11. He has good[3] qualities, but he lacks courage.   12. We know few people in our building[4].   13. They sent him a package[5] filled with toys.   14. The majority of women like to travel.   15. Today they use[6] machines for all sorts of things.

___
[3] *good qualities* = **qualités**   [4] Use **immeuble**.   [5] Use **colis**.   [6] Use a form of **se servir de**.

PATTERN PRACTICE: the use of the noun alone after **de**

Pattern 4

YOU HEAR   Avez-vous du travail? (trop)
YOU SAY   J'ai trop de travail.

Pattern 5

YOU HEAR   Je vois des taxis dans la rue.
YOU SAY   Je ne vois pas de taxis dans la rue.

Pattern 6

YOU HEAR   Nous avons un appartement.
YOU SAY   Nous n'avons pas d'appartement.

Pattern 7

YOU HEAR   Est-ce que c'est du café italien?
YOU SAY   Non, ce n'est pas du café italien.

Pattern 8

YOU HEAR   Ce n'est pas du café italien.
YOU SAY   Nous n'avons pas de café italien.

Pattern 9

YOU HEAR   Jacques a besoin des timbres que vous avez achetés.
YOU SAY   Nous avons aussi besoin de timbres.

EXERCICE D'ENSEMBLE

F. *Traduisez en français. Expliquez oralement chaque emploi de l'article partitif ou du* **de.**

1. One sees a lot of students without hats.   2. Invite some entertaining people for[1] dinner.   3. In that house there are some very valuable pictures.   4. They aren't Japanese; they are Chinese.

___
[1] à dîner

5. It is necessary to learn as soon as possible to get along without money.   6. If you want to please[2] your wife, buy her a fur coat. 7. You have courage to[3] speak so frankly.   8. I learned with regret that you will no longer be with us next year.   9. In the army they do not want women for dangerous missions.   10. There are elegant[4] hotels in all the large cities.   11. If you need cigarettes, you have only to tell me.   12. The majority of the pilots are strong men. 13. There are many[5] people who would like to have his position[6]. 14. There are still some poor areas which have no schools.   15. We spent long hours in Notre-Dame.   16. If you have neither pencil nor paper, you can return home.   17. These aren't amateurs; they are true artists.   18. There are many interesting things to see when one travels.   19. We lack soap.   20. There is enough room[6] in the car for everyone.   21. I know some young men who are really old. 22. Certain authors write with ease, but I write with difficulty. 23. Don't go to[7] that café; they serve bad wine there.   24. I have just bought a beautiful leather suitcase for my trip.

---

[2] Use a form of **faire plaisir à.**   [3] **pour**   [4] First write this sentence with **élégant** following its noun, then write it with **élégant** preceding its noun.   [5] Use **bien.**   [6] **place**   [7] **dans**

Problem Words

47. return

(a) When *return = give back*

Guy ne m'a pas encore **rendu** mon magnétophone.   *Guy has not yet returned my tape recorder to me.*

The verb **rendre** means *to return* in the sense of *give back*.

(b) When *return = come back*

Revenez le plus tôt possible.   Return ⎫ *as soon as possible.* Come back ⎭

The verb **revenir** means *return* in the sense of *come back*.

(c) When *return = go back*

Je ne **retournerai** pas tout de suite à Paris.

$I \ will \ not \begin{cases} \text{return} \\ \text{go back} \end{cases} to \ Paris \ at \ once.$

The verb **retourner** means *return* in the sense of *go back*.

CAUTION: Do NOT use «retourner» when you mean *return* in the sense of *come back*. The verb **retourner** does not have the all-inclusive meaning of the English *return*.

(d) When *return = return home*

Tu devrais parler à Georges; il **est rentré** à trois heures du matin.

You should speak to George; he $\left.\begin{array}{l} returned \\ came \ back \ home \end{array}\right\}$ *at three in the morning.*

The verb **rentrer** means *return* in the sense of *return home*.

48. room

(a) How to express *room* witho ut indicating the type of room

Combien de **pièces** y a-t-il dans ce château?

How many rooms are there in that castle?

The general word for *room* is **la pièce.**

(b) When *room = bedroom*

Est-ce que Madame Renaud loue des **chambres?**

Does Mrs. Renaud rent rooms?

The word **chambre** indicates a *bedroom*.

(c) When a *room* is used for meetings

Nous avons besoin d'une grande **salle** pour notre prochaine réunion.

We need a large room for our next meeting.

The word **salle** indicates a room used for meetings.

(d) When *room* = *space*

Il n'y a pas beaucoup de **place** dans   *There isn't much* room *in your car.*
ta voiture.

When *room* = *space*, the French use **place**.
Note that **le salon** is the formal living room, but the room where
the family lives is **la salle de séjour.**

49. save

(a) When *save* means *to save from destruction*

Marius m'**a sauvé** la vie.	*Marius* saved *my life.*
L'inondation a tout emporté; on n'a rien pu **sauver.**	*The flood took everything; we couldn't* save *anything.*

The verb **sauver** indicates *saving a person or a thing from destruction.*
It is most often used to refer to saving persons.

(b) When *save* means *to keep*

Nous **avons gardé** quelques fruits   *We* saved *some fruit for your friends.*
pour vos amis.

The verb **garder** means *save* in the sense of *to keep.*

(c) How to say *save money*

Jean **a fait des économies** pour s'acheter une moto.	*John* has been saving up *in order to buy himself a motorcycle.*
J'ai donné une tirelire aux enfants pour les encourager à **économiser.**	*I gave a piggy bank to the children to encourage them* to save.
Économisez votre argent au lieu de le dépenser inutilement.	Save *your money instead of spending it uselessly.*

The expression **faire des économies** is used to mean *to save money;*
the verb **économiser** is likewise used to mean *to save money*, but not
always in quite the same sense.

(d) When *save* is expressed by **mettre de côté**

Je **mettrai** mes notes **de côté,** elles   *I will* save *my notes; they can be useful*
pourront vous être utiles plus   *to you later.*
tard.

Les Berger **ont mis** assez **de côté**   *The Bergers saved enough to have a nice*
pour se faire construire une belle   *house constructed for themselves.*
maison.

The expression **mettre de côté** means *save* in the sense of *put aside*
something for later use, whether it be money or something else.

50. sit

(**a**) How to say that *someone is sitting = seated*

La dame **assise** devant moi avait   *The lady* {sitting / seated} *in front of me had such*
une coiffure si haute que je ne   *a high hair-do that I couldn't see any-*
pouvais rien voir.   *thing.*

When **assis** is used as a pure adjective, it means *sitting* or *seated.*

Tout le monde **est assis**; on peut   *Everyone is* {sitting down / seated} ; *we can*
commencer.   *begin.*

When **assis** follows the verb **être,** it is also an adjective. When *is
sitting* (or its equivalent in other tenses) expresses a state rather than
an action, it must be expressed by a form of **être assis.**

CAUTION: Do NOT express *is sitting* by the verb «s'asseoir»; rather,
use a form of **être assis.**

(**b**) How to say that *someone is sitting down*

Après avoir chanté l'hymne na-   *After singing the national anthem, every-*
tional, tout le monde **s'est assis.**   *one sat down.*

When *sit down* indicates an action rather than a state, a form of the
verb **s'asseoir** must be used.
Note the difference between:

Elle **est assise.**   *She is sitting* (= is seated).
Elle **s'est assise.**   *She sat down.*

G. *Remplacez les mots anglais par leur équivalent français.*

1. Est-ce que le voisin nous (*returned*) notre scie?   2. Les enfants sont
trop grands; il leur faut une (*room*) à chacun.   3. Il y a bien des

façons de (*save*). 4. Ouf! Quelle journée! Je suis content de (*sit down*). 5. Cela vaut toujours la peine de (*save*). 6. Le maire devrait faire construire une plus grande (*room*) pour les fêtes. 7. Attendez-moi; je (*will return*) dans un instant. 8. On a pu (*save*) tous les papiers importants de l'incendie. 9. On est content de se remettre au travail en (*returning*) de vacances. 10. Inutile d'acheter ce buffet; il n'y aurait pas de (*room*) dans la salle à manger. 11. Même dans les moments les plus durs, je (*saved*) de l'argent. 12. Les Arnoux ont acheté une maison de dix (*rooms*) dans la banlieue. 13. Marguerite s'est cassé la jambe et (*will not return*) faire du ski. 14. Lucie a fait un grand nettoyage; elle ne (*saved*) que quelques objets. 15. L'étudiant qui (*is sitting*) au cinquième rang s'endort toujours pendant le cours.

H. *Traduisez en français. Attention aux mots en italique.*

1. If you didn't smoke, you would *save* a great deal of money. 2. How can that family live in those two *rooms?* 3. Guy will *return* to Japan next year. 4. Marie-Claire bought some pretty green curtains for her *room*. 5. I *save* all the stamps I receive from abroad for Régis. 6. Juliette *sat down* on the sofa and began to cry. 7. *Save* for your old age. 8. In what *room* will the tournament be held? 9. *Return* home early this evening, since we are going out. 10. I like houses with a lot of *room*. 11. My old grandmother *was sitting* in her arm-chair near the window. 12. Their dog *saved* a child's life. 13. I am willing to lend you that book if you promise to *return* it to me. 14. When Roland receives his check, he always *saves* ten percent of it. 15. I didn't know that you had already *returned*.

Verb Review

Review the verbs **prendre** and **rire** according to the outline on page 283.

CHAPTER 14

The Passive Voice and the Causative Construction

I. The Passive Voice

When the subject of the sentence acts, we say that the sentence is in the ACTIVE VOICE. When the subject of the sentence is acted upon, we say that the sentence is in the PASSIVE VOICE.

ACTIVE VOICE	PASSIVE VOICE
John found *the money.*	*The money* was found *by John.*
The teacher will correct *that examination.*	*That examination* will be corrected *by the teacher.*

In the two above examples, note:

(a) The subject of the sentence in the active voice, (*John, teacher*) becomes the object of the preposition *by* and is called the 'agent' of the sentence in the passive voice.

(b) The object of the sentence in the active voice, (*money, examination*) becomes the subject of the sentence in the passive voice.

(c) The verb of the sentence in the passive voice is in the same tense as the verb of the sentence in the active voice.

(d) The verb of the sentence in the passive voice is made up of a form of the auxiliary *to be* + THE PAST PARTICIPLE of the verb in the active voice.

187

1. How is the passive voice formed in French?

Cet escroc **sera mis** en prison.	*This swindler* will be put *in prison.*
Les enfants **étaient** toujours **récompensés** pour leurs bonnes notes.	*The children* were *always* rewarded *for their good marks.*
La maison **a été vendue** hier.	*The house* was sold *yesterday.*

In French, the passive voice is made up of

> a form of the auxiliary verb **être** + PAST PARTICIPLE

2. How and with what does the past participle of a verb in the passive voice agree?

(See examples in §1.)

The past participle of a verb in the passive voice agrees in gender and number with the subject of the sentence.

3. By what preposition is the agent usually introduced in French?

Cet article sera certainement lu <u>**par**</u> **tout le monde.**	*That article will certainly be read* by everyone.
Ce roman a été écrit <u>**par**</u> **un Russe.**	*That novel was written* by a Russian.
Cette maison a été détruite <u>**par**</u> **l'incendie.**	*This house was destroyed* by the fire.

In French, **par** usually introduces the phrases indicating the agent.

The agent is the person or the thing by which the action of a sentence in the passive voice is caused or performed.

4. When is de used to introduce the phrase indicating the agent?

Elle était aimée <u>**de**</u> **tous.**	*She was loved* by all.
Le Président était suivi <u>**de**</u> **plusieurs ministres.**	*The President was followed* by several ministers.
Il sera accompagné <u>**de**</u> **deux secrétaires.**	*He will be accompanied* by two secretaries.
La maison était entourée <u>**d'un**</u> **jardin.**	*The house was surrounded* by a garden.

The preposition **de** is less strong than **par**. It usually follows verbs which indicate a state, a mental action, or an habitual action, where the role of the agent is less dynamic.

Also, certain verbs are normally followed by **de,** as, for example, **entourer de, couvrir de, remplir de,** etc.

5. If a verb can be followed by both *par* and *de*, what determines whether *par* or *de* should introduce the phrase indicating the agent?

Les verres ont été de nouveau remplis **par** le garçon.

Les verres étaient remplis **de** vin.

L'enfant qui allait tomber a été saisi **par** son frère.

L'enfant était saisi **de** terreur.

Irène était très aimée **par** son fiancé.

Irène était aimée **de** ses amis.

One can almost always use **par** to introduce a phrase indicating the agent unless the past participle is habitually followed by **de.**

The preposition **par** is dynamic, the preposition **de** is weaker. When the role of the agent is forceful, **par** is likely to be used, when the role of the agent is less active, **de** is often found. The preposition **par** is likely to indicate an action that took place at one time; both **par** and **de** may indicate habitual actions.

A. *Mettez les verbes des phrases suivantes à la voix passive en employant le temps indiqué.*

1. (PASSÉ COMPOSÉ) Cette chambre (réserver) par Monsieur et Madame Arnaud, mais ils ne peuvent pas venir. 2. (PRÉSENT DE L'INDICATIF) Les fleurs (récolter) pour en faire des parfums. 3. (PRÉSENT DU SUBJONCTIF) J'aimerais que Charlotte (inviter) à votre soirée. 4. (FUTUR) Les manifestations (interdire) à l'Université. 5. (IMPARFAIT) Ce restaurant (tenir) par les parents de Pierre. 6. (FUTUR) Si le coup réussit, ce peuple (gouverner) par des gens capables de tout. 7. (PASSÉ DU SUBJONCTIF) Je ne crois pas que ce poème (écrire) par Georges. 8. (IMPARFAIT) Les hommes les plus influents (inviter) chez le maire. 9. (PASSÉ COMPOSÉ) Le petit garçon du voisin (mordre) par son chien. 10. (FUTUR) Dépêchez-vous, sinon toutes les cerises (cueillir).

B. *Traduisez en français.*

1. I wonder why Mr. Lenoir is being watched by the police. 2. Considerable sums are being spent each year by the state. 3. The accused was being defended by Maître Olivier. 4. Everything they

had was lost in this fire.   5. The new ambassador was received by the President.

PATTERN PRACTICE: using the passive

Pattern 1

YOU HEAR   Son livre sera publié demain.
YOU SAY   Son livre a été publié hier.

Pattern 2

YOU HEAR   On a réparé ma voiture.
YOU SAY   Ma voiture a été réparée.

6. How does French often avoid an English passive when there is no agent expressed in the English sentence?

On a donné le prix au meilleur élève.	*The prize* was given *to the best pupil.*
On verra l'éclipse demain soir.	*The eclipse* will be seen *tomorrow evening.*

Although the passive is by no means uncommon in French, it is not used as frequently as in English. There are certain verbs with which it is never used, other verbs with which it is not used in certain tenses, still others where it could be used but sounds somewhat unnatural. Long experience in speaking French is necessary to develop a precise feeling for when a French sentence sounds natural in the passive and when it does not. But French has various other ways of expressing certain sentences which English puts into the passive.

To express an English passive in a sentence where there is no agent, French often uses the indefinite pronoun **on** + VERB IN ACTIVE VOICE.

C. *Traduisez en français en évitant la voix passive.*

1. Why was I awakened at six o'clock?   2. How is this sentence translated?   3. That was said at the beginning of the hour.   4. The prizes will be distributed to the pupils Saturday morning.   5. The door was opened to allow[1] a little more air to come in.   6. Bridge will be played after the reception.   7. Christmas carols are always

---

[1] *allow to come in* = **laisser entrer**

sung in the month of December. 8. That evening[2] the doors were locked at 8:30. 9. French is spoken in that store. 10. His name was[3] taken out of the telephone book.

---

[2] In time expressions referring to the past, how is *that* expressed?   [3] *take out* = **enlever**

PATTERN PRACTICE: avoiding the passive voice

Pattern 3

    YOU HEAR   Cette maison sera vendue la semaine prochaine.
    YOU SAY   On vendra cette maison la semaine prochaine.

7. How does French often avoid an English passive when an agent is expressed in the English sentence?

Un célèbre humoriste **a dit** cela.	*That* was said *by a famous humorist.*
Ceux qui l'ont vu n'**oublieront** pas cet incident.	*That incident* will not be forgotten *by those who saw it.*

French often uses the active voice to express an idea which English might express with a sentence in the passive voice. Some French verbs are not normally used in the passive voice.

D. *Traduisez en français en évitant la voix passive.*

1. That explosion was heard by several persons. 2. The boss would be liked by everyone if he were more patient. 3. All the money for the family was earned by the oldest brother. 4. This doctor had been criticized by several of his colleagues. 5. The problem was explained to the students by the teacher. 6. That talk will be given[1] by a well-known specialist. 7. The car was driven by a sixteen-year-old boy[2]. 8. By whom was that man seen?

---

[1] Use a form of **faire**.   [2] The French say: *a boy of sixteen years.*

8. How does French express an English passive sentence whose subject would be the indirect object in the active sentence?

Le notaire montrera le testament **aux héritiers** jeudi.	The heirs will be shown *the will* by the notary *Thursday.*
On a permis à Suzanne de passer le week-end chez les Grillet.	Suzanne was allowed *to spend the weekend at the Grillets.*

Consider the passive and active forms of the following English sentence:

>Passive: *I was given* the book by a friend.
>Active: A friend *gave* the book *to me*.

The subject of the passive sentence is *I*. This *I* would become *to me* in the active sentence. Thus, the subject of the passive sentence is the indirect object of the active sentence. As you can see from the examples above, this is not the case in French.

The indirect object of the active form of a French sentence CAN-NOT become the subject of the passive form of that sentence. Instead, French expresses the sentence in the active voice only.

E. *Traduisez en français.*

1. We were forbidden to enter that room. 2. The workmen were promised a raise in[1] pay. 3. You will be given the necessary information by my secretary. 4. We were served coffee and sandwiches in the plane. 5. The students were told to come back the next day. 6. The defendant was asked by the lawyer where he had been that evening. 7. You will be sent some samples by the salesman of that company[2]. 8. We were shown some snapshots at the Arnauds'[3]. 9. The children were allowed to go to the movies yesterday evening.

---

[1] de [2] maison [3] In French, proper names do not take an -*s* in the plural. The plural is indicated by the plural form of the definite article.

9. When is the English passive expressed by a French reflexive?

Ce produit **se vend** partout. *That product* is sold *all over.*
Ça ne **se fait** pas ici. *That* isn't done *here.*

The reflexive form of a French verb is often used to express an English passive when the sentence describes a general rather than a specific action.

Compare the following three sentences, each of which has a different meaning, although English uses approximately the same construction in each.

a. Ce livre **se vend** partout. *That book* is sold *everywhere.*

Here, French uses the reflexive form of the verb to describe a general action.

b. Ce livre **est vendu.**   *That book* is sold.

Here, a form of **être** + PAST PARTICIPLE describes a state, so that **vendu** is an adjective, and the sentence is not in the passive voice at all.

c. Ce livre **a été vendu** hier.   *That book* was sold *yesterday*.

Here, **a été vendu** is a real passive which describes one specific action.

10. In what other way is the reflexive form of a French verb used to express an English passive?

Mon ami **s'appelle** Jean Colin.   *My friend* is called *Jean Colin.*
Orléans **se trouve** au sud de Paris.   *Orleans* is located *to the south of Paris.*

The reflexive forms of certain French verbs are used idiomatically where English uses the passive voice. Each verb of this type must be learned individually with its meaning.

F. *Traduisez en français.*

1. Everything is done automatically in that factory.   2. The Pyrenees are situated between France and Spain.   3. That telephone is used[1] only in case of an[2] emergency.   4. Green[3] was worn a great deal last year.   5. That is said, but it[4] isn't written.   6. Hundreds[5] of novels are published each year.

---

[1] Use a form of **employer.**   [2] Omit in French.   [3] Supply the definite article.   [4] ça
[5] Here *hundreds* is a noun.

II. The Causative Construction

11. What is the causative construction? With what verb does French express it?

Le professeur **fera lire** les élèves.   *The teacher* will have *the pupils* read·
Notre voisin **a fait peindre** la maison.   *Our neighbor* had *the house* painted.

The causative construction expresses the idea of 'having something done' or of 'having someone do something' — of causing something to be done or of causing someone to do something.

In English, this idea is expressed by *have* + INFINITIVE or *have* + PAST PARTICIPLE.

NOTE: When the infinitive follows a form of *have*, it is used without *to*.

In French, the causative is expressed by **faire** + INFINITIVE. The causative always has at least one object and often it has two objects.

NOTE: Consider the sentence: **Le professeur fera lire les élèves.** In this sentence, **les élèves** is the object of the verb **fera,** and the subject of the infinitive **lire.**

Now consider the sentence: **Notre voisin a fait peindre la maison.** Here, **la maison** is the object of the verb **peindre.**

In a sentence with a causative construction, the object is sometimes governed by a form of **faire,** sometimes by the INFINITIVE following **faire.** In either case, the pronoun of the causative behave in the same way.

12. When the causative has only one object, what kind of object is it?

Nous **ferons écrire les enfants.**	*We*'ll have the children write.
Ils **faisaient écrire des lettres.**	*They used to* have letters written.

When a causative has only one object, it is always a direct object whether a person or a thing.

G. *Traduisez en français.*

1. The teacher doesn't have Roger[1] work, because he was sick.
2. Our neighbors are having a garage[1] built. 3. Why did you have your father-in-law[1] come? 5. Tomorrow I'll have your typewriter[1] repaired. 5. We'll have those records[1] played later.

---

[1] In the causative construction in French, the noun object follows the infinitive directly.

PATTERN PRACTICE: the causative with one noun object

Pattern 4

YOU HEAR Je lave ma voiture tous les samedis.
YOU SAY Je fais laver ma voiture tous les samedis.

13. When a causative construction has two objects—usually a person and a thing—what kind of objects are they?

Nous avons fait étudier **sa leçon à Lucie.**   *We had* <u>Lucy</u> *study* her lesson.

Je ferai ranger **ses affaires à Jean.**   *I'll have* <u>John</u> *put* his things *in order.*

When a causative construction has two objects, the thing is the direct object and the person the indirect object.

NOTE: Occasionally, a causative construction has two personal objects. In such cases, the person performing the action is the agent and the person receiving the action is the direct object.

Le président fera présenter **le conférencier par son collègue.**   *The president will have* <u>his colleague</u> *introduce* the speaker.

14. Sometimes the use of the indirect object for the person causes ambiguity. How may this ambiguity be avoided?

J'ai fait écrire une lettre **par mon frère.**   *I had* my brother *write a letter.*

Il fait lire ce roman **par tous ses amis.**   *He has* all his friends *read that novel.*

In cases where the use of **à** + PERSONAL OBJECT could result in ambiguity, it is not incorrect to use that construction for the causative, but such a sentence is often made clearer by using instead **par** + PERSONAL OBJECT.

NOTE: Equally correct is: **J'ai fait écrire une lettre à mon frère.** But this could mean either: "I had a letter written to my brother," or, "I had my brother write a letter." Likewise equally correct is: **Il fait lire ce roman à tous ses amis.** But this could mean either: "He has all his friends read that novel," or, "He has that novel read to all his friends."

H. *Traduisez en français.*

1. We had his parents correct his mistakes.   2. Mr. Géré had his wife pack[1] his suitcase.   3. Businessmen have their secretaries[2] write their letters.   4. I will have the cleaning woman wash the windows.   5. That teacher has all his students copy the same poem.

---

[1] *pack a suitcase* = **faire une valise**   [2] Use the singular in French.

15. When the causative construction governs a pronoun object, what is the position of the pronoun object?

Jacques **fera lire** le testament de son oncle.

Jacques **le fera lire.**

Nous **ferons réparer** notre voiture demain.

Nous **la ferons réparer** demain.

La ville **a fait abattre** cette vieille maison au propriétaire.

La ville **la lui a fait** abattre.

Mon père **m'a fait recommencer** mes devoirs.

Mon père **me les a fait recommencer.**

The pronoun objects of a causative construction normally precede the form of the verb **faire**. Pronouns come in their usual order.

NOTE: When the causative construction is in the affirmative imperative, pronoun objects follow the form of **faire**. Ex.: **Faites-le lire.**

16. When the verb *faire* is used in a compound tense, what about the agreement of its past participle with a preceding direct object?

Je **les ai fait** vendre.

I had them *sold.*

Où sont **les lettres que** nous **avons fait** copier?

Where are the letters *that we* had *copied?*

When the past participle of the verb **faire** is followed by an infinitive, the past participle of **faire** is always invariable. In other words, when it is used as part of the causative construction, the past participle of **faire** does not agree with its preceding direct object.

I. *Copiez les phrases françaises et traduisez en français les phrases anglaises. Attention à la position et à l'ordre des pronoms compléments.*

(Use the French sentence of the exercise as a model in translating the following English sentence. Watch the position and order of pronoun objects and the agreement of the past participle.)

1. Avez-vous fait construire le garage cette année? (*Yes, I had it constructed this year.*) 2. Ferez-vous envoyer ce paquet par avion? (*Yes, I'll have it sent by plane.*) 3. Faisiez-vous travailler vos élèves pendant les week-ends? (*Yes, I used to have them work during the weekends.*) 4. M. Duchamp a-t-il fait couper ces beaux arbres? (*No, he didn't have them cut down.*) 5. Le médecin vous a-t-il fait prendre un nouveau remède?

(*No, he didn't have me take any.*)   6.   Claude vous a-t-il fait conduire sa voiture? (*Yes, he had me drive it.*)   7.   Leur mère a-t-elle fait ranger leurs jouets aux enfants? (*Yes, she had them put them away.*)

PATTERN PRACTICE: the position of pronoun objects governed by a causative

Pattern 5

YOU HEAR   Nous avons fait venir le médecin.
YOU SAY   Nous l'avons fait venir.

Problem Words

51. soon

(**a**) When *soon* is expressed by **bientôt**

Ma fille aura **bientôt** vingt ans.   *My daughter will* soon *be twenty years old.*

The common word for *soon* is **bientôt**. But **bientôt** is not usually modified.

(**b**) When *soon* is expressed by **tôt**

Ne venez pas <u>si</u> **tôt**.   *Don't come <u>so</u> soon.*
Vous avez parlé <u>trop</u> **tôt**.   *You spoke <u>too</u> soon.*
Il aurait fallu faire cela **plus** tôt.   *You should have done that* sooner.

To express *soon* modified by an adverb, use **tôt**. Also, **tôt** is used in the expression **tôt ou tard,** which means *sooner or later.*

(**c**) Expressions embodying *soon*

> **dès que** (common)
> **aussitôt que** (mainly literary)   *as soon as*

> **dès que possible**
> **aussitôt que possible**
> **le plus tôt possible**   *as soon as possible*
> **au plus tôt**

52. spend

(a) When it is a question of *spending money*

Vous **dépensez** beaucoup trop d'ar-   *You* spend *much too much* money *for*
gent pour des choses superflues.   *superfluous things.*

The verb **dépenser** is used when it is a question of *spending money.*

(b) When it is a question of *spending time*

Nous **avons passé deux semaines**   *We* spent two weeks *in Portugal.*
au Portugal.
J'ai **passé une heure** à écrire cette   *I* spent an hour *writing that letter.*
lettre.

The verb **passer** is used when it is a question of *spending time.*

CAUTION: The verb **passer** must NOT be followed by the present
participle to express the idea of spending a given amount of time
doing something. French expresses this construction by **à** + INFINI-
TIVE.

53. stop

(a) When *stop* may be expressed by **cesser**

Le bruit **a cessé.**   *The noise* stopped.
Tiens! Il **a cessé de neiger.**   *Look! It* has stopped snowing.
Quand est-ce que les gens du dessus   *When will the people upstairs* stop
cesseront de faire tout ce bruit?   making *all that noise?*

The verb **cesser** never takes a direct object. It is most often used
with **de** + INFINITIVE, although it may be used as in the first example
when a thing is the subject of the verb.

(b) When *stop* may be expressed by **arrêter**

Arrêtez donc **la voiture** un peu plus   Stop the car *a little more gently.*
doucement.

The verb **arrêter** is usually followed by a direct object. It is sometimes followed by **de** + INFINITIVE.

(c) When *stop* may be expressed by **s'arrêter**

Nous **nous sommes arrêtés** pour admirer la vue.	*We* stopped *to admire the view.*
Je ne peux pas **m'arrêter** si près du carrefour.	*I can't* stop *so near the crossing.*

The reflexive form **s'arrêter** is used when no object follows. It is sometimes followed by **de** + INFINITIVE.

54. such

(a) How to say *such a* + NOUN

Avez-vous jamais entendu **une histoire pareille?**

Avez-vous jamais entendu **une histoire comme ça?**   } *Have you ever heard* such a story?

Avez-vous jamais entendu **une telle histoire?**

The English *such* + NOUN may be expressed by **un tel** + NOUN, **un** + NOUN + **pareil,** and by **un** + NOUN + **comme ça.**

(b) How to say *such a* + ADJECTIVE

Je n'ai jamais entendu une histoire **aussi drôle.**

Je n'ai jamais entendu une histoire **aussi drôle que ça.**   } *I never heard* such a funny *story.*

The English *such a* + ADJECTIVE may be expressed by **aussi** +AD-JECTIVE or **aussi** + ADJECTIVE + **que ça.**

J. *Remplacez les mots anglais par leur équivalent français.*

1. Pourquoi Nicolas est-il rentré (*sooner*) que toi?   2. Où (*will you spend*) les trois mois d'été?   3. Voulez-vous (*stop*) votre taxi au coin de la rue?   4. Si Marcel ne revient pas (*soon*), je m'en vais.   5. J'ai dû (*stop*) plusieurs fois en route pour me reposer.   6. Personne ne peut (*spend*) tant d'argent sans se ruiner.   7. (*As soon as*) vous recevrez sa lettre, prévenez-moi.   8. Je ne peux rien entendre; (*stop*) l'aspirateur, s'il te plaît.   9. Quand Thomas (*stops*) de travailler, c'est pour dormir.

K. *Traduisez en français. Attention aux mots en italique.*

1. You'll come to see me *soon*, won't you? 2. Ah, that Micheline! She never *stops* talking! 3. I never saw *such* a hard exercise! 4. *Stop* making that noise! 5. If you *spend* your money like that, you won't go[1] far. 6. Come *soon* enough to have[2] dinner with us. 7. If you need information, *stop* someone on[3] the street. 8. *Such a* man should be the mayor of the city. 9. I *stopped* to have[4] lunch at the Hôtel de la Poste. 10. We are invited to *spend* the evening at Dr.[5] Beaugendre's. 11. Come[6] and see me *as soon as* possible. 12. Won't it ever *stop* raining? 13. I have rarely heard *such a* boring lecture. 14. Have you ever seen *such a* monster?

---

[1] Use a form of **aller loin.** [2] *have dinner* = **dîner** [3] **dans** [4] *have lunch* = **déjeuner** [5] Use the article before such titles. [6] French uses **venir** + INFINITIVE.

Verb Review

Review the verbs **savoir** and **suivre** according to the outline on page 283.

CHAPTER 15

The verb *devoir*

The verb **devoir** constitutes a difficulty to an English-speaking person, because no one English verb corresponds exactly to the French verb **devoir**. Each tense of **devoir** has its own translation, and in some tenses **devoir** may have several meanings, according to the context.

1. What meanings may *devoir* have in the present tense?

M. Guillot **doit** arriver demain.	*Mr. Guillot* is to *arrive tomorrow.*
Vous **devez** partir tout de suite.	*You* must (have to) *leave at once.*
Anne **doit** beaucoup aimer la musique.	*Anne* must *like* (probably *likes*) *music a great deal.*
Votre fils **doit** lire beaucoup.	*Your son* must *read* $\begin{cases} \text{(has *to read*)} \\ \text{(probably *reads*)} \end{cases}$ *a great deal.*

In the present tense, **devoir** means either *is to* (*am to, are to*) or *must.*

But *must* itself has two possible meanings: *has to* and *probably does.*

In the second example above, *must* clearly means *have to.* The *must* of the third example clearly means *probably does.* But in the fourth example, there are two possibilities. "*Your son must read a great deal*", may mean: *Your son has to read a great deal,* or: *Your son probably reads a great deal.* When the two possible interpretations are present, the context decides.

201

A. *Traduisez en anglais les phrases suivantes. Attention au verbe* **devoir.**
Si vous traduisez ce verbe par must, *indiquez le sens de* must.

1. Mon collègue *doit* me rendre mon livre demain, et je vous le
passerai.   2. Si vous *devez* leur écrire, faites-le tout de suite.   3. Il
doit y avoir des ours dans cette forêt.   4. On *doit* toujours faire de
son mieux.   5. Le professeur *doit* nous expliquer ces règles cette
semaine.

PATTERN PRACTICE: the use of the present of **devoir**

Pattern 1

> YOU HEAR   Il faut que je parte demain.
>
> YOU SAY   Je dois partir demain.

Pattern 2

> YOU HEAR   Vous parlez probablement plusieurs langues.
>
> YOU SAY   Vous devez parler plusieurs langues.

2. What meanings may *devoir* have in the imperfect?

M. Guillot **devait** arriver ce matin. *Mr. Guillot* was to *arrive this morning.*
Gilbert **devait** travailler plus dur *Gilbert* had to *work harder to catch up.*
  pour se rattraper.
Ces gens-là **devaient** être très riches. *Those people* must have been *(prob-ably were)* very rich.

Votre fils **devait** lire beaucoup. *Your son*$\begin{cases}\text{used to have } to\ read \\ \text{probably used to } read\end{cases}$
  a great deal.

In the imperfect **devoir** sometimes means *was to* (*were to*), sometimes *had to*, and sometimes *must have.* (Occasionally, the imperfect of
devoir has other less common meanings.)

3. When does the imperfect of *devoir* mean *had to* and when *must have*?

Claude **devait** finir son travail avant *Claude* had to *finish his work before*
  de s'occuper de nous.   *turning his attention to us.*
Cet homme **devait** savoir plusieurs *That man* must have known *(probably*
  langues.   *knew) several languages.*

When the imperfect of **devoir** represents the past of the English
must = have to, it is often translated by *had to.*

When the imperfect of **devoir** is the past of the English *must =
probably does*, it is usually translated by *must have = probably did*.

When the imperfect of **devoir** is expressed by the English *must have*,
it normally represents an habitual state or action. Even though *must
have* looks like an English present perfect, it corresponds to the French
imperfect of **devoir**. The best way to determine the proper translation is to rephrase the sentence, using the word *probably* + THE MAIN
VERB.

B. *Traduisez en anglais les phrases suivantes. Attention au verbe* **devoir.**

1. Nous *devions* partir demain, mais c'est impossible. 2. Avant de
sortir le soir, nous *devions* montrer à nos parents ce que nous avions
fait. 3. Votre voisin *devait* être bien embarrassé chaque fois que
vous lui racontiez cette histoire. 4. Quand Florence habitait chez
nous, elle *devait* passer l'après-midi à garder les enfants. 4. Les
Lemire *devaient* faire le tour du monde cet été, mais ils n'ont pas pu.

PATTERN PRACTICE: the use of the imperfect of **devoir**

Pattern 3

    YOU HEAR   Il fallait toujours que nous arrivions à l'heure.
    YOU SAY   Nous devions toujours arriver à l'heure.

Pattern 4

    YOU HEAR   Votre collègue comprenait probablement l'espagnol.
    YOU SAY   Votre collègue devait comprendre l'espagnol.

4. What two meanings may *devoir* have in the compound past?

J'**ai dû** travailler toute la nuit pour faire mes devoirs.	*I* had to *work the whole night to do my exercises.*
Guy **a dû** se faire mal en tombant.	*Guy* must have *hurt himself* (probably *hurt himself*) *when he fell.*
Leurs portes étaient fermées à clé; les voisins **ont dû** entrer par la fenêtre.	*Their doors were locked; the neighbors* must have *entered* ⎱ probably *entered* ⎰ *through the window.*

In the compound past, the verb **devoir** sometimes means *had to*,
which is the past of *must = has to*. This is clearly the case in the first
example above. It sometimes means *must have = probably did*, which

is the past of *must* = *probably does*. This is clearly the case in the second example above. But in the third example, either possibility is present, and the context must decide.

When the imperfect of **devoir** means *must have*, it describes a customary state or action, whereas when the compound past of **devoir** means *must have*, it indicates a past action at one definite past time.

C. *Traduisez en anglais les phrases suivantes. Attention au verbe* **devoir.**

1. Si vous étiez chez les Lagarde, vous *avez dû* voir Pierre. 2. Personne ne parlait anglais ici; Agnès *a dû* aller en Angleterre pour l'apprendre. 3. Comme il n'y avait pas assez de place dans la voiture, nous *avons dû* laisser les enfants à la maison. 5. Juliette n'est pas encore là; elle *a dû* se tromper de route.

PATTERN PRACTICE: the use of the compound past of **devoir**

Pattern 5

> YOU HEAR Il a fallu que je finisse mon travail avant de sortir.
> YOU SAY   J'ai dû finir mon travail avant de sortir.

Pattern 6

> YOU HEAR Il est probable que Félix est parti ce matin.
> YOU SAY   Félix a dû partir ce matin.

5. What does *devoir* mean in the conditional?

On annonce le froid; vous **devriez** mettre un manteau.	*They say it will be cold; you* should *put on an overcoat.*
Les Lepic **devraient** être plus patients avec leurs enfants.	*The Lepics* ought to *be more patient with their children.*

In the conditional, **devoir** means *should, ought to.*

6. What does *devoir* mean in the past conditional?

Les Aubry n'**auraient** pas dû acheter cette voiture.	*The Aubrys* should not *have* bought *that car.*
Vous **auriez dû** nous dire que vos parents seraient là.	*You* ought to have *told us that your parents would be there.*

In the past conditional, **devoir** means *should have, ought to have.*

D. *Traduisez en anglais. Attention au verbe* **devoir.**

1. Les Bréger *auraient dû* prendre l'avion pour venir ici.   2. Nous *devrions* leur dire de quoi il s'agit.   3. Georges, tu *devrais* aider ton frère à finir sa leçon.   4. Robert *aurait dû* faire cela quand je le lui ai demandé.   5. Ce film est très drôle; vos amis *devraient* aller le voir.

PATTERN PRACTICE: the conditional and past conditional of **devoir**

Pattern 7

> YOU HEAR   J'irai chez les Minard demain.
> YOU SAY   Je devrais aller chez les Minard demain.

Pattern 8

> YOU HEAR   Robert n'est pas parti avant onze heures.
> YOU SAY   Robert aurait dû partir avant onze heures.

7. In what other ways does French express the idea of *must = has to?*

Il faut que vous vous couchiez plus tôt.	You must *go to bed earlier.*
Nous étions obligés de surveiller cet enfant tout le temps.	We used to have to *watch that child all the time.*

Note the following equivalents:

Je dois + INFINITIVE	**Il faut que je** + SUBJUNCTIVE	**Je suis obligé de** + INFINITIVE
Je devais + INFINITIVE	**Il fallait que je** + SUBJUNCTIVE	**J'étais obligé de** + INFINITIVE
J'ai dû + INFINITIVE	**Il a fallu que je** + SUBJUNCTIVE	**J'ai été obligé de** + INFINITIVE
Je devrai + INFINITIVE	**Il faudra que je** + SUBJUNCTIVE	**Je serai obligé de** + INFINITIVE

In the present, imperfect, compound past, and future, the INFINITIVE appropriate tenses of *must = have to* may also be expressed by forms of **il faut que** + SUBJUNCTIVE and by forms of **être obligé de** + INFINITIVE.

The **il faut que** construction is somewhat stronger than **devoir.** When *must* is expressed by forms of **être obligé de,** it is about the equivalent of *to be obliged to.* Sometimes, but not always, any of the three forms may be used to express the same idea.

E. *Traduisez en français chaque phrase de trois façons différentes.*

1. We used to have to work every day except Sunday. 2. Yesterday I had to leave at five o'clock. 3. Our friends have to stay in Bordeaux this evening. 4. The Leclercs[1] will have to move next week.

---

[1] In French, the plural form of proper names does not take an -*s*.

EXERCICES D'ENSEMBLE

F. *Remplacez par la forme convenable de* **devoir** *les mots anglais entre parenthèses.*

1. Nous (*had to*) prendre l'autocar pour aller à Paris hier. 2. Même si cela vous ennuie, vous (*must*) faire cette visite. 3. Les acteurs (*must have been*) furieux chaque fois qu'ils lisaient les critiques de M. Lafont. 4. Georges (*has to*) finir cette affaire avant de partir. 5. Maurice est seul; nous (*should have*) l'inviter pour dimanche. 6. Je (*am to*) passer mon examen aujourd'hui. 7. Madame Gervaise est toute pâle, elle (*must*) être malade. 8. François (*must have*) perdre sa montre, il n'en porte plus. 9. Les Gaspard (*were to*) arriver ce matin; je me demande pourquoi ils ne sont pas là. 10. Vous (*should*) acheter une nouvelle voiture. 11. Le gardien (*had to*) nous ouvrir la porte chaque fois que nous arrivions tard dans la nuit.

G. *Traduisez en français les phrases suivantes, en employant dans chaque phrase une forme du verbe* **devoir.**

1. You *should* always *knock* before entering a room[1]. 2. Mrs. Henriot was always very elegant; her husband *must have spent* a lot of money on[2] her. 3. The visitors *must not touch* the paintings. 5. We *had to hand in* our papers[3] yesterday morning. 4. Huber *was to write* me every day, but I have received only one letter from him. 6. George doesn't have any money; *he must have spent* it last week. 7. Our neighbors have a new boat; they *must be* rich. 8. My friends are late; they *should have taken* a taxi. 9. We *are to eat* at grandmother's today. 10. When I was young, I used to *have to get up* at six in[4] the morning.

---

[1] pièce [2] pour [3] Not **papiers.** [4] du

Problem Words

55. take

(**a**) When *take* is expressed by **prendre**

Qui **a pris** la voiture?   *Who* took *the car?*

The verb **prendre** is the commonest way to express *take*. But it cannot be used indiscriminately to express *take*.

(**b**) When *take* is expressed by **porter**

Le chauffeur **a porté** nos valises au   *The driver* took *our suitcases to the taxi.*
taxi.

When *take* is the equivalent of *carry to*, it is usually expressed by **porter.**

(**c**) When *take* is expressed by **emporter**

N'**emporte** pas la télévision dans ta   *Don't* take *the television into your room.*
chambre.

When *take* means *to carry something away*, it may be expressed by **emporter.**

(**d**) When *take* is expressed by **mener**

Nous **avons mené nos invités** au   *We* took *our guests to the restaurant.*
restaurant.

French has several ways of expressing *to take a person* (*somewhere*). When the verb **mener** is used, the destination must be indicated.

(**e**) When *take* is expressed by **emmener**

J'**emmène** Françoise ce soir.   *I* am taking *Frances* (with me) *this evening.*

J'**emmène** Françoise **au cinéma** ce   *I* am taking *Frances to the movies*
soir.   *this evening.*

The verb **emmener** means *to take someone away*. It may be used either with or without the destination.

NOTE: In certain cases, forms of the verb **amener** may also be used to express the idea of taking *a person away*, but **amener** also has the meaning of *bringing a person*.

(f) How to say *to take time to* . . .

Le menuisier **a mis** cinq jours $\begin{cases} \text{à} \\ \text{pour} \end{cases}$ *The carpenter* took *five days* to do *that work.* **faire** ce travail.

The idiomatic **mettre** + period of time + **à** (or **pour**) + INFINITIVE expresses *to take so much time to do something*.

(g) How to say *to take an examination*

Nous **passons notre examen** à deux heures.   *We* take our test *at two o'clock.*

The expression **passer un examen** means *to take an examination*.

(h) How to say *to take a course*

Suivez-vous **des cours** intéressants?   Are *you* taking *interesting* courses?

The expression **suivre un cours** means *to take a course*. It is becoming more and more common to say **prendre un cours,** but it is best for the learner to avoid this expression.

(i) How to say *to take a magazine*

Je **m'abonne à** plusieurs revues.
Je **suis abonné à** plusieurs revues. $\Big\}$ *I* take *several magazines.*

When *take = subscribe to*, French uses **s'abonner à** or **être abonné à**.

(j) How *take* is expressed by **faire** in some expressions

There are many idiomatic expressions with **faire** which English expresses with *to take*, such as

faire une promenade	*take a walk*
faire un tour	*take a stroll*
faire un voyage	*take a trip*

56. teach

(a) When *teach* is expressed by **enseigner**

Qui **a enseigné votre classe** pendant votre absence?	*Who taught your class during your absence?*
Mademoiselle Bouillet **enseigne les mathématiques** au lycée.	*Miss Bouillet teaches mathematics in high school.*

The verb **enseigner** is used with a direct object to mean *teach*. The direct object may be the subject taught, but not normally the person taught. For instance, to express in French: *Mr. Duparc teaches John*, one would have to say something like: **Monsieur Duparc est le professeur de Jean.**

Qui **enseignera** le latin **à Philippe?**	*Who will teach Latin to Philip?*

The verb **enseigner** may also be used with a direct object indicating <u>what</u> is taught and an indirect object indicating <u>who</u> is taught.

(b) When *teach* may be expressed by **apprendre**

C'est un ami brésilien qui **nous a appris le portugais.**	*It is a Brazilian friend who taught us Portuguese.*
C'est un ami brésilien qui **a appris le portugais à Brigitte.**	*It is a Brazilian friend who taught Brigitte Portuguese.*

The basic meaning of **apprendre** is *learn*. But it means *teach* when it is followed by a direct object denoting the thing taught and an indirect object indicating the person taught.

Ma mère **a appris à ma sœur à jouer** du piano.	*My mother taught my sister to play the piano.*

The verb **apprendre** means *teach* when followed by a *personal indirect object* + **à** + INFINITIVE.

57. time

(a) When *time* is expressed by **le temps**

Je n'ai pas **le temps** de réparer la radio.	*I don't have the time to repair the radio.*
Combien de **temps** faut-il pour faire cela?	*How much time is needed to do that?*

The general word for *time* is **le temps**.

The following expressions are used with **temps**:

à temps	*in time* (*for*)
en même temps	*at the same time*
de temps en temps	*from time to time*

In certain contexts **le temps** means *weather*.

(b) When *time* is expressed by **la fois**

Robert a dû répéter son explication trois **fois**.	*Robert had to repeat his explanation three* times.
Chaque **fois** que tu viens il pleut.	*It rains each* time *you come.*

The word **fois** is somewhat synonymous with *occasion*. It is used with numerals as well as with other words which indicate quantity.

(c) When *time* is expressed by **heure**

Quelle **heure** est-il?	*What* time *is it?*
C'est **l'heure** du thé.	*It is tea* time.

The word **heure** is used to ask *what time it is* and sometimes to indicate the *time* of a given function. When it tells time in sentences such as: **Il est cinq heures,** it is expressed by *o'clock* in English.

(d) When *time* is expressed by **le moment**

En ce moment nous apprenons le latin.	At this time *we are learning Latin.*
A ce moment-là j'étais en France.	At that time *I was in France.*

The word **moment** indicates *a point in time;* **en ce moment** means *now* or *at this time,* **à ce moment-là** means *then* or *at that time.*

(e) When *time* is expressed by **l'époque**

A cette époque-là nous n'avions pas le téléphone.	At that time *we didn't have a telephone.*

The word **époque** indicates a longer period of time than does **moment** and usually refers to a time which is farther in the past.

(f) How to express *have a good time*

Passez une bonne soirée.	Have a good time this evening.
Nous **avons fait un excellent séjour** en France cet été.	*We* had a very good time *in France this summer.*
Les enfants **se sont bien amusés** au cirque.	*The children* had a very good time *at the circus.*

The French have no word-for-word translation of the English expression *to have a good time*. The verb **s'amuser** is often used to express this idea, but, depending on the occasion also other expressions such as those found in the above examples are used.

H. *Remplacez les mots anglais par leur équivalent français.*

1. Il faut (*take*) Pierrot à la leçon de danse tous les jeudis. 2. Nous parlions justement de vous (*at the time*) où vous êtes entré. 3. Lucienne voudrait (*take*) une revue de mode de Paris. 4. Il ne faut jamais regretter le (*time*) passé. 5. Cette lettre est importante; je la (*will take*) moi-même à la poste. 6. Il faut réussir à ce concours pour (*teach*) dans un lycée. 7. Ce film est excellent; je l'ai vu trois (*times*). 8. En juin la plus grande partie des élèves (*take*) des examens. 9. Je crois que nous (*will have a good time*) chez les Barois. 10. Si tu veux me faire plaisir, (*take*) les enfants au jardin zoologique. 11. C'est Florence qui me (*taught*) à nager quand j'avais quatre ans. 12. Nous n'avons plus besoin de ces affaires; vous pouvez les (*take*) chez vous. 13. (*At the time*) où j'habitais Londres, les choses n'étaient pas faciles. 14. Il faut (*take*) les choses un peu plus au sérieux, mon ami. 15. C'est toi qui a permis à Pierre de (*take*) l'auto? 16. A quelle (*time*) est le dernier métro? 17. Jeannot (*takes*) un journal de sport. 18. Depuis son mariage, Lucie n'a plus le temps de (*take*) des cours.

I. *Traduisez en français. Attention aux mots en italique.*

1. Someone *has taken* the silverware. 2. If you don't have *time* to write, telephone me Sunday. 3. Will you *take* Mr. Galant to the laboratory? 4. At what *time* do you want to see me? 5. I wonder who *taught* Rose to cook. 6. I think I am going to *take* another magazine. 7. Did you have a good *time* last night? 8. Don't forget to *take* your suit to the cleaner's. 9. Louise *teaches* art, and her sister

teaches history.   10. Susan *is taking* some Spanish courses[1].   11. Claude can't *take* us; his car is too small.   12. Felix arrived just at the *time* when I was leaving.   13. Did Peter pass the examination he *took* last week?   14. Every *time* he comes, Paul brings us something. 15. When are you going to *take* your vacation?   16. At the *time* of my grandparents there wasn't any television[2].   17. I *took* an hour to read that novel.

---

[1] **cours d'espagnol**   [2] Use the definite article.

Verb Review

Review the verbs **tenir** and **valoir** according to the outline on page 283.

CHAPTER 16

Constructions with Prepositions

I. Prepositions of Place

TO, IN, AT

In French, *in, at* and *to* are all expressed by the same preposition before proper nouns used as place names. The preposition used depends on whether the place name is a city, a masculine country, or a feminine country or continent.

1. What preposition of place is used to express *in, at,* and *to* with cities?

Nous sommes **à** Paris.　　　　*We are* in (at) *Paris.*
Gérard va **à** Tours.　　　　　*Gerard is going* to *Tours.*

The preposition **à** is used before cities to express the English prepositions *in, at* or *to.*

2. How can one determine the gender of countries in French?

la France • **la** Grèce • **la** Belgique • **la** Suisse • **la** Bolivie • **la** Chine

All countries ending in **-e** are feminine except **le Mexique.**

le Canada • **le** Japon • **le** Portugal • **le** Danemark • **le** Pérou

All countries not ending in **-e** are masculine.

NOTE: These rules hold with the well-known and well-established countries, but they do not always seem to apply to the so-called "emerging countries," where uniform usage has not yet been well determined.

213

3. What preposition of place is used to express *in* or *to* before feminine countries and continents?

Michel est **en** France.	*Michael is* in *France.*
Louise va **en** France.	*Louise is going* to *France.*
Maurice a passé deux ans **en** Afrique.	*Maurice spent two years* in *Africa.*

French uses **en** to express both *in* and *to* before feminine countries and continents.

4. What preposition of place is used to express *in* or *to* before masculine countries?

Charlotte est **au** Danemark.	*Charlotte is* in *Denmark.*
Gilbert va **au** Danemark.	*Gilbert is going* to *Denmark.*
Restez-vous longtemps **aux** États-Unis?	*Are you staying* in *the United States for a long time?*
Nous allons **aux** États-Unis l'année prochaine.	*We are going* to *the United States next year.*

French uses **à** + DEFINITE ARTICLE to express *in* or *to* before masculine countries.

NOTE: Although the same preposition **à** and **en** is used to express both *in* and *to* with French place names, this does not ordinarily lead to ambiguity. **Je suis allé en France** clearly means *I went to France,* **Je suis allé au Canada** clearly means *I went to Canada.* **J'ai passé un an en France** clearly means *I spent a year in France,* **J'ai passé un an au Canada** clearly means *I spent a year in Canada.*

In sentences with the verb **voyager,** however, a problem does exist. **J'ai voyagé en France cet été** means *I traveled in France this summer,* and not "I traveled to France this summer." To avoid ambiguity in expressing the idea of traveling *to a place,* it is best to use the verb **aller.** Ex.: **Je suis allé en France cet été.**

5. What preposition of place is used before modified countries, cities, and continents?

(a) if the modifying phrase or adjective is an integral part of the place name

Il habite **à** la Nouvelle Orléans.	*He lives* in *New Orleans.*
Nous allons **en** Amérique du Sud.	*We are going* to *South America.*
Le Maroc, l'Algérie et la Tunisie sont **en** Afrique du Nord.	*Morocco, Algeria and Tunisia are* in *North Africa.*

If the modifying phrase or adjective is an integral part of the place name, the same preposition would be used as if the place were not modified.

(b) if the modifying phrase or adjective is not an integral part of the place name

Quelle université est située **dans la** Belgique flamande?	*What university is located* in the *Flemish part of Belgium?*
Nous avons passé des journées **dans le** vieux Paris.	*We spent days* in *old Paris.*

When a place name is modified by an adjective or phrase which is not an integral part of the name, **dans** + DEFINITE ARTICLE is used to express *in* or *to*. But this construction is rather rare.

A. *Remplacez les tirets par la préposition convenable.*

1. Beaucoup de catholiques vont _____ Rome pour voir le Vatican.
2. Quand vous serez _____ Naples, allez donc voir les ruines de Pompéi.   3. Quand j'étais _____ Angleterre, j'aimais prendre le thé à quatre heures.   4. Puisque vous aimez les sports d'hiver, allez passer l'hiver _____ Canada.   5. Nous avons renoncé à aller _____ Chine, c'est un trop long voyage.   6. Ces jeunes Français passeront un mois _____ États-Unis pour étudier la chimie.   7. Quand vous serez _____ Danemark, vous verrez que presque tout le monde parle anglais.

B. *Traduisez en français.*

1. They want to spend their vacation in Madrid, but they do not know Spanish.   2. If you want to go to Canada, I advise you to take the train at eight in[1] the evening.   3. Many Americans went to Germany during and after the war.   4. Our friends were[2] to come back, but they want to stay in Portugal in April.   5. A large number of American engineers work[3] in Mexico.   6. I took some very beautiful photographs on arriving in Japan and some others[4] while I was in China.   7. We did not stay in Russia long[5] enough to learn Russian.   8. This old man would now like to go back to Italy to see his relatives.

---

[1] **du**   [2] Use a form of **devoir.**   [3] This verb is in the plural.   [4] **d'autres**   [5] **assez longtemps pour**

PATTERN PRACTICE: *in*, *at*, and *to* with place names

Pattern 1

    YOU HEAR   France
    YOU SAY   Cet été je vais en France.

FROM

6. How is *from* expressed with cities?

Je suis parti **de** Paris hier pour voir   *I left Paris yesterday to see the surround-*
les environs.   *ing country.*

    With cities, *from* is expressed by **de.**

7. How is *from* expressed with feminine countries and continents?

Nous sommes revenus **de** France la   *We returned* from *France last week.*
semaine dernière.
Philippe partira-t-il **d'**Angleterre la   *Will Philip leave England next week?*
semaine prochaine?

    Before feminine countries and continents, *from* is expressed by **de.**

8. How is *from* expressed with masculine countries?

Nos cousins sont partis **du** Canada   *Our cousins left Canada yesterday.*
hier.
Quand reviendrez-vous **du** Portu-   *When will you come back* from *Portugal?*
gal?

    Before masculine countries, *from* is expressed by **de** + DEFINITE
ARTICLE (**du, de l', des**).

C. *Remplacez les tirets par l'équivalent français de* from.

1. Il part _____ Japon la semaine prochaine à cause de la situation
politique. 2. A votre accent, je devine que vous venez _____ Belgique.
3. Des avions partent tous les jours _____ Canada pour l'Europe.
4. Ces messieurs viennent _____ Lyon pour montrer leurs étoffes de
soie. 5. Beaucoup de gens qui reviennent _____ Mexique sont contents de retrouver la cuisine américaine. 6. Les Russes ne peuvent
pas toujours sortir librement _____ Russie. 7. Si vous allez _____
France en Angleterre, prenez donc l'avion.

D. *Traduisez en français.*

1. I like to take the boat when I go from Japan to the United States.
2. It is sometimes difficult to say whether someone comes from the United States or from England. 3. We are coming back from Greece delighted[1] by the beauty of that country. 4. He is coming back from Spain, where he spent the whole month of July. 5. When you come back from Portugal, will you know how to speak Portuguese?

---

[1] **enchantés par**

PATTERN PRACTICE: *from* with place names

Pattern 2

    YOU HEAR   France
    YOU SAY   Jean est revenu de France lundi.

II. Verb + Preposition + Infinitive

9. What words does French use to join a verb to a following infinitive?

Je **voudrais aller** en France.	*I* should like <u>to</u> go *to France.*
Nous **avons commencé à lire.**	*We* began <u>to</u> read.
Les ouvriers **ont refusé de travailler.**	*The workmen* refused <u>to</u> work.

Some verbs are followed directly by an infinitive, some verbs require **à** before an infinitive, some require **de** before an infinitive, a few require still other prepositions.

10. How can one determine which construction to use before an infinitive?

Ils **viendront voir** leur nouveau petit-fils la semaine prochaine.	*They* will come to see *their new grandson next week.*
Nous **voulons régler** cette affaire le plus tôt possible.	*We* want to take care *of this matter as soon as possible.*

Verbs of motion (**aller, venir**) and the common verbs of wishing (**vouloir, désirer**) are followed directly by the infinitive.

Le mari de Janine lui **a demandé**   *Janine's husband asked her to be saving.*
de faire des économies.

Nous avons **regretté d'**apprendre   *We were sorry to learn of his very hasty*
son départ si précipité.   *departure.*

Verbs of telling, asking, ordering, advising, etc. (someone to do something) and most verbs of emotion (**craindre, avoir peur, regretter, s'étonner,** etc.) are followed by **de** before an infinitive.

But except for these, the preposition to be used after each verb before an infinitive must be learned.

11. Which verbs require no preposition before an infinitive?

The following are the commonest verbs which are followed directly by the infinitive:

aimer	*like*	falloir	*be necessary*
aimer mieux	*prefer*	laisser	*leave, allow, let*
aller	*go, be going*	oser	*dare*
compter	*intend*	pouvoir	*can, be able*
croire	*believe*	préférer	*prefer*
désirer	*desire, wish*	savoir	*know, know how*
devoir	*am to, must*	sembler	*seem*
entendre	*hear*	venir	*come*
espérer	*hope*	voir	*see*
faire	*do, make, have*	vouloir	*want, wish*

12. Which verbs require de before an infinitive?

The following are the commonest verbs which require **de** before an infinitive:

avoir peur de	*be afraid*	finir de	*finish*
cesser de	*cease*	ordonner de	*order*
craindre de	*fear*	oublier de	*forget*
décider de	*decide*	permettre de	*permit*
défendre de	*forbid*	prier de	*beg, ask, pray*
demander de	*ask*	promettre de	*promise*
se dépêcher de	*hurry*	refuser de	*refuse*
dire de	*tell*	regretter de	*regret*
écrire de	*write*	remercier de	*thank*
empêcher de	*prevent*	tâcher de	*try*
essayer de	*try*		

13. Which verbs require à before an infinitive?

The following are the commonest verbs which require **à** before an infinitive:

aider à	*help*	demander à*	*ask*
s'amuser à	*amuse oneself*	enseigner à	*teach*
apprendre à	*learn, teach*	s'habituer à	*accustom oneself*
arriver à	*succeed*	hésiter à	*hesitate*
avoir à	*have*	inviter à	*invite*
commencer à	*begin*	recommencer à	*begin again*
consentir à	*consent*	réussir à	*succeed*
continuer à	*continue*	songer à	*think, dream*
se décider à	*decide*	tarder à	*delay in*

E. *Remplacez les tirets par une préposition s'il[1] y a lieu.*

1. —Allô chérie, j'ai invité le patron ____ dîner chez nous ce soir. 2. J'avais un oiseau en cage, mais je l'ai laissé ____ partir. 3. Dépêche-toi ____ finir ton travail pour qu'on puisse sortir. 4. Je n'aime pas qu'il s'amuse ____ faire des expériences de chimie dans la maison. 5. Ne parlez pas si fort, ils peuvent ____ arriver d'un moment à l'autre. 6. Cessez ____ bavarder avec votre voisin, ou prenez la porte. 7. Il faut ____ vivre, et je vais ____ essayer ____ gagner un peu plus d'argent. 8. Il vient d'avoir cinquante ans et il a décidé ____ se remarier. 9. Commencez ____ économiser de l'argent dès que possible. 10. J'aime mieux ____ sortir quand il pleut, l'air est plus pur. 11. Oseriez-vous ____ répéter ce que vous venez de dire? 12. Beaucoup de réfugiés refusent absolument ____ retourner dans leurs pays.

---

[1] *if one is necessary*

F. *Remplacez les tirets par une préposition s'il y a lieu.*

1. Il est malade, mais il continue ____ faire ses classes. 2. J'ai été un peu brusque, je crains ____ l'avoir vexé. 3. Faites un petit effort pour apprendre ____ parler correctement. 4. A partir de demain, je veux ____ travailler dix heures tous les jours. 5. Je regrette ____ ne pas être plus riche. 6. Il est bon de savoir ____ faire plusieurs métiers. 7. Bien des Américains espèrent ____ aller un jour en Europe. 8. J'ai cru qu'ils ne se décideraient jamais ____ partir.

---

* The verb **demander** + AN INDIRECT OBJECT requires **de** before an infinitive. Comparez: Il demande **à** venir. Il demande à son ami **de** venir.

9. Il faut s'habituer ____ vivre dans l'incertitude.   10. Si vous voulez un chat, nous cherchons ____ placer les nôtres.   11. S'il tarde ____ rentrer, sa femme imagine qu'il a eu un accident.   12. On doit ____ réfléchir avant de parler.

G. *Traduisez en français. Attention aux prépositions.*

1. His wife prevents him from playing poker with his friends.   2. I completely forgot to telephone him[1] today, and it's too late now. 3. Several friends will help me paint my house.   4. Don't hesitate to interrupt me if you have a question.   5. As soon as one speaks of France, Anne begins[2] to dream.   6. We spoke of politics, but I didn't succeed in changing his opinion.   7. Few people like to write long letters.   8. If you want to see him, come quickly, because he is going to leave.   9. Look at that man; he seems to want to speak to us.

---

[1] Which type of object is this?   [2] Use a form of **se mettre**.

PATTERN PRACTICE: the use of prepositions before an infinitive

Pattern 3

    YOU HEAR   Cet élève a peur
    YOU SAY   Cet élève a peur de parler français.

Pattern 4

    YOU HEAR   Vous allez
    YOU SAY   Vous allez sortir ce soir.

III. The *à* + *de* Verbs

14. How does French express the idea 'to tell someone to do something'?

J'ai dit à mon frère de partir tout   *I told my brother to leave immediately.*
de suite.

Le père a promis à ses enfants de   *The father promised his children to*
leur apporter des jouets.   *bring them some toys.*

Certain verbs require **à** before a noun object and **de** before a following infinitive in French but not necessarily in English. These may be called the **à + de** verbs. Among these are:

conseiller à quelqu'un de	*advise someone to*	Je **conseille à Paul de** partir.
défendre à quelqu'un de	*forbid someone to*	Il **défend à Marie de** sortir.
demander à quelqu'un de	*ask someone to*	Elle **demande à sa mère de** venir.
dire à quelqu'un de	*tell someone to*	Je **dis à mon frère de** se taire.
écrire à quelqu'un de	*write someone to*	Nous **écrivons à Guy de** rester.
ordonner à quelqu'un de	*order someone to*	Il **ordonne au soldat de** tirer.
permettre à quelqu'un de	*permit someone to*	Je **permets à Jean d'**entrer.
promettre à quelqu'un de	*promise someone to*	Elle **promet à Henri de** lui écrire.
téléphoner à quelqu'un de	*telephone someone to*	Il **téléphone à Claude de** revenir.

H. *Traduisez en français.*

1. Telephone your father to send you some money. 2. After that trouble[1], I advised Gerard to leave town[2]. 3. If you want to marry my daughter, promise me to come to work here every day. 4. There are always people who want to forbid others[2] to do what they wish. 5. Ask your uncle to buy you a car, since he is rich. 6. If he comes, tell Mr. Fondeville to leave his address and I'll write him. 7. You are wrong to[3] permit your children to do everything[4] they wish. 8. I'll write my friends to come to get[5] you at the airport.

---

[1] **histoire**   [2] Use the definite article.   [3] **de**   [4] **tout ce que**   [5] **chercher**

PATTERN PRACTICE: the **à + de** verbs

Pattern 5

    YOU HEAR   dire

    YOU SAY   J'ai dit à Pierre de rester à Paris.

IV. Verb (+ Preposition) + Noun

15. How do the verb + noun constructions in French compare with those in English?

Nous **attendons** le train.	*We are* waiting for *the train.*
Je **suis entré dans** la maison.	*I* entered *the house.*
Il **pense à** ses examens.	*He* is thinking of *his examinations.*

While many VERB + NOUN constructions are the same in French and English, some verbs require a preposition before a noun in French but not in English, and others require a preposition before a noun in English but not in French. Still other verbs require one preposition in English, another in French.

16. What are some common verbs which require a direct object in French but a preposition before the object in English?

attendre	*wait for*	Paul **attend** son ami.
chercher	*look for*	Marie **cherche** son livre.
demander	*ask for*	Pierre **demande** cinq cents francs.
écouter	*listen to*	Nous **écoutons** la musique.
payer	*pay for*	Il **a payé** cet objet mille francs.
regarder	*look at*	Je **regarde** le plan de Paris.

The verbs listed above require a direct object in French.

17. What are some common verbs which require a preposition before the object in French but a direct object in English?

s'approcher de	*approach*	Nous nous **approchons de** la rivière.
assister à	*attend*	Il **assiste à** la réunion.
changer de	*change*	Elle **a changé de** robe.
entrer dans	*enter*	Qui **entre dans** la salle?
échapper à	*escape*	Le soldat **a échappé à** la mort.
s'échapper de	*escape*	Le voleur **s'est échappé de** prison.
jouer à	*play*	Je **joue au** football et **aux** échecs.
jouer de	*play*	Elle **joue du** piano et **du** violon.
manquer de	*lack*	Je **manque de** renseignements.
se marier avec	*marry*	Denise **se marie avec** Jean-Pierre.
obéir à	*obey*	Paul **obéit à** son père.
plaire à	*please*	Yvonne **plaît à** tout le monde.

répondre à	*answer*	Je **réponds à** la lettre.
résister à	*resist*	Il **résiste à** la tentation.
ressembler à	*resemble*	Maurice **ressemble à** son frère.
se servir de	*use*	Ils **se servent de** la machine à écrire.
se souvenir de	*remember*	Je **me souviens de** la guerre.

The verbs listed above require a preposition before the object in French.

NOTE: The verb **échapper à** means *to escape getting into something*, **s'échapper de** means *to escape from something one has gotten into*.

The construction **jouer à** means *to play a game*, the construction **jouer de** means *to play a musical instrument*.

18. What are some common verbs which require one preposition in French and another in English?

s'intéresser à	*be interested in*	Il **s'intéresse à** la musique.
s'occuper de	*busy oneself with*	Je **m'occupe de** la maison.
penser à	*think of*	Il **pense à** son travail.
penser de	*think of*	Que **pensez-vous de** cet homme?
remercier de	*thank for*	Il **a remercié** sa mère **de** son cadeau.
rire de	*laugh at*	Nous **rions de** ce clown.
songer à	*think of*	Il **songe à** son voyage en France.

The verbs listed above require one preposition in French and another in English.

NOTE: The construction **penser à** means *to think of someone or something*, the construction **penser de** is used in questions *to ask one's opinion of someone or something*.

The verb **remercier** may also be followed by **pour** before a noun. Ex.: Il **a remercié** sa mère **pour** son cadeau.

I. *Remplacez les expressions anglaises entre parenthèses par les équivalents français.*

(Each sentence has a verb which entails the use or non-use of a preposition. In certain sentences, it may be necessary to combine a preposition with the definite article.)

1. Je (*am looking for*) une bonne réponse à sa lettre, mais c'est difficile.
2. Certains élèves peuvent travailler en (*listening to*) la radio.
3. (*Look at*) bien le ciel et vous verrez peut-être des satellites.

4. Avec cette foule il sera impossible de (*approach*) la scène.   5. Sauve qui peut! Un ours (*has escaped from*) sa cage.   6. Il faut de longues années d'étude pour (*play*) le violon en virtuose.   7. Trop de familles (*lack*) argent.   8. Chacun rêve de (*marry*[1]) la personne idéale.   9. Il y a des gens qui croient pouvoir (*escape*) la maladie.   10. Tout évolue et il est impossible de (*resist*) longtemps les changements. 11. (*Concern yourself with*[2]) vos affaires.   12. Il faut le (*thank for*) les fleurs qu'il m'a envoyées.   13. Ce n'est pas gentil de (*laugh at*) une personne qui tombe.   14. Il (*is waiting for*) son amie, mais je sais qu'elle ne viendra pas.

---

[1] Use a form of **se marier**.   [2] Use a form of **s'occuper**.

J. *Traduisez en français. Attention aux prépositions.*

1. Live in the present; do not think too much of the past.   2. I attended a fine concert last evening.   3. They change cars every other year.   4. I have lost my key, but I can enter my house through the window.   5. It is amusing to[1] play chess.   6. Formerly, women used to obey their husbands[2].   7. He is spending a fortune to please that woman.   8. Do not wait to answer those letters.   9. He does not resemble his father at all[3].   10. Today one uses[4] forks and knives to eat.   11. She doesn't like sports; she is interested in poetry. 12. What do you think of the work of that pupil?

---

[1] **de**   [2] French uses the singular in such cases.   [3] Place directly after **pas**.   [4] Use a form of **se servir**.

V. The *It is* + Adjective + Infinitive Constructions

19. What construction follows the impersonal *Il est* + adjective?

Il est impossible **de** partir aujour-   It is *impossible* to *leave today.*
d'hui.

Il serait difficile **de** lui donner cet   It would be *hard* to *give him that money.*
argent.

The construction used with the impersonal **il est** + ADJECTIVE is:

> (impersonal) **il est** + ADJECTIVE + **de** + INFINITIVE (+ idea)

NOTE: In conversational French, this impersonal **il** may always be replaced by **ce,** and the following construction is exactly the same as though the impersonal **il** were used.

20. What construction follows idea + C'est + adjective?

Est-ce que cet écrivain écrit vraiment bien? **C'est difficile à** dire.

Does that author really write well? It's hard to *say.*

Votre frère est-il bon élève? Non, et **c'est impossible à** comprendre.

Is your brother a good student? No, and it's impossible to *understand.*

When **c'est** + adjective refers to a preceding idea without gender or number, the following construction is used:

> IDEA in preceding sentence + **c'est** + ADJECTIVE + **à** + INFINITIVE

K. *Remplacez les tirets par* **à** *ou* **de,** *selon le cas.*

1. —Les planètes sont-elles habitées? —Peut-être, mais c'est impossible ____ prouver. 2. Il sera bientôt possible ____ aller dans la lune. 3. Il est agréable ____ prendre un petit cognac après un bon repas. 4. —Comment avez-vous fait pour apprendre à jouer si bien? —C'est difficile ____ expliquer. 5. Les candidats ont discuté pendant une heure. C'était interessant ____ écouter. 6. Il n'est pas toujours facile ____ dire ce qui est bien et ce qui est mal. 7. Vous l'avez vraiment vu voler cette montre? C'est difficile ____ croire.

L. *Traduisez en français.*

1. It is interesting to see a football[1] game between two good teams. 2. Man is master of his destiny. It's easy to say. 3. It is necessary to write a great many letters, even if it is sometimes boring to do. 4. It is annoying to go to the movies all alone. 5. It is difficult to understand certain scientific theories. 6. It is amusing to observe people in the street. 7. Maurice wants to buy an airplane. It's impossible to believe. 8. It is polite to answer[2] letters[3] immediately. 9. I'm going to paint my house. It's easy to do. 10. It is restful to interrupt one's[4] work from time to time. 11. Mark is so stubborn

---

[1] *football game* = **match de football**   [2] By what preposition is **répondre** followed?   [3] The definite article is necessary, since this noun is used in a general sense.   [4] Use a form of **son.**

that it is useless to try to convince him.   12. Jack says that he is
capable of writing a novel. It is hard to imagine.   13. Mr. Laroque
does not believe that his son was at my house last night, but it's easy
to prove.   14. It is impossible to get[5] to the top of that mountain.
15. It is interesting to hear the candidates discuss their ideas.

---

[5] Use a form of **arriver à.**

PATTERN PRACTICE : *It is* + adjective constructions

Pattern 6

YOU HEAR   Parler français est facile.
YOU SAY   Il est facile de parler français.

VI. Verbal Constructions after Prepositions; Constructions with *pour*

Most English prepositions are followed by the present participle.
One says *on arriving, in coming, by working, without leaving*, etc. But this
is not usually the case in French.

21. What verbal construction usually follows a French preposition?

Ne partez pas **sans laisser** votre   *Don't go away* without leaving *your*
adresse.   *address.*

All French prepositions except **en** are followed by the infinitive.

When we use the term infinitive, we mean SIMPLE INFINITIVE, for
it is by far the most common infinitive to be used. But there is also a
COMPOUND INFINITIVE which is made up of the infinitive of **avoir** or
être and the past participle of the main verb. The compound infinitive is also known as the PAST INFINITIVE.

Simple infinitive	*Compound infinitive*
parler	avoir parlé
finir	avoir fini
venir	être venu(e)(s)
se laver	s'être lavé(e)(s)

22. By what verbal construction is the preposition en followed?

En entrant dans le café, nous avons   On entering *the café, we saw Robert*
vu Robert et Marie.   *and Marie.*

The preposition **en** is followed by the present participle. (For a complete treatment of **en** + PRESENT PARTICIPLE, see pages 64–65.)

---

23. When is a French preposition followed by the compound infinitive?

Les voisins ont puni leur fils **pour**   *The neighbors punished their son* for
avoir cassé nos vitres.   breaking *our windowpanes.*

When the verbal action after a preposition clearly takes place before the action of the main verb of the sentence, the compound infinitive is used in order to preserve the time distinction.

---

24. What French construction is used to express the English before + verb + -ing?

Regardez à droite et à gauche **avant**   *Look left and right* before crossing *the*
de traverser la rue.   *street.*

French uses **avant de** + INFINITIVE for the English *before* + VERB + *-ing.*

---

25. What French construction is used to express the English after + verb + -ing?

Après avoir lu le journal, je me   After reading *the newspaper, I got*
suis mis au travail.   *down to work.*

French uses **après** + COMPOUND INFINITIVE to express the English *after* + VERB + *-ing.*

---

26. How does French express purpose?

Notre voisin a acheté ce terrain   *Our neighbor bought this land* to plant
pour planter des arbres fruitiers.   *some fruit trees.*

To express purpose, English uses $\begin{cases} to \\ in\ order\ to \end{cases}$ + VERB. French uses the preposition **pour** + THE INFINITIVE to indicate purpose.

27. When may the preposition *pour* **be omitted before the infinitive in purpose phrases?**

Jean **est venu** (pour) **travailler**   *John* came (in order) to work *with*
avec Daniel aujourd'hui.   *Daniel today.*
Nous **sommes allés** à la ferme (pour)   *We* went *to the farm* (in order) to get
chercher du lait.   *some milk.*

In purpose phrases, the preposition **pour** is usually omitted after forms of **aller** and **venir** and sometimes after other verbs of motion. When **pour** is used after forms of **aller** and **venir,** it emphasizes the idea of purpose much as *in order to* does in English. The preposition **pour** is also often used when several words separate the main verb and the infinitive.

28. How does French express the idea of *enough . . . to* **and** *too much . . . to* **or** *too . . . to?*

Louise chante **assez** bien **pour** faire   *Louise sings well* enough to *be in the*
partie du chœur.   *choir.*
Nous avons **trop** à faire **pour** partir   *We have* too much to *do to leave now.*
maintenant.
Jacques est **trop** jeune **pour** rester   *Jack is* too *young* to *stay out after nine*
dehors après neuf heures du soir.   *o'clock at night.*

French expresses the idea of *enough . . . to* by **assez . . . pour** and of *too much . . . to* and *too . . . to* by **trop . . . pour.**

M. *Remplacez l'infinitif entre parenthèses par la forme convenable du verbe, s'il y a lieu.*

1. Pourquoi êtes-vous venu ici sans (téléphoner) pour me prévenir?
2. Il faut aller au Maroc pour (acheter) un beau tapis.   3. Après (monter) dans ma chambre, j'ai relu toutes les lettres de Pierre.
4. En (parler) à mon voisin, j'ai appris ce qui s'était passé.   5. Faites peser mes lettres avant de les (mettre) à la poste.   6. Nous avons commencé par (ouvrir) toutes les fenêtres.   7. Michel a répondu après (réfléchir) un moment.   8. Au lieu de (se[1] plaindre), vendez donc votre voiture.   9. Je me suis intéressé à la science en (lire) la biographie de Pasteur.   10. Jean est encore parti sans (fermer) la porte.   11. On apprend mieux quelque chose en l'(expliquer) à d'autres.

---

[1] Even in the infinitive form, the reflexive object must agree in person with the subject of the sentence. In what person is the subject of an imperative sentence?

N. *Traduisez en français.*

1. Paul is too proud to admit his error.   2. Someone came to ask for some information[1] concerning[2] Jack.   3. We left after hearing the announcement of the results.   4. Robert is old[3] enough to have a motorcycle.   5. Did you come to our house only to see our cats? 6. The children went to play at the neighbor's.   7. Before leaving for Paris, reserve a room in a good hotel.   8. You are intelligent enough to understand those things.   9. Paul went to get[4] some books at the library.   10. I am too tired to go out this evening.   11. Correct your mistakes before erasing the sentences.   12. At what time will you come to get[4] me?

---

[1] Use the plural.   [2] **sur**   [3] **âgé**   [4] **chercher**

PATTERN PRACTICE: **avant de** + infinitive

Pattern 7

YOU HEAR   J'ai eu des doutes en prenant cette décision.
YOU SAY   J'ai eu des doutes avant de prendre cette décision.

PATTERN PRACTICE: **après** + compound infinitive

Pattern 8

YOU HEAR   J'ai eu des doutes en prenant cette décision.
YOU SAY   J'ai eu des doutes après avoir pris cette décision.

Problem Words

58. very much

Ways of expressing *very much* and *very many*

J'ai **énormément** à faire.
J'ai **des tas de choses** à faire.   } *I have* very much *to do.*
J'ai **une quantité de choses** à faire.

Ces étudiants ont **énormément** de livres à lire.
Ces étudiants ont **des tas** de livres à lire.   } *Those students have* very many *books to read.*
Ces étudiants ont **une quantité** de livres à lire.

Depending on the exact sentence, *very much* and *very many* may be expressed by **énormément de, une quantité de, un tas de, des tas de**[1], and other like expressions. In familiar speech, the French sometimes say **beaucoup** twice, so that one might hear: **J'ai beaucoup beaucoup à faire**, and: **Ces étudiants ont beaucoup beaucoup de livres à lire**. This latter construction should be avoided in writing.

CAUTION: In French, **très** cannot modify **beaucoup**. Therefore, *very much* and *very many* cannot be expressed by «très beaucoup».

---

[1] The expressions **un tas de** and **des tas de** are colloquial.

59. visit

(a) How to say *to visit a person*

Hier je **suis allé voir Monsieur Moreau**.	*Yesterday I* visited Mr. Moreau.

The commonest way of saying *to visit a person* is **aller voir quelqu'un**.

Il faudra **faire une visite aux voisins**.	*We must* visit the neighbors.

Another way of saying *to visit a person* is **faire une visite à quelqu'un**.

Nous **avons rendu visite à Madame de Rosemont**.	*We* visited (paid a visit to) Mrs. de Rosemont.

More formal and therefore less common is **rendre visite à quelqu'un**.

CAUTION: Do NOT use the verb «visiter» to express the idea of *visiting a person*. The commonest way of saying *to visit a person* is **aller voir une personne**.

(b) How to say *to visit a place*

Avez-vous **visité le Louvre?**	*Did you* visit the Louvre?
Quand nous étions en Italie, nous **avons visité Naples**.	*When we were in Italy, we* visited Naples.

Ne manquez pas de **visiter les vieux**   *Don't fail* to visit the old sections *of*
quartiers de Paris.   *Paris.*

The verb **visiter** is used to express the idea of *visiting a place*.

60. while

(**a**) When to express *while* by **pendant que**

Attendez-moi dans la voiture **pen-**   *Wait for me in the car* while *I go and get*
dant que je vais chercher les   *the children.*
enfants.

When *while* means *during the time that*, it is expressed by **pendant
que.**

(**b**) When to express *while* by **tandis que**

Marc travaille bien, **tandis que**   *Mark works well* while *Joseph doesn't*
Joseph ne fait pas grand-chose.   *do much of anything.*

When *while* means *whereas*, it is expressed by **tandis que.** (Pronounced either [tɑ̃dikə] or [tɑ̃diskə]).

Sometimes **tandis que** is also used in the sense of *during the time
that*, but it is best for the learner to reserve **tandis que** for *while =
whereas*.

61. wish

(**a**) How to *wish someone something*

Je vous **souhaite** un bon voyage.   *I* wish *you a good trip.*

The verb **souhaiter** is used to *wish someone something*.

(**b**) How **désirer** expresses *wish*

Pauline **désire** toujours avoir ce   *Pauline always* wishes *to have what*
qu'ont les autres.   *others have.*

The verb **désirer** means *wish* or *desire*. It may be used in the spoken
language but is much less common than the verb **vouloir.**

(**c**) How to express *wish* by the conditional of **vouloir** and **aimer**

François $\begin{cases} \textbf{voudrait} \\ \textbf{aimerait} \end{cases}$ être très riche.   *Francis wishes that he were very rich.*

The conditional of **aimer** and **vouloir** is used with the INFINITIVE to express wish when the subject of the main and subordinate clauses are the same in the English sentence.

Nous $\begin{cases} \textbf{voudrions} \\ \textbf{aimerions} \end{cases}$ que Roger vienne   *We* wish (*that*) *Roger would come with*
avec nous.   *us.*

The conditional of **aimer** and **vouloir** + **que** + subjunctive is used to express wish when the subject of the main and subordinate clauses are different in both the English and French sentences.

O. *Remplacez les mots anglais par leur équivalent français.*

1. Vincent est marié, mais il (*visits*) sa mère tous les jours.   2. Vous avez accepté sa proposition tout de suite (*while*) vous auriez dû discuter.   3. Le directeur (*wishes*) vous parler.   4. Il peut bien être fatigué, il a (*very much*) travaillé.   5. Nous (*visited*) plusieurs musées à Rome.   6. Je travaillerai au bureau (*while*) tu seras chez Martine. 7. Les Marcellin sont revenus de la mer; nous devrions (*visit them*). 8. Je (*wish*) que tu m'apprennes à jouer de la guitare.   9. Il fait bon chez vous (*while*) il fait toujours froid chez nous.   10. Si vous n'avez pas le temps de (*visit*) la ville, montez au moins sur la colline. 11. Jean a un examen aujourd'hui; (*wish*)-lui bonne chance.

P. *Traduisez en français. Attention aux mots en italique.*

1. If I have time, I will *visit* you Friday afternoon.   2. I *wish* you a[1] Happy New Year.   3. Louis learned Arabic *while* he was in Africa. 4. This morning I *visited* my former teacher.   5. I have always *wished* to travel.   6. I speak only one language, *while* Alexander speaks twelve.   7. Have you ever *visited* Athens?   8. I *wish* I could go to Portugal this year.   9. I would be glad to see Madeleine again; I like her *very much*.

───────────
[1] **une bonne année**

Verb Review

Review the verbs **venir** and **vivre** according to the outline on page 283.

CHAPTER 17

Problem Prepositions

I. English Words which are both Prepositions and Conjunctions

Certain English words, such as *after, as, before,* and *since* are sometimes used as prepositions, to introduce a prepositional phrase, and sometimes as conjunctions, to introduce a dependent clause, which has its own subject and verb. It is important to know when such English words are used as a preposition and when as a conjunction, for French often uses one word to express the English preposition and another to express the English conjunction.

Among the most common English words used both as a preposition and a conjunction are:

PREPOSITION	CONJUNCTION

1. after

après*	après que
Nous sommes partis **après** l'annonce des résultats.	Nous sommes partis **après que** Jean a annoncé les résultats.
We left after the announcement of the results.	*We left after John announced the results.*

Après is used to express English *after* when a preposition and **après que** when conjunction.

---

* For après + VERBAL CONSTRUCTION, see page 227, §25.

2. as

comme	**comme**
Monsieur Brunot est ici **comme** professeur de russe.	**Comme** j'ai du travail à finir, je ne peux pas aller chez vous.
Mr. Brunot is here as *a Russian teacher.*	As *I have work to finish, I cannot go to your house.*

Sometimes **comme** is used to express the English *as* both when a preposition and a conjunction. When **comme** is used as a preposition, it is often followed directly by its noun (without any indefinite article). On the other hand, note: **Il parle comme un professeur. Il conduit comme un fou.** As a conjunction, **comme** means *as = because.*

en	**à mesure que**
Il s'est conduit **en** véritable ami.	**A mesure** qu'il vieillissait, il devenait moins sévère.
He behaved as *a true friend.*	As *he got older, he became less strict.*

The preposition **en** sometimes means *as,* and in such cases it is followed by its noun without an indefinite article.

The conjunction **à mesure que** means *as = in proportion as.*

3. before

avant	**avant que**
Nous sommes partis **avant** l'annonce des résultats.	Nous sommes partis **avant que** Jean annonce les résultats.
We left before *the announcement of the results.*	*We left* before *John announced the results.*

The conjunction **avant que** is always followed by the subjunctive, and both the present and past subjunctive are found with it. Thus: «Nous sommes partis **avant que** Jean **ait annoncé** les résultats» is also correct.

4. because

à cause de	**parce que**
Je suis resté à la maison **à cause de** la pluie.	Je suis resté à la maison **parce qu'**il pleuvait.
I stayed home because of *the rain.*	*I stayed home* because *it was raining.*

The English preposition *because of* is expressed in French by **à cause de** and is followed by a noun or pronoun, whereas the English conjunction *because* is expressed in French by **parce que** and is followed by a clause.

5. but

sauf	mais
Tout le monde est parti **sauf** Suzanne.	Georges est parti, **mais** où est-il allé?
Everyone left but *Suzanne.*	*George left,* but *where did he go?*

The word *but* is usually a conjunction. However, it is occasionally used as a preposition, and then it is equivalent to the English *except*. The preposition *but* may be expressed in several ways*, the most common of which is probably **sauf.**

6. for

pour	car
Nous avons fait cela **pour** vous.	Nous avons fait cela, **car** vous n'étiez pas ici.
We did that for *you.*	*We did that,* for *you were not here.*

The commonest way of expressing *for* as a preposition is **pour.****
The conjunction *for* is always expressed by **car,** and its meaning is somewhat similar to that of *because*.

7. since

depuis	depuis que
Philippe est chez nous **depuis** jeudi.	Philippe est chez nous **depuis que** ses parents sont partis pour la Suisse.
Philip has been with us since *Thursday.*	*Philip has been with us* since *his parents left for Switzerland.*

When *since* indicates time, it is expressed by **depuis** as a preposition and by **depuis que** as a conjunction.

---

* For other ways, see page 241, §18.   ** For other ways, see page 242, §19.

Note that the preposition **depuis** and its equivalents are usually followed by the present in French where English uses the present perfect.

When *since* = *because*, it is a conjunction and is expressed in French by **puisque**.

puisque

Puisque vous partez pour la Suisse, Philippe peut venir chez nous.

Since *you are leaving for Switzerland, Philip can come to our house.*

8. until

jusqu'à	jusqu'à ce que
Nous resterons ici **jusqu'à** dimanche.	Nous resterons ici **jusqu'à ce que** vous reveniez.
We'll stay here until *Sunday.*	*We'll stay here* until *you come back.*

As a preposition, **jusqu'à** expresses the English *until;* as a conjunction, French expresses *until* by **jusqu'à ce que** and the verb of the dependent clause is always in the subjunctive.

A. *Remplacez les mots anglais indiqués entre parenthèses par l'équivalent français.*

1. Nous vous traiterons tout à fait (*as a*) camarade.   2. Marie a retrouvé toutes ses clés (*but*) celle de sa voiture.   3. Roland regrette de ne pas avoir connu Françoise (*before*) elle se marie.   4. Vous viendrez me voir (*after*) la classe.   5. Je m'ennuyais (*before*) votre arrivée.   6. Il ne faut pas renoncer à un projet (*because*) on a des difficultés.   7. (*Since*) nous sommes ici, il pleut tous les jours.   8. Cherchez (*until*) vous trouviez la solution de ce problème.   9. Ma colère montait (*as*) son avocat parlait.

B. *Remplacez les mots anglais indiqués entre parenthèses par l'équivalent français.*

1. Il ne faut pas négliger votre famille (*because of*) vos affaires.   2. Je vous dirai mon opinion (*after*) vous aurez vu ce dossier.   3. (*Since*) votre séjour en Europe, vous n'êtes plus le même.   4. Je voulais vous voir, (*but*) je n'ai pas pu.   5. (*Before*) son accident, il faisait toutes

sortes de sports.   6. (*Since*) vous êtes debout, voulez-vous m'apporter le dictionnaire?   7. Cet argent leur permettra de vivre (*until*) la fin du mois.   8. Tu ne peux pas trouver mieux (*as a*) ami.

C. *Traduisez en français.*

1. The children will come[1] home immediately after the movies. 2. I visited every country in Europe but Spain.   3. Juliette was becoming[2] more and more worried as time went by.   4. Mr. Forestier will give you a good job after you have done[3] your military service. 5. We'll not go out this evening because of the snow.   6. Since my operation, I am[4] much better.   7. Almost everyone left before Mr. Ponsard's lecture.   8. Mark and Irene danced until six o'clock in[5] the morning.   9. Doctor Beauchamp went to that convention as a specialist.   10. Do what you wish until I come back.   11. Victor has many shortcomings, but he is very nice.   12. All that happened because you were careless.   13. As we have little time, we'll take an[6] airplane.   14. Since you like the theater, why don't you go there more often?   15. The director would like to speak to you before you leave.   16. The astronaut was received in his native city as a hero.

---

[1] *come home* = **rentrer**   [2] *become worried* = **s'inquiéter**   [3] What tense does French use here?
[4] *be much better* = **aller beaucoup mieux**   [5] **du**   [6] Use the definite article.

II. Other English Prepositions which Pose Problems in French

Certain English prepositions pose problems in French (1) because they may also be used as another part of speech, in which case they are expressed by two different words according to their function; (2) because some English prepositions have several connotations, each of which is expressed in a special way in French.

The words presented in this section are all used as prepositions some of the time. Sometimes it seems sufficient just to give the French equivalent, at times examples best show the differences, other times an explanation of usage appears clearest.

9. about

(a) *concerning* = **de, sur, au sujet de, à propos de**

Nous parlions **de** votre nouvelle secrétaire.	*We were speaking* about *your new secretary.*
Paul nous a écrit plusieurs lettres **sur** son voyage.	*Paul wrote us several letters* about *his trip.*
Qu'est-ce que vous avez à dire **au sujet** de votre conduite?	*What do you have to say* about *your behavior?*
Personne n'a rien dit **à propos de** mon absence.	*No one said anything* about *my absence.*

When *about* means *concerning*, it is a preposition and is sometimes expressed by **de** (especially after forms of **parler**), sometimes by **sur**, sometimes by **au sujet de** or **à propos de**. At times, but not always, several of these words could express *about* in the same sentence.

(b) *approximately* = **environ, vers, à peu près, -aine** (appended to a cardinal numeral)

J'ai vu **environ** dix appartements.	*I saw* about *ten apartments.*
Michel est arrivé **vers** six heures.	*Michael came at* about *six o'clock.*
C'est **à peu près** ce que j'ai dit.	*That's* about *what I said.*
Il s'est passé une **vingtaine** d'années.	About *twenty years went by.*

The word **environ** modifies a numeral. The preposition **vers** is usually found before expressions of time of day. When the suffix **-aine** is appended to a cardinal numeral, it indicates an approximation. The expression **à peu près** may be used for **environ**, but it may also modify words other than numerals.

(c) *be about to* = **être sur le point de**

Nous étions **sur le point de** partir.	*We were* about *to leave.*

10. above

Les avions volent souvent **au-dessus des** nuages.	*Airplanes often fly* above *the clouds.*

The preposition *above* meaning *over, in or to a higher place* is expressed in French by **au-dessus de**.

11. according to

Selon ⎫
Suivant ⎬ Voltaire, il faut cultiver   *According to Voltaire, one must culti-*
D'après ⎭   *vate one's garden.*
son jardin.

The English preposition *according to* is expressed by **selon, suivant,** and **d'après,*** which are normally interchangeable.

12. across

Marc a couru après son chien **à**   *Mark ran after his dog* across *the fields.*
travers les champs.

Je l'ai vu **traverser** la place **en**   *I saw him* run across *the square.*
courant.

Je l'aurais salué, mais il était **de**   *I would have greeted him, but he was*
l'autre côté de la rue.   across *the street.*

Nous **avons traversé** le pont.   *We* went across *the bridge.*

The preposition *across* is often expressed by **à travers.** But when *across* means *on the other side of,* the French say **de l'autre côté de,** and *to run across* is **traverser en courant.** The idea of *to go across* is often expressed by using the verb **traverser.**

13. after

On l'**a appelé** Victor **d'après** son   *They* named *him Victor* after *his god-*
parrain.   *father.*

The preposition *after* is usually **après,** but *to name after* is **appeler d'après.**

14. along

Il est agréable de se promener **le**   *It is pleasant to walk* along *the Seine.*
long de la Seine.

Il y a des voitures stationnées tout   *There are cars parked all* along *the*
le long de la rue.   *street.*

Il **a suivi le chemin** jusqu'au pont.   *He went* along *the road up to the*
                                             bridge.

The preposition *along* is usually expressed by **le long de.** But *to go along the road* is **suivre le chemin (la route)** and *to go along the street* is **suivre la rue.**

---

* See §13 below for another use of **d'après.**

D. *Remplacez le mot anglais indiqué entre parenthèses par l'équivalent français.*

1. George fume (*about*) vingt-cinq cigarettes par jour.   2. Claude et Sophie se promènent (*along*) la rivière.   3. Avez-vous vu ce qui se passe (*across*) la frontière?   4. Hier, j'ai entendu parler (*about*) votre voyage.   5. C'est (*about*) la même chose.   6. (*According to*) le traité, il n'y aura plus de douane entre ces pays.   7. Il y avait des fleurs tout (*along*) le sentier.   8. J'ai entendu une conférence (*about*) l'énergie atomique.   9. Ils se sont revus (*at about*) six heures et demie. 10. (*After*) qui avez-vous appelé votre fils Christian?   11. (*According to*) les experts, on ne peut pas construire un pont à cet endroit. 12. Donnez-moi (*about twenty*) francs.   13. Qu'est-ce que c'est que ce fil (*above*) le pont?   14. Il ne faut pas vous inquiéter (*about*) vos enfants.   15. (*According to*) les journaux, on trouvera bientôt le coupable.   16. Je n'aime pas avoir des gens bruyants dans l'appartement (*above*) me.   17. Je voudrais vous demander des renseignements (*about*) les hôtels à Paris.

E. *Traduisez en français.*

1. I think that writer was born about 1900.   2. According to his father, Francis doesn't work enough.   3. We went along the road up to the white house.   4. After the lecture, we went home.   5. Have you heard about George's accident?   6. Our friends traveled across the whole country on a motorcycle.   7. There were about two hundred people before the library.   8. We had some good discussions about modern music.   9. We called my daughter Rose after her grandmother.   10. The little boy ran across the street.   11. Louise spoke before the class about her trip to Mexico.   12. According to Mr. Parain, they are going to build a new city hall.   13. Our friends were about to telephone us when we arrived.   14. My friend lives across the street.   15. The sun was directly above us.   16. There are about thirty girls in the dormitory.   17. It's about all I have to do. 18. Professor Martin wrote me about my examination.

15. at

With nouns, *at* is usually expressed by **à** or **dans**.
The preposition *at* with place names is taken up on page 213.

With the connotation of *at the home of* or *at the place of business of* or *in the country of*, *at* is often expressed by **chez**. Note the uses of **chez** in the following sentences.

Nous irons passer la soirée **chez les Moreau.**	*We'll go to spend the evening* at the Moreaus.
Chez nous on dîne à six heures du soir.	In our country* *we eat at six in the evening.*
N'oublie pas de passer **chez le boulanger** à ton retour.	*Don't forget to go* to the bakery *on your return.*
On retrouve cette même idée **chez tous les grands écrivains.**	*One finds this same idea* in the works of all the great writers.

16. before

Il y a un tableau **devant** la classe.	*There is a blackboard* before *the class.*
Venez **avant** huit heures.	*Come* before *eight o'clock.*
Nous avons **déjà** fait ça. Nous avons fait ça **avant.** }	*We did that* before.

The preposition *before* is expressed by **devant** when it indicates place and means *in front of* and by **avant** when it indicates *time*. As an adverb, *before* may be expressed by **déjà, avant,** and **auparavant.**

17. down

Ils **sont**** **descendus** tout de suite.	*They* came down *at once.*
Nous **avons**** **descendu** la rue.	*We* went down *the street.*

The English *down* is often part of the French verb **descendre,** which may mean *to come down* or *to go down*. The English *to go down the street* is expressed in French by **descendre la rue.**

18. except

Tout le monde m'a félicité **sauf** **à part** } M. Gervais. **excepté**	*Everyone congratulated me* except *Mr. Gervais.*

The English *except* may be expressed by **sauf, à part,** and **excepté.**

---

* In this sentence, **chez nous** may also mean *at our house.*
** Intransitive verbs of motion are usually conjugated with **être,** but when a verb of motion governs a direct object, it becomes transitive and is then conjugated with **avoir.**

19. for (time)

Nos amis sont chez nous **depuis**   *Our friends have been with us for two*
quinze jours.   *weeks.*

When an action begins in the past and is still going on in the
present, French uses **depuis** with the present to express *for*.*

Nos amis sont restés chez nous   *Our friends stayed at our house (for)*
(**pendant**) quinze jours.   *two weeks.*

A completed action describing a certain duration of time uses
pendant with the compound past, where English uses *for*. This **pendant** may be omitted, just as *for* may be omitted in the English
sentence.

Ces jeunes gens voyageront en   *These young men will travel in Africa*
Afrique **pendant** quinze jours.   *for two weeks.*

In the future *for* is usually expressed by **pendant.**

J'irai à Paris **pour** quinze jours.   *I'll go to Paris for two weeks.*
Pour combien de temps partirez-   *For how long will you be gone?*
vous?

However, with verbs of motion the future is often used with **pour**
to express duration of time.

20. in

(**a**) The preposition *in* with place names is taken up on pages 213–215.

(**b**) *in* + A COMMON NOUN

Nos amis sont **au** restaurant.   *Our friends are in the restaurant.*
Jacques est **dans** sa chambre.   *Jack is in his room.*

The usual word for *in* is **dans,** but **à** + DEFINITE ARTICLE is often
used to express *in the*.

(**c**) *in* + **matin, après-midi, soir**

Ne faites pas de bruit **le soir** après   *Don't make any noise in the evening*
dix heures.   *after ten o'clock.*

---

* For other ways of expressing this idea, see page 113.

For *in the morning, in the afternoon,* and *in the evening* French says **le matin, l'après-midi,** and **le soir** without the preposition **dans.**

(**d**) *in* to express time required to do something

Monsieur Goulet travaille très vite; il pourrait réparer votre télévision **en une heure.**	*Mr. Goulet works very fast; he could fix your television set* in an hour.

To indicate the length of time required to do something, French uses **en** to express the English *in.*

(**e**) *in* to express time at which an action can begin

Je n'ai pas le temps maintenant, mais je pourrais réparer votre télévision **dans trois jours.**	*I don't have time now, but I could fix your television set* in (meaning 'after') three days.

To indicate the moment at which an action can begin, French uses **dans** to express the English *in.*

(**f**) *in* used to introduce a phrase of manner

Madame Renard parle **d'une voix très douce.**	*Mrs. Renard speaks* in a very soft voice.

Phrases of manner are often introduced by the preposition **de.**

(**g**) — *o'clock in the* —

Je me suis réveillé **à deux heures du matin.**	*I woke up* at two o'clock in the morning.

In expressions such as **deux heures du matin, trois heures de l'après-midi,** and **huit heures du soir,** the English *in the* is expressed in French by **de** + DEFINITE ARTICLE.

F. *Remplacez les mots anglais indiqués entre parenthèses par leur équivalent français.*

1. Paul fait tout bien (*except*) ses leçons de musique.   2. Vous êtes fou de dépenser votre argent (*in*) une façon aussi extravagante.   3. Couchez-vous de bonne heure (*in the evening*).   4. Jean a passé le week-end (*at*) les Biéville.   5. (*For*) dix jours on ne savait pas où ils étaient.   6. Je viens de parler à Nicole; elle était (*in*) mauvaise humeur.   7. Le petit a dormi jusqu'à quatre heures (*in the afternoon*).

8. Nous partirons (*for*) huit jours.   9. (*In*) Molière il y a toujours des choses amusantes.   10. Marc a fait ses devoirs (*in*) vingt minutes. 11. Nous regardons la télévision (*for*) deux heures.   12. Dépéchez-vous, le train part (*in*) une demi-heure.   13. Cela ne se passe pas comme ça (*at*) les Italiens.   14. Son mari lui a répondu (*in*) un ton ferme.   15. (*For*) combien de temps partirez-vous à Londres?

G. *Traduisez en français.*

1. Those boys have been playing here for an hour.   2. My alarm clock rang at six o'clock in the morning.   3. I will go to Portugal for three days.   4. Your little boy went down the street a little while ago. 5. Do you want to see me at your home or in your office?   6. I saw Mr. Lebrun at the barber's.   7. I'll begin that work in a half hour. 8. We get up early in the morning.   9. I slept a great deal during my illness.   10. Everyone came except Michael.   11. In Balzac one finds extraordinary characters[1].   12. I can finish that book in an hour.   13. One is always well received at their home.   14. We read that before.

---

[1] Not **caractères**. See page 40.

21. in spite of

Malgré le mauvais temps, je vais sortir ce soir.   In spite of *the bad weather, I'm going out this evening.*

The English *in spite of* is expressed in French by **malgré.**

22. instead of

Au lieu d'un cadeau, j'ai donné de l'argent à Jacques.   Instead of *a gift, I gave Jack some money.*

The English *instead of* is expressed in French by **au lieu de,** which may be followed by a noun, a pronoun, or an infinitive.

23. out of

(a) *out of* = **hors de**

Votre ami est **hors de** danger main-tenant.   *Your friend is* out of *danger now.*

The commonest equivalent of *out of* is **hors de.**

(b) *out of = without*

Vous êtes toujours **sans** argent.   *You are always* out of *money.*

When *out of* means *without*, it is expressed by **sans.**

(c) *out of* between numerals (one *out of* three)

Un étudiant **sur** cinq a déjà visité   *One student* out of *five has already*
la France.   *visited France.*

When *out of* is used idiomatically between numerals in phrases
such as *two out of three*, French expresses *out of* by **sur.**

(d) *go out of, come out of, fall out of*

Louis **est sorti de** la maison avec   *Louis* came out of *the house with his*
son chien.   *dog.*

Votre carte d'identité **est tombée**   *Your identification card* has fallen out
de votre portefeuille.   *of your billfold.*

The verbs *come out of* and *go out of* are expressed by **sortir de,** and
fall out of is expressed by **tomber de.**

24. toward

Tout le monde s'est précipité **vers**   *Everyone rushed* toward *the door.*
la porte.

Vers la fin de la journée, je me sens   *Toward the end of the day I feel tired.*
fatigué.

The word *toward* is usually expressed by **vers,** whether it indicates
motion or means *about* with an expression of time.

Il faut être loyal **envers** ses amis.   *One must be loyal* toward *one's friends.*
Quelle est son attitude **envers** ses   *What is his attitude* toward *his parents?*
parents?

Used figuratively in referring to a person, *toward* is expressed by
envers.

25. under

Le métro passe **sous** la Seine.   *The subway goes* under *the Seine.*

The commonest way of expressing *under* is **sous.**

Les Delorme habitent **au-dessous de** nous. — *The Delormes live* under *us.*

Raymond a quinze employés **au-dessous de** lui. — *Raymond has fifteen employees* under *him.*

However, *under* and *underneath* are expressed by **au-dessous de** when used figuratively and when *under* does not mean *immediately under.*

26. up

Je **monte** cet escalier cinq fois par jour. — *I go up that stairway five times a day.*

En sortant de son bureau, Monsieur Glantin **a remonté la rue.** — *On leaving his office, Mr. Glantin went up the street.*

The English *up* is often part of the French verb. Two of the common expressions which express *up* are **monter,** meaning *to go up,* and **remonter la rue,** which means *to go up the street.*

27. with

(a) *with* = **avec**

Je vous ai vu **avec** une dame hier soir. — *I saw you* with *a lady yesterday evening.*

The common way of expressing *with* is **avec.**

(b) *with* = **de** after verb or adjective

Son bureau est toujours **couvert de** poussière. — *His desk is always* covered with *dust.*

Es-tu **content de** ta voiture? — *Are you* satisfied with *your car?*

Certain verbs and adjectives are regularly followed by **de** in French and their English equivalents are followed by *with.*

(c) *with* = **chez**

Louise habite **chez** sa tante. — *Louise lives* with *her aunt.*

Chez Verlaine, la musicalité des mots est très importante. — *With Verlaine, the musical quality of the words is very important.*

When *with* means *at the house of* or *in the case of* + A PERSON, French generally uses **chez.**

(d) *with* in phrases of manner = **de**

Françoise regardait sa montre **d'un   *Frances was looking at her watch* with
air anxieux.**   an anxious air.

French phrases of manner are introduced by **de**. Sometimes this **de** is expressed in English by *with*, sometimes by *in*.

(e) *with* in phrases of characteristic = **à** + ARTICLE

Cette brune **aux yeux bleus** a beau-   *That brunette* with blue eyes *has a
coup de charme.   great deal of charm.*

French uses **à** + DEFINITE ARTICLE to indicate a characteristic of a person. English uses the preposition *with* in the same way.

(f) *with* to express attitude or manner of a part of the body = DEFINITE ARTICLE

Louis dort toujours **la bouche ou-   *Louis always sleeps* with his mouth
verte.**   open.

English uses *with* to express attitude or manner of a part of the body, whereas French uses the DEFINITE ARTICLE without a preposition.

H. *Remplacez par l'équivalent français les mots anglais entre parenthèses.*

1. Restez à la maison (*instead of*) vous fatiguer.   2. Je suis allé en classe (*in spite of*) la neige.   3. Connaissez-vous ce jeune homme (*with*) cheveux roux?   4. Les enfants (*under*) sept ans paient demi-place.   5. Cet homme est toujours (*out of*) travail.   6. Nous nous sommes dirigés (*toward*) le centre de la place.   7. Nous sommes très satisfaits (*with*) vos progrès.   8. Êtes-vous toujours indulgents (*toward*) vos amis?   9. Comment trouvez-vous la famille qui habite (*under*) vous?   10. Nous habitons (*at*) mes beaux-parents.   11. Dans ce pays, deux personnes (*out of*) sept savent une langue étrangère.   12. La terre était couverte (*with*) neige.   13. Aidez-moi à mettre ce bureau (*toward*) la fenêtre.   14. Achetez une voiture (*instead of*) une moto.

I. *Traduisez en français.*

1. He looked at me with his mouth open. 2. Read instead of looking at television. 3. Who is that girl with bare feet? 4. What is your
attitude toward foreigners? 5. Are you satisfied[1] with your new job?
6. What fell out of your pocket? 7. My son lives at his grandmother's. 8. Toward the end of the play, everybody was laughing.
9. What do you have under your coat? 10. The room was filled
with smoke. 11. Don't forget to go to the dentist's before going to
Alain's. 12. Our friends came to see us in spite of the bad weather.
13. One girl out of three gets married before the age of twenty[2].
14. Who just came out of the office? 15. I hope that your brother
is out of danger. 16. My brother-in-law has been out of work for a
month. 17. When Mr. Saunier came out of the hotel, he went up
the street.

---

[1] content [2] Supply **ans.**

Problem Words

62. would

(**a**) When *would* is used to express a condition

Je **partirais** tout de suite si j'avais   *I* would leave *immediately if I had*
le temps.   *time.*

The word *would* is often a part of the conclusion of an English conditional sentence. In this case, French puts the verb in the CONDI-
TIONAL.

Que **ferais**-tu à ma place?   *What* would *you* do *in my place?*

Sometimes *would* is the auxiliary of the verb of an implied condition, that is, one in which the *if*-clause is missing but is implied. The
above sentence, for instance, means: *What would you do if you were I?*
In an implied condition French uses the CONDITIONAL of the verb of
the sentence to express the English *would*.

(**b**) When *would* means *used to*

Je **partais** de bonne heure tous les   *I* would (= used to) *leave early every*
matins.   *morning.*

When *would = used to*, it indicates a customary past action, and in
such cases the IMPERFECT of the verb must be used.

CAUTION: Whenever you find *would* in an English sentence which you wish to express in French, determine whether *would* is part of a condition or whether it is used to describe a customary action and is the equivalent of *used to*. If *would* is the equivalent of *used to*, use the imperfect rather than the conditional.

63. year

(a) When *year* is expressed by **année**

En quelle **année** êtes-vous né?	*In what* year *were you born?*
Cette **année**-là il a beaucoup neigé.	*That* year *it snowed a great deal.*
J'ai passé beaucoup d'**années** en France.	*I spent many* years *in France.*
Ma troisième **année** à l'université a été très amusante.	*My third* year *at the university was very entertaining.*

The most common word for *year* is **année**. It should be used except in the cases stated in (**b**).

(b) When *year* is expressed by **an**

Nous avons passé **trois ans** en France.	*We spent three* years *in France.*
Nous y retournons **tous les ans**.	*We go back there* every year.
Sans indiscrétion, combien gagnez-vous **par an**?	*If it isn't indiscreet to ask, how much do you earn* a year?

The word **an** is used for *year* when it is modified by a cardinal numeral, in the expressions **tous les ans** (*every year*) and **par an** (*per year*), and occasionally in other circumstances.

64. yes

(a) When *yes* is expressed by **oui**

—Êtes-vous arrivé hier?	*"Did you arrive yesterday?"*
—**Oui,** je suis arrivé hier.	*"Yes, I arrived yesterday."*

The usual word for *yes* is **oui**; it indicates the speaker's agreement with the previous statement or question.

(b) When *yes* is expressed by **si**

—**N'êtes**-vous **pas** arrivé hier?	*"Didn't you arrive yesterday?"*
—**Si,** je suis arrivé hier.	*"Yes, I arrived yesterday."*

—Guy **ne** comprend **pas** bien l'an-   *"Guy* doesn't *understand English well."*
glais.

—**Si,** il le comprend bien.   "Yes, *he does understand it well."*

After a negative statement or question, **si** is used for *yes.* It contradicts the preceding statement or question.

65. young men

How to express the plural of **jeune homme**

Il y avait **des jeunes gens** et des   *There were* some young men *and some*
jeunes filles à cette réception.   *young ladies at that reception.*

Lucile voudrait connaître **des jeunes**   *Lucille would like to get acquainted with*
gens avec qui elle puisse sortir.   *some young men with whom she*
                                           could go out.

The plural of **jeune homme** is **jeunes gens.** A frequent meaning of **jeunes gens** is therefore *young men.* The expression **les jeunes hommes** seldom occurs, and you should avoid using it.

Les **jeunes gens** s'amusent beaucoup   Young people *have a very good time*
pendant la traversée en bateau.   *during a boat trip.*

The term **jeunes gens** also means *young people.* The context must decide where **jeunes gens** means *young men* and where *young people.*

J. *Remplacez les mots anglais peur leur équivalent français.*

1. Dans quelques (*years*) j'espère savoir plusieurs langues.   2. Ces (*young men*) avec leurs cheveux longs ressemblent à des filles.   3. Nos amis mexicains ne sont pas retournés dans leur pays depuis dix (*years*).   4. —Pourquoi ne prenez-vous pas le train de cinq heures? —Parce que je (*would arrive*) au milieu de la nuit.   5. —Je ne parle pas bien le français. __(*Yes*), vous le parlez fort bien.   6. Agnès ne veut sortir qu'avec des (*young men*) de son âge.   7. Le patron change de voiture (*every year*).   8. Quand je préparais mes examens, je (*would get up*) à six heures du matin.   9. —Voulez-vous m'accompagner chez les Bridoux? —(*Yes*), volontiers.

K. *Traduisez en français. Attention aux mots en italique.*

1 I think I could go to France in[1] two *years.*   2 *Would* you lend me your car this weekend?   3. Our cousins from Pontigny come to see

----
[1] dans

us twice a *year*.   4. "Do you like that music?" "*Yes*, very much."
5. Robert and Roger are very serious *young men*.   6. In^2 what *year*
did you come to the United States?   7. When we were young, we
would go to church every Sunday.   8. I found the first *year* of medicine the most difficult.   9. "Haven't you seen Alain?" "*Yes*, he's
coming."

---

^{2} en

Verb Review

Review the verbs **voir** and **vouloir** according to the outline on page
283.

The Texts

To the Student

There follow eight texts from twentieth century French authors. Each of these selections presents an image or an experience which reveals some aspect of life and which gives the passage an interest in itself as well as constituting a part of a complete work.

Each text is interesting in content and could be studied uniquely for subject matter. Each has its peculiar style and might be examined from the point of view of the author's literary technique.

In addition to having esthetic and intellectual qualities, each selection contains examples of various syntactical constructions common in present-day French. To facilitate your study of these texts from a grammatical point of view, we have edited them with questions and comments on the language.

Since no French author writes in order to illustrate only certain syntactical points, these texts naturally contain many different kinds of constructions. From each, we have chosen certain significant grammatical topics on which to focus your attention.

* * *

These texts may be assigned to you for study at any time during your course.

If the earlier texts are assigned toward the beginning of the course, you will find in them questions based on grammatical constructions which you will not as yet have studied in the course. But that does not matter. It is stimulating to be confronted with a construction for the first time in an author, to study its usage there without any previous knowledge of it, and then later to delve into the same subject in a more organized and formal fashion. The fact that you have already examined a topic in a text will help you to understand it better when you take it up in detail.

If the texts are assigned toward the end of the course, you will probably be able to answer many of the questions from what you have already learned in the course. But if you cannot answer the questions from what you have observed in the example of the selection and from what you already know about French grammar, look in the index to find the topic under discussion and read the references to it which you find there.

In making questions on the grammar of the texts, we have tried to avoid repeating questions on the same types of grammar in succeeding texts except where it seemed wise to do so in order to emphasize the importance of knowing certain difficult aspects of the language. But your instructor may ask you questions on these points of grammar in every text in order to review them.

Your instructor may direct you to analyze a text grammatically for home preparation, and then, when you come to class, spend some time discussing all aspects of the texts. To this end, you should read the passage carefully, think of it from all points of view, and be able to answer the various types of questions your instructor may ask.

Texte N° 1

Jean Cocteau

Homme extraordinaire, universel, romancier, dramaturge, essayiste, mais poète avant tout, mêlé à tous les mouvements d'avant-garde dans l'art et la littérature, Jean Cocteau a «étonné» son époque. Nul n'est resté jeune plus longtemps que ce magicien et ne s'est plus intéressé à la jeunesse.

A la sortie d'un lycée, une fin d'après-midi à Paris, une bataille a lieu à coups de boules de neige entre deux groupes de garçons d'une douzaine d'années. Le chef d'un des camps est Dargelos, le héros de son école. Il vient de lancer brutalement une boule de neige sur un jeune camarade qui l'admire. Celui-ci, blessé, tombe évanoui; on le transporte dans la loge du concierge, et le censeur vient voir ce qui se passe.

Dargelos était[1] debout dans la porte. Derrière la porte se pressaient[1] des têtes curieuses. Gérard pleurait[1] et tenait[1] la main de son ami.

—Racontez, Dargelos, dit[2] le censeur.

5 —Il n'y a rien à raconter, m'sieur. On lançait[3] des boules de[4] neige. Je lui en ai jeté[5] une. Elle devait[6] être très dure. Il l'a reçue[7] en pleine poitrine, il a fait «ho!» et il est tombé comme ça. J'ai d'abord cru[8] qu'il saignait du nez à cause d'une autre boule de neige.

—Une boule de neige ne défonce pas la poitrine.

10 —Monsieur, monsieur, dit alors l'élève qui répondait au nom de Gérard, il avait entouré[9] une pierre avec de la neige.

—Est-ce[10] exact? questionna le censeur.

Dargelos haussa les[11] épaules.

—Vous ne répondez pas?

15 —C'est[10] inutile. Tenez, il ouvre les[11] yeux, demandez-lui . . .

255

Le malade se ranimait. Il appuyait la tête contre la manche de
son camarade.

—Comment vous sentez-vous?

—Pardonnez-moi . . .

—Ne vous excusez pas, vous êtes malade, vous vous êtes évanoui. 20

—Je me rappelle.

—Pouvez-vous me dire à la suite de quoi vous vous êtes évanoui?

—J'avais reçu une boule de neige dans la poitrine.

—On ne se trouve pas mal en recevant une boule de neige!

—Je n'ai rien[12] reçu d'autre.   25

—Votre camarade prétend que cette boule de neige cachait une
pierre.

Le malade vit que Dargelos haussait les épaules.

—Gérard est fou, dit-il. Tu es fou. Cette boule de neige était une
boule de neige. Je courais, j'ai dû avoir une congestion.   30

Le censeur respira[13].

Dargelos allait sortir. Il se ravisa[14] et on pensa[14] qu'il marchait vers
le malade. Arrivé en face du comptoir où les concierges vendent des
porte-plume, de l'encre, des sucreries, il hésita, tira des sous de sa
poche, les posa sur le rebord et prit en échange un de ces rouleaux de 35
réglisse qui[15] ressemblent à des lacets de bottine et que[15] sucent les
collégiens. Ensuite, il traversa la loge, porta la main à sa tempe dans
une sorte de salut militaire et disparut.

Les Enfants terribles
(Extrait)

© *Éditions Gallimard*

NOTES AND QUESTIONS

1. You notice that the selection starts with four verbs in the imperfect
   tense. What do these verbs do for the selection? Why did the author
   put them in the imperfect rather than in the simple past?

2. What sort of word order does **dit le censeur** exemplify? Whenever a
   like phrase follows part of a conversation, it is always in inverted word
   order.

3. Why is this form of the verb **lancer** written with a **ç** (**c cédille**)?

4. Analyze the expression **de neige.** Of what two parts of speech does it consist? How would **boule de neige** be expressed in English? What then is the function of **de neige?** Can you make a generalization concerning this sort of case? Your generalization should read something like this: "English often uses a noun as an adjective. In like cases, French uses **de** + NOUN and places them after the word they modify."

5. The verb **lancer** in the previous sentence was in the imperfect. Why does Dargelos now switch to the compound past?

6. How would you express **devait être** in English? If you are not sure, look up the imperfect of **devoir** on page 202, §§2, 3.

7. With what does **reçue** agree? What is the rule for the agreement of a past participle of a verb conjugated with the auxiliary **avoir?**

8. This is a verb of mental action, yet it is in the compound past rather than the imperfect. Why?

9. What tense is **avait entouré?** Why would such a tense be used here rather than the compound past?

10. What type of **ce** is this? To what does it refer? If you are not sure, see page 103, which discusses this in reference to demonstrative pronouns.

11. How would you say in English: **Dargelos haussa les épaules? Il ouvre les yeux?** What rule for the use of the French definite article applies in this case? If you are not sure, consult page 73 in the chapter on possessives. Find another example of this same construction in the following sentences.

12. In this sentence, notice the position of **rien** in a compound tense. What generalization can you make concerning the position of **rien** in a compound tense? Also, notice the **d'** in the expression **rien d'autre** (*nothing else*). In French, an indefinite is always separated from a following adjective by **de.**

13. The verb **respirer** often means *breathe*, but breathing is a continuous operation. Here the simple past is used, and therefore, what would the meaning of **respirer** as used here be?

14. The verbs **se ravisa** and **pensa** constitute mental actions. Why are they put in the simple past here?

15. Note the relative pronouns **qui** and **que.** Both refer to **ces rouleaux de réglisse.** Why is **qui** used in one instance and then **que?**

Texte N° 2

COLETTE

Colette est célèbre pour sa finesse, son esprit enjoué, le charme de son style. Par sa peinture sensible de l'amour et son observation originale de la nature, elle donne vie à tout un monde de tendresse et de fraîcheur. Dans *La Maison de Claudine* elle raconte des souvenirs d'enfance.

La petite fille de treize ans passe ses vacances dans la maison familiale avec son grand frère et Maurice, un camarade d'études de celui-ci. Elle est d'abord secrètement amoureuse de lui, mais elle se raisonne et ils deviennent de bons amis. Quand elle apprend qu'il va se marier, elle joue subtilement de sa coquetterie et, avec un plaisir mêlé de tristesse, elle réussit pour la première fois à troubler un homme.

C'est en écoutant[1] causer les deux jeunes gens que j'appris le mariage, encore assez lointain, de Maurice. Un jour que[2] nous étions seuls au[3] jardin, je m'enhardis[4] jusqu'à lui demander le portrait de sa fiancée. Il me le tendit: une jeune fille souriante, jolie, extrêmement coiffée, enguirlandée de mille ruches de dentelle. 5

—Oh! dis-je maladroitement, la[a] belle robe!

Il rit si franchement que je ne m'excusai pas.

—Et qu'allez-vous faire, quand vous serez[5] marié?

Il cessa de rire et me regarda.

—Comment, ce que je vais faire? Mais je suis déjà presque avocat[6], 10
tu[7] sais!

—Je sais. Et elle, votre fiancée, que fera-t-elle, pendant que vous serez avocat?

—Que[8] tu es drôle! Elle sera ma femme, voyons.

—Elle mettra d'autres[9] robes avec beaucoup de petites ruches? 15

—Elle s'occupera de notre maison, elle recevra . . . Tu te moques de moi? Tu sais très bien comment on vit quand on est marié.

---

[a] *What a beautiful dress!* The definite article is sometimes used to modify a noun in an exclamation.

—Non, pas très bien. Mais je sais comment nous vivons[10] depuis un mois et demi.

20 —Qui donc, «nous»?

—Vous, mon frère et moi[11]. Vous êtes bien[12], ici? Étiez-vous heureux? Vous nous aimez?

Il leva ses[13] yeux noirs vers le toit d'ardoises brodé de jaune, vers la glycine en sa seconde floraison, les arrêta un moment sur moi et 25 répondit comme à lui-même:

—Mais oui . . .

—Après, quand vous serez marié, vous ne pourrez plus, sans doute, revenir ici, passer les vacances? Vous ne pourrez plus jamais vous promener à côté de mon frère, en tenant mes deux nattes par 30 le bout, comme des rênes?

Je tremblais de tout mon corps, mais je ne le quittais pas des yeux. Quelque chose changea[14] dans son visage. Il regarda autour de lui, puis il parut mesurer, de la tête aux pieds, la fillette qui s'appuyait à un arbre et qui levait la tête en lui parlant, parce qu'elle n'avait pas 35 encore assez grandi. Je me souviens qu'il ébaucha une sorte de sourire contraint, puis il haussa les épaules, répondit assez sottement:

—Dame, non, ça va de soi[15] . . .

Il s'éloigna vers la maison sans ajouter[16] un mot et je mêlai pour la première fois, au grand regret enfantin que j'avais de perdre bien- 40 tôt Maurice, un petit chagrin victorieux de femme.

> *La Maison de Claudine*
> (Extrait)
>
> © *Libraire Ernest Flammarion*

NOTES AND QUESTIONS

1. Here, the present participle is used with **en.** When the present participle is used with **en,** to what word in the sentence does it refer? If you are not sure, see pages 64–65. Find another example of the present participle with **en** in this selection.

2. The expression **un jour que** means *a day when.* You learned on page 133 that *when,* relative, is normally **où.** However, when the antecedent indicating a period of time is modified by **un** or **une,** it is fairly common to find *when* expressed by **que,** although it may also be expressed by **où.**

3. The expression **au jardin** means *in the garden*. Notice that French often uses **au** instead of **dans le** for the English *in the*. There is no general rule to determine which is used, and sometimes either is used.

4. The expression **je m'enhardis** means *I became bold*. Comment on the use of the reflexive verb and especially of the compound past and the simple past of the reflexive verb to express the English *become* + ADJECTIVE. If you are not sure of this usage, see page 27, §5(c) and page 71, §19(e).

5. English would use the present tense here. Under what conditions does French use the future in constructions in which English uses the present? Find another similar example several lines down.

6. English would say: *I am already almost a lawyer*. When does French omit the indefinite article where English would use it?

7. The little girl has been using the **vous** form when speaking to Maurice. Why does he use the **tu** form when answering her? Notice the use of **vous** and **tu** throughout this text.

8. Note that here **que** is used as an exclamation. English would say: *How funny you are!* French also uses **comme** in such cases, so that **Comme tu es drôle!** is equally possible.

9. Why is **d'** used instead of **des**? If you are not sure, consult page 175, §4.

10. How does English express . . . **nous vivons depuis un mois et demi?** Give the general rule for the use of the present tense in such constructions.

11. What kind of pronoun is **moi**? Why is it used here?

12. Here, **bien,** which is more often an adverb, is used as an adjective with a special meaning. What does **bien** mean here? Note that **bien** may be used as an adjective when it is in the predicate after a form of **être.** It is much less frequently used thus to modify a noun directly.

13. You have learned that when the subject of the sentence acts with a part of the body, French normally uses the article where English uses a possessive adjective. Yet here, French uses a possessive adjective — because the part of the body is modified. When a part of the body is modified, French tends to use the possessive adjective just as does English.

14. Why is an **e** inserted between the stem and ending of this form of the verb **changer?**

15. The disjunctive form of the reflexive pronoun **se,** which is **soi,** is used in what circumstances? If you are not sure, see page 50.

16. The French **sans ajouter un mot** would be expressed in English by *without adding a word*. Thus, after a preposition English uses a present participle where French uses an infinitive.

Texte N° 3

Marguerite Duras

Des nombreuses femmes écrivains d'aujourd'hui, Marguerite Duras est parmi les plus connues dans la littérature et dans le cinéma. Elle fait partie de l'école du «nouveau roman», surtout par sa technique de stricte observation, qui donne à ses œuvres un air neutre, détaché. Mais ce qu'elle écrit est toujours évocateur et souvent poignant.

Cette scène à trois voix est l'ouverture du drame passionnel qui va bientôt se dérouler. Un professeur de piano questionne en vain le petit garçon à qui l'on impose des leçons de musique alors qu'il rêve d'autres choses.

—Veux-tu lire ce[a] qu'il y a d'écrit au-dessus de ta partition? demanda la dame.

—Moderato cantabile, dit l'enfant.

La dame ponctua cette réponse d'un[1] coup de crayon sur le clavier.

5 L'enfant resta[2] immobile, la[3] tête tournée vers sa partition.

—Et qu'est-ce que ça veut dire, moderato cantabile?

—Je[b] sais pas.

Une femme, assise à trois mètres de là, soupira.

—Tu es sûr de ne pas[4] savoir ce que ça veut dire, moderato canta-
10 bile? reprit la dame.

L'enfant ne répondit pas. La dame poussa un cri d'impuissance étouffé, tout[5] en frappant de nouveau le clavier de son crayon. Pas[6] un cil dē l'enfant ne bougea. La dame se retourna.

—Madame Desbaresdes[c] quelle[d] tête vous avez là, dit-elle.

15 Anne Desbaresdes soupira une nouvelle fois.

—A[e] qui le dites-vous, dit-elle.

---

[a] *what is written.* The **d'** in this expression is the **de** which separates a modifying adjective from an indefinite pronoun in expressions such as **rien de difficile, quelque chose de beau,** etc.
[b] In familiar spoken French, the **ne** of the negative **ne . . . pas** is often slurred over or entirely omitted.
[c] Desbaresdes is pronounced [debared].
[d] *what a stubborn child*   [e] *You're telling me!*

L'enfant, immobile, les yeux baissés, fut seul à se souvenir que le
soir venait d'éclater. Il en[7] frémit.

—Je te l'ai dit la dernière fois, je te l'ai dit l'avant-dernière fois, je
te l'ai dit cent fois, tu es sûr de ne pas le savoir?   20

L'enfant ne jugea pas bon de répondre. La dame reconsidéra une
nouvelle fois l'objet qui était devant elle. Sa fureur augmenta.

—Ça recommence, dit tout bas Anne Desbaresdes.

—Ce qu'il y a, continua la dame, ce qu'il y a, c'est que tu ne veux
pas le dire.   25

Anne Desbaresdes aussi reconsidéra cet enfant de ses pieds jusqu'à
sa tête mais d'une[8] autre façon que la dame.

—Tu vas le dire tout de suite, hurla la dame.

L'enfant ne témoigna aucune surprise. Il ne répondit toujours[9]
pas. Alors la dame frappa une troisième fois sur le clavier, mais si 30
fort que le crayon se cassa[10]. Tout à côté des mains de l'enfant.
Celles-ci[11] étaient à peine écloses, rondes, laiteuses encore. Fermées
sur elles-mêmes, elles ne bougèrent pas.

—C'est un enfant difficile, osa dire Anne Desbaresdes, non sans
une[12] certaine timidité.   35

L'enfant tourna la tête vers cette voix, vers elle, vite, le[f] temps de
s'assurer de son existence, puis il reprit sa pose d'objet, face à la
partition. Ses mains restèrent fermées.

—Je ne veux pas savoir s'il est difficile ou non, Madame Desbaresdes, dit la dame. Difficile ou pas, il faut qu'il obéisse, ou[g] bien.   40

Dans le temps qui suivit ce propos, le bruit de la mer entra par la
fenêtre ouverte. Et avec lui, celui, atténué, de la ville au cœur de
l'après-midi de ce printemps. . . .

—Une dernière fois. Tu es sûr de ne pas le savoir? . . .

L'enfant ouvrit sa[13] main, la déplaça et se[13] gratta légèrement le 45
mollet. Son geste fut désinvolte et peut-être la dame convint-elle de
son innocence?

—Je sais pas, dit-il, après s'être[14] gratté.

Les couleurs du couchant devinrent tout à coup si glorieuses que
la blondeur de cet enfant s'en trouva modifiée.   50

—C'est facile, dit la dame un peu plus calmement.

Elle se moucha longuement.

---

[f] **le temps de** = *long enough to*   [g] *or else*

—Quel enfant j'ai là, dit Annes Desbaresdes joyeusement, tout de
même, mais quel enfant j'ai fait là, et comment se fait-il qu'il me
55 soit[15] venu avec cet entêtement-là . . .

La dame ne crut pas bon de relever tant d'orgueil.

—Ça veut dire, dit-elle à l'enfant — écrasée — pour la centième
fois, ça veut dire modéré et chantant.

—Modéré et chantant, dit l'enfant totalement en[h] allé où?

60 La dame se retourna.

—Ah, je[i] vous jure.

Moderato cantabile
(Extrait)

© *Les Éditions de Minuit*

---

[h] **en allé où** = *blankly* (lit. *gone off . . . where?*) [i] (In a tone of exasperation) *honestly!*

NOTES AND QUESTIONS

1. What is the meaning of **d'un coup de crayon?** What is the function of **de** in such a phrase? If you are not sure, see page 247, §27(**d**).

2. Notice that although **resta** seems to indicate a state, it is in the simple past because it constitutes a new phase of the action and by so doing forwards the action of the narrative.

3. How would we express **la tête tournée** in English? How does French use the article with parts of the body in such cases? Find another example of the same use of the article in the text. This case is discussed on page 78, §10 of the grammar.

4. Here we find both parts of the negation without an intervening verb. When a negative modifies a simple infinitive, the two parts of the negation precede this infinitive.

5. How would you express **tout en frappant** in English? How does **tout** affect the meaning of **en frappant?**

6. Here, **pas** precedes **ne,** which is unusual. Make a generalization as to the positions of **ne** and **pas** in a French sentence.

7. How would you express this **en** in English? Remember that **en** usually takes the place of **de** + NOUN.

8. How would you express **d'une autre façon** in English? What is the function of **de** in such a phrase? If you are not sure, see page 243, §20(**f**).

9. Here, **toujours** does not mean *always.* What does it mean?

10. In English, we would say: *The pencil broke.* No reflexive pronoun would be used. But in French many verbs require a reflexive object to complete their meaning.

11. What is the meaning of **celles-ci** in this sentence? To what word does it refer?

12. The preposition **sans** normally is followed directly by an indefinite noun without an article. But here, note that **une certaine timidité** has, as a matter of fact, an element of definiteness, hence the use of the article.

13. Note first of all the use of the possessive adjective with an unmodified part of the body. Perhaps more frequent is **L'enfant ouvrit la main.** In the second part of the sentence, we find **se gratta légèrement le mollet.** When is the REFLEXIVE OBJECT + THE ARTICLE used in French where English would use only a possessive adjective?

14. What verbal construction is used after the preposition **après?** And why is this verb conjugated with the auxiliary **être?**

15. What is the basic reason for the use of the subjunctive here? If you are in doubt, see page 144. And why would the past rather than the present subjunctive be required?

Texte N° 4

Alain Robbe-Grillet

D'abord ingénieur, Alain Robbe-Grillet est devenu le maître du «nouveau roman», de l'école dite du regard. Il rejette l'appareil psychologique traditionnel et semble ne faire qu'enregistrer avec minutie ce qui frappe la vue et l'imagination d'une personne. Il donne aux objets une grande importance: ils ont chez lui une substance, une épaisseur qui révèle mieux le monde des hommes.

Sa vision s'applique particulièrement bien à un paysage comme cette plage où marchent trois enfants qui se rendent à l'école; le temps qui s'écoule est marqué par le soleil, la mer, le sable, les empreintes des pas, la falaise et la troupe d'oiseaux qui arpente le rivage. Les enfants avancent fragiles dans la nature; le plus petit détail, la moindre description contribuent à donner une dimension nouvelle à la scène et une vie intense aux personnages que le lecteur accompagne pas à pas et dont il partage les sensations.

Trois[1] enfants marchent[2] le long d'une grève. Ils s'avancent[3], côte
à côte, se tenant par la main. Ils ont sensiblement la même taille, et
sans doute aussi le même âge : une douzaine[4] d'années. Celui[5] du
milieu, cependant, est un peu plus petit que les deux autres.

5 Hormis ces[1] trois enfants, toute la longue[6] plage est déserte. C'est[7]
une bande de sable assez large, uniforme, dépourvue de[8] roches isolées[9] comme de trous d'eau, à peine inclinée entre la falaise abrupte[9],
qui paraît sans issue, et la mer.

Il fait très beau. Le soleil éclaire le sable jaune d'une lumière
10 violente, verticale. Il n'y a pas un[10] nuage dans le ciel. Il n'y a pas,
non plus, de[10] vent. L'eau est bleue, calme, sans la moindre ondulation venant du large, bien que la plage soit[11] ouverte sur la mer
libre, jusqu'à l'horizon.

Mais à intervalles réguliers, une vague soudaine, toujours la même,
15 née à quelques mètres du bord, s'enfle brusquement et déferle aussitôt, toujours sur la même ligne. On n'a pas alors l'impression que
l'eau avance[3], puis se retire ; c'est, au contraire, comme si tout ce
mouvement s'exécutait[12] sur place. Le gonflement de l'eau produit
d'abord une légère[13] dépression, du côté de la grève, et la vague
20 prend un peu de recul, dans un bruissement de graviers roulés ; puis
elle éclate et se répand, laiteuse, sur la pente, mais pour regagner
seulement le terrain perdu. C'est à peine si une montée plus forte,
çà et là, vient mouiller un instant quelques décimètres supplémen-
taires.

25 Et tout reste de nouveau immobile, la mer, plate et bleue, exactement arrêtée à la même hauteur sur le sable jaune de la plage, où[14]
marchent côte à côte les trois enfants.

Ils sont blonds, presque de la même couleur que le sable : la peau
un peu plus foncée, les cheveux un peu plus clairs. Ils sont habillés
30 tous les trois de la même façon, culotte courte et chemisette, l'une et
l'autre en grosse toile d'un bleu délavé. Ils marchent côte à côte, se
tenant par la main, en ligne droite, parallèlement à la mer et parallèlement à la falaise, presque à égale distance des deux, un peu plus
près de l'eau pourtant. Le soleil, au zénith, ne laisse pas d'ombre à
35 leur pied.

Devant eux le sable est tout à fait vierge, jaune et lisse depuis le rocher jusqu'à l'eau. Les enfants s'avancent en ligne droite, à une vitesse régulière, sans faire le plus petit[6] crochet, calmes et se tenant par la main. Derrière eux le sable, à peine humide, est marqué des trois lignes d'empreintes laissées par leurs[1] pieds nus, trois successions 40 régulières d'empreintes semblables et pareillement espacées, bien creuses, sans bavures.

Les enfants regardent droit devant eux. Ils n'ont pas un coup d'œil vers la haute[6] falaise, sur leur gauche, ni vers la mer dont les petites vagues éclatent périodiquement, sur l'autre côté. A plus forte 45 raison ne se retournent-ils pas, pour contempler derrière eux la distance parcourue. Ils poursuivent leur chemin, d'un pas égal et rapide.

Devant eux, une troupe d'oiseaux de mer arpente le rivage, juste à la limite des vagues. Ils progressent parallèlement à la marche des 50 enfants, dans le même sens que ceux-ci[15], à une centaine[4] de mètres environ. Mais, comme les oiseaux vont beaucoup moins vite, les enfants se rapprochent d'eux. Et tandis que la mer efface au fur et à mesure les traces des pattes étoilées, les pas des enfants demeurent inscrits avec netteté dans le sable à peine humide, où les trois lignes 55 d'empreintes continuent de s'allonger.

Instantanés
(Extrait)

© *Les Éditions de Minuit*

NOTES AND QUESTIONS

1. Numerals, demonstrative adjectives and possessive adjectives are known as limiting adjectives, for they limit the meaning of the noun they modify rather than describing it. Where are limiting adjectives placed in relation to the noun they modify?

2. The verb **marchent** and all the other verbs in the selection are in the present tense. What effect does the use of the present tense throughout the selection give?

3. In this passage we find both the reflexive form **s'avancer** and the non-

reflexive form **avancer.** It is difficult to explain exactly when one and when the other is used, but it may be noted that **avancer** is used with both persons and things, whereas **s'avancer** seems to be limited in use to persons.

4. The suffix **-aine** is used on both **douzaine** and **centaine.** What effect does the addition of **-aine** to a cardinal number have on that number?

5. What kind of pronoun is **celui?** This sort of pronoun must be followed by what types of words? Can they be followed by two types of words at the same time?

6. What position in respect to their noun do certain short adjectives such as **long, petit** and **haut** have? Notice that they do not have the more usual position of descriptive adjectives, possibly because they are short and common.

7. This is the introductory **ce.** Under what conditions can this **ce** be used?

8. The noun **roche** is indefinite rather than definite. Why is it preceded by **de** rather than **des?**

9. In the expressions **roches isolées** and **falaise abrupte,** each adjective is descriptive and therefore follows its noun. Notice that when an adjective follows its noun, it is in a more emphatic position than when it precedes its noun, and that it then indicates how this noun is different from all other nouns of the same category — that is, **roches isolées** are different from all other **roches.**

10. Here we find **pas un nuage** but **pas de vent.** Normally, the negative **pas** is followed by **de.** When **un** follows **pas,** as in **pas un nuage,** the emphasis is on **un** — *not a single cloud.*

11. What in the nature of the meaning of the relative adverb **bien que** would require that it be followed by the subjunctive?

12. How would you express **s'exécutait** in English? Certain French reflexives are regularly expressed in English by a passive. It is difficult to explain this construction, but in such cases the subject of the sentence acts upon itself by means of the reflexive object.

13. The descriptive adjective **léger** usually follows its noun. What is its meaning here? Why does it precede its noun here?

14. Note the word order of **où marchent côte à côte les trois enfants.** The French could also use our English word order and say **où les trois enfants marchent côte à côte,** but is is more natural in a situation like this to put the subject at the end of the sentence for reasons of rhythm and emphasis.

15. Here we find a demonstrative pronoun followed by **-ci** but with no corresponding **ceux-là.** What is the meaning of **ceux-ci** in this case? To what noun does it refer?

Texte N° 5

ANTOINE DE SAINT-EXUPÉRY

Homme d'action, pilote de ligne à l'époque héroïque de l'aviation, puis pilote de guerre, Saint-Exupéry était en même temps un grand écrivain. L'avion lui a donné une nouvelle vision du monde qu'il a exprimée dans ses œuvres. Il n'est pas possible de voler toujours dans les étoiles; aussi Saint-Exupéry a-t-il cherché à établir une civilisation plus humaine, fondée sur le devoir et la solidarité.

Fabien est un aviateur, pionnier des vols de nuit en Amérique du Sud. Il devrait arriver à sa base de Buenos-Aires, mais il a été pris dans un cyclone dont il est le jouet. Sa jeune femme l'ignore encore et téléphone à l'aéroport, comme d'habitude, pour être rassurée sur l'homme qu'elle aime.

La femme de Fabien téléphona.

La nuit de chaque retour elle calculait[1] la marche du courrier de Patagonie: «Il décolle de Trelew . . .» Puis se rendormait[1, 2]. Un peu plus tard: «Il doit[3] approcher de San Antonio, il doit[3] voir ses lumières . . .» Alors elle se levait[1], écartait les rideaux, et jugeait[1] le ciel: 5 «Tous ces nuages le gênent . . .» Parfois la lune se promenait comme un berger. Alors la jeune femme se recouchait[1, 2], rassurée par cette lune et ces étoiles, ces milliers de présences autour de son mari. Vers[4] une heure, elle le sentait proche: «Il ne doit[3] plus être bien loin, il doit voir Buenos-Aires . . .» Alors, elle se levait[1] encore, et lui[5] pré- 10 parait[1] un repas, un café bien chaud: «Il fait si froid, là-haut . . .» Elle le recevait[1] toujours, comme s'il descendait d'un sommet de neige: «Tu n'as pas froid? —Mais non! —Réchauffe-toi quand même . . .» Vers une heure et quart tout était prêt. Alors elle téléphonait. 15

Cette nuit, comme les autres, elle s'informa:

—Fabien a-t-il atterri?

Le secrétaire qui l'écoutait se troubla un peu:

—Qui parle?

—Simone Fabien. 20

—Ah! une minute . . .

Le secrétaire, n'osant rien dire, passa l'écouteur au chef de bureau.

268

—Qui est là?

—Simone Fabien.

25 —Ah! . . . que désirez-vous, madame?

—Mon mari a-t-il atterri?

Il y eut un silence qui dut[6] paraître inexplicable, puis on répondit simplement:

—Non.

30 —Il a du[7] retard?

—Oui . . .

Il y eut un nouveau silence.

—Oui, du retard.

—Ah! . . .

35 C'était un «Ah!» de chair blessée. Un retard ce n'est rien . . . ce n'est rien . . . mais quand il se prolonge . . .

—Ah! . . . Et à quelle heure sera-t-il ici?

—A quelle heure il sera ici? Nous . . . Nous ne savons pas.

Elle se heurtait maintenant à un mur. Elle n'obtenait que l'écho 40 même de ses questions.

—Je vous en prie, répondez-moi[8]! Où se trouve-t-il? . . .

—Où il se trouve? Attendez . . .

Cette inertie lui faisait mal. Il[9] se passait quelque chose, là, derrière ce mur.

45 On se décida[10]:

—Il a décollé de Commodoro à dix-neuf heures trente.

— Et depuis?

—Depuis? . . . Très retardé . . . Très retardé par le mauvais temps . . .

50 —Ah! Le mauvais temps . . .

Quelle[11] injustice, quelle fourberie dans cette lune étalée là, oisive, sur Buenos-Aires! La jeune femme se rappela soudain qu'il fallait deux heures à peine pour[12] se rendre de Commodoro à Trelew.

—Et il vole depuis six heures vers Trelew! Mais il vous envoie des 55 messages! Mais que[13] dit-il? . . .

—Ce qu'il nous dit? Naturellement par un temps pareil . . . vous comprenez bien . . . ses messages ne s'entendent[14] pas.

—Un temps pareil!

—Alors, c'est convenu, Madame, nous vous téléphonons[15] dès que 60 nous savons[15] quelque chose.

—Ah! vous ne savez rien . . .

—Au revoir, Madame . . .

—Non! non! Je veux parler au Directeur!

—M. le Directeur est très occupé, Madame, il est en conférence . . .

—Ah! ça m'est égal! Ça m'est bien égal! Je veux lui parler!   65

Le chef de bureau s'épongea:

—Une minute . . .

Il poussa la porte de Rivière:

—C'est Mme Fabien qui veut vous parler.

«Voilà, pensa Rivière, voilà ce que je craignais». Les éléments 70
affectifs du drame commençaient à se montrer.

Vol de nuit
(Extraits)

© *Éditions Gallimard*

NOTES AND QUESTIONS

1. In the second paragraph are a series of verbs in the imperfect. Why is the imperfect used in this passage?

2. The verbs **se rendormait** and **se recouchait** both have the prefix **re-**. How does this prefix modify the meaning of those verbs?

3. What meaning does **doit** have in this paragraph?

4. When the preposition **vers** is used with a time expression, what does it mean?

5. Here **lui** means *for him* — and is an indirect object. By definition, the indirect object is the person or thing *to* or *for* whom something is said or done.

6. What meaning does **dut** have in this sentence? How is it related in meaning to **doit** in question 3?

7. What is the meaning of **Il a du retard?** What is the function of **du** in this expression?

8. Under what conditions does the object pronoun **me** become **moi?** Notice that it becomes **moi** when placed in an emphatic position.

9. This **Il** is merely introductory and impersonal. In English we might say: *There was something happening.*

10. The verb **décider** is found in both the simple and the reflexive form. When the reflexive form is used, it has the sense of *to make up one's mind.*

11. Normally interrogative, what function does **quelle** have here? If you are not sure, consult page 4.

12. What function does the preposition **pour** perform before an infinitive?

13. In this sentence we find **que,** interrogative, used as the object of a question. But in the following sentence, which is an indirect question, this **que** becomes **ce que,** which is normal in such cases. Consider the change from direct to indirect question: **Que dit-il?** becomes **Dites-moi ce qu'il dit.**

14. What is the meaning of **s'entendent?** What function does this reflexive form of the verb serve?

15. Both **téléphonons** and **savons** are in the present where we would expect the future, since it is a question of future action. But the speaker is using a familiar style, where less attention is given to tenses and where the present is used for vividness.

Texte N° 6

Albert Camus

Lui aussi engagé dans l'histoire, Albert Camus a eu une influence considérable sur sa génération. Il a reçu le prix Nobel de littérature en 1957 pour une œuvre «mettant en lumière les problèmes qui se posent de nos jours à la conscience des hommes». Depuis ses premiers livres, comme L'Étranger, il a beaucoup évolué, à la recherche de valeurs comme la justice et la fraternité.

Meursault est un homme curieux, presque une caricature de l'homme «absurde», c'est-à-dire désaccordé, étranger à ce monde. Petit employé, il vit strictement dans le présent, selon ses sensations. Condamné pour avoir tué un homme plus ou moins volontairement, mais surtout parce qu'il n'a pas pleuré le jour de l'enterrement de sa mère et n'a pas voulu jouer le jeu hypocrite de la société, il va mourir. En prison, il devient un autre homme. Dans cette scène finale, il vient de chasser dans une grande colère l'aumônier, qui lui volait les précieux moments qui lui restent à vivre; il repense à sa mère qui, dans son asile de vieillards, s'était «fiancée» à un vieux pensionnaire; il savoure les impressions qui lui viennent du port d'Alger et il se laisse aller à une dernière méditation.

Lui[1] parti, j'ai retrouvé le[2] calme. J'étais épuisé et je me suis jeté sur ma couchette. Je crois que j'ai dormi[3] parce que je me suis réveillé avec des étoiles sur le[4] visage. Des bruits de campagne montaient jusqu'à moi. Des odeurs de[5] nuit, de[5] terre et de[5] sel rafraîchissaient

mes[4] tempes. La merveilleuse[6] paix de cet été endormi entrait en moi 5
comme une marée. A ce moment, et à la limite de la nuit, des sirènes
ont hurlé. Elles annonçaient des départs pour un monde qui maintenant m'était à jamais indifférent. Pour la première fois depuis bien
longtemps, j'ai pensé[7] à maman. Il m'a semblé[7] que je comprenais[7]
pourquoi à la fin d'une vie elle avait pris[8] un «fiancé», pourquoi elle 10
avait joué[8] à recommencer. Là-bas, là-bas aussi, autour de cet asile
où des vies s'éteignaient, le soir était comme une trêve mélancolique.
Si près de la[2] mort, maman devait s'y sentir libérée et prête à tout
revivre. Personne, personne n'avait[9] le droit de pleurer sur elle. Et
moi[1] aussi, je me suis senti prêt à tout[10] revivre. Comme si cette 15
grande colère m'avait purgé[11] du mal, vidé d'espoir[12], devant cette
nuit chargée de[12] signes et d'étoiles[12], je m'ouvrais pour la première
fois à la tendre indifférence du monde. De l'éprouver si pareil à moi,
si fraternel enfin, j'ai senti que j'avais été heureux, et que je l'étais[13]
encore. Pour que tout soit[14] consommé, pour que je me sente[14] moins 20
seul, il me restait à souhaiter qu'il y ait[15] beaucoup de spectateurs le
jour de mon exécution et qu'ils m'accueillent avec des cris de haine.

L'Étranger
(Extrait)

© *Éditions Gallimard*

NOTES AND QUESTIONS

1. Whenever a personal pronoun is found in a position other than its normal one, a disjunctive form is used. This is because the disjunctive form
   is an emphatic form — it makes the pronoun stand out.

2. Why is the definite article used with this noun?

3. What mode is used after forms of the verb **croire?**

4. French uses the article with **visage,** a possessive adjective with **tempes**
   in this passage. English would use a possessive adjective with both. We
   can say that French tends to use the definite article with parts of the
   body, but we cannot say that it always uses the definite article in such
   cases.

5. Each of these **de** phrases would be expressed in English by placing the
   noun before **odeurs** and making it an adjective: *night odors, earthy odors,
   salt odors.*

6. Why is the descriptive adjective **merveilleuse** placed before its noun?

7. Why are the verbs **j'ai pensé** and **a semblé** in the compound past whereas **comprenais** is in the imperfect?

8. The two pluperfects **avait pris** and **avait joué** are past tenses. How are they used in contrast to the compound past?

9. Why is **ne** used here?

10. Some words may be several parts of speech. What part of speech is **tout** here? What factor determines what part of speech a word is?

11. Here, the pluperfect is used in a contrary-to-fact condition. The pluperfect indicative is regularly used after **si** and **comme si** in such constructions.

12. Why is **de** used here rather than **de** + ARTICLE?

13. The **l'** in **l'étais** is an example of the «neuter» **le,** that is, the invariable **le** which is used to refer to a previous adjective and which is used with a form of the verb **être.** The French requires this **le** to complete its meaning: ". . . I had been happy and I am *it* still."

14. Why would the subjunctive be used after the conjunction **pour que?**

15. Why would the subjunctive be used after the verb **souhaiter?**

Texte N° 7

Marcel Proust

Marcel Proust, qui appartenait à la haute société parisienne, a peint son monde dans un long roman, *A la Recherche du temps perdu,* que sa profondeur psychologique et son art font considérer comme un des plus grands du siècle. A côté de l'étude des passions, Proust s'intéresse au passage du temps; son œuvre est fondée, comme il l'a dit lui-même, sur «l'édifice immense du souvenir».

Voici le début d'un célèbre passage. Le narrateur, qui nous a parlé de son enfance heureuse à Combray, pense que le temps a détruit tout ce passé. Mais un jour il goûte à une petite madeleine trempée dans du thé et est saisi par un violent sentiment de joie. Son esprit, provoqué, se met en quête; il rappellera enfin à la conscience une sensation analogue d'autrefois, qui fera revivre pour l'écrivain tout le passé de Combray.

. . . Un jour d'hiver, comme je rentrais à la maison, ma mère, voyant que j'avais froid, me proposa de me[1] faire prendre, contre mon habitude, un[2] peu de thé. Je refusai d'abord et, je ne sais pourquoi, me ravisai. Elle envoya chercher un de ces gâteaux courts et dodus appelés[3] Petites Madeleines qui semblent avoir été moulés 5 dans la valve[a] rainurée d'une coquille de Saint-Jacques. Et bientôt, machinalement, accablé[3] par la morne[4] journée et la perspective d'un triste[4] lendemain, je portai à mes lèvres une cuillerée du[5] thé où j'avais laissé s'amollir un morceau de madeleine. Mais à l'instant même où la gorgée mêlée des miettes du gâteau toucha mon palais, 10 je tressaillis, attentif à ce qui se passait d'extraordinaire en moi. Un plaisir délicieux m'avait envahi, isolé[b], sans la notion de sa cause. Il m'avait aussitôt rendu[6] les vicissitudes de la vie indifférentes, ses désastres inoffensifs, sa brièveté illusoire, de la même façon qu'opère[7] l'amour, en me remplissant d'une essence précieuse: ou plutôt cette 15 essence n'était pas en moi, elle était moi. J'avais cessé de me sentir médiocre, contingent, mortel. D'où avait pu me venir cette puissante joie? Je sentais qu'elle était liée au goût du thé et du gâteau, mais qu'elle le dépassait infiniment[8], ne devait pas être de la même nature. D'où venait-elle? Que signifiait-elle? Où[9] l'appréhender? Je bois[10] 20 une seconde[11] gorgée où je ne trouve rien de[12] plus que la première, une troisième qui m'apporte un peu moins que la seconde. Il[13] est temps que je m'arrête, la vertu du breuvage semble diminuer. Il[14] est clair que la vérité que je cherche n'est pas en lui, mais en moi. Il l'y[15] a éveillée, mais ne la connaît pas, et ne peut que répéter indéfini- 25 ment[8], avec de moins en moins de force, ce même témoignage que je ne sais pas interpréter et que je veux au moins pouvoir[16] lui rede- mander et retrouver intact, à ma disposition, tout à l'heure, pour un éclaircissement décisif. Je pose la tasse et me tourne vers mon esprit. C'est à lui de trouver la vérité. Mais comment? 30

A la Recherche du temps perdu
(Extrait)

© *Éditions Gallimard*

---

[a] grooved mold of a patty-shell of the type used to serve creamed shell-fish
[b] (had) isolated (me from the outside world)

NOTES AND QUESTIONS

1. When a form of the verb **faire** is followed by the infinitive, it constitutes a special construction. What is this construction called? What is the meaning of **me faire prendre un peu de thé?** What kind of object is **me?** If you are not sure of this construction, see pages 193–195.

2. What is the difference in meaning of **un peu de thé** and **peu de thé?** If you are not sure, see page 124.

3. What part of the verb is **appelés?** Notice that here it is partly an adjective, partly a verb. It is an adjective in that it modifies **gâteaux** and agrees with it in gender and number; it is a verb in that it indicates action and is followed by a complement just as any other form of the verb **appeler** could be. Likewise, **accablé** refers to **je** and is followed by a phrase introduced by **par.**

4. What stylistic effect is attained by placing the adjective before its noun in **la morne journée** and **un triste lendemain?**

5. Normally, one would expect **une cuillerée de thé.** Why in this case do we find **une cuillerée du thé?** Note that at the end of the sentence we find the more usual construction **un morceau de madeleine.**

6. What is the meaning of the verb **rendre** in the expression **Il m'avait aussitôt rendu les vicissitudes de la vie indifférentes . . .?** When do forms of **rendre** have this meaning?

7. Notice that in the clause **qu'opère l'amour,** the verb precedes the subject. This word order is often used in order to attain a certain balance of rhythm, which is attained by placing the verb between the relative pronoun object and the noun subject.

8. From what you observe in **infiniment** and **indéfiniment,** what can you say concerning the formation of adverbs whose adjective form ends in a vowel in the masculine singular?

9. Notice the use of the infinitive in the sentence: **Où l'appréhender?** The sentence means: *Where could it be seized?* French sometimes uses the infinitive in this way in direct questions expressing deliberation.

10. Up to this point, the author has been speaking in the past tense. Why does he now go over to the present?

11. The author uses **second** to express the English *second*. In present-day French, **second** and **deuxième** are used interchangeably.

12. Notice that an indefinite pronoun is always separated from a following modifying adjective by the preposition **de**.

13. The verb **arrête** is subjunctive in **Il est temps que je m'arrête.** Why? If you are not sure, see pages 144–145.

14. But the verb **est** is indicative in **Il est clair que la vérité . . . n'est pas en lui.** Why?

15. The combination **l'y** is a contraction of **la y**. Comment on the position of these two pronouns when they are used together. If you are not sure, see page 46, §7.

16. In the clause **je veux pouvoir lui redemander,** there are two infinitives: **redemander** is dependent on **pouvoir,** and **pouvoir** is dependent on **veux**. Why is the infinitive used after **je veux** rather than **que** + SUBJUNCTIVE? If you do not know, consult page 142.

Texte Nº 8

Jacques Prévert

Jacques Prévert est un des rares poètes d'inspiration populaire qui a connu un grand succès. Il s'attaque avec mordant à tous ceux qui, par intérêt ou par leur profession, empêchent le bonheur des hommes. Il prend contre eux le parti des humbles, des rêveurs, des amoureux, des enfants, des oiseaux, des fleurs, et chante la vie qui peut être «si jolie». Son style, bien à lui, est riche en jeux de mots, énumérations fantaisistes, associations d'idées bizarres et images neuves.

Ce poème est un sujet philosophique traité avec humour. Il y a, sans doute, de tristes choses dans la vie; il faut y faire face mais ne pas s'abandonner aux idées noires, car la vie est là, ensoleillée aussi, qui nous invite et par laquelle il est bon de se laisser griser un peu.

Chanson des escargots qui vont à l'enterrement

A l'enterrement d'une feuille morte
Deux escargots s'en vont[1, 2]
Ils ont la[3] coquille noire
Du crêpe autour des cornes
5   Ils s'en vont dans le noir
Un très beau soir d'automne[4]
Hélas quand ils arrivent
C'est déjà le printemps[5]
Les feuilles qui étaient mortes[6]
10   Sont toutes ressuscitées
Et les deux escargots
Sont très désappointés
Mais voilà[7] le soleil
Le soleil qui leur dit
15   Prenez prenez la peine
La peine de vous asseoir
Prenez un verre de[8] bière
Si le cœur vous en[9] dit
Prenez si ça[10] vous plaît
20   L'autocar pour Paris
Il partira ce soir
Vous[a] verrez du pays
Mais ne prenez pas le deuil
C'est[b] moi[11] qui vous le dis[11]
25   Ça noircit le blanc de l'œil
Et puis ça enlaidit
Les histoires de cercueils
C'est[12] triste et pas joli
Reprenez vos couleurs
30   Les couleurs de la vie

---

[a] *You will see places*   [b] *I am the one who is telling you*

Alors toutes les bêtes
Les arbres et les plantes
Se mettent à chanter
A chanter à tue-tête
La vraie chanson vivante[13]   35
La chanson de l'été
Et[c] tout le monde de boire
Tout le monde de trinquer
C'est[14] un très joli soir
Un joli soir d'été   40
Et les deux escargots
S'en retournent chez eux
Ils s'en vont très émus
Ils s'en vont très heureux
Comme ils ont beaucoup[15] bu   45
Ils titubent un p'tit peu
Mais là-haut dans le ciel
La lune veille sur eux.

Paroles

© *Éditions Gallimard*

NOTES AND QUESTIONS

1. Notice that the author has not punctuated his poem. The unpunctuated verse gives a certain stylistic effect.

2. The form **s'en vont** comes from the verb **s'en aller,** meaning *to go away* or *to go off*. This verb is normally used without any designation of place.

3. How would you say **Ils ont la coquille noire** in English? French uses a different type of sentence. If you are not sure, see page 77, §9.

4. In the expression **soir d'automne,** what function does **de** + NOUN perform? How would we express this idea in English?

5. Explain the use of the definite article with **printemps.**

6. The combination **étaient mortes** might be expressed in two different ways in English. What are they? Analyze each one grammatically.

---

[c] *And everybody starts drinking, everybody starts clinking glasses*

7. The word **voilà** is really **vois là** and is equivalent to the English *there is* used to point out.

8. Notice the use of **de** + NOUN in **verre de bière.** This usage is general, e.g., **tasse de café,** etc.

9. What is the relative position of **en** in reference to other object pronouns?

10. What kind of pronoun is **ça?** To what does it refer? When is it used rather than **cela?**

11. What is the use of the disjunctive pronoun **moi** here? And why is the form **dis** used rather than **dit?**

12. What type of **ce** is this?

13. Here is a word in **-ant.** Is it a present participle? What about its agreement? If you do not know, consult page 64.

14. What kind of **ce** is this? Under what conditions is it used?

15. What is the position of most adverbs not ending in **-ment** when used in clauses with compound tenses?

Verbs

The Organization of the French Verb

To be able to use the French verb adequately, you must know the forms of the present, imperfect, future and compound past of the indicative, the conditional, and the present and past subjunctive of each type of regular verb and of the common irregular verbs. To have a complete picture of the verb, you should also know the other compound tenses, the simple past, and the imperfect subjunctive of these verbs.

Regular verbs may be classified as follows:

1. **-er** verbs
2. **-ir** verbs which insert **-iss-** in the plural of the present, throughout the imperfect, and in the present subjunctive
3. **-ir** verbs which do not insert **-iss-** anywhere
4. **-re** verbs

In addition to these, you should know the forms of verbs in **-cevoir**, such as **recevoir**, verbs in **-aindre** and **-eindre**, such as **craindre** and **peindre**, verbs with past participles in **-ert**, such as **ouvrir**, and the following frequently used irregular verbs:

aller	être	rire
avoir	faire	savoir
boire	falloir	suivre
courir	lire	tenir
croire	mettre	valoir
devoir	mourir	venir
dire	pouvoir	vivre
écrire	prendre	voir
envoyer		vouloir

Once you know the forms of an irregular verb such as **prendre,** you can also handle its compounds, such as **apprendre** and **comprendre.**

Regular verbs are formed on the verb stem which is found by taking the infinitive ending from the infinitive:

INFINITIVE	STEM
1. **donn**-er	**donn-**
2. **fin**-ir	**fin-**
3. **dorm**-ir	**dorm-**
4. **perd**-re	**perd-**

281

Both types of **-ir** verbs have peculiarities.

Verbs of the type of **finir** insert an **-iss-** between the stem and the ending in the present participle, the plural forms of the present indicative, throughout the imperfect indicative, and in the present subjunctive.

Verbs of the type of **dormir** drop the last consonant of the stem before adding the endings in the singular of the present indicative.

Irregular verbs are formed on several stems.

In order to get a complete picture of the verb and thus facilitate learning it, it is helpful to know the five principal parts of the verb and also to know which tenses are formed from each of these principal parts.

Below are the five principal parts of the regular verbs and of some of the irregular verbs. The stems are in boldface type.

INFINITIVE	PRESENT PARTICIPLE	PAST PARTICIPLE	PRESENT *(singular)*	SIMPLE PAST *(singular)*
donner	**donn**ant	**donn**é	je **donne**	je **donne**
finir	**finiss**ant	**fini**	je **finis**	je **finis**
dormir	**dorm**ant	**dorm**i	je **dors**	je **dormis**
perdre	**perd**ant	**perd**u	je **perds**	je **perdis**
recevoir	**recev**ant	**reç**u	je **reçois**	je **reçus**
craindre	**craign**ant	**craint**	je **crains**	je **craignis**
ouvrir	**ouvr**ant	**ouvert**	j'**ouvre**	j'**ouvris**
boire	**buv**ant	**bu**	je **bois**	je **bus**
écrire	**écriv**ant	**écrit**	j'**écris**	j'**écrivis**
faire	**fais**ant	**fait**	je **fais**	je **fis**
venir	**ven**ant	**venu**	je **viens**	je **vins**

There follows a list of the five principal parts of the verb along with the tenses derived from each principal part:

INFINITIVE	PRESENT PARTICIPLE	PAST PARTICIPLE	PRESENT	SIMPLE PAST
future	plural of	compound past	singular of	simple past
conditional	present imperfect indicative present subjunctive	pluperfect indicative future perfect past conditional past anterior «passé surcomposé» past subjunctive pluperfect subjunctive	present	imperfect subjunctive

Here is the conjugation of the verb **boire** with the tenses arranged under the principal part from which each is derived.

INFINITIVE	PRESENT PARTICIPLE	PAST PARTICIPLE	PRESENT INDICATIVE	SIMPLE PAST
boire	**buvant**	**bu**	je **bois**	je **bus**
			tu bois	tu bus
	PLURAL OF PRESENT INDICATIVE	COMPOUND PAST INDICATIVE	il boit	il but
FUTURE				nous bûmes
je boirai	nous buvons	j'ai bu, etc.		vous bûtes
tu boiras	vous buvez			ils burent
il boira	ils boivent			
nous boirons		PLUPERFECT INDICATIVE		IMPERFECT SUBJUNCTIVE
vous boirez		j'avais bu, etc.		que je busse
ils boiront	IMPERFECT INDICATIVE			que tu busses
	je buvais			qu'il bût
CONDITIONAL	tu buvais	FUTURE PERFECT		que nous bussions
je boirais	il buvait	j'aurai bu, etc.		que vous bussiez
tu boirais	nous buvions			qu'ils bussent
il boirait	vous buviez	PAST CONDITIONAL		
nous boirions	ils buvaient	j'aurais bu, etc.		
vous boiriez				
ils boiraient		PAST ANTERIOR		
	PRESENT SUBJUNCTIVE	j'eus bu, etc.		
	que je boive			
	que tu boives	PASSÉ SURCOMPOSÉ		
	qu'il boive	j'ai eu bu, etc.		
	que nous buvions			
	que vous buviez	PAST SUBJUNCTIVE		
	qu'ils boivent	que j'aie bu, etc.		
		PLUPERFECT SUBJUNCTIVE		
		que j'eusse bu, etc.		

The regular and the common irregular verbs are conjugated by tenses on pages 284–301. This is practical for easy reference, but the verbs will be easier to learn if you rearrange them by stems as shown in the above conjugation of the verb **boire.**

At the end of each lesson are two verbs to be reviewed. If your instructor directs you to do so, learn to write each tense under the proper principal part as above. To find the forms you do not know, consult pages 284–301.

The conjugation of the verb

INFINITIVE AND PARTICIPLES	INDICATIVE			
	PRESENT	IMPERFECT	SIMPLE PAST	FUTURE
1. **-er** *verbs* **parler** (*speak*) parlant parlé	parle parles parle parlons parlez parlent	parlais parlais parlait parlions parliez parlaient	parlai parlas parla parlâmes parlâtes parlèrent	parlerai parleras parlera parlerons parlerez parleront
	COMPOUND PAST	PLUPERFECT	PAST ANTERIOR	FUTURE PERFECT
	ai parlé as parlé a parlé avons parlé avez parlé ont parlé	avais parlé avais parlé avait parlé avions parlé aviez parlé avaient parlé	eus parlé eus parlé eut parlé eûmes parlé eûtes parlé eurent parlé	aurai parlé auras parlé aura parlé aurons parlé aurez parlé auront parlé
	PRESENT	IMPERFECT	SIMPLE PAST	FUTURE
2. **-ir** *verbs* **finir** (*finish*) finissant fini	finis finis finit finissons finissez finissent	finissais finissais finissait finissions finissiez finissaient	finis finis finit finîmes finîtes finirent	finirai finiras finira finirons finirez finiront
	COMPOUND PAST	PLUPERFECT	PAST ANTERIOR	FUTURE PERFECT
	ai fini as fini a fini avons fini avez fini ont fini	avais fini avais fini avait fini avions fini aviez fini avaient fini	eus fini eus fini eut fini eûmes fini eûtes fini eurent fini	aurai fini auras fini aura fini aurons fini aurez fini auront fini
	PRESENT	IMPERFECT	SIMPLE PAST	FUTURE
3. **-re** *verbs* **perdre** (*lose*) perdant perdu	perds perds perd perdons perdez perdent	perdais perdais perdait perdions perdiez perdaient	perdis perdis perdit perdîmes perdîtes perdirent	perdrai perdras perdra perdrons perdrez perdront
	COMPOUND PAST	PLUPERFECT	PAST ANTERIOR	FUTURE PERFECT
	ai perdu as perdu a perdu avons perdu avez perdu ont perdu	avais perdu avais perdu avait perdu avions perdu aviez perdu avaient perdu	eus perdu eus perdu eut perdu eûmes perdu eûtes perdu eurent perdu	aurai perdu auras perdu aura perdu aurons perdu aurez perdu auront perdu

La conjugaison du verbe

CONDITIONAL	IMPERATIVE	SUBJUNCTIVE	
PRESENT CONDITIONAL		**PRESENT**	**IMPERFECT**
parlerais		parle	parlasse
parlerais	parle	parles	parlasses
parlerait		parle	parlât
parlerions	parlons	parlions	parlassions
parleriez	parlez	parliez	parlassiez
parleraient		parlent	parlassent
PAST CONDITIONAL		**PAST**	**PLUPERFECT**
aurais parlé		aie parlé	eusse parlé
aurais parlé		aies parlé	eusses parlé
aurait parlé		ait parlé	eût parlé
aurions parlé		ayons parlé	eussions parlé
auriez parlé		ayez parlé	eussiez parlé
auraient parlé		aient parlé	eussent parlé
PRESENT CONDITIONAL		**PRESENT**	**IMPERFECT**
finirais		finisse	finisse
finirais	finis	finisses	finisses
finirait		finisse	finît
finirions	finissons	finissions	finissions
finiriez	finissez	finissiez	finissiez
finiraient		finissent	finissent
PAST CONDITIONAL		**PAST**	**PLUPERFECT**
aurais fini		aie fini	eusse fini
aurais fini		aies fini	eusses fini
aurait fini		ait fini	eût fini
aurions fini		ayons fini	eussions fini
auriez fini		ayez fini	eussiez fini
auraient fini		aient fini	eussent fini
PRESENT CONDITIONAL		**PRESENT**	**IMPERFECT**
perdrais		perde	perdisse
perdrais	perds	perdes	perdisses
perdrait		perde	perdît
perdrions	perdons	perdions	perdissions
perdriez	perdez	perdiez	perdissiez
perdraient		perdent	perdissent
PAST CONDITIONAL		**PAST**	**PLUPERFECT**
aurais perdu		aie perdu	eusse perdu
aurais perdu		aies perdu	eusses perdu
aurait perdu		ait perdu	eût perdu
aurions perdu		ayons perdu	eussions perdu
auriez perdu		ayez perdu	eussiez perdu
auraient perdu		aient perdu	eussent perdu

The conjugation of the verb

INFINITIVE AND PARTICIPLES	INDICATIVE			
	PRESENT	IMPERFECT	SIMPLE PAST	FUTURE
4. **2d** *class*	dors	dormais	dormis	dormirai
-ir *verbs*	dors	dormais	dormis	dormiras
dormir	dort	dormait	dormit	dormira
(*sleep*)	dormons	dormions	dormîmes	dormirons
dormant	dormez	dormiez	dormîtes	dormirez
dormi	dorment	dormaient	dormirent	dormiront
	COMPOUND PAST	PLUPERFECT	PAST ANTERIOR	FUTURE PERFECT
	ai dormi	avais dormi	eus dormi	aurai dormi
	as dormi	avais dormi	eus dormi	auras dormi
	a dormi	avait dormi	eut dormi	aura dormi
	avons dormi	avions dormi	eûmes dormi	aurons dormi
	avez dormi	aviez dormi	eûtes dormi	aurez dormi
	ont dormi	avaient dormi	eurent dormi	auront dormi
	PRESENT	IMPERFECT	SIMPLE PAST	FUTURE
5. **-oir** *verbs*	reçois	recevais	reçus	recevrai
recevoir	reçois	recevais	reçus	recevras
(*receive*)	reçoit	recevait	reçut	recevra
recevant	recevons	recevions	reçûmes	recevrons
reçu	recevez	receviez	reçûtes	recevrez
	reçoivent	recevaient	reçurent	recevront
	COMPOUND PAST	PLUPERFECT	PAST ANTERIOR	FUTURE PERFECT
	ai reçu	avais reçu	eus reçu	aurai reçu
	as reçu	avais reçu	eus reçu	auras reçu
	a reçu	avait reçu	eut reçu	aura reçu
	avons reçu	avions reçu	eûmes reçu	aurons reçu
	avez reçu	aviez reçu	eûtes reçu	aurez reçu
	ont reçu	avaient reçu	eurent reçu	auront reçu
	PRESENT	IMPERFECT	SIMPLE PAST	FUTURE
6. *Intransitive verb*	entre	entrais	entrai	entrerai
of motion	entres	entrais	entras	entreras
entrer	entre	entrait	entra	entrera
(*enter*)	entrons	entrions	entrâmes	entrerons
entrant	entrez	entriez	entrâtes	entrerez
entré	entrent	entraient	entrèrent	entreront
	COMPOUND PAST	PLUPERFECT	PAST ANTERIOR	FUTURE PERFECT
	suis entré(e)	étais entré(e)	fus entré(e)	serai entré(e)
	es entré(e)	étais entré(e)	fus entré(e)	seras entré(e)
	est entré(e)	était entré(e)	fut entré(e)	sera entré(e)
	sommes entré(e)s	étions entré(e)s	fûmes entré(e)s	serons entré(e)s
	êtes entré(e)(s)	étiez entré(e)(s)	fûtes entré(e)(s)	serez entré(e)(s)
	sont entré(e)s	étaient entré(e)s	furent entré(e)s	seront entré(e)s

La conjugaison du verbe

CONDITIONAL	IMPERATIVE	SUBJUNCTIVE	

PRESENT CONDITIONAL		PRESENT	IMPERFECT
dormirais		dorme	dormisse
dormirais	dors	dormes	dormisses
dormirait		dorme	dormît
dormirions	dormons	dormions	dormissions
dormiriez	dormez	dormiez	dormissiez
dormiraient		dorment	dormissent

PAST CONDITIONAL		PAST		PLUPERFECT	
aurais	dormi	aie	dormi	eusse	dormi
aurais	dormi	aies	dormi	eusses	dormi
aurait	dormi	ait	dormi	eût	dormi
aurions	dormi	ayons	dormi	eussions	dormi
auriez	dormi	ayez	dormi	eussiez	dormi
auraient	dormi	aient	dormi	eussent	dormi

PRESENT CONDITIONAL		PRESENT	IMPERFECT
recevrais		reçoive	reçusse
recevrais	reçois	reçoives	reçusses
recevrait		reçoive	reçût
recevrions	recevons	recevions	reçussions
recevriez	recevez	receviez	reçussiez
recevraient		reçoivent	reçussent

PAST CONDITIONAL		PAST		PLUPERFECT	
aurais	reçu	aie	reçu	eusse	reçu
aurais	reçu	aies	reçu	eusses	reçu
aurait	reçu	ait	reçu	eût	reçu
aurions	reçu	ayons	reçu	eussions	reçu
auriez	reçu	ayez	reçu	eussiez	reçu
auraient	reçu	aient	reçu	eussent	reçu

PRESENT CONDITIONAL		PRESENT	IMPERFECT
entrerais		entre	entrasse
entrerais	entre	entres	entrasses
entrerait		entre	entrât
entrerions	entrons	entrions	entrassions
entreriez	entrez	entriez	entrassiez
entreraient		entrent	entrassent

PAST CONDITIONAL		PAST		PLUPERFECT	
serais	entré(e)	sois	entré(e)	fusse	entré(e)
serais	entré(e)	sois	entré(e)	fusses	entré(e)
serait	entré(e)	soit	entré(e)	fût	entré(e)
serions	entré(e)s	soyons	entré(e)s	fussions	entré(e)s
seriez	entré(e)(s)	soyez	entré(e)(s)	fussiez	entré(e)(s)
seraient	entré(e)s	soient	entré(e)s	fussent	entré(e)s

The conjugation of the verb

INFINITIVE AND PARTICIPLES	INDICATIVE			
	PRESENT	IMPERFECT	SIMPLE PAST	FUTURE
7. *Reflexive verb*	me lave	me lavais	me lavai	me laverai
	te laves	te lavais	te lavas	te laveras
	se lave	se lavait	se lava	se lavera
se laver	nous lavons	nous lavions	nous lavâmes	nous laverons
(wash	vous lavez	vous laviez	vous lavâtes	vous laverez
oneself)	se lavent	se lavaient	se lavèrent	se laveront
se lavant				
lavé	COMPOUND PAST	PLUPERFECT	PAST ANTERIOR	FUTURE PERFECT
	me suis lavé(e)	m'étais lavé(e)	me fus lavé(e)	me serai lavé(e)
	t'es lavé(e)	t'étais lavé(e)	te fus lavé(e)	te seras lavé(e)
	s'est lavé(e)	s'était lavé(e)	se fut lavé(e)	se sera lavé(e)
	nous	nous	nous	nous
	sommes lavé(e)s	étions lavé(e)s	fûmes lavé(e)s	serons lavé(e)s
	vous êtes lavé(e)(s)	vous étiez lavé(e)(s)	vous fûtes lavé(e)(s)	vous serez lavé(e)(s)
	se sont lavé(e)s	s'étaient lavé(e)s	se furent lavé(e)s	se seront lavé(e)s
	PRESENT	IMPERFECT	SIMPLE PAST	FUTURE
8. *Auxiliary verb*	ai	avais	eus	aurai
	as	avais	eus	auras
	a	avait	eut	aura
avoir	avons	avions	eûmes	aurons
(have)	avez	aviez	eûtes	aurez
ayant	ont	avaient	eurent	auront
eu				
	COMPOUND PAST	PLUPERFECT	PAST ANTERIOR	FUTURE PERFECT
	ai eu	avais eu	eus eu	aurai eu
	as eu	avais eu	eus eu	auras eu
	a eu	avait eu	eut eu	aura eu
	avons eu	avions eu	eûmes eu	aurons eu
	avez eu	aviez eu	eûtes eu	aurez eu
	ont eu	avaient eu	eurent eu	auront eu
	PRESENT	IMPERFECT	SIMPLE PAST	FUTURE
9. *Auxiliary verb*	suis	étais	fus	serai
	es	étais	fus	seras
	est	était	fut	sera
être	sommes	étions	fûmes	serons
(be)	êtes	étiez	fûtes	serez
étant	sont	étaient	furent	seront
été				
	COMPOUND PAST	PLUPERFECT	PAST ANTERIOR	FUTURE PERFECT
	ai été	avais été	eus été	aurai été
	as été	avais été	eus été	auras été
	a été	avait été	eut été	aura été
	avons été	avions été	eûmes été	aurons été
	avez été	aviez été	eûtes été	aurez été
	ont été	avaient été	eurent été	auront été

La conjugaison du verbe

CONDITIONAL	IMPERATIVE	SUBJUNCTIVE	

PRESENT CONDITIONAL

		PRESENT	IMPERFECT
me laverais		me lave	me lavasse
te laverais	lave-toi	te laves	te lavasses
se laverait		se lave	se lavât
nous laverions	lavons-nous	nous lavions	nous lavassions
vous laveriez	lavez-vous	vous laviez	vous lavassiez
se laveraient		se lavent	se lavassent

PAST CONDITIONAL / PAST / PLUPERFECT

		PAST	PLUPERFECT
me serais lavé(e)		me sois lavé(e)	me fusse lavé(e)
te serais lavé(e)		te sois lavé(e)	te fusses lavé(e)
se serait lavé(e)		se soit lavé(e)	se fût lavé(e)
nous serions lavé(e)s		nous soyons lavé(e)s	nous fussions lavé(e)s
vous seriez lavé(e)(s)		vous soyez lavé(e)(s)	vous fussiez lavé(e)(s)
se seraient lavé(e)s		se soient lavé(e)s	se fussent lavé(e)s

PRESENT CONDITIONAL / PRESENT / IMPERFECT

		PRESENT	IMPERFECT
aurais		aie	eusse
aurais	aie	aies	eusses
aurait		ait	eût
aurions	ayons	ayons	eussions
auriez	ayez	ayez	eussiez
auraient		aient	eussent

PAST CONDITIONAL / PAST / PLUPERFECT

		PAST	PLUPERFECT
aurais eu		aie eu	eusse eu
aurais eu		aies eu	eusses eu
aurait eu		ait eu	eût eu
aurions eu		ayons eu	eussions eu
auriez eu		ayez eu	eussiez eu
auraient eu		aient eu	eussent eu

PRESENT CONDITIONAL / PRESENT / IMPERFECT

		PRESENT	IMPERFECT
serais		sois	fusse
serais	sois	sois	fusses
serait		soit	fût
serions	soyons	soyons	fussions
seriez	soyez	soyez	fussiez
seraient		soient	fussent

PAST CONDITIONAL / PAST / PLUPERFECT

		PAST	PLUPERFECT
aurais été		aie été	eusse été
aurais été		aies été	eusses été
aurait été		ait été	eût été
aurions été		ayons été	eussions été
auriez été		ayez été	eussiez été
auraient été		aient été	eussent été

The conjugation of the verb

INFINITIVE AND PARTICIPLES	INDICATIVE			
	PRESENT	IMPERFECT	SIMPLE PAST	COMPOUND PAST
10. **acquérir** (*acquire*) acquérant acquis	acquiers acquiers acquiert acquérons acquérez acquièrent	acquérais acquérais acquérait acquérions acquériez acquéraient	acquis acquis acquit acquîmes acquîtes acquirent	ai acquis as acquis a acquis avons acquis avez acquis ont acquis
11. **aller** (*go*) allant allé	vais vas va allons allez vont	allais allais allait allions alliez allaient	allai allas alla allâmes allâtes allèrent	suis allé(e) es allé(e) est allé(e) sommes allé(e)s êtes allé(e)(s) sont allé(e)s
12. **asseoir*** (*seat*) asseyant assis	assieds assieds assied asseyons asseyez asseyent	asseyais asseyais asseyait asseyions asseyiez asseyaient	assis assis assit assîmes assîtes assirent	me suis assis(e)* t'es assis(e) s'est assis(e) nous sommes assis(es) vous êtes assis(e)(s) se sont assis(es)
assoyant	assois assois assoit assoyons assoyez assoient	assoyais assoyais assoyait assoyions assoyiez assoyaient		
13. **battre** (*beat*) battant battu	bats bats bat battons battez battent	battais battais battait battions battiez battaient	battis battis battit battîmes battîtes battirent	ai battu as battu a battu avons battu avez battu ont battu
14. **boire** (*drink*) buvant bu	bois bois boit buvons buvez boivent	buvais buvais buvait buvions buviez buvaient	bus bus but bûmes bûtes burent	ai bu as bu a bu avons bu avez bu ont bu

* This verb is usually used in its reflexive form **s'asseoir** (*to sit*). For this reason, the reflexive forms of the compound past and imperative are given.
Certain tenses of this verb have two forms.

La conjugaison du verbe

FUTURE	CONDITIONAL	IMPERATIVE	SUBJUNCTIVE PRESENT	IMPERFECT
acquerrai	acquerrais		acquière	acquisse
acquerras	acquerrais	acquiers	acquières	acquisses
acquerra	acquerrait		acquière	acquît
acquerrons	acquerrions	acquérons	acquérions	acquissions
acquerrez	acquerriez	acquérez	acquériez	acquissiez
acquerront	acquerraient		acquièrent	acquissent
irai	irais		aille	allasse
iras	irais	va	ailles	allasses
ira	irait		aille	allât
irons	irions	allons	allions	allassions
irez	iriez	allez	alliez	allassiez
iront	iraient		aillent	allassent
assiérai	assiérais		asseye	assisse
assiéras	assiérais	assieds-toi*	asseyes	assisses
assiéra	assiérait		asseye	assît
assiérons	assiérions	asseyons-nous	asseyions	assissions
assiérez	assiériez	asseyez-vous	asseyiez	assissiez
assiéront	assiéraient		asseyent	assissent
assoirai	assoirais		assoie	
assoiras	assoirais	assois-toi	assoies	
assoira	assoirait		assoie	
assoirons	assoirions	assoyons-nous	assoyions	
assoirez	assoiriez	assoyez-vous	assoyiez	
assoiront	assoiraient		assoient	
battrai	battrais		batte	battisse
battras	battrais	bats	battes	battisses
battra	battrait		batte	battît
battrons	battrions	battons	battions	battissions
battrez	battriez	battez	battiez	battissiez
battront	battraient		battent	battissent
boirai	boirais		boive	busse
boiras	boirais	bois	boives	busses
boira	boirait		boive	bût
boirons	boirions	buvons	buvions	bussions
boirez	boiriez	buvez	buviez	bussiez
boiront	boiraient		boivent	bussent

* This verb is usually used in its reflexive form **s'asseoir** (*to sit*). For this reason, the reflexive forms of the compound past and imperative are given.

The conjugation of the verb

INFINITIVE AND PARTICIPLES	INDICATIVE			
	PRESENT	IMPERFECT	SIMPLE PAST	COMPOUND PAST
15. **conduire** (*lead*) conduisant conduit	conduis conduis conduit conduisons conduisez conduisent	conduisais conduisais conduisait conduisions conduisiez conduisaient	conduisis conduisis conduisit conduisîmes conduisîtes conduisirent	ai conduit as conduit a conduit avons conduit avez conduit ont conduit
16. **connaître** (*be acquainted*) connaissant connu	connais connais connaît connaissons connaissez connaissent	connaissais connaissais connaissait connaissions connaissiez connaissaient	connus connus connut connûmes connûtes connurent	ai connu as connu a connu avons connu avez connu ont connu
17. **courir** (*run*) courant couru	cours cours court courons courez courent	courais courais courait courions couriez couraient	courus courus courut courûmes courûtes coururent	ai couru as couru a couru avons couru avez couru ont couru
18. **craindre** (*fear*) craignant craint	crains crains craint craignons craignez craignent	craignais craignais craignait craignions craigniez craignaient	craignis craignis craignit craignîmes craignîtes craignirent	ai craint as craint a craint avons craint avez craint ont craint
19. **croire** (*believe*) croyant cru	crois crois croit croyons croyez croient	croyais croyais croyait croyions croyiez croyaient	crus crus crut crûmes crûtes crurent	ai cru as cru a cru avons cru avez cru ont cru
20. **devoir** (*owe, have to*) devant dû, due*	dois dois doit devons devez doivent	devais devais devait devions deviez devaient	dus dus dut dûmes dûtes durent	ai dû as dû a dû avons dû avez dû ont dû

* The masculine singular form of the past participle is written with the circumflex accent to distinguish it from the word **du**. All other forms are written without the accent (**dû, due, dus, dues**).

La conjugaison du verbe

FUTURE	CONDITIONAL	IMPERATIVE	SUBJUNCTIVE PRESENT	IMPERFECT
conduirai	conduirais		conduise	conduisisse
conduiras	conduirais	conduis	conduises	conduisisses
conduira	conduirait		conduise	conduisît
conduirons	conduirions	conduisons	conduisions	conduisissions
conduirez	conduiriez	conduisez	conduisiez	conduisissiez
conduiront	conduiraient		conduisent	conduisissent
connaîtrai	connaîtrais		connaisse	connusse
connaîtras	connaîtrais	connais	connaisses	connusses
connaîtra	connaîtrait		connaisse	connût
connaîtrons	connaîtrions	connaissons	connaissions	connussions
connaîtrez	connaîtriez	connaissez	connaissiez	connussiez
connaîtront	connaîtraient		connaissent	connussent
courrai	courrais		coure	courusse
courras	courrais	cours	coures	courusses
courra	courrait		coure	courût
courrons	courrions	courons	courions	courussions
courrez	courriez	courez	couriez	courussiez
courront	courraient		courent	courussent
craindrai	craindrais		craigne	craignisse
craindras	craindrais	crains	craignes	craignisses
craindra	craindrait		craigne	craignît
craindrons	craindrions	craignons	craignions	craignissions
craindrez	craindriez	craignez	craigniez	craignissiez
craindront	craindraient		craignent	craignissent
croirai	croirais		croie	crusse
croiras	croirais	crois	croies	crusses
croira	croirait		croie	crût
croirons	croirions	croyons	croyions	crussions
croirez	croiriez	croyez	croyiez	crussiez
croiront	croiraient		croient	crussent
devrai	devrais		doive	dusse
devras	devrais	dois	doives	dusses
devra	devrait		doive	dût
devrons	devrions	devons	devions	dussions
devrez	devriez	devez	deviez	dussiez
devront	devraient		doivent	dussent

The conjugation of the verb

INFINITIVE AND PARTICIPLES	INDICATIVE			
	PRESENT	IMPERFECT	SIMPLE PAST	COMPOUND PAST
21. dire (*say, tell*) disant dit	dis dis dit disons dites disent	disais disais disait disions disiez disaient	dis dis dit dîmes dîtes dirent	ai dit as dit a dit avons dit avez dit ont dit
22. écrire (*write*) écrivant écrit	écris écris écrit écrivons écrivez écrivent	écrivais écrivais écrivait écrivions écriviez écrivaient	écrivis écrivis écrivit écrivîmes écrivîtes écrivirent	ai écrit as écrit a écrit avons écrit avez écrit ont écrit
23. envoyer (*send*) envoyant envoyé	envoie envoies envoie envoyons envoyez envoient	envoyais envoyais envoyait envoyions envoyiez envoyaient	envoyai envoyas envoya envoyâmes envoyâtes envoyèrent	ai envoyé as envoyé a envoyé avons envoyé avez envoyé ont envoyé
24. faire (*do, make*) faisant* fait	fais fais fait faisons faites font	faisais* faisais faisait faisions faisiez faisaient	fis fis fit fîmes fîtes firent	ai fait as fait a fait avons fait avez fait ont fait
25. falloir** (*be necessary*) fallu	il faut	il fallait	il fallut	il a fallu
26. fuir (*flee*) fuyant fui	fuis fuis fuit fuyons fuyez fuient	fuyais fuyais fuyait fuyions fuyiez fuyaient	fuis fuis fuit fuîmes fuîtes fuirent	ai fui as fui a fui avons fui avez fui ont fui
27. lire (*read*) lisant lu	lis lis lit lisons lisez lisent	lisais lisais lisait lisions lisiez lisaient	lus lus lut lûmes lûtes lurent	ai lu as lu a lu avons lu avez lu ont lu

* The **ai** of the stem of these forms is pronounced like mute **e** [ə].
** Used in third person singular only.

La conjugaison du verbe

	CONDITIONAL	IMPERATIVE	SUBJUNCTIVE	
FUTURE			PRESENT	IMPERFECT
dirai	dirais		dise	disse
diras	dirais	dis	dises	disses
dira	dirait		dise	dît
dirons	dirions	disons	disions	dissions
direz	diriez	dites	disiez	dissiez
diront	diraient		disent	dissent
écrirai	écrirais		écrive	écrivisse
écriras	écrirais	écris	écrives	écrivisses
écrira	écrirait		écrive	écrivît
écrirons	écririons	écrivons	écrivions	écrivissions
écrirez	écririez	écrivez	écriviez	écrivissiez
écriront	écriraient		écrivent	écrivissent
enverrai	enverrais		envoie	envoyasse
enverras	enverrais	envoie	envoies	envoyasses
enverra	enverrait		envoie	envoyât
enverrons	enverrions	envoyons	envoyions	envoyassions
enverrez	enverriez	envoyez	envoyiez	envoyassiez
enverront	enverraient		envoient	envoyassent
ferai	ferais		fasse	fisse
feras	ferais	fais	fasses	fisses
fera	ferait		fasse	fît
ferons	ferions	faisons	fassions	fissions
ferez	feriez	faites	fassiez	fissiez
feront	feraient		fassent	fissent
il faudra	il faudrait		il faille	il fallût
fuirai	fuirais		fuie	fuisse
fuiras	fuirais	fuis	fuies	fuisses
fuira	fuirait		fuie	fuît
fuirons	fuirions	fuyons	fuyions	fuissions
fuirez	fuiriez	fuyez	fuyiez	fuissiez
fuiront	fuiraient		fuient	fuissent
lirai	lirais		lise	lusse
liras	lirais	lis	lises	lusses
lira	lirait		lise	lût
lirons	lirions	lisons	lisions	lussions
lirez	liriez	lisez	lisiez	lussiez
liront	liraient		lisent	lussent

The conjugation of the verb

INFINITIVE AND PARTICIPLES	INDICATIVE			
	PRESENT	IMPERFECT	SIMPLE PAST	COMPOUND PAST
28. mettre (*put*) mettant mis	mets mets met mettons mettez mettent	mettais mettais mettait mettions mettiez mettaient	mis mis mit mîmes mîtes mirent	ai mis as mis a mis avons mis avez mis ont mis
29. mourir (*die*) mourant mort	meurs meurs meurt mourons mourez meurent	mourais mourais mourait mourions mouriez mouraient	mourus mourus mourut mourûmes mourûtes moururent	suis mort(e) es mort(e) est mort(e) sommes mort(e)s êtes mort(e)(s) sont mort(e)s
30. naître (*be born*) naissant né	nais nais naît naissons naissez naissent	naissais naissais naissait naissions naissiez naissaient	naquis naquis naquit naquîmes naquîtes naquirent	suis né(e) es né(e) est né(e) sommes né(e)s êtes né(e)(s) sont né(e)s
31. ouvrir (*open*) ouvrant ouvert	ouvre ouvres ouvre ouvrons ouvrez ouvrent	ouvrais ouvrais ouvrait ouvrions ouvriez ouvraient	ouvris ouvris ouvrit ouvrîmes ouvrîtes ouvrirent	ai ouvert as ouvert a ouvert avons ouvert avez ouvert ont ouvert
32. peindre (*paint*) peignant peint	peins peins peint peignons peignez peignent	peignais peignais peignait peignions peigniez peignaient	peignis peignis peignit peignîmes peignîtes peignirent	ai peint as peint a peint avons peint avez peint ont peint
33. plaire (*please*) plaisant plu	plais plais plaît plaisons plaisez plaisent	plaisais plaisais plaisait plaisions plaisiez plaisaient	plus plus plut plûmes plûtes plurent	ai plu as plu a plu avons plu avez plu ont plu
34. pleuvoir* (*rain*) pleuvant plu	il pleut	il pleuvait	il plut	il a plu

* Used only in third person singular.

La conjugaison du verbe

	CONDITIONAL	IMPERATIVE	SUBJUNCTIVE	
FUTURE			PRESENT	IMPERFECT
mettrai	mettrais		mette	misse
mettras	mettrais	mets	mettes	misses
mettra	mettrait		mette	mît
mettrons	mettrions	mettons	mettions	missions
mettrez	mettriez	mettez	mettiez	missiez
mettront	mettraient		mettent	missent
mourrai	mourrais		meure	mourusse
mourras	mourrais	meurs	meures	mourusses
mourra	mourrait		meure	mourût
mourrons	mourrions	mourons	mourions	mourussions
mourrez	mourriez	mourez	mouriez	mourussiez
mourront	mourraient		meurent	mourussent
naîtrai	naîtrais		naisse	naquisse
naîtras	naîtrais	nais	naisses	naquisses
naîtra	naîtrait		naisse	naquît
naîtrons	naîtrions	naissons	naissions	naquissions
naîtrez	naîtriez	naissez	naissiez	naquissiez
naîtront	naîtraient		naissent	naquissent
ouvrirai	ouvrirais		ouvre	ouvrisse
ouvriras	ouvrirais	ouvre	ouvres	ouvrisses
ouvrira	ouvrirait		ouvre	ouvrît
ouvrirons	ouvririons	ouvrons	ouvrions	ouvrissions
ouvrirez	ouvririez	ouvrez	ouvriez	ouvrissiez
ouvriront	ouvriraient		ouvrent	ouvrissent
peindrai	peindrais		peigne	peignisse
peindras	peindrais	peins	peignes	peignisses
peindra	peindrait		peigne	peignît
peindrons	peindrions	peignons	peignions	peignissions
peindrez	peindriez	peignez	peigniez	peignissiez
peindront	peindraient		peignent	peignissent
plairai	plairais		plaise	plusse
plairas	plairais	plais	plaises	plusses
plaira	plairait		plaise	plût
plairons	plairions	plaisons	plaisions	plussions
plairez	plairiez	plaisez	plaisiez	plussiez
plairont	plairaient		plaisent	plussent
il pleuvra	il pleuvrait		il pleuve	il plût

The conjugation of the verb

INFINITIVE AND PARTICIPLES	INDICATIVE			
	PRESENT	IMPERFECT	SIMPLE PAST	COMPOUND PAST
35. **pouvoir** (*be able*) pouvant pu	peux, puis peux peut pouvons pouvez peuvent	pouvais pouvais pouvait pouvions pouviez pouvaient	pus pus put pûmes pûtes purent	ai pu as pu a pu avons pu avez pu ont pu
36. **prendre** (*take*) prenant pris	prends prends prend prenons prenez prennent	prenais prenais prenait prenions preniez prenaient	pris pris prit prîmes prîtes prirent	ai pris as pris a pris avons pris avez pris ont pris
37. **rire** (*laugh*) riant ri	ris ris rit rions riez rient	riais riais riait riions riiez riaient	ris ris rit rîmes rîtes rirent	ai ri as ri a ri avons ri avez ri ont ri
38. **savoir** (*know*) sachant su	sais sais sait savons savez savent	savais savais savait savions saviez savaient	sus sus sut sûmes sûtes surent	ai su as su a su avons su avez su ont su
39. **suivre** (*follow*) suivant suivi	suis suis suit suivons suivez suivent	suivais suivais suivait suivions suiviez suivaient	suivis suivis suivit suivîmes suivîtes suivirent	ai suivi as suivi a suivi avons suivi avez suivi ont suivi
40. **tenir** (*hold, keep*) tenant tenu	tiens tiens tient tenons tenez tiennent	tenais tenais tenait tenions teniez tenaient	tins tins tint tînmes tîntes tinrent	ai tenu as tenu a tenu avons tenu avez tenu ont tenu

La conjugaison du verbe

	CONDITIONAL	IMPERATIVE	SUBJUNCTIVE	
FUTURE			PRESENT	IMPERFECT
pourrai	pourrais		puisse	pusse
pourras	pourrais		puisses	pusses
pourra	pourrait		puisse	pût
pourrons	pourrions		puissions	pussions
pourrez	pourriez		puissiez	pussiez
pourront	pourraient		puissent	pussent
prendrai	prendrais		prenne	prisse
prendras	prendrais	prends	prennes	prisses
prendra	prendrait		prenne	prît
prendrons	prendrions	prenons	prenions	prissions
prendrez	prendriez	prenez	preniez	prissiez
prendront	prendraient		prennent	prissent
rirai	rirais		rie	risse
riras	rirais	ris	ries	risses
rira	rirait		rie	rît
rirons	ririons	rions	riions	rissions
rirez	ririez	riez	riiez	rissiez
riront	riraient		rient	rissent
saurai	saurais		sache	susse
sauras	saurais	sache	saches	susses
saura	saurait		sache	sût
saurons	saurions	sachons	sachions	sussions
saurez	sauriez	sachez	sachiez	sussiez
sauront	sauraient		sachent	sussent
suivrai	suivrais		suive	suivisse
suivras	suivrais	suis	suives	suivisses
suivra	suivrait		suive	suivît
suivrons	suivrions	suivons	suivions	suivissions
suivrez	suivriez	suivez	suiviez	suivissiez
suivront	suivraient		suivent	suivissent
tiendrai	tiendrais		tienne	tinsse
tiendras	tiendrais	tiens	tiennes	tinsses
tiendra	tiendrait		tienne	tînt
tiendrons	tiendrions	tenons	tenions	tinssions
tiendrez	tiendriez	tenez	teniez	tinssiez
tiendront	tiendraient		tiennent	tinssent

The conjugation of the verb

INFINITIVE AND PARTICIPLES	INDICATIVE			
	PRESENT	IMPERFECT	SIMPLE PAST	COMPOUND PAST
41. **vaincre** (*conquer*) vainquant vaincu	vaincs vaincs vainc vainquons vainquez vainquent	vainquais vainquais vainquait vainquions vainquiez vainquaient	vainquis vainquis vainquit vainquîmes vainquîtes vainquirent	ai vanicu as vaincu a vaincu avons vaincu avez vaincu ont vaincu
42. **valoir** (*be worth*) valant valu	vaux vaux vaut valons valez valent	valais valais valait valions valiez valaient	valus valus valut valûmes valûtes valurent	ai valu as valu a valu avons valu avez valu ont valu
43. **venir** (*come*) venant venu	viens viens vient venons venez viennent	venais venais venait venions veniez venaient	vins vins vint vînmes vîntes vinrent	suis venu(e) es venu(e) est venu(e) sommes venu(e)s êtes venu(e)(s) sont venu(e)s
44. **vivre** (*live*) vivant vécu	vis vis vit vivons vivez vivent	vivais vivais vivait vivions viviez vivaient	vécus vécus vécut vécûmes vécûtes vécurent	ai vécu as vécu a vécu avons vécu avez vécu ont vécu
45. **voir** (*see*) voyant vu	vois vois voit voyons voyez voient	voyais voyais voyait voyions voyiez voyaient	vis vis vit vîmes vîtes virent	ai vu as vu a vu avons vu avez vu ont vu
46. **vouloir** (*wish, want*) voulant voulu	veux veux veut voulons voulez veulent	voulais voulais voulait voulions vouliez voulaient	voulus voulus voulut voulûmes voulûtes voulurent	ai voulu as voulu a voulu avons voulu avez voulu ont voulu

La conjugaison du verbe

	CONDITIONAL	IMPERATIVE	SUBJUNCTIVE	
FUTURE			PRESENT	IMPERFECT
vaincrai	vaincrais		vainque	vainquisse
vaincras	vaincrais	vaincs	vainques	vainquisses
vaincra	vaincrait		vainque	vainquît
vaincrons	vaincrions	vainquons	vainquions	vainquissions
vaincrez	vaincriez	vainquez	vainquiez	vainquissiez
vaincront	vaincraient		vainquent	vainquissent
vaudrai	vaudrais		vaille	valusse
vaudras	vaudrais	vaux	vailles	valusses
vaudra	vaudrait		vaille	valût
vaudrons	vaudrions	valons	valions	valussions
vaudrez	vaudriez	valez	valiez	valussiez
vaudront	vaudraient		vaillent	valussent
viendrai	viendrais		vienne	vinsse
viendras	viendrais	viens	viennes	vinsses
viendra	viendrait		vienne	vînt
viendrons	viendrions	venons	venions	vinssions
viendrez	viendriez	venez	veniez	vinssiez
viendront	viendraient		viennent	vinssent
vivrai	vivrais		vive	vécusse
vivras	vivrais	vis	vives	vécusses
vivra	vivrait		vive	vécût
vivrons	vivrions	vivons	vivions	vécussions
vivrez	vivriez	vivez	viviez	vécussiez
vivront	vivraient		vivent	vécussent
verrai	verrais		voie	visse
verras	verrais	vois	voies	visses
verra	verrait		voie	vît
verrons	verrions	voyons	voyions	vissions
verrez	verriez	voyez	voyiez	vissiez
verront	verraient		voient	vissent
voudrai	voudrais		veuille	voulusse
voudras	voudrais	veuille	veuilles	voulusses
voudra	voudrait		veuille	voulût
voudrons	voudrions		voulions	voulussions
voudrez	voudriez	veuillez	vouliez	voulussiez
voudront	voudraient		veuillent	voulussent

Verbs with Spelling Changes

A. Verbs in -cer

Since **c** is pronounced like **s** only before **e** and **i** and like **k** before **a, o,** and **u,** verbs whose infinitives end in **-cer** change **c** to **ç** when the **c** is followed by **a, o,** or **u,** in order to preserve the *s* sound of the **c.** Changes are made then in the tenses below and in the imperfect subjunctive.

EXAMPLE: **effacer.**

PRESENT PARTICIPLE	PRESENT INDICATIVE	IMPERFECT INDICATIVE	SIMPLE PAST
effaçant	j'efface	j'effaçais	j'effaçai
	tu effaces	tu effaçais	tu effaças
	il efface	il effaçait	il effaça
	nous effaçons	nous effacions	nous effaçâmes
	vous effacez	vous effaciez	vous effaçâtes
	ils effacent	ils effaçaient	ils effacèrent

B. Verbs in -ger

Since **g** is pronounced like *g* in *get* before **a, o,** and **u,** and like *s* in *pleasure* before **e** and **i,** verbs whose infinitives end in **-ger** insert **e** between **g** and the next vowel whenever that vowel is not **e** or **i.** Changes are made then, in the tenses below and in the imperfect subjunctive.

EXAMPLE: **changer.**

PRESENT PARTICIPLE	PRESENT INDICATIVE	IMPERFECT INDICATIVE	SIMPLE PAST
changeant	je change	je changeais	je changeai
	tu changes	tu changeais	tu changeas
	il change	il changeait	il changea
	nous changeons	nous changions	nous changeâmes
	vous changez	vous changiez	vous changeâtes
	ils changent	ils changeaient	ils changèrent

C. Verbs in -yer

Verbs in **-yer** (**-ayer, -oyer, -uyer**) change **y** to **i** before a mute **e** in the following syllable. This change occurs throughout the present except for the **nous** and **vous** forms and throughout the entire future and conditional.

EXAMPLE: **nettoyer.**

PRESENT INDICATIVE	PRESENT SUBJUNCTIVE	FUTURE	CONDITIONAL
je nettoie	que je nettoie	je nettoierai	je nettoierais
tu nettoies	que tu nettoies	tu nettoieras	tu nettoierais
il nettoie	qu'il nettoie	il nettoiera	il nettoierait
nous nettoyons	que nous nettoyions	nous nettoierons	nous nettoierions
vous nettoyez	que vous nettoyiez	vous nettoierez	vous nettoieriez
ils nettoient	qu'ils nettoient	ils nettoieront	ils nettoieraient

D. Verbs in -e- + $\begin{cases} \text{a single} \\ \text{consonant} \end{cases}$ + -er

Many verbs, such as **mener, lever,** and **acheter,** whose stems end in unaccented **e** plus a single consonant, place a grave accent (`) over this **e** whenever the following syllable also has a mute **e**. This indicates that the pronunciation of the **e** [ə] of the stem becomes **è** [ɛ]. The grave accent is found throughout the singular and in the third person plural of the present indicative and subjunctive and throughout the entire future and conditional of all these verbs.

EXAMPLE: **mener.**

PRESENT INDICATIVE	PRESENT SUBJUNCTIVE	FUTURE	CONDITIONAL
je mène	que je mène	je mènerai	je mènerais
tu mènes	que tu mènes	tu mèneras	tu mènerais
il mène	qu'il mène	il mènera	il mènerait
nous menons	que nous menions	nous mènerons	nous mènerions
vous menez	que vous meniez	vous mènerez	vous mèneriez
ils mènent	qu'ils mènent	ils mèneront	ils mèneraient

E. Verbs in **-é-** $+\begin{cases}\text{a single}\\\text{consonant}\end{cases}+$ **-er**

Verbs whose stems end in **é** followed by a single consonant change this **é** to **è** throughout the singular and in the third person plural of the present indicative and present subjunctive, that is, in those forms in which the following syllable has a mute **e**. In the future and conditional the **é** is retained in writing, but this **é** is usually pronounced **è** because a vowel tends to open in a closed syllable.[1]

EXAMPLE: **espérer**

PRESENT INDICATIVE	PRESENT SUBJUNCTIVE	FUTURE	CONDITIONAL
j'espère	que j'espère	j'espérerai	j'espérerais
tu espères	que tu espères	tu espéreras	tu espérerais
il espère	qu'il espère	il espérera	il espérerait
nous espérons	que nous espérions	nous espérerons	nous espérerions
vous espérez	que vous espériez	vous espérerez	vous espéreriez
ils espèrent	qu'ils espèrent	ils espéreront	ils espéreraient

F. Verbs in **-eler** and some in **-eter**

Verbs in **-eler** and a few verbs in **-eter** double the **l** or **t** when the next syllable contains a mute **e**. This change takes place in the singular and third person plural of the present indicative and of the present subjunctive and throughout the future and conditional.

EXAMPLE: **appeler.**

PRESENT INDICATIVE	PRESENT SUBJUNCTIVE	FUTURE	CONDITIONAL
j'appelle	que j'appelle	j'appellerai	j'appellerais
tu appelles	que tu appelles	tu appelleras	tu appellerais
il appelle	qu'il appelle	il appellera	il appellerait
nous appelons	que nous appelions	nous appellerons	nous appellerions
vous appelez	que vous appeliez	vous appellerez	vous appelleriez
ils appellent	qu'ils appellent	ils appelleront	ils appelleraient

---

[1] The fact that the mute **e** of the infinitive drops out in pronunciation closes the preceding syllable, thus tending to open the **e**; e.g., j'espérerai [ʒɛsperre]; il espérerait [ilɛsperre]; tu céderas [tysɛdra].

French-English Vocabulary

French-English Vocabulary

ABBREVIATIONS

adj.	adjective	*irr. sp.*	irregular spelling	*pers.*	person
adv.	adverb	*m.*	masculine	*prep.*	preposition
cond.	conditional	*n.*	noun	*pres.*	present
conj.	conjugated	*obj.*	object	*pron.*	pronoun
conjunc.	conjunction	*p.*	page	*rel.*	relative
f.	feminine	*part.*	participle	*sing.*	singular
fut.	future	*pl.*	plural	*sp*	simple past
inf.	infinitive	*pp*	past participle	*subjunc.*	subjunctive
interrog.	interrogative			*v.*	verb

* aspirate *h* (2) -ir verbs which do not insert -iss-; all other -ir verbs insert -iss-.

Verbs whose principal parts are given are irregular, and their conjugations may be found on pp. 284–301. The use of the principal parts is explained on page 283. Verbs followed by (*conj. like* . . .) are irregular and follow the pattern of the verb indicated.

Verbs followed by (*irr. sp.* **A** to **F**) undergo a spelling change in certain forms. The letter refers to the appropriate type of change explained on pp. 302–304.

This vocabulary contains all words used in the text and in the *Pattern Practice Manual* except words which have the same form in English and French and certain words of which the French spelling is so near to the English that they are easily recognizable.

A

à at; with; in; by; **à votre accent** by your accent; **c'est à lui** it is up to him

a (*pres. of* **avoir**) has; **il y a** there is, there are; **il y a un an** a year ago

abandonner abandon; **s'abandonner** give way (to)

abattre (*conj. like* **battre**) tear down

abord: d'abord at first

aboyer (*irr. sp.* **C**) bark

abrupt steep

absence *f.* absence

absolu absolute

absolument absolutely

absurde absurd; living in the absurd; alienated

accent *m.* accent; **à votre accent** from your accent

accablé overwhelmed; weary

accepter accept

accompagner accompany

accord *m.* agreement

accueillir receive; welcome

acheter (*irr. sp.* **D**) buy

acte *m.* act

acteur *m.* actor

actif (*f.* **active**) active

actrice *f.* actress

actuel (*f.* **actuelle**) present day

addition *f.* check (in a restaurant)

adieu *m.* goodbye; **faire ses adieux** say goodbye

admirer admire

adresse *f.* address

adresser (**s'**)(**à**+*n.*) go to; ask at; apply

adverbe *m.* adverb

affaire *f.* affair; thing; deal; business; **les affaires** business; one's things

affectif (*f.* **affective**) emotional

affiche *f.* poster; bulletin

afin que in order that

Afrique *f.* Africa; **Afrique du Nord** North Africa

âge *m.* age

âgé old

agent *m.* policeman

agir act; **s'agir de** to be a question of, to be about

agréable pleasant, agreeable

aider (+*person*+**à**+*inf.*) help

aille (*pres. subjunc. of* **aller**) go

ailleurs elsewhere

aimer (+*inf.*) like; love

air *m.* air; appearance; **avoir l'air** (+ *adj.; de* + *inf.*) look; seem

aise *f.* ease; **être à l'aise** be comfortable

ait (*pres. subjunc. of* **avoir**) has; have

ajouter add

alcool *m.* alcohol

algèbre *m.* algebra

Alger Algiers, a city on the seacoast of North Africa, capital of Algeria

Algérie *f.* Algeria

Allemagne *f.* Germany

allemand German

aller (**allant, allé, je vais, j'allai**) (+ *inf.*) go; **aller voir** go and see, visit; **ça va de soi** that goes without saying; **cette robe vous va bien** this dress fits you well, this dress looks very becoming on you; **s'en aller** go away, leave; start on one's way

allergie *f.* allergy

allié *m.* ally

allô hello

allonger (**s'**)(*irr. sp.* **B**) stretch out

allons bon there now

allumer light; turn on the lights

alors then; **alors que** when; whereas

Alpes *f. pl.* Alps

ambassadeur *m.* ambassador

amer (*f.* **amère**) bitter

américain American

Amérique *f.* America; **Amérique du Sud** *f.* South America

ami *m.* friend

amie *f.* friend; **bonne amie** girl friend

amitié *f.* friendship; **dites-lui mes amitiés** give him my best regards

amollir (**s'**) soften

amour (*m. in sing., f. in pl.*) love

amoureusement lovingly

Verbs with spelling changes are explained on pp. 302–304.

amoureux *m. pl.* people in love
amoureux (*f.* **amoureuse**) in love
amusant entertaining; amusing
amuser entertain; **s'amuser** (à + *inf.*)
have fun; have a good time; amuse
oneself
an *m.* year
analogue similar
ancien (*f.* **ancienne**) old; former
anglais English
Angleterre *f.* England
anglican Anglican
animal *m.* (*pl.* **animaux**) animal
année *f.* year
annonce *f.* announcement
annoncer (*irr. sp.* **A**) announce; say;
herald
anthropologie *f.* anthropology
anxieux (*f.* **anxieuse**) anxious; worried
apercevoir (*conj. like* **recevoir**) (+ *n.*)
notice; catch sight of; **s'apercevoir**
(**de** + *n;* **que** + *clause*) notice, realize
appareil *m.* apparatus; machine
appartement *m.* apartment
appartenir (*conj. like* **tenir**) belong
appeler (*irr. sp.* **F**) call; **s'appeler** be
called, be named
applaudir applaud
appliquer (**s'**) apply oneself; work hard
at
apporter bring
apprécier appreciate
appréhender seize
apprendre (*conj. like* **prendre**) (*thing* +
à + *person;* à + *inf.*) learn; teach;
apprendre par cœur memorize, learn
by heart
approcher (**de** + *n.*) approach; **s'approcher** (**de** + *n.*) approach
approuver approve
appuyer (*irr. sp.* **C**) lean; **s'appuyer**
lean
après after; afterwards; **d'après** according to; after
après-midi *m. or f.* afternoon
arbre *m.* tree, **arbre fruitier** fruit tree
Arc de Triomphe *m.* Arch of Triumph
ardemment ardently
ardoise *f.* slate
argent *m.* money
Argentine *f.* Argentina

armé armed
armée *f.* army
armoire *f.* cupboard; a large piece of
furniture used as a wardrobe
arpenter walk along; stride along; strut
along
arrangé set
arranger (*irr. sp.* **B**) fix; arrange;
s'arranger come out all right, manage
arrêt *m.* stop; **sans arrêt** without stopping, ceaselessly
arrêter (**de** + *inf.*) stop; arrest; fix;
s'arrêter (**de** + *inf.*) stop
arrivée *f.* arrival
arriver arrive, reach; happen
art *m.* art; **beaux-arts** fine arts
artiste *m. or* ^f. artist
asile *m.* home (for the aged)
aspirateur *m.* vacuum cleaner
asseoir (**asseyant, assis, j'assieds,
j'assis**) sit; seat; **s'asseoir** sit down
assez enough; rather
assiette *f.* plate
assis (*pp and sp of* **asseoir**) seated; sitting
assister (à + *n.*) attend, be present at
assurer (**s'**) make sure, assure oneself
astronomie *f.* astronomy
Atlantique *m.* Atlantic
atomique atomic, nuclear
attaquer attack
attendre (+ *n.*) wait; wait for; expect
s'attendre (à + *n.*) expect
attentif (*f.* **attentive**) attentive
attention *f.* attention; **faire attention à**
watch out for; pay attention to; **faire
bien attention** pay special attention
to; be very careful about; **faites
attention** look out
attentivement attentively
atténué attenuated, subdued
atterrir land
attraper catch
au to the; **au revoir** goodbye
aucun any; **ne . . . aucun** no; none
audacieux (*f.* **audacieuse**) audacious;
bold
au-dessus above
augmentation *f.* raise
augmenter increase; raise
aumônier *m.* chaplain
auprès near

aurai, aurais (*fut. and cond. of* **avoir**) will have; would have
aussi also; so, therefore
aussitôt at once, immediately; **aussitôt que** as soon as
auteur *m.* author
auto *f.* car, auto
autobus *m.* (city) bus
autocar *m.* (interurban) bus
automatique automatic
automne *m.* autumn, fall
automobile *f.* car
autour around
autre other
autrement differently; otherwise
Autriche *f.* Austria
auxiliaire auxiliary
avancer (*irr. sp.* **A**) advance, move forward; **s'avancer** advance; approach
avant before; ahead; formerly; **avant-dernier** next to the last; **avant-hier** the day before yesterday; **avant tout** above all
avant-garde *f.* avant-garde; pioneer
avec with
avenir *m.* future
aventure *f.* adventure
aventurer (**s'**) venture
avertir warn; inform
aveugle blind
avez (**avoir**) have
aviateur *m.* flier
avion *m.* airplane
avis *m.* opinion; **changer d'avis** change one's mind
avocat *m.* lawyer
avoir (**ayant, eu, j'ai, j'eus**) (**à** + *inf.*) have; **avoir de la chance** be lucky; **ce qu'il y a** the trouble is; **il y a** there is, there are; ago
avouer confess; admit
ayant (*pres. part. of* **avoir**) having
azur blue; **Côte d'Azur** French Riviera

B

baccalauréat *m.* baccalaureate (state examination given students after seven years of the French lycée)
bagage *m.* baggage

bague *f.* ring
bain *m.* bath
baissé lowered
baisser lower
bal *m.* dance
ballon *m.* ball
Balzac, Honoré de (1799–1850) French realistic novelist of the nineteenth century
bande *f.* strip; tape (for tape recorder)
banlieue *f.* suburbs
banque *f.* bank; **billet de banque** *m.* banknote
banquier *m.* banker
barbe *f.* beard
bas (*f.* **basse**) low; **tout bas** in a whisper
base *f.* base; airport
Bastille *f.* square in Paris, formerly the site of the state prison taken and destroyed by the people on July 14, 1789
bataille *f.* battle
bateau *m.* boat; **faire du bateau** take a boatride; go boating; **traversée en bateau** boat trip
bâtiment *m.* building
battre (**battant, battu, je bats, je battis**) beat; **se battre** fight; **se battre à coups de boules de neige** have a snowball fight
bavarder talk; chat
bavure smudge; **sans bavure** perfect, unblemished
beau (before vowel sound **bel**; *f.* **belle**) beautiful; handsome; **il fait beau** the weather is good
beaucoup much, many, a great deal, a great many, a lot
bébé *m.* baby
Belge *m.* Belgian
Belgique *f.* Belgium
belle (*f. of* **beau**) beautiful; **la belle saison** the summer months
berger *m.* shepherd; **l'étoile du Berger** Venus
besoin *m.* need; **avoir besoin** (**de** + *n.*; **de** + *inf.*) need
bête *f.* beast; animal
beurre *m.* butter
bibliothèque *f.* library
bicyclette *f.* bicycle

Verbs with spelling changes are explained on pp. 302–304.

bien well; well-off; comfortable; good; indeed; very; very much; right; **bien que** although; **ou bien** or else; **qu'on est bien** how comfortable we are; **vouloir bien** be willing; **vous comprenez bien** you must understand
bientôt soon
bière f. beer
bifteck m. steak
bijou m. jewel
bijoutier m. jeweler
billet m. ticket; **billet de banque** banknote
biographie f. biography
biologie f. biology
bistrot m. a small café or restaurant (patronized principally by the working class)
bizarre odd, strange; outlandish
blanc (f. **blanche**) white
blessé m. the wounded man
blesser wound
bleu blue
blondeur f. blondness
boire (**buvant, bu, je bois, je bus**) drink
bois m. wood
boîte f. box
Bolivie f. Bolivia
bon (f. **bonne**) good; fit; **allons bon** there now; **bon marché** cheap; **il fait bon** it is cozy, it is comfortably warm
bonbon m. candy
bonheur m. happiness
bonjour good morning, hello
bonne f. maid
bonnet m. cap
bord m. edge
bottine f. shoe; boot; **lacet de bottine** boot lace
bouche f. mouth
boudin m. black pudding
bouger (irr. sp. **B**) move
bougie f. candle
boulanger m. baker; **chez le boulanger** at the bakery
boule f. ball; **se battre à coups de boules de neige** have a snowball fight
bout m. end; tip
bouteille f. bottle

boxe f. boxing
bras m. arm
Brésil m. Brazil
brésilien (f. **brésilienne**) Brazilian
breuvage f. drink
brièveté f. brevity
brillant brilliant; bright
broder embroider
brosser brush
bruissement m. slight sound, rustling
bruit m. noise; rumor
brune f. brunette
brusque blunt; brusk
brusquement suddenly; bruskly
brutalement brutally
bruyant noisy
bu, bus (pp and sp of **boire**) drunk; drank
Buenos-Ayres Buenos-Aires, capital of Argentina
bureau m. desk; office; **bureau de tabac** tobacco shop; **chef de bureau** head clerk
but m. aim
buvant (pres. part. of **boire**) drinking

C

ça that; it; **çà et là** here and there
cacher hide
cacheter (irr. sp. **F**) seal
cadeau m. gift; **faire un cadeau** give a present
café m. coffee; café, coffee house
cahier m. notebook
calculer calculate; estimate
calme m. peace; calm; (adj.) calm
calmement calmly
camarade m. or f. friend; pal; **camarade d'études** school friend
camp f. camp; team
campagne f. country; countryside; landscape; **maison de campagne** country home
Camus, Albert (1913–1960) French novelist, essayist, and playright
Canada m. Canada
candidat m. candidate
cantabile [kantabile] (Italian) melodious; **moderato cantabile** musical term meaning that the piece is to be melodious and moderately paced

capable capable, able; **capable de tout** capable of anything
capitaine *m.* captain
capitale *f.* capital
capitalisme *m.* capitalism
car (*conjunc.*) for
caractère *m.* character (attributes or features which distinguish a person)
carré square
carrefour *m.* crossing; crossroad
carte *f.* card; map; **carte d'identité** identification card; **carte postale** postcard; **carte de visite** visiting card
cas *m.* case
casser break; **se casser** break
cathédrale *f.* cathedral
Catholique *m. or f.* Catholic
cause *f.* cause; **à cause de** because of
causer talk; chat; cause
caviar *m.* caviar
ce (*adj.*) this; that; (*pron.*) this; that; it; he; she; they
célèbre famous
célibataire *m.* bachelor
celui (*f.* **celle**) this one, that one; the one; **celui-ci** this one, that one; the latter
censeur *m.* vice-principal in charge of attendance and discipline in a **lycée**
cent hundred
centaine *f.* about a hundred
cependant however
cercueil *m.* coffin
cerise *f.* cherry
certain some; certain
certainement certainly
cesse: sans cesse constantly, ceaselessly
cesser (**de** + *inf.*) stop, cease
cet this, that
cette (*f. of* **ce**) this, that
chagrin *m.* sorrow; chagrin
chair *f.* flesh
chaise *f.* chair
chaleur *f.* heat
chambre *f.* bedroom
champagne *m.* champagne
Champs-Élysées avenue in Paris leading from the Place de la Concorde to the Place de l'Étoile
chance *f.* luck; **avoir de la chance** be lucky

changement *m.* change
changer (*irr. sp.* **B**) change; **changer d'avis** change one's mind
chanson *f.* song
chantant melodious
chanter sing
chanteuse *f.* singer
chapeau *m.* hat
chaque each
chargé loaded; overloaded; **chargé de** filled with
charger (**se**) (**de** + *inf.*) take care
charmant charming
charme *m.* charm
chasse *f.* hunt, hunting; **aller à la chasse** go hunting
chasser hunt, throw out, chase away
chat *m.* cat
château *m.* castle
chaud hot; warm; **j'ai chaud** I am warm; **il fait chaud** it is warm; it is hot
chauffeur *m.* driver; chauffeur
chaussure *f.* shoe; *pl.* footwear; shoes
chauve bald
chef *m.* head, leader; chief; **chef de bureau** head clerk
chemin *m.* road; path; way
cheminée *f.* fireplace
chemisette *f.* short-sleeved shirt
chèque *m.* check
cher (*f.* **chère**) dear; expensive
chercher (+ *n.*) look for; meet; go and get; pick up (**à** + *inf.*) try to, seek to; **envoyer chercher** send for
chérie *f.* dear
cheval *m.* (*pl.* **chevaux**) horse
cheveux *m. pl.* hair
chez at; with; in; at the house of; in the case of; **allez chez vous** go home; **chez le directeur** to the director's office; **chez nous** at our house; in our country; **chez qui** at whose home
chien *m.* dog
chimie *f.* chemistry
Chine *f.* China
chinois Chinese
chocolat *m.* chocolate; candy
chœur *m.* choir
choisir choose
chose *f.* thing; **pas grand-chose** not much, not very much

Verbs with spelling changes are explained on pp. 302–304.

chouette *f.* owl
Cid *m.*: Le Cid is a play written by Corneille in 1636
ciel *m.* sky
cigare *m.* cigar
cil *m.* eyelash
cinéma *m.* movie; movies
cinq five
cinquante fifty
cinquième fifth
cirer wax; shine; **toile cirée** oilcloth
cirque *m.* circus
citron *m.* lemon
clair clear, light; obvious; **clair de lune** *m.* moonlight
classe *f.* class; classroom; **faire une classe** teach
classique classical
clavier *m.* keyboard
clé *f.* key; **fermer à clé** lock
client *m.* client; custom; patron
climatiser air-condition
cloche *f.* bell
clou *m.* nail
clown *m.* clown
Cocteau, Jean (1889–1963) French writer of the twentieth century
cœur *m.* heart; **apprendre par cœur** memorize; **au cœur de** in the middle of; **avoir mal au cœur** be nauseated
cognac *m.* brandy
coiffée with one's hair dressed; **extremement coiffée** with a high style hairdo
coiffeur *m.* hairdresser; barber
coiffure *f.* hairdo
coin *m.* corner
colère *f.* anger; **en colère** angry; **se mettre en colère** get angry
Colette, Sidonie Gabriel (1873–1954) French woman novelist
colis *m.* package
colle *f.* glue
collectionner collect
collégien *m.* secondary school student
collègue *m. or f.* colleague
coller (+ *person*) (*colloquial*) fail (someone in a test or course)
colline *f.* hill
combien how much; how many; **tous les combien** how often

Combray fictitious French village in works of Marcel Proust
comédie *f.* comedy; play
comédien *m.* actor; comedian
commander order (a meal)
comme as; like; as well as; since; **comme si** as if; **comme d'habitude** as usual; **comme il faut** properly
commencement *m.* beginning
commencer (*irr. sp.* **A**) begin
comment how; what; What! What do you mean; **comment trouvez-vous** what do you think of
commissaire *m.* police commissioner
commission *f.* errand; **faire des commissions** go shopping
commode convenient
Commodoro a city in Argentina
communisme *m.* communism
communiste *m.* communist
compagnie *f.* company; firm
complètement completely
compliqué complicated
comporter require; include; comprise; behave
composé compound; **passé composé** compound past
composition *f.* composition; theme
comprendre (*conj. like* **prendre**) understand; comprise
comprenez (**comprendre**) understand; **vous comprenez bien** you must understand
compte *m.* account; **se rendre compte (de** + *n.*)** realize
compter count; (+ *inf.*) expect; intend
comptoir *m.* counter
concierge *m. or f.* house-porter; janitor; caretaker
conclure conclude; **l'affaire sera conclue** the deal will be closed
concours *m.* competitive examination
condamner condemn
condition *f.* condition; social level; **à condition que** provided that
conduire (**conduisant, conduit, je conduis, je conduisis**) drive; take; **se conduire** behave
conduite *f.* behavior
conférence *f.* lecture; **en conférence** in conference, at a meeting

Irregular verbs are conjugated on pp. 284–301.

conférencier *m.* speaker; lecturer
conflit *m.* conflict
confort *m.* comfort
confortable comfortable
connaissance *f.* acquaintance; knowledge; **faire la connaissance de** get acquainted with, meet
connaître (connaissant, connu, je connais, je connus) know, be acquainted with
connu well known, famous
consciencieux (*f.* consciencieuse) conscientious
conseil *m.* piece of advice; *pl.* advice
conseiller (à + *person* + de + *inf.*) advise
consolant consoling
consommer consummate; accomplish; consume
construire (*conj. like* conduire) build
contempler view
contenir (*conj. like* tenir) contain
contenter satisfy
contingent accidental
continuellement continually; incessantly
continuer (à + *inf.*) continue; keep on
contraint forced
contraire *m.* contrary; **au contraire** on the contrary
contribuer contribute
convenable proper
convenir (*conj. like* venir) agree; be proper, be suiting; **convenir de** accept; **quelque chose convient** something is proper, something is suitable
convenu agreed; OK
convertir convert
convive *m. or f.* guest
copain *m.* pal, chum, close friend
copie *f.* paper (to hand in); (school) exercise
copier copy
coquetterie *f.* coquetry; desire to please a man; flirtatious attitude
coquille *f.* shell
corne *f.* horn
corps *m.* body
correctement correctly
correspondant *m.* correspondent
corriger (*irr. sp.* B) correct
costume *m.* suit

côte *f.* coast; **côte à côte** side by side; **Côte d'Azur** French Riviera
côté *m.* side; **à côté de** near, beside, alongside of; in addition to; **à côté de** in the direction of; on the side of; **mettre de côté** save; **tout à côté** right near
cou *m.* neck
couchant *m.* sunset
coucher put to bed; spend the night; **se coucher** go to bed; (*n.*) *m.* bedtime
couchette *f.* cot
couleur *f.* color
couloir *m.* corridor
coup *m.* blow; "coup"; **coup d'œil** glance; **se battre à coups de boules de neige** have a snowball fight; **coup de tonnerre** thunderclap; **d'un coup de crayon** with the tap of a pencil; **tout à coup** all of a sudden; **tout d'un coup** all of a sudden
coupable guilty; (*n.*) *m. or f.* the guilty one
couper cut; cut down
cour *f.* yard; court yard; court; **faire la cour** make love
courageux (*f.* courageuse) brave
courant running; **au courant** informed
courir (courant, couru, je cours, je courus) run
courrier *m.* mail
cours *m.* course; **cours de vacances** summer courses
course *f.* errand; race
court short
couteau *m.* knife
coûteux (*f.* coûteuse) expensive
couvert (*pp of* couvrir) covered; (*n.*) *m.* cover; knives, forks, and spoon used for eating; **enlever le couvert** clear the table; (*adj.*) covered
couverture *f.* blanket
craie *f.* chalk
craignais (*imperfect of* craindre) feared
craindre (craignant, craint, je crains, je craignis) fear
cravate *f.* tie
crayon *m.* pencil; **d'un coup de crayon** with the tap of a pencil
créer create
crème *f.* cream

Verbs with spelling changes are explained on pp. 302–304.

créneau *m.* battlement
crêpe *m.* crepe; mourning band
creux (*f.* creuse) hollow
cri *m.* cry; pousser un cri utter a cry
crier yell; cry out
criminel *m.* criminal
critique *f.* criticism; review
critiquer criticize
crochet hook; faire un crochet swerve
croire (croyant, cru, je crois, je crus)
  believe; croire bon deem fit
croisade *f.* crusade
croisé crossed; mots croisés crossword
  puzzle
croiser cross
cru, crus (*pp and sp of* croire) believed
cruel (*f.* cruelle) cruel
cuillerée *f.* spoonful
cueillir pick
cuisine *f.* kitchen; cooking
cuisinière *f.* cook
culotte *f.* kneepants
cultiver cultivate
curieux (*f.* curieuse) curious; odd;
  strange; inquisitive
cyclone *m.* hurricane

D

d'abord at first
dame *f.* lady; dame! (*interjection*) why,
  of course
Danemark *m.* Denmark
dangereux (*f.* dangereuse) dangerous
dans in, on
danse *f.* dancing; leçon de danse
  dancing lesson
danser dance
danseuse *f.* dancer
dater date
de of; from; by; in; out of; with
déborder overflow
debout standing; puisque vous êtes
  debout since you are up
début *m.* beginning
décapotable *f.* convertible (car)
déchirer tear up
décider (de + *inf.*) decide; se décider
  (à + *inf.*) make up one's mind
décimètre *m.* decimeter: a unit of the

metric system equivalent to about 4
  inches
décisif (*f.* décisive) decisive
décision *f.* decision; prendre une
  décision make a decision, make up
  one's mind
décoller (speaking of airplanes) take off
découper cut; cut out
décourager (*irr. sp.* B) discourage
découvrir (*conj. like* ouvrir) discover
défendre defend; (à + *person* + de +
  inf.) forbid
défendu forbidden
déferler break
défoncer (*irr. sp.* A) smash
dehors outside
déjà already
déjeuner have the noon meal; have
  breakfast; (*n.*) *m.* noon meal (main
  meal in France)
délacer (*irr. sp.* A) free
délavé faded
délicieux (*f.* délicieuse) delightful
demain tomorrow
demander ask; (à + *person* + de + *inf.*)
  ask someone to; (à + *inf.*) ask to
déménager (*irr. sp.* B) move
demeurer remain
demi half; demi-heure half an hour;
  demi-place half price (for a seat)
démission *f.* resignation
démonstratif demonstrative
dent *f.* tooth
dentelle *f.* lace
départ *m.* departure
dépasser go beyond; go around
dépêcher (se) (de + *inf.*) hurry
déplacer (*irr. sp.* A) shift
dépourvu without
dépression *f.* hollow, fall
depuis since; from; for
déranger (*irr. sp.* B) disturb, bother
dernier (*f.* dernière) last
dérouler (se) unfold; develop; take
  place
derrière behind; la porte de derrière
  the back door
dès que as soon as; dès que possible as
  soon as possible
désaccordé out of tune
désappointé disappointed

Irregular verbs are conjugated on pp. 284–301.

désastre *m.* disaster
descendre come down; go down; descend
désert deserted
désinvolte natural
désirer (+ *inf.*) wish, desire
désolé sorry
dessin *m.* drawing
dessus upstairs; on it
détaché detached
détruire (*conj. like* conduire) destroy
dette *f.* debt
deuil *m.* mourning; prendre le deuil go into mourning
deux two; vous deux both of you
devant before
devenir (*conj. like* venir) become
deviner guess
devoir (pp. 201–205) (devant, dû, je dois, je dus) have to, must, ought to; should probably + *verb;* (*n.*) *m.* duty, exercise
diable *m.* devil
diamant *m.* diamond
dictionnaire *m.* dictionary
Dieu *m.* God
difficile difficult
dimanche *m.* Sunday
diminuer diminish
dîner dine, have dinner
diplomatique diplomatic
diplôme *m.* diploma
dire (disant, dit, je dis, je dis) (à + *person* + de + *inf.*) say; tell; à qui le dites-vous You're telling me! c'est-à-dire that is to say; vouloir dire mean
directeur *m.* director; manager
diriger (*irr. sp.* B) direct; se diriger go
disant (*pres. participle of* dire) saying
discours *m.* speech
discret (*f.* discrète) discreet
discuter discuss; argue about
disparaître (*conj. like* connaître) disappear
disque *m.* (phonograph) record
distingué distinguished
distribuer distribute
dit (*pres. and pp of* dire) say; said; so called; si le cœur vous en dit if you so desire

divers various, different
dix ten
docteur *m.* doctor
dodu plump, filled out; puffy
doigt *m.* finger
doit (*pres. of* devoir) must; has to; is to; probably does
domestique *m. or f.* servant
donc then; thus; therefore; now; allez donc voir be sure and see; entrez donc do come in; pensez donc think of it; qui donc who is that; whom do you mean?
donner give; donner sur look out upon
dormir (2) sleep
dos *m.* back
dossier *m.* file
douane *f.* customs
doucement gently
douleur *f.* pain; suffering; sorrow
doute *m.* doubt; sans doute probably
douteux (*f.* douteuse) doubtful
doux (*f.* douce) mild; soft
douzaine *f.* dozen
dramaturge *m.* dramatist
drame *m.* drama; drame passionnel drama of passion
drapeau *m.* flag
droit *m.* study of law; justice; law; (*adj.*) right; straight; tout droit erect; straight ahead
droite *f.* right
drôle funny; odd
du of the
dû, due (*pp of* devoir) had to, etc.; due to
dur hard
Duras, Marguerite (1914–   ) contemporary French writer
durer last

E

eau *f.* water
ébaucher begin; start to display
écarter pull aside
échange *m.* exchange
échanger exchange
échapper (à + *n.*) escape, avoid; s'échapper (de + *n.*) escape

Verbs with spelling changes are explained on pp. 302–304.

écharpe *f.* scarf
éclaircissement *m.* elucidation; enlightenment
éclairé lighted
éclairer light
éclater burst; break out; flash; **le soir venait d'éclater** evening had just come (upon them)
éclos open; grown; **à peine éclos** not yet fully shaped
école *f.* school
économies *f. pl.* savings; **faire des économies** save
économiser save
écouler (**s'**) elapse, pass
écouter (+ *n.*) listen; listen to
écouteur *m.* receiver
écrasé crushed; overwhelmed
écrire (**écrivant, écrit, j'écris, j'écrivis**) write; **machine à écrire** *f.* typewriter
écrivain *m.* writer
édifice *m.* building; framework, structure
effacer (*irr. sp.* **A**) erase; obliterate
effrayer (*irr. sp.* **C**) scare, frighten
effroyable frightful
égal equal; **cela m'était égal** it did not make any difference to me
église *f.* church
égratignure *f.* scratch
élancer (**s'**) (*irr. sp.* **A**) dart forth
électricité *f.* electricity; **panne d'électricité** power failure
élève *m. or f.* pupil
élevé high; brought up; **bien élevé** well-mannered; **mal élevé** ill-mannered, ill bred
élire (*conj. like* **lire**) elect
éloigner keep away; **s'éloigner** go off
élu (*pp of* **élire**) elected
embarrassé embarrassed
embouteillage *m.* traffic jam
émigrer emigrate
emmener (*irr. sp.* **D**) take away; take along
emparer (**s'**) (**de** + *n.*) seize
empêcher (*n.* + **de** + *inf.*) hinder, prevent
empereur *m.* emperor
emploi *m.* use
employé *m.* clerk; employee; **petit employé** minor office clerk

employer (*irr. sp.* **C**) use
empoigner seize
emporter take away (a thing)
empreinte *f.* imprint
emprunter borrow
ému moved
en in; to; as; while; by
enchanté delighted
encore again; still; yet; **encore un mot** one more word
encourageant encouraging
encre *f.* ink
encrier *m.* inkwell
endormi asleep; sleeping
endormir (**s'**) (2) fall asleep
endroit *m.* place
endurci hardened; confirmed
énergie *f.* energy; power
enfance *f.* childhood
enfant *m. or f.* child
enfantin childish
enfin finally, at last; in short, anyway; well
enfler (**s'**) swell; rise
engagé engaged, involved
engager (*irr. sp.* **B**) hire
enguirlandé decorated, festooned
enhardir (**s'**) pick up enough courage, become bold enough
enjoué sprightly
enlaidir become ugly; make ugly
enlever (*irr. sp.* **D**) take away; take off; **enlever le couvert** clear the table
ennui *m.* boredom; trouble
ennuyer (*irr. sp.* **C**) bore; bother; **s'ennuyer** get bored; be lonesome; be bored
ennuyeux (*f.* **ennuyeuse**) annoying; boring
énorme enormous
énormément very much; considerably
enregistrer record; register
enseigner (*thing* + **à** + *person; person* + **à** + *inf.*) teach
ensemble together; **exercices d'ensemble** summing up exercises
ensoleillé sunny
ensuite then
entendre hear; **s'entendre** be heard; get along
entendu agreed

Irregular verbs are conjugated on pp. 284–301.

enterrement *m.* burial
entêtement *m.* stubbornness
enthousiasme *m.* enthusiasm
entouré surrounded
entourer (de + *n.*) surround; cover over
entre between
entrée *f.* entrance; beginning
entrer (dans + *n.*) enter; penetrate
envahir invade; come over
enveloppe *f.* envelope
envelopper wrap; wrap up
envers toward
envie *f.* wish, desire; **avoir envie de** feel like
envier envy
environ about, approximately
environs *m. pl.* surroundings; surrounding territory
envoler (s') take off (in an airplane flight)
envoyer, envoyant, envoyé, j'envoie, j'envoyai) send; **envoyer chercher** send for
épais (*f.* **épaisse**) thick
épaisseur *f.* depth
épaule *f.* shoulder; **hausser les épaules** shrug one's shoulders
épidémie *f.* epidemic
éponger (s') (*irr. sp.* **B**) wipe the sweat from one's forehead
époque *f.* time; period
épouser (+ *person*) marry
éprouver feel; experience
épuisé exhausted
erreur *f.* mistake
escalier *m.* stairway
escargot *m.* snail
escroc *m.* swindler
espacé spaced
Espagne *f.* Spain
espagnol Spanish
espérer (*irr. sp.* **E**) (+ *inf.*) hope; expect
espion *m.* spy
espoir *m.* hope
esprit *m.* spirit; wit; mind
essayer (*irr. sp.* **C**) (de + *inf.*) try
essayiste *m.* essayist
essence *f.* essence; gasoline
essuyer (*irr. sp.* **C**) wipe
établir establish
étaler display

étant (*pres. part. of* **être**) being
état *m.* state; shape
États-Unis *m. pl.* United States
été (*v.*) (*pp of* **être**) been; (*n.*) *m.* summer
éteindre (*conj. like* **peindre**) turn off; **s'éteindre** come to an end
éternel (*f.* **éternelle**) eternal
étoffe *f.* fabric; material; cloth
étoile *f.* star; **avec des étoiles sur le visage** stars were shining in my face; **l'étoile du Berger** Venus
étoilé star-shaped
étonnant astonishing; remarkable; surprising
étonné surprised
étonner astonish; surprise; **s'étonner** be surprised
étouffé stifled
étranger *m.* foreigner; estranged man; stranger; **à l'étranger** abroad; (*adj.*) (*f.* **étrangère**) foreign; estranged, alienated
être (**étant, été, je suis, je fus**) be; **être à l'aise** be comfortable; **ne pas être en reste** be equal to the situation; **vous n'en seriez pas là** you wouldn't be in such a fix; (*n.*) *m.* being
étroit narrow; close
étude *f.* study; **camarade d'étude** school friend
étudiant *m.* (college) student
eu, eus (*pp and sp of* **avoir**) had
eux *m.* them
évader (s') escape
évanoui unconscious; fainted
évanouir (s') faint
éveiller awaken; arouse
événement *m.* event
évidemment obviously
évident obvious
éviter (de + *inf.*) avoid
évocateur suggestive; meaningful, inspiring
évoluer develop; evolve
exact true; correct
exactement exactly
examen *m.* examination; **passer un examen** take an examination
examiner examine
excepté except
excuser (s') apologize

Verbs with spelling changes are explained on pp. 302–304.

exécuter (s') take place
exercice m. exercise; exercices d'ensemble summing-up exercises
existence f. existence; life
exister exist
expérience f. experience; experiment
expliquer explain
exporter export
exposer exhibit
exposition f. fair
exprimer express
extraordinaire extraordinary
extrêmement extremely; extrêmement
coiffé with a high style hairdo

F

fabriquer make; manufacture
face f. face; d'en face on the opposite
side (of the street); face à facing;
faire face à face up to; accept
fâché angry; sorry
fâcher (se) (contre + person) get angry
facilement easily
façon f. manner; way; de la même
façon in the same way
facteur m. mailman
faculté f. college or school of a university,
including buildings and teaching staff
faible weak
faim f. hunger; avoir faim be hungry
faire (faisant, fait, je fais, je fis) (+
inf.) do; make; carry out; have (done);
faire l'accord make the agreement;
faire ses adieux say goodbye; faire
attention look out; pay attention;
faire du bateau go boating; faire un
cadeau give a present; faire du cheval
go horseback riding; faire ses classes
teach one's classes; faire la connaissance de get acquainted with; meet;
faire face à face up to; accept; faire
des farces play tricks; play jokes;
faire froid be cold; faire de la gymnastique exercise; faire une lettre
write a letter; faire mal hurt; faire de
son mieux do one's best; faire de la
musique play music; faire partie de
belong to, be part of; faire une
période militaire do a short tour of

military duty; faire plaisir à please,
give pleasure to; faire une promenade
take a walk; faire du ski go skiing;
faire des sports participate in sports;
faire une valise pack a suitcase;
faire venir send for: il a fait «ho» he
exclaimed "ho"; il fait bon it's cozy;
it is comfortably warm; se faire mal
hurt oneself; se faire du souci worry
falaise f. cliff
falloir (—, fallu, il faut, il fallut) (+
inf.) must, be necessary; comme il faut
properly; il faut it takes; one must;
il me faut I need
familial (adj.) family
famille f. family; famille nombreuse
large family
fantaisiste whimsical; fanciful
farce f. farce; faire des farces play
tricks; play jokes
farine f. flour
fasse (pres. subjunc. of faire) make; do
fatigant tiring; tiresome
fatiguer tire
faut (pres. of falloir) must, has to; il
faut one must; it takes; comme il faut
properly; il me faut I need
faute f. mistake; sans faute without fail
fauteuil m. armchair
faux (f. fausse) false
favori (f. favorite) favorite
femme f. woman; wife; femme de
ménage cleaning woman; Les
Femmes savantes The Learned Women,
a play by Molière
fenêtre f. window
ferai, ferais (fut. and cond. of faire) will
make, will do; would make, would do
ferme f. farm; adj. firm
fermer close; fermer à clé lock
fermier m. farmer
féroce ferocious
fête f. holiday; festivity; celebration;
birthday
feu m. fire; feu rouge red light; traffic
light
feuille f. leaf; sheet
ficelle f. string; piece of string
fil m. wire
fille f. daughter; girl; jeune fille f. girl
fillette f. young girl; little girl

Irregular verbs are conjugated on pp. 284–301.

film *m.* film; movie
fils *m.* son
fin *f.* end
finesse *f.* subtlety; fineness; finesse
finir finish; **finir mal** end up badly; **finir par** end up by
flamand Flemish
flambé bright colored
fleur *f.* flower
floraison *f.* blooming
foie *m.* liver
fois *f.* time; **une fois pour toutes** once and for all
folle (*f. of* **fou**) crazy; reckless
foncé dark
fonder found
fontaine *f.* fountain
football *m.* football; ball
force *f.* strength; force
forêt *f.* forest
forme *f.* form
formidable marvelous
fort (*adj.*) loud; strong; (intellectually) good; *adv.* hard; very
fou (*before vowel sound* **fol.**, *f.* **folle**) crazy; reckless
foule *f.* crowd
fourberie *f.* trickery; deceit
fourchette *f.* fork
fourrure *f.* fur
fraîcheur *f.* freshness
frais (*f.* **fraîche**) fresh; cool
fraise *f.* strawberry
franc (*f.* **franche**) frank
Français *m.* Frenchman
français French
franchement frankly
frapper strike; knock
fraternel (*f.* **fraternelle**) fraternal
fraternité *f.* fraternity; brotherhood
frémir quiver, shudder; **il en frémit** it made him shudder
fréquemment frequently
fréquenter frequent, go to regularly
frère *m.* brother
frigidaire *m.* refrigerator
froid *m.* cold; **avoir froid** be cold; **il fait froid** it is cold
froidement coldly; cooly
fumer smoke
fur: au fur et à mesure gradually

fureur *f.* rage
furieux (*f.* **furieuse**) furious
fus, fut (*sp. of* **être**) was
fusil *m.* gun; rifle

G

gagner win; gain; earn
gant *m.* glove
garçon *m.* boy; waiter
garde *m.* watchman; guard
garder keep; watch
gardien *m.* watchman
Garonne *f.* river in southern France
gâteau *m.* cake
gâter spoil
gauche *f.* left
gazon *m.* lawn
gêner disturb; bother; embarrass
gens *m. pl.* people; **jeunes gens** young men; young people
gentil (*f.* **gentille**) nice
géographie *f.* geography
géologie *f.* geology
geste *m.* gesture
glissement *m.* sliding; sliding noise; swishing
glorieux (*f.* **glorieuse**) glorious
glycine *f.* glycine (kind of plant)
gonflement *m.* swelling
gorge *f.* throat
gorgée *f.* spoonful (*lit.* throatful)
goût *m.* taste
goûter taste; **goûter à quelque chose** take a snack, take a little of something
gouvernement *m.* government
gouverner govern
gracieux (*f.* **gracieuse**) graceful; gracious
grammaire *f.* grammar
grand great; large; **il est grand temps** it is high time
grand-chose much; **votre idée ne vaut pas grand-chose** your idea isn't worth much
grand-père *m.* grandfather
grandir grow
gratter scratch; **se gratter** scratch
gravier *m.* gravel
Grèce *f.* Greece

Verbs with spelling changes are explained on pp. 302–304.

grève *f.* beach
gris gray
griser intoxicate
gronder scold; grumble, rumble
gros (*f.* grosse) big; fat
guère scarcely, hardly
guéridon *m.* small, round table
guerre *f.* war; pilote de guerre military
pilot
guitare *f.* guitar
gymnastique *f.* exercise; faire de la
gymnastique exercise

H

* indicates an aspirate h

habiller dress; s'habiller dress
habiter (*place;* à + *place*) live; inhabit
habitude *f.* habit; comme d'habitude
as usual
habituer (s') (à + *inf.*) get used to
*haine *f.* hate
*haletant breathless, panting
harmonieux (*f.* harmonieuse) har-
monious
*hasard *m.* hazard; chance; au hasard
at random
*hausser raise; hausser les épaules shrug
one's shoulders
*haut high; à haute voix aloud
*hauteur *f.* height; level
*Haye, La *f.* The Hague, capital of the
Netherlands
*hélas alas
*héros *m.* hero
hésitation *f.* hesitation
hésiter hesitate
heure *f.* hour; o'clock; time; à l'heure
on time; de bonne heure early; tout
à la heure in a little while; a little
while ago
heureux (*f.* heureuse) happy
*heurter (se) (à + *n.*) run up against
hier yesterday; avant-hier the day before yesterday
histoire *f.* story; history; trouble
hiver *m.* winter
ho: faire «ho» exclaim "ho" (exclamation of pain or surprise)

*hocher nod; hocher la tête nod one's
head
homme *m.* man
*Hongrois *m.* Hungarian
hormis except for; outside of
*hors outside; hors de lui beside himself
hôte *m.* guest; host
hôtel *m.* hotel; hôtel de ville city hall
humain human
humble *m.* humble people, meek people
humeur *f.* humor; mood; de mauvaise
humeur in a bad mood
humide humid
humoriste *m.* humorist
humour *m.* humor; comic element
*hurler yell, howl
hymne *m.* hymn
hypocrite (*adj.*) hypocritical

I

ici here
idée *f.* idea
identité *f.* identification; carte d'identité identification card
ignorer not to know
illusoire illusory
image *f.* picture
imaginer imagine
imbécile *m. or f.* fool
immédiatement immediately
immense immense, vast
immobile motionless
imparfait *m.* imperfect (tense)
impatienter (s') become impatient
importer matter; be important
imposer impose
impossible impossible
impression *f.* impression
imprévu unforeseen
imprimer print
incendie *m.* fire
incertitude *f.* uncertainty
incliné sloping
inconnu unknown
incroyable unbelievable
inculpé *m.* accused one
indien (*f.* indienne) Indian
indifférence *f.* indifference
indifférent indifferent
indiquer indicate; show

individu *m.* man; individual (often with unfavorable connotation)
inertie *f.* inertia
inestimable priceless
inexplicable unexplainable
infiniment infinitely
infirmière *f.* nurse
influent influential
influer influence
informer (**s'**) (*sur* + *n.*) inquire for information; get information about
ingénieur *m.* engineer
ingrat *m.* ungrateful man
inoffensif (*f.* **inoffensive**) harmless
inondation *f.* flood
inquiéter (**s'**) (*irr. sp.* **E**) worry
inquiétude uneasiness
inscrire (*conj. like* **écrire**) inscribe
insister (**sur** + *thing;* **pour** + *inf.;* **pour que** + *subjunc.*) insist
inspecter inspect
instant *m.* instant; moment; **à l'instant même où** at the very moment when
insuffisant insufficient
insupportable unbearable
intention *f.* intention; **avoir l'intention de** intend to
interdire (*conj. like* **dire**) forbid
intéresser interest; **s'intéresser** (**à** + *n.*) be interested in
intérêt *m.* interest
interprète *m.* interpreter
interpréter (*irr. sp.* **E**) interpret
interrogatif (*f.* **interrogative**) interrogative
interroger (*irr. sp.* **B**) (*person* + **sur** + *n.*) question; quiz
interrompre interrupt
intervalle *m.* interval
introduire (*conj. like* **conduire**) introduce (something into); insert
inutile useless
invité *m.* guest
inviter (**à** + *inf.*) invite; entice
irai, irais (*fut. and cond. of* **aller**) will go; would go
isolé isolated
isoler isolate
issue *f.* exit; **sans issue** impassable
Italie *f.* Italy
italien (*f.* **italienne**) Italian

italique *m.* italics

J

jamais ever; never; **à jamais** forever; **ne . . . jamais** never
jambe *f.* leg
Japon *m.* Japan
jardin *m.* garden; park; **jardin zoologique** zoo
jardinier *m.* gardener
jaune yellow
Jeannot Johnnie
jeter (*irr. sp.* **F**) throw; **jeter les yeux** glance; **se jeter** throw oneself
jeu *m.* game; play; **jeu de mots** play on words, pun
jeudi *m.* Thursday
jeune young; **jeune fille** *f.* girl; **jeunes gens** *m.* young men; young people
jeunesse *f.* youth
joie *f.* joy
joli pretty
joliment nicely
jouer (**de** + instrument; **à** + game) play; **jouer de** make use of; turn on
jouet *m.* toy
joueur *m.* player
jour *m.* day; **au jour le jour** day by day; **dans les beaux jours** during the summer months; **de nos jours** in our days; in our time
journal *m.* newspaper; magazine; **journal de sport** sports magazine
journaliste *m.* newspaper man; journalist
journée *f.* day
jovial fun loving
joyeusement joyfully
juger (*irr. sp.* **B**) deem; judge; examine; scan; **juger bon** deem advisable
jurer swear; **je vous jure** (in a tone of exasperation) honestly!
jus *m.* juice
jusqu'à up to; as far as; to the point of
jusqu'à ce que (+ *subjunc.*) until
juste just
justice *f.* justice; **palais de justice** courthouse

K

kilo *m.* kilogram (2.2 pounds)

Verbs with spelling changes are explained on pp. 302–304.

L

là there; here; **çà et là** here and there
là-bas over there
là-haut up there
lac *m.* lake
lacet *m.* lace; **lacet de bottine** boot lace
laine *f.* wool
laisser (+ *inf.*) let; leave
lait *m.* milk
laiteux (*f.* **laiteuse**) milky; in milky foam
laitier *m.* milk dealer; milkman
lampe *f.* lamp
lancer (*irr. sp.* **A**) throw
langue *f.* language
lapin *m.* rabbit
large *m.* open sea; *adj.* wide
laver wash; **se laver** wash oneself
le, la, les (*definite article*) the; (*personal pron.*) him; her; it; them
leçon *f.* lesson; **leçon de danse** dancing lesson
lecteur *m.* reader
léger (*f.* **légère**) light; slight
lendemain *m.* next day; **le lendemain matin** the next morning
lent slow
lentement slowly
lequel (*f.* **laquelle**) (*interrog.*) which; which one; (*rel.*) whom; which
lettre *f.* letter; **faire une lettre** write a letter
leur (*pron.*) them, to them; (*adj.*) their; **le leur,** etc. theirs
lever (*irr. sp.* **D**) raise; lift; **se lever** get up
lèvre *f.* lip
libérer free, liberate
liberté *f.* freedom
libraire *m.* bookseller
libre free; open
librement freely
lier link; tie
lieu *m.* place; spot; **s'il y a lieu** if necessary; **au lieu de** instead; **avoir lieu** take place
ligne *f.* line; **pilote de ligne** commercial air pilot
limite *f.* limit; threshold; **à la limite de la nuit** at nightfall
linge *m.* dirty clothes; linen; laundry
lire (**lisant, lu, je lis, je lus**) read

lisant (*pres. part. of* **lire**) reading
lisse smooth
lit *m.* bed
livre *m.* book; *f.* pound
loge *f.* semi-public room at entrance of French *lycée* which adjoins the apartment of the *concierge*
loi *f.* law
loin far
lointain distant
Loire *f.* river in central France
Londres *m.* London
long (*f.* **longue**) long; **le long de** along
longuement at length
louer rent; reserve (a seat)
Louisiane *f.* Louisiana
loup *m.* wolf
lu, lus (*pp and sp. of* **lire**) read
lui him, to him; to her; it, to it; **bien à lui** typical, characteristic; **lui parti** once he had gone (*lit.* he having left)
lumière *f.* light; **mettre en lumière** throw light on
lundi *m.* Monday
lune *f.* moon; **clair de lune** *m.* moonlight
lutte *f.* wrestling; struggle
lycée *m.* French secondary school equivalent to American high school and junior college

M

machinalement mechanically
machine *f.* machine; **machine à écrire** typewriter
madeleine *f.* a small cupcake; a small sponge-cake
magasin *m.* store
magicien *m.* magician
magnétophone *m.* tape recorder
magnifique magnificent
maigre very thin, skinny; low (salary)
main *f.* hand; **porter la main à** put one's hand on; **se tenir par la main** hold hands
maintenant now
maire *m.* mayor
mais but; **mais non** why no; **mais oui** certainly; why yes
maïs *m.* corn
maison *f.* house; home; **maison de campagne** country home

Irregular verbs are conjugated on pp. 284–301.

maître *m.* teacher; master; leader; title given to lawyers
maîtriser control; master
majorité *f.* majority
mal *m.* evil; *adv.* badly; not well; **avoir mal** be sore; ache; **avoir mal au cœur** feel nauseated; **avoir mal à la tête** have a headache; **avoir un terrible mal de tête** have a terrible headache; **finir mal** end up badly; **mal élevé** ill-bred; **se sentir mal** feel sick; **se trouver mal** faint
malade *m. or f.* patient; sick person; *adj.* sick; **tomber malade** get sick
maladroitement clumsily, awkwardly
malgré in spite of
malheureux (*f.* **malheureuse**) unhappy
manche *f.* sleeve
manger (*irr. sp.* **B**) eat
manie *f.* mania
manquer (*pp.* 107–108) miss; lack
manteau *m.* overcoat
manuscrit *m.* manuscript
marchand *m.* merchant; storekeeper
marche *f.* walking; progress
marcher walk; run
mardi *m.* Tuesday
marée *f.* tide; flood
mari *m.* husband
mariage *m.* wedding; marriage
marier (*person* + **à** + *person*) marry; **se marier** (**avec** + *person*) marry; get married
Maroc *m.* Morocco
marquer mark; measure; indicate
Mars Mars
mars March
Marseille *f.* Marseilles
massif (*f.* **massive**) massive; large and heavy
match *m.* game
mathématiques *f. pl.* mathematics
matin *m.* morning
Mauresque *f.* Moorish woman
mauvais bad
me me, to me
mécanicien *m.* mechanic
méchant mean, vicious; bad; naughty
médecin *m.* doctor
Méditerranée *f.* Mediterranean
méfier (**se**) (**de** + *n.*) mistrust; distrust

meilleur better; best; **meilleur marché** cheaper; **de meilleure heure** earlier
mélancolique melancholy
mélanger (*irr. sp.* **B**) mix
mêlé mixed; involved in
mêler mix
même self; same; even; itself; mere; very; **quand même** even so, just the same; **tout de même** all the same
mémoires *m. pl.* memoirs
menacer (*irr. sp.* **A**) (**de** + *inf.*) threaten
ménage *m.* household; housework; **femme de ménage** *f.* cleaning woman
mener (*irr. sp.* **D**) lead, take (a person)
mensonge *m.* lie
menuisier *m.* carpenter
mer *f.* sea; **revenir de la mer** come back from the seaside
mercredi *m.* Wednesday
mère *f.* mother
mériter deserve
merveilleux (*f.* **merveilleuse**) marvelous
messieurs (*pl. of* **monsieur**) gentlemen
mesure *f.* measure; **à mesure que** as; **au fur et à mesure** gradually
mesurer measure; look over
méthodique methodical
métier *m.* trade; type of work
mètre *m.* meter (39.37 inches)
métro (*abbreviation for* **métropolitain**) *m.* subway
mettre (**mettant, mis, je mets, je mis**) put; put on; **mettre à la poste** mail; **mettre en lumière** throw light on; **mettre la table** set the table; **se mettre** become; **se mettre à** begin; **se mettre au travail** set oneself to work; **se mettre en colère** get angry; **se mettre en quête** set out in search of
meuble *m.* (piece of) furniture
meubler furnish
Mexique *f.* Mexico
midi *m.* noon
miel *m.* honey
miette *f.* crumb
mieux better; best; **faire de son mieux** do one's best
milieu *m.* middle
militaire military
militant militant

Verbs with spelling changes are explained on pp. 302–304.

mille thousand
millier *m.* thousand
ministre *m.* minister
minute *f.* minute; **une minute** just a minute
minutie *f.* attention to minute detail
mis (*pp and sp of* **mettre**) put
Misanthrope, Le *The Misanthrope*, a play by Molière
misérable *m. or f.* scoundrel; unfortunate person
mode *f.* fashion; style
moderato (Italian) moderate; **moderato cantabile** musical term meaning that the piece is to be melodious and moderately paced
modéré moderate; subdued
moderne modern
modifier modify
moi me, to me; self; I
moindre least; slightest
moins less; **de moins en moins** less and less; **du moins** at least; **à moins que** (**+** *subjunc.*) unless
Molière (1622–1673) French dramatist, writer of comedies
molle (*f. of* **mou**) soft; weak
mollet *m.* calf of the leg
moment *m.* moment; time; **ce n'est pas le moment** it isn't the proper time; **d'un moment à l'autre** from one minute to the next, at any time
monarque *m.* monarch
monde *m.* world; people; **tout le monde** everybody
monsieur *m.* (*pl.* **messieurs**) sir, Mr.; gentleman
mont *m.* small mountain
Mont Blanc *m.* highest peak of French Alps
montagne *f.* mountain
montée *f.* rise
monter go up; go up to; rise; climb; bring up; **monter dans une chambre** go to a room; **monter dans un train** get on a train
montre *f.* watch
montrer show; **se montrer** appear
moquer (**se**) (**de** **+** *n.*) make fun of; not care about
morceau *m.* piece
mordant *m.* pungency, sharpness

mordre bite
morne gloomy; drag
mort (*pp of* **mourir**) died; dead
mort *f.* death
mortel (*f.* **mortelle**) mortal
Moscou Moscow
mot *m.* word; **encore un mot** one more word; **jeu de mots** play on words, pun; **mots croisés** crossword puzzle
moto *f.* motorcycle; **en moto** on a motorcycle
motocyclette *f.* motorcycle
mou (*before vowel sound* **mol**; *f.* **molle**) weak; soft
moucher (**se**) blow one's nose
mouillé wet
mouiller wet, moisten; **se mouiller** get wet
mouler mold
moulu (*pp of* **mouler**) molded
mourir (**mourant, mort, je meurs, je mourus**) die
mouvement *m.* movement
moyen *m.* means; way
m'sieur (*colloquial for* **monsieur**) sir; Mr.
mur *m.* wall
musée *m.* museum
musicalité *f.* musical quality
musique *f.* music; **faire de la musique** play music
mystérieux (*f.* **mystérieuse**) mysterious
mythe *m.* myth

N

nager (*irr. sp.* **B**) swim
naïf (*f.* **naïve**) naïve
narrateur *m.* narrator
natif (*f.* **native**) native
nationalité *f.* nationality
natte *f.* braid of hair
naturellement naturally
né (*pp of* **naître**) born
négatif *m.* negative
négliger (*irr. sp.* **B**) neglect
neige *f.* snow; **se battre à coups de boules de neige** have a snowball fight
neiger (*irr. sp.* **B**) snow
netteté *f.* sharpness; clearness
nettoyage *m.* cleaning; **faire un grand nettoyage** do a thorough cleaning
nettoyer (*irr. sp.* **C**) clean

Irregular verbs are conjugated on pp. 284–301.

neuf nine
neuf (*f.* **neuve**) new
neutre neutral; impersonal
neuve (*f. of* **neuf**) new
neveu *m.* nephew
nez *m.* nose; **il saignait du nez** his nose was bleeding
ni neither; **ni . . . ni** neither . . . nor
Noël *m.* Christmas
noir *m.* dark; darkness; night; (*adj.*) black
noircir blacken
nom *m.* name
nombreux (*f.* **nombreuse**) many; numerous; **famille nombreuse** large family
nord *m.* north
Normandie *f.* Normandy, a province in northwestern France
Norvège *f.* Norway
nos (*pl. of* **notre**) our
notaire *m.* notary
note *f.* check; grade; note
notion *f.* idea; notion
notre (*possessive adj.*) our
nôtre (*possessive pron.*) ours
nourrissant nourishing
nouveau (*before vowel sound* **nouvel**; *f.* **nouvelle**) new; **à nouveau** again; **de nouveau** again, once more; **"nouveau roman"** school of writers, who, from 1950 on, searched for completely new forms for the novel
nouvel, nouvelle (*m. and f. of* **nouveau**) new
nouvelle *f.* a piece of news; **les nouvelles** *f. pl.* news; **nous avons de ses nouvelles** we've heard from him
Nouvelle-Orléans, la *f.* New Orleans
nu bare
nuage *m.* cloud
nuit *f.* night
nul (*pron.*) no one
nylon *m.* nylon

O

obéir (**à** + *n.*) obey
obéissant obedient
objet *m.* object
obligatoire compulsory
observation *f.* remark; observation
observer watch; observe

occasion *f.* opportunity
occupé busy
occuper (**s'**) (**de** + *n.*) take care of; turn one's attention to; take charge of; busy oneself with
odeur *f.* odor, smell
œil *m. sing.* (*m. pl.* **yeux**) eye; **coup d'œil** glance
œillet *m.* carnation
œuf *m.* egg
œuvre *f.* work
offenser offend
officier *m.* officer
offre *f.* offer
offrir (*conj. like* **ouvrir**) offer
oiseau *m.* bird; **oiseau de mer** sea bird
oisif (*f.* **oisive**) idle
olivier *m.* olive tree
ombre *f.* shade
on (*indefinite pron.*) one; we; you; they; people
oncle *m.* uncle
ondulation *f.* ripple; wave
opéra *m.* opera; opera house
opérer operate; work
opinion *f.* opinion, view
or *m.* gold
oralement orally
oranger *m.* orange tree
ordonner (**à** + *person* + **de** + *inf.*) order
ordre *m.* order; **à vos ordres** at your orders
oreille *f.* ear
organiser organize; plan
orgueil *m.* pride
original original; odd, strange, eccentric
Orléans French city on Loire between Paris and Tours
oser (+ *inf.*) dare
où where; in which; when; **au moment où** at the time when; **où que** wherever
oublier (**de** + *inf.*) forget
ouf! phew! (with a sigh of relief)
oui yes; **mais oui** certainly; why yes
ours *m.* bear
outre-tombe beyond the grave
ouvert open; exposed to
ouverture *f.* opening
ouvrier *m.* worker, workingman
ouvrir (**ouvrant, ouvert, j'ouvre, j'ouvris**) open; **s'ouvrir** lay open one's heart

Verbs with spelling changes are explained on pp. 302–304.

P

paie, paient (**payer**) pay
paille *f.* straw
pain *m.* bread
paix *f.* peace
palais *m.* palate; palace; **palais de justice** courthouse
pâle pale
pâleur *f.* paleness
panier *m.* basket
panne *f.* breakdown; **panne d'électricité** power failure
papier *m.* paper
paquet *m.* package
par through; by; with; for; per; **par ce temps** in such weather; **par jour** per day, each day
paragraphe *m.* paragraph
paraître (*conj. like* **connaître**) look, seem
parallèlement parallel
parcourir (*conj. like* **courir**) travel; go through
pardonner (**à** + *person* + **de** + *inf.*) pardon; forgive
pareil (*f.* **pareille**) same, identical; such a
pareillement similarly
parent *m.* parent; relative
parenthèse *f.* parenthesis
parfaitement perfectly
parfois sometimes
parfum *m.* perfume
Parisien *m.* Parisian
parler (**à** + *person;* **de** + *n.*) speak; talk
parmi among
parole *f.* (spoken) word
part *f.* part; **à part** except; **de ma part** for me, in my behalf
partager (*irr. sp.* **B**) share
parti *m.* party; **prendre le parti de** side with
participe *m.* participle
particulièrement particularly
partie *f.* part; **faire partie de** belong to, be a part of
partir (2) leave; go away; depart; **lui parti** once he had left (*lit.* he having left)
partition *f.* (musical) score
paru, parus (*pp and sp of* **paraître**) seemed, looked, appeared

pas *m.* step; footstep; **pas à pas** step by step
passage *m.* passage; passing
passé *m.* past; **passé composé** compound past; (*adj.*) past
passeport *m.* passport
passer (**à** + *inf.*) pass; pass by; give; spend (time); advance; **j'ai passé par là** I've gone through that; **passer un examen** take an examination; **se passer** happen; take place; be done; **il se passe quelque chose** something is happening; **se passer de** do without
passif (*f.* **passive**) passive
passionnant fascinating
passionnel (*f.* **passionnelle**) of love; of passion; **drame passionnel** drama of passion
pasteur *m.* minister (in church)
Pasteur, Louis (1822–1895) French scientist
Patagonie *f.* Patagonia, region in the southern part of South America
patron *m.* boss
patte *f.* paw; foot
pauvre *m.* poor man; (*adj.*) poor
payer (*irr. sp.* **C**) pay; pay for
pays *m.* country
paysage *m.* countryside; landscape
pêche *f.* fishing
peindre (**peignant, peint, je peins, je peignis**) paint; portray
peine *f.* trouble; difficulty; pain; grief; **à peine** slightly, scarcely; not very; **cela me fait de la peine** I am sorry; **valoir la peine** be worthwhile
peint (*pp. of* **peindre**) painted
peintre *m.* painter
peinture *f.* painting; portrayal
pelouse *f.* lawn
pendant during; **pendant que** while
pendule *f.* clock
penser (**à** + *n.*) think; think of; believe; (+ *inf.*) intend; (**à** + *inf.*) consider; (**de** + *n.*) have an opinion of
pension *f.* boarding house; boarding school
pensionnaire *m.* boarder
pente *f.* slope
perdre lose
père *m.* father

Irregular verbs are conjugated on pp. 284–301.

période *f.* period; **faire une période militaire** do a short tour of military duty
périodiquement periodically
permettre (*conj. like* **mettre**) (**à** + *person* + **de** + *inf.*) permit, allow
permis *m.* license; **permis de conduire** driver's license
Pérou *m.* Peru
perron *m.* porch
personnage *m.* character (in a literary work)
personne *f.* person
personne no one, nobody; **ne . . . personne** no one, nobody
perspective *f.* prospect
peser (*irr. sp.* **D**) weigh
petit *m.* baby; little boy; (*adj.*) small, little; **petit employé** minor office clerk; **un petit cognac** a small glass of brandy; **petits pois** *m. pl.* peas
petit-fils *m.* grandson
peu little; **à peu près** about, approximately; **un peu** a little, a bit
peuple *m.* people; masses
peur *f.* fear; **avoir peur** be afraid; **faire peur** scare
peut, peuvent, peux (**pouvoir**) can
pharmacien *m.* druggist; pharmacist
philosophique philosophical
photo *f.* photograph; snapshot
photographier photograph
phrase *f.* sentence
physiologie *f.* physiology
pianiste *m. or f.* pianist
piano *m.* piano
pièce *f.* play; room
pied *m.* foot
piège *m.* trap
pierre *f.* stone
Pierrot (*diminutive of* **Pierre**) little Peter
pilote *m.* pilot; **pilote de guerre** military pilot; **pilote de ligne** commercial air pilot
pilule *f.* pill
pionnier *m.* pioneer
pire (*comparative of* **mauvais**) worse
pisciculture *f.* pisciculture (fish raising)
piscine *f.* swimming pool
place *f.* seat; public square; place (space); spot; job; **sur place** on the spot

placer (*irr. sp.* **A**) place; find a home for
plage *f.* beach
plaindre (*conj. like* **craindre**) pity; feel sorry for; **se plaindre** (**de** + *n.*) complain
plaire (**plaisant, plu, je plais, je plus**) (**à** + *person*) please
plaisanter joke
plaisir *m.* pleasure; **faire plaisir à** please, give pleasure to
plaît (*pres. of* **plaire**) pleases; **s'il vous plaît** please; **si ça vous plaît** if you wish
plan *m.* plan; map (of a city)
plante *f.* plant
planter plant
plat flat
plein full; **en pleine poitrine** right in the chest, in the middle of the chest
pleurer cry
pleut (*pres. of* **pleuvoir**) it is raining; it rains
pleuvoir (**pleuvant, plu, il pleut, il plut**) rain
plu, plut (*pp and sp of* **pleuvoir**) rained
plu, plus (*pp and sp of* **plaire**) pleased
pluie *f.* rain
plupart *f.* majority
pluriel *m.* plural
plus more; most; **de plus en plus** more and more; **ne . . . plus** no more; no longer; **non plus** either; neither; not . . . either
plusieurs several
plutôt rather
poche *f.* pocket
poème *m.* poem
poids *m.* weight
poignant gripping
point *m.* point; period; **point de vue** point of view; **être sur le point de** be about to; (*adv.*) **ne . . . point** not at all
poire *f.* pear
pois *m.* pea; **petits pois** *m. pl.* peas
poisson *m.* fish
poitrine *f.* chest; **en pleine poitrine** right in the chest, in the middle of the chest
poli polite
policier *m.* policeman; **roman policier** *m.* detective story

Verbs with spelling changes are explained on pp. 302–304.

politique *f.* politics
polonais Polish
pomme *f.* apple; **pomme de terre** potato
pommier *m.* apple tree
Pompéi Pompeii
ponctuer punctuate; emphasize
pont *m.* bridge
populaire popular; well liked by the masses
population *f.* people
port *m.* seaport; port
porte *f.* door; doorway; **porte de derrière** back door; **prendre la porte** get out
portefeuille *m.* billfold
porte-monnaie *m.* pocket book
porte-plume *m.* penholder; pen
porter carry; bear; lift; raise; wear; **porter la main à** put one's hand on
portrait *m.* picture, portrait
portugais Portuguese
Portugal *m.* Portugal
poser pose; put down; **poser une question** ask a question; **un problème se pose** a problem presents itself
poste *m.* position, job
poste *f.* post office; **mettre à la poste** mail
poudre *f.* powder
poulet *m.* chicken
poupée *f.* doll
pour for; in order to; **pour que** in order that
pourquoi why
pourrai, pourrais (*fut. and cond. of* **pouvoir**) will be able to; would be able to
poursuivre (*conj. like* **suivre**) continue; pursue
pourtant however; yet
pourvu que provided that
pousser push; **pousser un cri** utter a cry
poussière *f.* dust
pouvoir (**pouvant, pu, je peux, je pus**) (+ *inf.*) can, be able to; may; **il se peut** it is possible; **puis-je** can I; may I; **sauve qui peut!** look out! run for your life!
pratiquant practicing
précieux (*f.* **précieuse**) precious

précipité hasty
précipiter (se) rush
préféré favorite
préférence *f.* preference; **de préférence** preferably
préférer (*irr. sp.* **F**) prefer
premier (*f.* **première**) first; prime
prendre (**prenant, pris, je prends, je pris**) (+ *thing* + **à** [*from*] + *person*) take; have; catch; **prendre une décision** make a decision; **prendre le deuil** go into mourning; **prendre le parti de** side with; **prendre la porte** get out; **prendre sa source** (of river) begin; **prendre tes responsabilités** assume some responsibility; **prendre un verre** have a drink
préparatif *m.* preparation
préparer prepare
près (**de** + *n.*) near; **à peu près** about, approximately
présent *m.* gift; (*adj.*) present
présenter (*person* + **à** + *person*) introduce
presque almost
presser rush; **se presser** crowd; peer
prêt (**à** + *inf.*) ready
prétendre claim
prêter lend
prévenir (*conj. like* **venir**) warn; inform; call (the doctor)
Prévert, Jacques (1900–   ) contemporary French poet
prévoir (*conj. like* **voir** *except in fut. and conditional*) foresee
prier (*person* + **de** + *inf.*) pray; ask; beg; **je vous prie** please
printemps *m.* spring
pris (*pp and sp of* **prendre**) taken; took
prisonnier *m.* prisoner
priver (**de** + *n.*) deprive
prix *m.* price; prize
problème *m.* problem; **poser un problème** present a problem
procédé *m.* process
prochain next
proche near
produire (*conj. like* **conduire**) produce; create
produit *m.* product
professeur *m.* professor; teacher
profiter (**de** + *n.*) take advantage of

Irregular verbs are conjugated on pp. 284–301.

profond deep
profondeur *f.* depth
programme *m.* program
progrès *m.* progress
progresser progress, advance
projet *m.* plan; project
prolonger (se) (*irr. sp.* **B**) last
promenade *f.* walk; **faire une promenade** take a walk
promener (se) (*irr. sp.* **D**) take a walk
promettre (*conj. like* **mettre**) (**à** + **person** + **de** + *inf.*) promise
promis (*pp and sp of* **promettre**) promised
pronom *m.* pronoun
prononcer (*irr. sp.* **A**) pronounce
propos *m.* remark; **à propos de** concerning
proposer propose; suggest
proposition *f.* proposition; proposal
propriétaire *m. or f.* owner; landlord, landlady
protestant *m.* protestant
protestation *f.* protest
Proust, Marcel (1871–1922) twentieth century French novelist
prouver prove
Provence *f.* a region of southern France
provoquer challenge; set into motion
prudence *f.* prudence, care
prudent cautious; prudent
psychologique psychological
pu, pus (*pp and sp of* **pouvoir**) could, was able
public *m.* audience
publier publish
puis then
puis, puisse (*pres. indic. and pres. subjunc. of* **pouvoir**) can, am able; may
puissant powerful; all-powerful, overwhelming
pull-over *m.* sweater
punir punish
pur pure
purger (*irr. sp.* **B**) purge
Pyrénées *f. pl.* Pyrenees

Q

quadrillé ruled in squares
quai *m.* wharf; quai; bank
quand when; **quand même** just the same, even so

quant à as for
quarante forty
quartier *m.* district
quatorze fourteen
quatre four
que that; which; what; whom; how; when; **qu'on est bien!** how comfortable one is!
quel (*f.* **quelle**) which; what; **quel que soit** whatever is
quelconque some sort of
quelque some
quelque chose something
quelqu'un someone
question *f.* question; **poser une question** ask a question
questionner question; inquire
quête *f.* quest; **se mettre en quête** set out in quest of something
qui who; whom; that; which; **à qui le dites-vous!** you're telling me! **qui que ce soit** whoever he is
quinze fifteen
quitter (+ *n.*) leave; **ne pas quitter quelqu'un des yeux** not to take one's eyes off someone
quoi what; **n'importe quoi** anything, anything whatever; **quoi que** whatever; **quoi qu'il en soit** however that may be, however the case may be
quoique although

R

raconter tell
radio *f.* radio
rafraîchir refresh
rage *f.* rabies
rainuré grooved
raison *f.* reason; **à plus forte raison** all the more
raisonnable reasonable
raisonner (se) reason with oneself; try to be reasonable
ramener (*irr. sp.* **D**) bring back
rang *m.* row
ranger (*irr. sp.* **B**) put in order; arrange; put away
ranimer (se) regain consciousness, come to
rapide fast

Verbs with spelling changes are explained on pp. 302–304.

rappeler (*irr. sp.* **F**) remind; call back
se rappeler (+ *n.*) remember
rapport *m.* report
rapporter bring back
rapprocher (**se**) draw near
raser shave; **se raser** shave oneself
rassurant reassuring
rassurer reassure
raviser (**se**) change one's mind
rayon *m.* ray
rebord *m.* edge
recette *f.* recipe
recevoir (**recevant, reçu, je reçois, je reçus**) receive; entertain
réchauffer (**se**) warm oneself
recherche *f.* search; **A la Recherche du temps perdu** *In Search of Lost Time,* novel of Marcel Proust
récolter harvest
recommander recommend
recommencer (*irr. sp.* **A**) do over; begin again; resume; make a fresh start; **ça recommence** "here we go again"
récompenser reward
reconnaître (*conj. like* **connaître**) recognize
reconsidérer reconsider; take another long look at
recoucher (**se**) go back to bed
reçu, reçus (*pp and sp of* **recevoir**) received
recul *m.* recoil, withdrawal, drawing back; **prendre du recul** withdraw
redemander ask again
rédiger (*irr. sp.* **B**) write; compose
réfléchir think; reflect
réfugié *m.* refugee
refuser (**de** + *inf.*) refuse
regagner regain
regard *m.* look; glance; observation
regarder (+ *n.*) look; look at
régime *m.* regime; diet
règlement *m.* rule
régler (*irr. sp.* **E**) settle
réglisse *f.* licorice
regret *m.* regret; grief
régulier (*f.* **régulière**) regular
régulièrement regularly
rejeter (*irr. sp.* **F**) reject
relatif (*f.* **relative**) relative
relativité *f.* relativity

relever (*irr. sp.* **D**) call attention to; point out
relire (*conj. like* **lire**) read again
relu, relus (*pp and sp of* **relire**) read again
remarier (**se**) marry again
remarquable remarkable
remarque *f.* remark
remarquer notice
remède *m.* remedy; medicine
remercier (*person* + **de** *or* **pour** + *thing; person* + **de** + *inf.*) thank
remettre (*conj. like* **mettre**) put back on again; hand in; turn in; put back; postpone
remis (*pp and sp of* **remettre**) put back on; handed in; postponed
remonter go up; **remonter la rue** go up the street
remplacer (*irr. sp.* **A**) replace
remplir fill; fill up; fill out; fulfill
renard *m.* fox
rencontrer meet (by chance)
rendez-vous *m.* date; appointment
rendormir (**se**) (2) go back to sleep
rendre return (something); (+ *adj.*) make; **se rendre** go; **se rendre compte** realize; **se rendre malade** make oneself sick
rêne *f.* rein
renommé famous
renoncer (*irr. sp.* **A**) give up; renounce
renseignement *m.* information
renseigner give information; **se renseigner** ask for information: get information, inform oneself
rentrer return; come back home; go back home; come back in
renverser overthrow; tip over
renvoyer (*conj. like* **envoyer**) dismiss
répandre (**se**) spread out
répandu common
réparation *f.* repair
réparer repair, fix
repas *m.* meal
répéter (*irr. sp.* **E**) repeat
répondre (**à** + *n.*) answer, reply to
reposer (**se**) rest
repousser push aside; push back
reprendre (*conj. like* **prendre**) resume; regain; continue
représentation *f.* show; performance

Irregular verbs are conjugated on pp. 284–301.

repris (*pp and sp of* **reprendre**) resumed; regained; continued
république *f.* republic
réputé famous; well known
réserver reserve; make a reservation
résister (**à** + *n.*) resist
respirer breathe; take a breath; feel relieved
responsabilité *f.* responsibility; **prendre tes responsabilités** assume some responsibility
ressembler (**à** + *n.*) look like, resemble
ressource *f.* resource
ressusciter resuscitate; come to life again
reste *m.* remainder; **ne pas être en reste** be equal to the situation; not be backward
rester remain; stay; stand; **il me reste à** I'll have to; **il ne me reste rien** I have nothing left
résultat *m.* result
retard *m.* delay; **avoir du retard** be late; **être en retard** be late
retarder delay
retéléphoner telephone again
retenir (*conj. like* **tenir**) reserve
retirer (**se**) withdraw
retour *m.* return; **à ton retour** when you return
retourner return, go back; turn again; **se retourner** turn around; look back **s'en retourner** go back
retraite *f.* retreat; **prendre sa retraite** retire
retraverser cross again
retrouver find; discover; find once more; **j'ai retrouvé le calme** peace came over me again
réunion *f.* meeting
réussi successful
réussir (**à** + *n.*; **à** + *inf.*) succeed
réveiller awaken; **se réveiller** wake up
révéler (*irr. sp.* **E**) reveal; discover
revenir (*conj. like* **venir**) return; come back
revenu *m.* income
rêver (**de** + *n.*; **de** + *inf.*) dream
rêveur *m.* dreamer
reviendrai, reviendrais (*fut. and cond. of* **revenir**) will, would come back

revivre (*conj. like* **vivre**) live again; relive; come back to life
revoir (*conj. like* **voir**) see again; **se revoir** meet again; **au revoir** goodbye
revue *f.* magazine
Rhin *m.* Rhine
Rhône *m.* Rhone, a river whose source is in Switzerland, and which flows through France, and empties into the Mediterranean near Marseilles
rhume *m.* cold
ri, rit (*pp, pres., sp of* **rire**) laughed; laughs; laughed
riche rich
rideau *m.* curtain
rien nothing; **ne . . . rien** nothing; **servir à rien** be useless
rire (**riant, ri, je ris, je ris**) (**de** + *n.*) laugh; **rire de quelqu'un** make fun of someone
rivière *f.* river; stream; tributary
Robbe-Grillet, Alain (1922–   ) contemporary French writer
robe *f.* dress
roche *f.* rock
rôle *m.* role; part
roman *m.* novel; **roman policier** detective story; (*adj.*) Romance; "**nouveau roman**" school of writers who, from 1950 on, searched for completely new forms for the novel
romancier *m.* novelist
rond *n.* circle; **tourner en rond** run around in circles; (*adj.*) round
rosier *m.* rosebush
rôti *m.* roast beef; a roast; (*adj.*) roasted
rouge red; **feu rouge** red light; traffic light
rougeole *f.* measles
rouleau *m.* roll
rouler drive; go; roll; move
route *f.* way; road; **en route** on the way; **se tromper de route** take the wrong road
roux (*f.* **rousse**) (referring to hair) red, reddish
ruche *f.* ruche (pleated strip of lace or ribbon); frilling
rue *f.* street
ruine *f.* ruin
ruiner (**se**) ruin oneself

Verbs with spelling changes are explained on pp. 302–304.

rusé sly; tricky
russe Russian
Russie *f.* Russia

S

sa (*f. of* **son**) his; her; its
sable *m.* sand
sac *m.* bag; handbag
sachant (*pres. part. of* **savoir**) knowing
sache, sachiez (*pres. subjunctive of* **savoir**) know
sacré sacred
sacrifier (**se**) sacrifice oneself
sage wise; (speaking of behavior) good, well-behaved
saigner bleed; **il saignait du nez** his nose was bleeding
Saint-Exupéry, Antoine de (1900–1944) twentieth century French novelist
sais, sait (*pres. of* **savoir**) know
saisir seize
saison *f.* season; **la belle saison** the summer months
sale dirty
salle *f.* room (for meetings); **salle à manger** dining room; **salle de séjour** living room
salon *m.* drawing room; living room
saluer greet
salut *m.* salute; salvation
samedi *m.* Saturday
San Antonio city in Argentina
sans without; **sans doute** probably
santé *f.* health
satellite *m.* satellite
sauce *f.* sauce; gravy
sauf except; but
saurai, saurais (*fut. and cond. of* **savoir**) will know; would know
sauvage wild
sauver save; **sauve qui peut!** look out! run for your life!
savant *m.* scientist; (*adj.*) learned; **Les Femmes savantes** *The Learned Women,* a play by Molière
savoir (**sachant, su, je sais, je sus**) know; (+ *inf.*) know how to
savourer enjoy
savoureux (*f.* **savoureuse**) tasty
scène *f.* scene; stage
scie *f.* saw

science *f.* science; **homme de science** scientist
sec (*f.* **sèche**) dry
secondaire secondary
secrétaire *m. or f.* secretary
secrètement secretly
Seine *f.* French river which crosses Paris
séjour *m.* stay, sojourn; **salle de séjour** living room
sel *m.* salt
selon according to
semaine *f.* week
semblable similar
sembler (+ *inf.*) seem
sens *m.* way; direct; meaning; **dans un sens** in a way
sensible sensitive
sensiblement more or less; perceptibly, noticeably
sentiment *m.* feeling; sensation
sentir (2) feel; **se sentir** feel; **se sentir mal** feel sick
séparer separate
serai, serais (*fut. and cond. of* **être**) will be; would be
sérieux (*f.* **sérieuse**) serious; **au sérieux** seriously
serrer shake; press; **serrer les dents** clench one's teeth
serrure *f.* lock
service *m.* service; silverware
serviette *f.* towel; briefcase
servir (2) serve; **ne servir à rien** be useless; **se servir de** use; make use of
seul alone; lonely; only; solely; single; **être seul à** be the only one to
sévère strict
si so; yes; **si riches qu'ils soient** however rich they are
siamoise *f.* cotton fabric
Sibérie *f.* Siberia
siècle *m.* century
sien (*f.* **sienne**) his; hers; its
signe *m.* sign
signifier mean
silence *m.* silence
silencieusement silently
silencieux (*f.* **silencieuse**) silent
simplement simply
singulier *m.* singular; (*adj.*) (*f.* **singulière**) singular; strange

Irregular verbs are conjugated on pp. 284–301.

sinon otherwise
sirène *f.* siren
six six
ski *m.* ski; **faire du ski** go skiing
socialisme *m.* socialism
société *f.* society; firm, company
sœur *f.* sister
soi oneself; **en soi** in itself; **ça va de soi** it goes without saying
soif *f.* thirst; **il a soif** he is thirsty
soigner take care of, care for
soigneusement carefully
soir *m.* evening
soirée *f.* evening; party
soixante sixty
soldat *m.* soldier
soleil *m.* sun
solidarité *f.* solidarity
sombre dark; **il fait sombre** it is dark
sommeil *m.* sleep; **avoir sommeil** be sleepy
sommet *m.* peak
son, sa, ses his; her; its; one's
sonner ring
sonnerie *f.* ring; doorbell
Sorbonne *f.* the building which houses the *Faculté des Lettres* of the University of Paris
sort *m.* fate
sorte *f.* sort
sortie *f.* exit; **à la sortie de l'école** after school
sortir (2) leave, go out
sot (*f.* **sotte**) foolish; silly
sottement foolishly; sheepishly
sou *m.* penny, cent
souci *m.* worry; **se faire du souci** worry
soucoupe *f.* saucer
soudain (*adj.*) sudden; (*adv.*) suddenly
souffrir (*conj. like* **ouvrir**) suffer
souhaiter wish
soulier *m.* shoe
souligner underline
soupe *f.* soup
souper *m.* supper; evening meal
soupirer sigh
source *f.* source; **prendre sa source** (of a river) begin
sourcil *m.* eyebrow
sourd deaf
souriant smiling

sourire (*conj. like* **rire**) (**à** + *n.*) smile; (*n.*) *m.* smile
sous-sol *m.* basement
souvenir (se) (*conj. like* **venir**) (**de** + *n.*; **de** + *inf.*) remember; (*n.*) *m.* souvenir; memory; remembrance; recollection; keepsake
souvent often
spectacle *m.* show
spectateur *m.* spectator
splendide marvelous
sport *m.* sport; **faire des sports** participate in sports; **journal de sport** sports magazine
sportif (*f.* **sportive**) sport loving; inclined toward sports
squelette *m.* skeleton
stationner park
strictement strictly
style *m.* style
stylo *m.* fountain pen
su, sus (*pp and sp of* **savoir**) known; knew; learned, found out
subjonctif *m.* subjunctive
subtilement subtly
succès *m.* success
sucer (*irr. sp.* **A**) suck
sucre *m.* sugar
sucrerie *f.* candy
sud *m.* south
Suède *f.* Sweden
suédois Swedish
suffire (**suffisant, suffi, je suffis, je suffis**) suffice
suis (*pres. of* **être**) I am; (*pres. of* **suivre**) I, you follow
Suisse *f.* Switzerland
suite *f.* continuation; aftermath, consequence; **à la suite** as a result; **tout de suite** right now, right away, immediately
suivant (*adj.*) following; next; (*prep.*) according to
suivre (**suivant, suivi, je suis, je suivis**) follow; **suivre un cours** take a course
sujet *m.* subject; **au sujet de** about, concerning
superbe superb
superflu superfluous
supplémentaire supplementary
sur on; out of

Verbs with spelling changes are explained on pp. 302–304.

sûr sure
surprenant surprising
surprise *f.* surprise, astonishment
surtout especially; above all; mostly
surveiller watch over
symphonie *f.* symphony
système *m.* system

T

tabac *m.* tobacco; **bureau de tabac** tobacco shop
table *f.* table; **mettre la table** set the table; **table de nuit** night stand
tableau *m.* picture; painting; **tableau noir** blackboard
tact *m.* tact
taille *f.* height
tailler cut
tandis que while, whereas
tant so much
tante *f.* aunt
taper type, typewrite
tapis *m.* rug
tard late
tarder (à + *inf.*) be late; delay, put off
tasse *f.* cup
taudis *m.* slum; hovel, shack
taxi *m.* taxi, taxicab, cab
technique *f.* technique
téléphoner (à + *person*) telephone
télévision *f.* television; television set
tellement so; so much
témoignage *m.* testimony
témoigner show; witness
tempe *f.* temple (part of body)
temps *m.* time; weather; tense; **en même temps** at the same time; **il est grand temps** it is high time; **par ce temps** in this weather; **le temps de** long enough to
tendance *f.* tendency
tendre (*v.*) hold out; extend; give; (*adj.*) tender
tendresse *f.* tenderness
tenez look here!
tenir (**tenant, tenu, je tiens, je tins**) hold; keep; **se tenir** be; stand; **se tenir par la main** hold hands
terminer finish
terrain *m.* ground; land; tract of land; field

terre *f.* earth; land; **pomme de terre** *f.* potato
terreur *f.* terror
testament *m.* will
tête *f.* head; **hocher la tête** nod one's head; **quelle tête** what a stubborn person
thé *m.* tea
théâtre *m.* theater
théologie *f.* theology
théorie *f.* theory
thèse *f.* thesis; dissertation
tiens look
tigre *m.* tiger
timbre *m.* stamp
timidité *f.* timidity
tire-lire *f.* piggy bank
tirer take out; pull; shoot; pull the trigger; (**sur** + *person*) shoot at
tiret *m.* dash
tiroir *m.* drawer
tituber stagger
toile *f.* linen; **toile cirée** oilcloth
toit *m.* roof
tomber fall; **tomber malade** get sick
ton *m.* tone
tonnerre *m.* thunder; **coup de tonnerre** thunder clap
tôt early; soon
totalement completely
toucher touch
toujours always; still
tour *m.* stroll; trip; trick; **faire le tour du monde** take a trip around the world
touriste *m.* tourist
tourmenter torment; bother
tourner turn; **tourner en rond** turn around in circles
Tours French city southwest of Paris in Loire valley
tout (*m. pl.* **tous**) (*adj.*) all, every; whole; **tout le monde** everyone; **tous les samedis** every Saturday
tout (*pron.*) everything; **avant tout** above all; **une fois pour toutes** once and for all; **capable de tout** capable of anything
tout (*adv.*) very, quite; **tout à côté** right near; **tout à coup** all of a sudden; **tout à fait** quite, completely; **tout à l'heure** in a little while; a little while

Irregular verbs are conjugated on pp. 284–301.

ago; **tout bas** in a whisper; **tout droit** erect; straight ahead; **tout de même** all the same; **tout de suite** immediately, right now; **tout en lisant** while reading

traditionnel (*f.* **traditionnelle**) traditional

traduction *f.* translation

traduire (*conj. like* **conduire**) translate

train *m.* train; **en train de** in the act of

traité *m.* treaty

traiter treat

traître *m.* traitor

tranquille quiet, calm; **nous avons été tranquilles** we were in peace

tranquillement calmly

transatlantique *m.* ocean liner

transmettre (*conj. like* **mettre**) transmit

transport *m.* transportation

transporter carry

travail *m.* work; job; **se mettre au travail** set to work

travailleur (*f.* **travailleuse**) hard working; industrious

travers: à travers across

traversée *f.* crossing; **traversée en bateau** boat trip

traverser cross

treize thirteen

Trelew city in Argentina

tremblant shivering

trembler shake

tremper wet; soak; dunk

trente thirty

très very

trésor *m.* treasure

tressaillir start; give a start

trêve *f.* truce; solace

trimestre *m.* trimester; (school) quarter

trinquer clink glasses; toast

triste sad

tristesse *f.* sadness

trois three

tromper deceive; **se tromper de route** take the wrong road

trou *m.* hole

troubler trouble; move; **troubler (se)** become upset; become embarrassed

troupe *f.* flock

trouver find; **comment trouvez-vous** what do you think of; **se trouver** be; be found, be located; lie; **se trouver**

mal faint; **se trouver mieux** feel better

tue-tête: à tue-tête at the top of one's voice

tuer kill

Tunisie *f.* Tunisia

tutoyer (*irr. sp.* **C**) use the "**tu**" form in speaking to someone

U

un a, an; one

uniforme *m.* uniform; (*adj.*) uniform

universel (*f.* **universelle**) universal; versatile and universal

usé worn out

usine *f.* factory

utile useful

V

va (*pres. of* **aller**) goes; **ça va de soi** it goes without saying

vacances *f. pl.* vacation; **cours de vacances** summer courses; **en vacances** on a vacation

vaccin *m.* vaccine

vache *f.* cow

vague *f.* wave

vaille (*pres. subjunc. of* **valoir**) be worth

vaisselle *f.* dishes; **faire la vaisselle** do the dishes

valeur *f.* value

valide valid, good

valise *f.* suitcase; **faire une valise** pack a suitcase

valoir (**valant, valu, je vaux, je valus**) be worth; **il vaut mieux** it is better; **valoir la peine** be worth the trouble; **votre idée ne vaut pas grand-chose** your idea isn't worth much

valve *f.* valve (a half shell)

Vatican *m.* Vatican, papal headquarters in Rome

vaut (*pres. of* **valoir**) is worth

veau *m.* veal

vécu, vécus (*pp and sp of* **vivre**) lived

veille *f.* watch

veiller watch; **veiller sur quelqu'un** watch over someone

vendeuse *f.* salesgirl; saleswoman

vendre sell

vendredi *m.* Friday

Verbs with spelling changes are explained on pp. 302–304.

venir (venant, venu, je viens, je vins)
come; **faire venir** send for; **venez me
voir** come and see me; **venir de** have
just (**il vient d'arriver** he has just
arrived)
vent *m.* wind
ventre *m.* belly; abdomen; stomach
verbe *m.* verb
verglas *m.* ice
vérité *f.* truth
Verlaine, Paul (1844–1896) French
symbolist poet
verrai, verrais (*fut. and cond. of* **voir**)
will see; would see
verre *m.* glass; **prendre un verre** have
a drink
vers toward; around; about
vert green
vertu *f.* virtue
vestiaire *m.* cloak room
vétérinaire *m.* veterinary
veut (*pres. of* **vouloir**) wants, wishes
vexer vex; hurt
viande *f.* meat
victorieux (*f.* **victorieuse**) victorious
vider empty
vie *f.* life
vieillard *m.* old man; *m. pl.* old people
vieillir grow old
viens, vient, viennent (*pres. of* **venir**)
comes; come
vierge untouched
vieux (*before vowel sound* **vieil**; *f.* **vieille**)
old
vif (*f.* **vive**) alert
ville *f.* city; town; **en ville** downtown;
hôtel de ville city hall
vin *m.* wine
vingt twenty
vingtaine *f.* about twenty
violent violent; very strong
virtuose *m.* virtuoso
visage *m.* face; **avec des étoiles sur le
visage** stars were shining on my face
vision *f.* vision; point of view
visiter visit (a place)
visiteur *m.* visitor
vit (*sp of* **voir**) saw; (*pres. of* **vivre**) lives
vite quick; quickly, fast;
vitesse *f.* speed
vitre *f.* window pane
vivant living; merry
vivre (vivant, vécu, je vis, je vécus) live
voici here is, here are

voilà there is, there are; here it is; **les
voilà** here they come
voir (voyant, vu, je vois, je vis) see;
notice; **aller voir** go and see; visit;
venez me voir come and see me; **voir
du pays** see places
voisin *m.* neighbor
voiture *f.* car
voix *f.* voice; **à haute voix** aloud; **à
trois voix** between three people
vol *m.* flight; theft
volant flying
voler fly; rob
volet *m.* shutter
voleur *m.* thief
volontairement willingly; voluntarily
volonté *f.* will
volontiers willingly; with pleasure
Voltaire (1694–1778) eighteenth century
writer of philosophical novels, essays,
poems, and plays
vont (*pres. of* **aller**) go
vos (*pl. of* **votre**) your
votre (*pl.* **vos**) your
voudrai, voudrais (*fut. and cond. of*
vouloir) will want; would like
vouloir (voulant, voulu, je veux, je
voulus) want; wish; desire; **voulez-
vous** will you please; **vouloir bien** be
willing; **vouloir dire** mean
vous you; **vous deux** both of you
voyage *m.* trip; **faire un voyage** take
a trip
voyager (*irr. sp.* **B**) travel
voyageur *m.* traveller
voyant (*pres. part. of* **voir**) seeing
voyons (**voir**) we see; come now; look
here
vrai true; real
vraiment really
vu (*pp of* **voir**) seen
vue *f.* view; sight

Y

y there; in it
yeux (*m. pl. of* **œil**) eyes; **jeter les yeux**
glance; **quitter quelqu'un des yeux**
take one's eyes off someone

Z

zoologique zoological; **jardin zoologique**
zoo

Irregular verbs are conjugated on pp. 284–301.

English-French Vocabulary

English-French Vocabulary

adj.	adjective	*irr. sp.*	irregular spelling	*pers.*	person
adv.	adverb	*m.*	masculine	*prep.*	preposition
cond.	conditional	*n.*	noun	*pres.*	present
conj.	conjugated	*obj.*	object	*pron.*	pronoun
conjunc.	conjunction	*p.*	page	*rel.*	relative
f.	feminine	*part.*	participle	*sing.*	singular
fut.	future	*pl.*	plural	*sp*	simple past
inf.	infinitive	*pp*	past participle	*subjunc.*	subjunctive
interrog.	interrogative			*v.*	verb

* aspirate *h*   (2) **-ir** verbs which do not insert **-iss-**; all other **-ir** verbs insert **-iss-**.

Page references immediately following the English word refer to explanations of the word in question.

Verbs whose principal parts are given are irregular, and their conjugations may be found on pp. 284–301. The use of the principal parts is explained on page 283. Verbs followed by (*conj. like* . . .) are irregular and follow the pattern of the verb indicated.

Verbs followed by (*irr. sp.* **A** to **F**) undergo a spelling change in certain forms. The letter refers to the appropriate type of change explained on pp. 302–304.

A

a un, une

able capable; **be able** pouvoir (pouvant, pu, je peux, je pus) ($+$ *inf.*)

about (p. 238) de; sur; environ; à peu près; vers; au sujet de; à propos de; **about that** à ce sujet; **be about to** être sur le point de; **talk about** parler de

above (p. 238) sur; au-dessus de

abroad à l'étranger; **from abroad** de l'étranger

absence absence *f.;* **in the absence** en l'absence

absent absent

absolutely absolument

accent accent *m.*

accident accident *m.*

according to (p. 239) selon, suivant, d'après

accused (*n.*) accusé *m.*

accustomed: **get accustomed to** s'habituer (à $+$ *inf.*)

ache (*v.*) faire mal; **I have a headache** j'ai mal à la tête

acquaintance connaissance *f.;* relation *f.*

across (p. 239) à travers; de l'autre côté de; **run across** traverser en courant; **travel across** traverser

act agir

action action *f.*

actress actrice *f.*

actually (p. 12) vraiment, réellement; en fait, à vrai dire

address adresse *f.*

admire admirer

admit admettre (*conj. like* mettre)

adopt adopter

adore adorer

adventure aventure *f.*

advice (pp. 12–13) conseil *m.;* **a piece of advice** un conseil *m.*

advise conseiller (à $+$ *person* $+$ de $+$ *inf,*); **advise against** déconseiller

affair affaire *f.*

afraid: **be afraid** avoir peur, craindre; **become afraid** *compound past of* avoir peur, prendre peur

Africa Afrique *f.*

after (pp. 227, 233, 239) après; d'après; **after hearing** après avoir entendu

afternoon après-midi *m. or f.*

again (p. 13) encore, encore une fois, de nouveau, à nouveau; re- $+$ *verb*

against contre; **advise against** déconseiller

age âge *m.;* **old age** vieillesse *f.,* **vieux jours** *m. pl.*

ago il y a; **a little while ago** tout à l'heure; **a month ago** il y a un mois

agree (pp. 13–14) s'accorder; consentir (à $+$ *inf.*); être d'accord

agreed d'accord, c'est entendu, entendu

aim but *m.*

air air *m.;* **in the air** en l'air

airplane avion *m.*

airport aéroport *m.*

alarm clock réveil *m.*

Alexander Alexandre

all tout (*f.* toute, *m. pl.* tous); **all the same** quand même; **all the while** (p. 65) tout en; **not at all** pas du tout

allow laisser (*person* $+$ *inf.*); permettre (à $+$ *person* $+$ de $+$ *inf.*); **I was allowed** j'ai pu

almost presque

alone seul; **leave me alone** laissez-moi tranquille

along (p. 239) le long de; **get along** se débrouiller; **go along the road** suivre le chemin

already déjà

although bien que, quoique

always toujours

amateur amateur *m.*

ambassador ambassadeur *m.*

ambitious ambitieux (*f.* ambitieuse)

America Amérique *f.*

American Américain *m.;* **South American** Sud-Américain *m.*

amuse amuser; **amuse oneself** s'amuser (à $+$ *inf.*)

amusing amusant

anger colère *f.*

angry fâché; en colère; vexé; **get angry** se mettre en colère; se fâcher

Verbs with spelling changes are explained on pp. 302–304.

animal animal *m.*
Anne Anne
anniversary anniversaire *m.*
announcement annonce *f.*
annoying ennuyeux (*f.* ennuyeuse)
answer répondre (à + *n.*)
any du, de la, des; quelque; (*obj. pron.*)
en; any at all pas du tout; in any case
en tout cas; not any pas de, ne . . .
aucun; not any more ne . . . plus
anyone quelqu'un; not . . . anyone
ne . . . personne
anything quelque chose; not . . . anything ne . . . rien
apartment appartement *m.*
approach approcher (de + *n.*); s'approcher (de + *n.*)
April avril
Arabic (*n.*) arabe *m.*
ardent ardent
are sont; se trouvent; are to doivent;
there are il y a
area région *f.*
aren't you n'est-ce pas
arm bras *m.*
armchair fauteuil *m.*
army armée *f.*
arrest arrêter
arrive arriver
art art *m.*
artist artiste *m. or f.*
as (pp. 22, 234) comme; as . . . as
aussi . . . que; as for quant à; as
long as tant que; as soon as dès que
ashamed: be ashamed avoir honte
ask demander (*thing* + à + *person;* à +
person + de + *inf.*); ask a question
poser une question; ask for something demander quelque chose; ask
of someone demander à quelqu'un;
he asked my pardon il m'a demandé
pardon
astrology astrologie *f.*
astronaut astronaute *m. or f.*
at (pp. 213–215, 240–241) à; chez; at
length longuement; at once tout de
suite; not at all pas du tout
Athens Athènes
attend (p. 82) aller à; assister à
attention attention *f.*
attentively attentivement
attitude attitude *f.*

author auteur *m.*
automatically automatiquement
awaken réveiller; se réveiller
away: right away tout de suite

B

back (*n.*) dos *m.*
back: come back revenir; come back
home rentrer; go back retourner
bad (*n.*) mauvais *m.* (*adj.*) mauvais
ball danse *f.*, bal *m.*
Balzac Balzac
barber coiffeur *m.*
bare nu
bark aboyer (*irr. sp.* C)
bathe se baigner
be être (étant, été, je suis, je fus); be
able pouvoir (pouvant, pu, je peux,
je pus); be better aller mieux; être
mieux; valoir mieux; be mistaken se
tromper; be warm avoir chaud; be
well aller bien; be willing vouloir bien
beach plage *f.*
beautiful beau (*before vowel sound* bel;
f. belle)
beauty beauté *f.*
because (pp. 240–241) parce que; because of à cause de
become (pp. 27, 71) devenir (*conj. like*
venir); become afraid prendre peur;
become frightened s'effrayer; become interested in s'intéresser à; it
became cold il a fait froid
bed lit *m.; go to bed se coucher
before (pp. 227, 234, 241) (time) avant
+ *n. or pron.*), avant de (+ *inf.*), avant
que (+ *subjunc.*); (place) devant
begin commencer (à + *inf.*) (*irr. sp.* A),
se mettre (à + *inf.*)
beginning commencement *m.*
believe croire (croyant, cru, je crois,
je crus) (+ *inf.;* + *person;* à + *thing;*
en + *person* [with the sense of *to have
faith in*])
belong appartenir (*conj. like* tenir)
best (*adj.*) meilleur; (*adv.*) mieux
better (pp. 27–28) (*adj.*) meilleur; (*adv.*)
mieux; be better valoir mieux, être
mieux; (referring to health) aller
mieux

Irregular verbs are conjugated on pp. 284–301.

between entre
big grand
billfold portefeuille *m.*
bird oiseau *m.*
bit: a bit un peu
blame blâmer
blanket couverture *f.*
blue bleu
boat bateau *m.*
book livre *m.;* telephone book annuaire *m.*
bored ennuyé; be bored s'ennuyer (*irr. sp.* C)
boring ennuyeux (*f.* ennuyeuse)
born: be born naître (naissant, né, je nais, je naquis); he was born il est né
boss patron *m.*
both les deux, tous les deux; both of you vous deux
bother déranger (*irr. sp.* B); ennuyer (*irr. sp.* C)
boy garçon *m.*
brave courageux (*f.* courageuse)
break casser
bridge (*over river*) pont *m.;* (*game*) bridge *m.*
briefcase serviette *f.*
brilliantly brillamment
bring (pp. 28–29) (*a thing*) apporter; (*a person*) amener (*irr. sp.* D)
brother frère *m.;* brother-in-law beau-frère *m.;* oldest brother aîné *m.,* frère aîné
brush brosser
Brussels Bruxelles
build construire (*conj. like* conduire)
building immeuble *m.;* bâtiment *m.,* édifice *m.*
bus (*within city*) autobus *m.;* (*between cities*) autocar *m.*
business affaire *f.;* les affaires *f. pl.;* businessman homme d'affaires *m.*
busy (p. 67) occupé; be busy être en train de; he was busy writing il était occupé à écrire, il était en train d'écrire
but (p. 235) (*conjunc.*) mais; (*prep.*) sauf, excepté
buy acheter (*irr. sp.* D)
by par; de; en; by falling en tombant; by plane par avion, en avion; by the time quand; go by passer

C

café café *m.*
call appeler (*irr. sp.* F); téléphoner (à + *person*)
can (p. 29) pouvoir (pouvant, pu, je peux, je pus); (*know how*) savoir (sachant, su, je sais, je sus)
Canada Canada *m.*
candidate candidat *m.*
capable capable
car voiture *f.,* auto *f.,* automobile *f.*
care soin *m.,* prudence *f.*
careless négligent
carnation œillet *m.*
carol: Christmas carol cantique de Noël *m.*
case cas *m.;* in any case en tout cas; in case of en cas de
cat chat *m.*
catch attraper; catch sight of apercevoir (*conj. like* recevoir)
Catholic catholique
caught pris
celebrate célébrer
certain certain
chair chaise *f.*
change (pp. 38–40) (*v.*) (*irr. sp.* B) changer; change one's mind changer d'avis; (*m.*) changement *m.;* (*small*) change monnaie *f.*
character (p. 40) personnage *m.;* caractère *m.*
charm charme *m.*
charming charmant
chat bavarder
chauffeur chauffeur *m.*
cheap bon marché
check chèque *m.*
chess échecs *m. pl.*
child enfant *m.* or *f.*
Chinese chinois
Christmas Noël *m.;* Christmas carol cantique de Noël *m.*
church église *f.*
cider cidre *m.*
cigaret cigarette *f.*
city ville *f.;* city hall hôtel de ville *m.,* mairie *f.*
claim prétendre
class classe *f.,;* conversation class classe de conversation *f.*

Verbs with spelling changes are explained on pp. 302–304.

classmate camarade de classe *m. or f.*
cleaner teinturier *m.;* **to the cleaner's**
à la teinturerie; chez le teinturier
cleaning woman femme de ménage *f.*
clear évident
climate climat *m.*
clock: alarm clock réveil *m.*
close (*v.*) fermer (*adj.*) proche; **a close
friend** un ami intime *m.*
clothes habits *m. pl.;* vêtements *m. pl.*
club club *m.,* cercle *m.*
coat (*overcoat*) manteau *m.;* (*suitcoat*)
veste *m.*
coffee café *m.*
cold (*n.*) rhume *m.;* (*adj.*) froid; **it became cold** il a fait froid; **it was cold** il
faisait froid
colleague collègue *m.*
collection collection *f.*
colonel colonel *m.*
come venir (venant, venu, je viens, je
vins); **come back** revenir (*conj. like*
venir); **come back home** rentrer;
come and see me venez me voir;
come in entrer; **come to dinner** venir
dîner
comfortable confortable
company compagnie *f.;* maison *f.;*
société *f.*
completely complètement
concern: **concern oneself with** s'occuper (de + *n.*)
concerning (p. 238) au sujet de; sur;
concerning them à leur sujet
concert concert *m.*
condemn condamner
condition condition *f.;* **on the condition that** à (la) condition que
considerable considérable
continue continuer (à + *inf.*); **continue
on our way** continuer notre route
convention congrès *m.*
conversation conversation *f.;* **a conversation class** une classe de conversation *f.*
convince convaincre (*conj. like* vaincre)
cook faire la cuisine
copy copier; **copy again** recopier
correct (*v.*) corriger (*irr. sp.* **B**); (*adj.*)
exact
corridor corridor *m.;* couloir *m.*

cost prix *m.*
count compter (+ *inf.*)
country pays *m.;* (*opposite of city*) campagne *f.*
courage courage *m.*
course cours *m.;* **take a course** suivre un
cours; **course** (*of action*) démarche *f.;*
drop a course abandonner un cours,
laisser tomber un cours
cousin cousin *m.;* cousine *f.*
cream crème *f.;* **ice cream** glace *f.*
crime crime *m.*
criticize critiquer
cross traverser
crossword puzzle mots croisés *m. pl.*
crowd foule *f.*
cry pleurer
cultured cultivé
curious curieux (*f.* curieuse)
curtain rideau *m.*
cut couper
cute mignon (*f.* mignonne)

D

dance danse *f.;* bal *m.*
danger danger *m.*
dangerous dangereux (*f.* dangereuse)
dark brun; sombre
date rendez-vous *m.*
daughter fille *f.*
dawn aube *f.*
day (pp. 40–41) jour *m.;* journée *f.*
daylight jour *m.*
dead mort
deal: **a great deal** beaucoup
December décembre *m.*
decide décider (de + *inf.*), se décider
(à + *inf.*)
deep profond
deep-seated profond
defend défendre
defendant inculpé *m.*
delighted enchanté
demanding exigeant
democracy démocratie *f.*
Denmark Danemark *m.*
dentist dentiste *m.*
describe décrire (*conj. like* écrire)
desk bureau *m.*

Irregular verbs are conjugated on pp. 284–301.

destiny destinée *f.*
detective inspecteur *m.;* detective story roman policier *m.*
diamond diamant *m.*
die mourir (mourant, mort, je meurs, je mourus)
difference différence *f.*
different différent
difficult difficile
difficulty difficulté *f.*
dinner dîner *m.;* come to dinner venir dîner; have dinner dîner
directly directement
director directeur *m.*
discuss discuter
discussion discussion *f.*
dishes vaisselle *f. sing.* wash the dishes faire la vaisselle
disillusion désillusion *f.*
distance distance *f.;* in the distance au loin
distribute distribuer
do faire (faisant, fait, je fais, je fis); do without se passer de; do wrong faire du tort
doctor docteur *m.,* médecin *m.*
dog chien *m.*
dollar dollar *m.*
door porte *f.*
dormitory dortoir *m.,* résidence *f.*
doubt douter (de + *n.*)
doubtful douteux (*f.* douteuse)
down (p. 241) en bas; go down descendre; slow down ralentir
drawer tiroir *m.*
dream rêver (de + *n.;* de + *inf.*)
dress robe *f.*
drink boire (buvant, bu, je bois, je bus)
drive conduire (conduisant, conduit, je conduis, je conduisis)
drop (*a course*) abandonner, laisser tomber
duck canard *m.*
duty devoir *m.*

E

each chacun; each other se; l'un l'autre
earlier plus tôt; de meilleure heure
early (pp. 53–54) tôt, de bonne heure; en avance

earn gagner
ease facilité *f.*
easy facile; easy going indulgent
eat manger (*irr. sp.* B)
egg œuf *m.*
eight huit
either non plus
elbow coude *m.*
elegant élégant
else: something else autre chose
elsewhere ailleurs, autre part
emergency urgence *f.*
encourage encourager (*irr. sp.* B)
end (p. 54) fin *f.;* bout *m.*
energetically énergiquement
engineer ingénieur *m.*
England Angleterre *f.*
English (*n.*) Anglais *m.;* (*adj.*) anglais
enough assez
enter entrer (dans + *n.*)
entertaining amusant
erase effacer (*irr. sp.* A)
error erreur *f.,* faute *f.*
escape (pp. 54–55) échapper (à + *n.*); s'échapper (de + *n.*)
especially surtout
even même; even though bien que, quoique; tout en (+ *pres. participle*)
evening (pp. 40–41, 137) soir *m.;* soirée *f.;* evening party soirée *f.;* last evening hier soir
event événement *m.*
ever jamais
every (p. 55) chaque; tous les; every other year tous les deux ans
everyone (p. 55) tout le monde
everything (pp. 55–56, 129) tout; n'importe quoi; everything that tout ce qui, tout ce que
everywhere partout
evident évident
examination examen *m.*
excellent excellent
except (p. 241) sauf, à part, excepté
exchange (p. 40) échanger (*irr. sp.* B)
exercise devoir *m.,* exercice *m.*
exist exister; régner
exotic exotique
expect (pp. 67–68) attendre (+ *n.*); s'attendre (à + *n.*); compter (+ *n.*) what do you expect que voulez-vous

Verbs with spelling changes are explained on pp. 302–304.

expensive cher (*f.* chère)
experience expérience *f.*
explain expliquer
explosion explosion *f.*
exterior extérieur *m.*
extraordinary extraordinaire
eye œil *m.* (*pl.*) yeux

F

face figure *f.*
factory usine *f.*
fail (pp. 68–69) manquer (de + *inf.*); échouer (à un examen); coller (quelqu'un)
fair exposition *f.*
fall tomber; **fall out** tomber de
family famille *f.*
famous célèbre, connu
far loin
farmer fermier *m.*
fast rapide; vite
fate sort *m.*
father père *m.*
father-in-law beau-père *m.*
favorite préféré
feel (pp. 69–70) sentir; se sentir; **feel well** se sentir bien; **How do you feel?** Comment allez-vous?
few peu; **a few** quelques
field champ *m.;* domaine *m.*
fifty cinquante
fight se battre (battant, battu, je bats, je battis)
fill remplir (de + *n.*)
film film *m.*
finally enfin, finalement
find trouver; **find again** retrouver; **find out** découvrir (*conj. like* ouvrir), apprendre (*conj. like* prendre)
fine excellent; beau (*before vowel sound* bel; *f.* belle); **those fine people** ces braves gens *m. pl.*
finger doigt *m.*
finish finir
fire incendie *m.*
first premier (*f.* première); **on the first floor** au rez-de-chaussée
fish poisson *m.*

five cinq
floor plancher *m.;* étage *m.;* **on the first floor** au rez-de-chaussée
Florida Floride *f.*
florist fleuriste *m. or f.*
flower fleur *f.*
fluently couramment
follow suivre (suivant, suivi, je suis, je suivis)
foolish stupide
foot pied *m.;* **on foot** à pied
football football *m.;* **football game** un match de football, une partie de football
for (pp. 235, 242) (*conjunc.*) car (*prep.*) pour; pendant; depuis, il y a . . . que, voilà . . . que
forbid défendre (à + *person* + de + *inf.*)
foreign étranger (*f.* étrangère)
foreigner étranger *m.*
forget oublier (de + *inf.*)
former ancien (*f.* ancienne); **the former** celui-là
formerly autrefois
fortune fortune *f.*
forty quarante
fountain pen stylo *m.*
four quatre
France France *f.*
Frances Françoise *f.*
Francis François *m.*
frankly franchement
Frederick Frédéric
free libre
French français; **French class** classe de français *f.*
Friday vendredi *m.*
friend ami *m.,* amie *f.;* **a close friend** un ami intime
frightened effrayé; **become frightened** s'effrayer (*irr. sp.* C)
frigidaire réfrigérateur *m.;* frigidaire *m.*
from de; **keep from** empêcher (+ *person* + de + *inf.*)
front: in front of devant
fruit fruit *m.*
full plein
fun: make fun of se moquer (de + *n.*)
funny amusant
fur fourrure *f.*
furious furieux (*f.* furieuse)

Irregular verbs are conjugated on pp. 284–301.

G

gain gagner; **gain ground** avancer (*irr. sp.* **A**)
game match *m.*, partie *f.;* **a football game** une partie de football, un match de football
garden jardin *m.*
general général *m.*
generous généreux (*f.* généreuse)
George Georges
German (*adj.*) allemand
Germany Allemagne *f.*
get (pp. 70–71) chercher; recevoir; prendre; faire; avoir; obtenir; atteindre; **get along** se débrouiller; **get angry** se fâcher; **get married** se marier; **get out of** sortir de; **get tired** se fatiguer; **get up** se lever (*irr. sp.* **D**); **it got warm** il a fait chaud
gift cadeau *m.;* **give a gift** faire un cadeau
girl jeune fille *f.*
give donner; consacrer; **give a lecture** faire une conférence
glad content, heureux (*f.* heureuse)
glance regard *m.*
go (pp. 81–82, 246) aller (allant, allé, je vais, j'allai); **go and see** aller voir; **go away** partir (2), s'en aller; **go back** retourner; **go by** passer; **go down** descendre; **go for a walk** aller se promener; **go out** sortir (2); **go to bed** se coucher; **go through** passer par; **go up** monter; remonter
going: easy going indulgent
golf golf *m.*
good (*n.*) bon *m.;* bien *m.* (*adj.*) bon; (*well-behaved*) sage; **good looks** beauté *f.;* **have a good time** s'amuser
goodbye au revoir
grandchild petit-fils *m.;* petite-fille *f.;* petits-enfants *m.* or *f. pl.*
grandmother grand-mère *f.*
grandparents grands-parents *m. pl.*
grave grave
great grand; **a great deal** beaucoup; **a great many** beaucoup
Greece Grèce *f.*
green vert
ground: gain ground avancer (*irr. sp.* **A**)
group groupe *m.*

H

hair cheveux *m. pl.*
hairdresser coiffeur *m.;* coiffeuse *f.*
half (*n.*) moitié *f.* (*adj.*) demi; **a half hour** une demi-heure
hall: city hall hôtel de ville *m.*, mairie *f.*
hand main *f.* **shake hands** se serrer la main
hand in remettre (*conj. like* mettre)
happen (pp. 82–84) se passer; arriver; se trouver; **it happened to me** cela m'est arrivé
happiness bonheur *m.*
happy heureux, content; **Happy New Year** Bonne Année, une Bonne Nouvelle Année
hard (*adj.*) dur; difficile
hard (*adv.*) dur
hateful méchant
have avoir (ayant, eu, j'ai, j'eus); (pp. 193–196, 201–205) (*causative*) faire (+ *inf.*) **have dinner** dîner; **have lunch** déjeuner; **have to** devoir, falloir, être obligé de
head tête *f.*
headache mal de tête *m.;* **have a headache** avoir mal à la tête
hear (p. 84) entendre; **hear of** entendre parler de; **hear that** entendre dire que
heartily de bon cœur
heaven ciel *m.*
heavy lourd
hell enfer *m.*
help aider (*person* + à + *inf.*)
her (*direct obj.*) la; (*indirect obj.*) lui; (*with prep.*) elle; (*adj.*) son, sa, ses
here ici; **here is, here are** voici
hero *héros *m.*
hesitate hésiter
high élevé; *haut
him (*direct obj.*) le; (*indirect obj.*) lui; (*with prep.*) lui
hire engager (*irr. sp.* **B**)
his (*adj.*) son, sa, ses; (*pron.*) le sien, la sienne, etc.
history histoire *f.*
hold tenir (tenant, tenu, je tiens, je tins); avoir lieu
home maison *f.;* **at home** chez soi; chez nous; **be home** être chez soi; **come**

Verbs with spelling changes are explained on pp. 302–304.

back home rentrer; **return home** rentrer
homework devoir *m.*
honor honneur *m.*
hope espérer (+ *inf.*) (*irr. sp.* E)
horseback: go horsebackriding faire du cheval, faire une promenade à cheval
hostile hostile
hotel hôtel *m.*
hour heure *f.;* **a half hour** une demi- heure
house maison *f.;* **at your house** chez vous
housework ménage *m.*
how comment; **how often** tous les combien; **know how to do something** (p. 95) savoir faire quelque chose
however cependant, pourtant; si (+ *adj.*); **however rich he is (may be)** si riche qu'il soit; **however that may be** quoi qu'il en soit
humble humble
hundred (*n.*) centaine *f.;* (*adj.*) cent
hurry se dépêcher (de + *inf.*)
hurt (*v.*) faire mal (à + *person*); **hurt oneself** se faire mal; (*adj.*) vexé
husband mari *m.*
hypothesis hypothèse *f.*

information information *f.;* renseignements *m. pl.*
inquire se renseigner
inspect inspecter
instead of (p. 244) au lieu de
insult insulte *f.*
intelligence intelligence *f.*
intelligent intelligent
intend (pp. 293–294) avoir l'intention de; compter (+ *inf.*); penser (+ *inf.*)
interest (*v.*) intéresser; s'intéresser (à + *n.*); (*n.*) intérêt *m.;* **take an interest in** s'intéresser (à + *n.*)
interested: become interested in s'intéresser (à + *n.*)
interesting intéressant
interior intérieur *m.*
interrupt interrompre
into dans; en
introduce (p. 94) présenter
invite inviter (à + *inf.*)
is est
isn't it? n'est-ce pas?
it (*subject*) il; elle; ce; ça; (*direct obj.*) le, la
Italian (*n.*) Italien *m.* (*adj.*) italien (*f.* italienne)
Italy Italie *f.*

I

I je; moi
ice glace *f.;* **ice cream** glace *f.;* **ice water** eau glacée
idea idée *f.*
if si
illness maladie *f.*
illustrated illustré
imagine imaginer
immediately immédiatement
import importer
important important
impression impression *f.*
in (pp. 213–215, 242–243) dans; en; à; de; **eight in the evening** huit heures du soir; **in that manner** de cette façon; **in the theater** au théâtre; **in two hours** dans deux heures; en deux heures
in spite of (p. 244) malgré
indifference indifférence *f.*

J

Jack Jacques
Japan Japon *m.*
Japanese japonais
job (p. 171) place *f.;* travail *m.;* position *f.;* situation *f.*
Johnnie Jeannot
joy joie *f.*
July juillet *m.*
June juin *m.*
just juste; **I have just done something** je viens de faire quelque chose

K

keep garder; **keep from** empêcher (*n.* + de + *inf.*)
kilometer kilomètre *m.* (⅝ of a mile)
kind aimable

Irregular verbs are conjugated on pp. 284–301.

kindness bonté *f.*
king roi *m.*
knife couteau *m.*
knock frapper; **there was a knock** (p. 94) on a frappé
know (pp. 94–95) (*something*) savoir (sachant, su, je sais, je sus); (*be acquainted with someone or something*) connaître (connaissant, connu, je connais, je connus); **know how to** savoir (+ *inf.*)

L

laboratory laboratoire *m.*
lack (pp. 107–108) manquer (de + *n.*)
ladder échelle *f.*
lady dame *f.; * femme *f.*
lake lac *m.*
language langue *f.*
large grand
last dernier (*f.* dernière); **last evening** hier soir; **last night** (p. 108) cette nuit; la nuit dernière
late (pp. 108–109) (*not early*) tard; (*not on time*) en retard
latter: the latter celui-ci; ce dernier
laugh (*v.*) rire (riant, ri, je ris, je ris) (de + *n.*); **laugh at** rire de, se moquer de; (*n.*) rire *m.*
Laura Laure
lawyer avocat *m.*
lazy paresseux (*f.* paresseuse)
learn apprendre (*conj. like* prendre)
leather cuir *m.*
leave (pp. 109–110) (*something somewhere*) laisser; (*a place*) quitter; partir (de + *n.*) (2); sortir (de + *n.*) (2); **leave me alone** laissez-moi tranquille
lecture conférence *f.*
leg jambe *f.*
lend prêter
length longueur *f.; * **at length** longuement
lesson leçon *f.*
letter lettre *f.*
library bibliothèque *f.*
lieutenant lieutenant *m.*
life vie *f.*
light lumière *f.*
like (*v.*) aimer; vouloir; (*prep.*) comme

lip lèvre *f.*
listen écouter; **listen to** écouter (+ *n.*)
little (*adj.*) petit; (*adv.*) (p. 124) peu; un peu
live (p. 124) habiter (+ *n.* or, à + *n.*, or, dans + *n.*); vivre (vivant, vécu, je vis, je vécus)
living room salle de séjour *f.; * salon *m.*
London Londres *m.*
long (p. 125) long (*f.* longue); **a long time** longtemps; **as long as** tant que; **how long** depuis quand, depuis combien de temps; combien de temps, pendant combien de temps
longer: no . . . longer ne . . . plus
look regarder; **look after** s'occuper (de + *n.*); **look at** regarder (+ *n.*); **look for** chercher (+ *n.*); **look well on someone** aller bien à quelqu'un
looking: good looking joli;beau
looks: good looks beauté *f.*
lose perdre
lot: a lot beaucoup
loud fort
Louvre Louvre *m.*
love aimer
luck chance *f.*
lunch déjeuner *m.; * **have lunch** déjeuner
Lyons Lyon

M

machine machine *f.*
magazine revue *f.; * magazine *m.*
mail mettre à la poste
main principal
majority plupart *f.; * majorité *f.*
make faire (faisant, fait, je fais, je fis); **make** + *adj.* (p. 126) rendre + *adj.; * **make fun of** se moquer de; **make a trip** faire un voyage
man homme *m.; * **businessman** homme d'affaires; **young man** jeune homme (*pl.* jeunes gens)
many beaucoup; **a great many** beaucoup; énormément, des tas de; **many times** bien des fois
March mars *m.*
Mark Marc
marriage mariage *m.*

Verbs with spelling changes are explained on pp. 302–304.

married marié; **get married** se marier
marry (p. 135) épouser; se marier avec;
marier (quelqu'un à quelqu'un)
marvelous superbe; merveilleux (*f.* merveilleuse)
master maître *m.*
mathematics mathématiques *f. pl.*
matter: what is the matter with me ce que j'ai
mayor maire *m.*
me me, moi
meager maigre
meal repas *m.*
mean vouloir dire; signifier
meet (p. 95) (*by appointment*) retrouver; (*by chance*) rencontrer; (*make the acquaintance of*) faire la connaissance de, connaître
meeting réunion *f.*
mention mentionner
Mexico Mexique *m.*
Michael Michel
midnight minuit *m.*
military militaire
milk lait *m.*
milliner modiste *f.*
mind esprit *m.;* **change one's mind** changer d'avis
mine le mien, la mienne, etc.; à moi
minute minute *f.*
miss (pp. 135–136) manquer; regretter
mission mission *f.*
mistake faute *f.;* erreur *f.*
mistaken: be mistaken se tromper
model mannequin *m.*
modern moderne
money argent *m.*
monster monstre *m.*
month mois *m.*
moon lune *f.*
more (p. 136) plus; **more and more** de plus en plus; **the more . . . the more** plus . . . plus; **no longer** ne . . . plus; **not any more** ne . . . plus
morning (pp. 40–41) matin *m.;* matinée *f.;* **the next morning** le lendemain matin, le matin suivant; **yesterday morning** hier matin
most plus; le plus
mother mère *f.*
mother-in-law belle-mère *f.*

motorcycle motocyclette *f.*, moto *f.;* **on a motorcycle** en moto
mountain montagne *f.*
mouth bouche *f.*
move bouger (*irr. sp.* **B**); remuer; (*change dwellings*) déménager (*irr. sp.* **B**)
movie cinéma *m.;* film *m.;* **movies** cinéma *m.*
much beaucoup; **so much** tellement; tant; **very much** (p. 229) beaucoup
music musique *f.*
musical musicien (*f.* musicienne)
must (pp. 201-205) devoir (devant, dû, je dois, je dus) (+ *inf.*); falloir (—, fallu, il faut, il fallut) (+ *inf.*); être obligé (de + *inf.*)
my mon, ma, mes

N

native natal; (*language*) maternel (*f.* maternelle)
natural naturel (*f.* naturelle)
nature nature *f.*
near près de, à côté de
necessary nécessaire; **it is necessary** il faut
necklace collier *f.*
need (*v.*) avoir besoin de; (*n.*) besoin *m.*
neighbor voisin *m.;* (*biblical sense*) prochain *m.*
neither . . . nor ni . . . ni
nervous nerveux (*f.* nerveuse)
never jamais; ne . . . jamais
new nouveau (*before vowel sound* nouvel; *f.* nouvelle)
news nouvelles *f. pl.;* **piece of news** nouvelle *f.*
newspaper journal *m.*
next (p. 137) prochain; suivant; **the next morning** le lendemain matin, le matin suivant
nice (*of persons*) gentil; (*of things*) joli; beau; **he is nice to us** il est gentil avec nous; **it is nice of him** c'est gentil de sa part
night nuit *f.*
nine neuf
no (*adj.*) aucun; ne . . . aucun; **no longer** ne . . . plus; **no more** ne . . . plus; (*adv.*) non

Irregular verbs are conjugated on pp. 284–301.

no one personne; ne . . . personne
noise bruit *m.*
noon midi *m.*
not ne . . . pas; **not any** pas de
nothing rien; ne . . . rien
notice (pp. 154–155) remarquer; voir; s'apercevoir (*conj. like* recevoir)
novel roman *m.*
now maintenant; **up to now** jusqu'à présent
number nombre *m.; (street, telephone)* numéro *m.*
numerous nombreux (*f.* nombreuse); beaucoup de
nylon nylon *m.*

O

obey obéir (à + *person*)
obliged obligé (de + *inf.*)
observe observer
o'clock heure *f.*
of de; **both of you** vous deux
office bureau *m.; (doctor's)* cabinet *m.*
often souvent; **how often** tous les combien
old vieux (*before vowel sound* vieil; *f.* vieille); âgé; **I was four years old** j'avais quatre ans
old age vieillesse *f.;* vieux jours *m. pl.*
oldest brother aîné *m.;* frère aîné
Oliver Olivier
on sur; dans; en; pour; à; **on the condition** à (la) condition; **on foot** à pied; **on a motorcycle** en moto; **on Saturdays** le samedi; **on the telephone** au téléphone; **on the way** en route; **try on** essayer (*irr. sp.* C)
once une fois; **at once** de suite; tout de suite
one un; on; **the one** celui qui; **no one** ne . . . personne
only seulement, ne . . . que
open (*v.*) ouvrir (ouvrant, ouvert, j'ouvre, j'ouvris); (*adj.*) ouvert
operation opération *f.*
opinion opinion *f.;* avis *m.*
opportunity (p. 155) occasion *f.;* possibilité *f.*
optimistic optimiste
or ou

orange orange *f.*
order (*v.*) ordonner; (*meal*) commander; (*prep.*); **in order to** pour
other autre; **each other** se; l'un l'autre; **every other year** tous les deux ans; **others** (*pron.*) les autres
out (pp. 254–255) dehors; **fall out** tomber de; **go out** sortir (2); **one out of three** un sur trois; **out of** hors de; **out of money** sans argent
overtake rattraper

P

package colis *m.*
page page *f.*
paint peindre (peignant, peint, je peins, je peignis)
painter *m.* peintre
painting tableau *m.;* peinture *f.*
paper (pp. 155–156) papier *m.;* copie *f.;* composition *f.; (newspaper)* journal *m.*
parade défilé *m.*
pardon pardon *m.;* **he asked my pardon** il m'a demandé pardon
parent parent *m.*
part partie *f.; (in a play)* rôle *m.*
party soirée *f.*
pass passer; **pass an examination** réussir à un examen
past passé *m.*
patient patient
pay (*v.*) payer (*irr. sp.* **A**); (*n.*) salaire *m.;* paie *f.*
peace paix *f.;* **in peace** en paix; **Peace Street** rue de la Paix
peaceful tranquille, calme, paisible
pen plume *f.;* **fountain pen** stylo *m.*
pencil crayon *m.*
people (pp. 156–157) gens *m. pl.;* on; personnes *f. pl.; (nation)* peuple *m.;* **those fine people** ces braves gens; **young people** jeunes gens *m. pl.*
per par
percent pour-cent *m.*
perfume parfum *m.*
perhaps peut-être
permit permettre (*conj. like* mettre) (à + *person* + de + *inf.*)
permission permission *f.*

Verbs with spelling changes are explained on pp. 302–304.

person personne *f.*
piano piano *m.;* **play the piano** jouer du piano
pick up ramasser; cueillir
picture tableau *m.;* peinture *f.*
picturesque pittoresque
piece (pp. 169–170) morceau *m.;* bout *m.;* (*of advice*) conseil *m.;* (*of paper*) feuille *f.*
pilot pilote *m.*
place (pp. 170–171) endroit *m.;* lieu *m.;* place *f.;* espace *m.;* **at their place** chez eux
plain: in plain daylight en plein jour
plant plante *f.*
play (*v.*) jouer (de + *instrument;* à + *game*); (*n.*) pièce *f.*
pleasant agréable
please plaire (plaisant, plu, je plais, je plus) (à + *person*); faire plaisir à; s'il vous plaît
pleasure plaisir *m.*
pocket poche *f.*
poetry poésie *f.*
point point *m.*
poker poker *m.*
Poland Pologne *f.*
police police *f.*
policeman agent *m.;* agent de police *m.;* policier *m.*
polite poli
politics politique *f. sing.*
poor pauvre
popular populaire
portrait portrait *m.*
Portugal Portugal *m.*
Portuguese portugais
position place *f.;* position *f.;* situation *f.*
possible possible
postcard carte postale *f.*
powerful puissant
practice pratique *f.*
preach prêcher
prefer préférer (*irr. sp.* **E**); aimer mieux
prepare préparer
present (*time*) présent *m.;* (*gift*) cadeau *m.*
president président *m.*
pressed together serré
pretty joli
prince prince *m.*

prison prison *f.*
prize prix *m.*
probable probable
probably probablement
problem problème *m.*
prodigy prodige *m.*
product produit *m.*
professor professeur *m.*
program programme *m.*
progress progrès *m.;* **make progress** faire des progrès
promise promettre (*conj. like* mettre) (à + *person* + de + *inf.*)
proud fier (*f.* fière)
prove prouver
provided that pourvu que (+ *subjunc.*)
public publique
publish publier
publisher éditeur *m.*
punish punir
pupil élève *m. or f.*
purple mauve
purse sac *m.*
put mettre (mettant, mis, je mets, je mis); **put down** baisser; **put on** mettre
puzzle: crossword puzzle les mots croisés *m. pl.*
Pyrenees Pyrénées *f. pl.*

Q

quality qualité *f.*
question (*v.*) questionner; interroger (*irr. sp.* **B**); (*n.*) question *f.;* **ask a question** poser une question
quickly vite
quiet tranquille, calme

R

radio radio *f.*
rain (*v.*) pleuvoir (pleuvant, plu, il pleut, il plut); (*n.*) la pluie
raise (*v.*) lever (*irr. sp.* **D**); (*n.*) augmentation *f.*
rapidly vite; rapidement
rare rare
rarely rarement

Irregular verbs are conjugated on pp. 284–301.

rather (pp. 171–172) plutôt; plutôt que de; assez; aimer mieux; au lieu de
read lire (lisant, lu, je lis, je lus)
real vrai
really vraiment
reason (p. 172) raison *f.;* **the reason for** la raison de; **the reason that** la raison pour laquelle
reassure rassurer
reassured rassuré
receive recevoir (recevant, reçu, je reçois, je reçus)
recently récemment
reception réception *f.*
recognize reconnaître (*conj. like* connaître)
recommend recommander
recommendation recommandation *f.*
record disque *m.*
red rouge
refuse refuser (de + *inf.*)
regret (*v.*) regretter; (*n.*) regret *m.*
relate raconter
relative parent *m.*
religion religion *f.*
remain rester
remarkable remarquable
remember se souvenir (*conj. like* venir) (de + *n.;* de + *inf.*); se rappeler (*irr. sp.* **F**) (+ *n.*)
repair réparer
repent se repentir (2)
reply (*v.*) répondre (à + *n.*); (*n.*) réponse *f.*
Republic République *f.*
require exiger (*irr. sp.* **B**)
resemble ressembler (à + *n.*)
reserve réserver, louer
resignation démission *f.*
resist résister (à + *n.*)
rest se reposer
restaurant restaurant *m.*
restful reposant
result résultat *m.*
résumé résumé *m.*
retirement retraite *f.*
return (*v.*) (pp. 182–183) (*come back*) revenir (*conj. like* venir); (*go back*) retourner; (*go back home*) rentrer; (*give back*) rendre; (*n.*) retour *m.*
reward récompenser

Rhone Rhône *m.*
rich riche
ridiculous ridicule
riding: go horseback riding faire du cheval, faire une promenade à cheval
right bon; juste; **right away** tout de suite; **be right** avoir raison
ring (*v.*) sonner; (*n.*) bague *f.*
river fleuve *m.;* rivière *f.*
Riviera Côte d'Azur *f.*
road route *f.;* chemin *m.;* **go along the road** suivre la route (le chemin)
roast rôti *m.*
roasted rôti
room (pp. 183–184) (*in general*) pièce *f.;* (*bedroom*) chambre *f.;* (*room for meetings*) salle *f.;* (*living room*) salle de séjour *f.;* salon *m.;* (*space*) place *f.*
rose rose *f.*
row rang *m.*
rub frotter
rule règle *f.*
rummage around fouiller
run courir (courant, couru, je cours, je courus); **run across** traverser en courant
rush se précipiter
Russia Russie *f.*
Russian russe

S

sad triste
salesman vendeur *m.;* représentant *m.*
same même; **all the same** quand même
sample échantillon *m.*
sandwich sandwich *m.*
satisfied content; satisfait
Saturday samedi *m.*
save (pp. 184–185) sauver; économiser; faire des économies; garder; mettre de côté
say dire (disant, dit, je dis, je dis) (à + *person* + de + *inf.*)
scarcely à peine
scarf écharpe *f.*
school école *f.*
scientific scientifique
scientist savant *m.*
season saison *f.*

Verbs with spelling changes are explained on pp. 302–304.

secretary secrétaire *m. or f.*
see voir (voyant, vu, je vois, je vis);
  come and see me venez me voir
seem sembler (+ *inf.*); paraître (*conj.*
  like connaître) (+ *inf.*); avoir l'air
  (+ *adj.; de* + *inf.*)
sell vendre
senator sénateur
send envoyer (envoyant, envoyé, j'envoie, j'envoyai)
sentence phrase *f.*
separate séparer
serious sérieux (*f.* sérieuse)
servant serviteur *m.;* domestique *m.*
serve servir (2)
service service *m.*
set (*v.*) (*the sun*) se coucher; (*n.*) (*television*) télévision *f.*
seven sept
several plusieurs
shake secouer; serrer; **shake hands** se
  serrer la main
sheet drap *m.*
shirt chemise *f.*
short court; **short story** conte *m.*
shortcoming défaut *m.*
should (p. 204) devrais, devrait, etc.
  conditional form of verb
shoulder épaule *f.*
show montrer
shrug hausser; **shrug one's shoulders**
  hausser les épaules
shut fermer
sick malade
sight vue *f.;* **catch sight of** apercevoir
  (*conj. like* recevoir) (+ *n.*)
silk soie *f.*
silly bête; sot (*f.* sotte)
silverware argenterie *f.*
since (pp. 113, 235–236) puisque;
  comme; depuis que; depuis
single seul
sister sœur *f.*
sit, sit down (p. 185) s'asseoir (s'asseyant, assis, je m'assieds, je m'assis)
  (*imperative*) asseyez-vous; **sitting** assis
situate situer
situation situation *f.*
six six
sixteen seize
skin peau *f.*

sleep dormir (2)
sleepy: be sleepy avoir sommeil
slight léger (*f.* légère)
slightest moindre
slow down ralentir
small petit
smile sourire *m.*
smoke (*v.*) fumer; (*n.*) fumée *f.*
snapshot photo *f.;* photographie *f.*
snow (*v.*) neiger; (*irr. sp.* **B**) (*n.*) neige *f.*
so si; tant; tellement; le; **so much** tant,
  tellement; **so that** pour que
soap savon *m.*
sofa sofa *m.;* canapé *m.*
soft doux (*f.* douce)
solve résoudre; (*pp*) résolu
soldier soldat *m.;* militaire *m.*
somber sombre
some (*adj.*) du, de la, de l', des; quelque;
  (*pron.*) quelques-uns; en
someone quelqu'un
something quelque chose; **something
  else** autre chose
sometimes quelquefois
somewhere quelque part
son fils *m.*
song chanson *f.*
soon (p. 197) tôt; bientôt; **as soon as**
  dès que
sore douloureux (*f.* douloureuse); **I have
  a sore throat** j'ai mal à la gorge
sorrow chagrin *m.;* **to my great sorrow**
  à mon vif regret
sorry désolé; **be sorry** regretter; **I'm
  sorry** pardon
sort sorte *f.*
soundly profondément
south sud *m.*
South American Sud-Américain *m.*
Spain Espagne *f.*
Spanish espagnol
speak parler
special particulier (*f.* particulière);
  spécial
specialist spécialiste *m.*
spend (p. 198) (*money*) dépenser; (*time*)
  passer
spite: in spite of (p. 244) malgré
sport sport *m.*
spring printemps *m.*
square place *f.*

Irregular verbs are conjugated on pp. 284–301.

stamp timbre *m.*
stand se tenir, se tenir debout; (*bear*) supporter
state état *m.*
station gare *f.*
stay rester
step (*course of action*) démarche *f.*
still encore
stocking bas *m.*
stop (pp. 198–199) cesser (de + *inf.*); arrêter (+ *n.;* de + *inf.*); s'arrêter (de + *inf.*) without stopping sans arrêt
store magasin *m.*
storm orage *m.*
story histoire *f.;* detective story roman policier *m.;* short story conte *m.*
strange étrange; curieux (*f.* curieuse)
stranger étranger *m.*
street rue *f.;* on the street dans la rue
stretch étendre; stretched out tendu; étendu
strong fort
stubborn entêté, têtu
student (*college*) étudiant *m.*, étudiante *f.;* (*grade and high school*) élève *m. or f.*
study (*v.*) travailler; étudier; (*n.*) étude *f.*
succeed réussir (à + *inf.*)
such (p. 199) tel (*f.* telle); aussi; comme ça; pareil (*f.* pareille)
suddenly soudain; tout à coup; tout d'un coup
suffer souffrir (*conj. like* ouvrir)
sugar sucre *m.*
suit costume *m.*
suitcase valise *f.*
sum somme *f.;* somme d'argent *f.*
summer été *m.*
sun soleil *m.;* there is sun il fait du soleil, il y a du soleil; the sun set le soleil s'est couché
Sunday dimanche *m.*
sunlight soleil *m.*
surprise étonner
surprised étonné
surprising étonnant
Susan Suzanne
suspect suspect *m.*
Sweden Suède *f.*
swim nager (*irr. sp.* B)

T

table table *f.*
take (pp. 207–208) prendre (prenant, pris, je prends, je pris); mener (*irr. sp.* D); emmener (*irr. sp.* D); amener (*irr. sp.* D); apporter; (= *subscribe to*) s'abonner à, être abonné à; take a course suivre un cours; take an interest in s'intéresser (à + *n.*); take a walk se promener (*irr. sp.* D), faire une promenade
talent talent *m.*
talk (*v.*) parler; (*n.*) causerie *f.;* give a talk faire une causerie
taxi taxi *m.*
tea thé *m.*
teach (p. 209) enseigner; apprendre (*conj. like* prendre)
teacher professeur *m.;* maître *m.*
team équipe *f.*
telephone (*v.*) téléphoner (à + *person*); (*n.*) téléphone *m.;* telephone book annuaire *m.;* telephone number numéro de téléphone
television télévision *f.;* television set télévision *f.*
tell dire (disant, dit, je dis, je dis) (à + *person* + de + *inf.*); raconter
ten dix
tender tendre
terrible terrible
than que; (*before numerals*) de
thank remercier (de *or* pour + *thing;* de + *inf.*)
that (*conjunc.*) que; so that pour que; (*demonstrative*) ce, cet, cette, ces; celui, etc.; cela; (*relative*) qui; que
the le, la, l', les
theater théâtre *m.;* in the theater au théâtre
their leur
then ensuite, puis; alors
theory théorie *f.*
there y; là; from there en; de là; there is, there are il y a; voilà
these ces
they ils; on; eux
thief voleur *m.*
thing chose *f.*
think penser (à + *n.*); croire (croyant, cru, je crois, je crus)

Verbs with spelling changes are explained on pp. 302–304.

third troisième
thirty trente
this ce, cet, cette
though bien que, quoique; **even though** quoique; bien que; tout en (+ *pres. participle*)
thought pensée *f.*
three trois
throat gorge *f.;* **I have a sore throat** j'ai mal à la gorge
through par; **go through** passer par; parcourir (*conj. like* écrire)
Thursday jeudi *m.*
tie cravate *f.*
time (pp. 209–211) temps *m.;* fois *f.;* heure *f.;* époque *f.;* moment *m.;* **by the time** quand; **for a long time** longtemps; **from time to time** de temps en temps; **have a good time** s'amuser, s'amuser bien; **many times** bien des fois; **on time** à l'heure
tired fatigué
title titre *m.*
to à; chez; dans; en
today aujourd'hui
together ensemble; **pressed together** serré
tomorrow demain
too trop
tool outil *m.*
top sommet *m.*
tourist touriste *m.*
tournament tournoi *m.*
toward (p. 245) vers; envers
town ville *f.*
toy jouet *m.*
train train *m.;* **by train** en train, par le train
translate traduire (*conj. like* conduire)
travel (*v.*) voyager (*irr. sp.* **B**) (p. 214); **travel across** traverser; (*n.*) voyage *m.*
traveller voyageur *m.*
trip voyage *m.;* **take a trip** faire un voyage
troop troupe *f.*
trouble histoire *f.;* ennuis *m. pl.*
true vrai
truly vraiment
truth vérité *f.*
try essayer (*irr. sp.* **C**) (de + *inf.*); chercher (à + *inf.*); **try on** essayer

turn around se retourner
twelve douze
twenty vingt
twice deux fois
twist tordre
two deux

U

ugly vilain
unbearable insupportable
under (pp. 245–246) sous; au-dessous de
understand comprendre (*conj. like* prendre)
uneasiness malaise *m.*
unfortunately malheureusement
United States États-Unis *m. pl.*
university université *f.*
unless à moins que (+ *subjunc.*)
until (p. 236) (*conjunc.*) jusqu'à ce que (+ *subjunc.*); (*prep.*) jusqu'à
up (p. 26) dessus; sur; en haut; **go up** remonter; monter; **up to now** jusqu'à présent
use se servir (de + *n.*); employer (*irr. sp.* **C**); **used to** (pp. 88–89) *a form of the imperfect tense*
useful utile
useless inutile

V

vacation vacances *f. pl.*
valuable précieux (*f.* précieuse); de prix; de valeur
vase vase *m.*
very très; **very much** (p. 229) beaucoup beaucoup; énormément, un tas de; des tas de
village village *m.*
violin violon *m.*
visit (pp. 230–231) (*a place*) visiter; (*a person*) aller voir; rendre visite à; faire une visite à
visitor visiteur *m.*
voice voix *f.*

W

wait attendre; **wait for** attendre (+ *n.*)
wake up réveiller; se réveiller
walk (*v.*) marcher; se promener (*irr. sp.* **D**); (*n.*) promenade *f.;* **go for a walk,**

Irregular verbs are conjugated on pp. 284–301.

take a walk aller se promener, faire une promenade, se promener (*irr. sp.* D)

want vouloir (voulant, voulu, je veux, je voulus) (+ *inf.*)

war guerre *f.*

warm chaud; be warm avoir chaud

wash laver; wash the dishes faire la vaisselle

waste gaspiller

watch (*v.*) regarder, observer; surveiller; (*n.*) montre *f.*

water eau *f;* ice water eau glacée

way route *f.;* manière *f.*, façon *f.;* continue on our way continuer notre route; in that way de cette façon; on the way en route

wear porter

weather temps *m.;* it is good weather il fait beau

week semaine *f.*

weekend week-end *m.*

well bien; well known connu, célèbre; bien connu

what (*interrog.*) qu'est-ce qui; que, qu'est-ce que; quoi; quel, quelle; comment; (*relative*) ce qui; ce que

whatever quoi que; quel que (*f.* quelle que)

when (p. 133) quand; où

where où

wherever où . . . que (+ *subjunc.*)

whether si

which (*interrog.*) quel, quelle; lequel, laquelle; (*rel.*) qui; que; lequel; quoi

while (pp. 65, 227) (*at the same time*) pendant que; (*whereas*) tandis que; a little while ago tout à l'heure; all the while tout en (+ *pres. participle*)

white blanc (*f.* blanche)

who (*interrog.*) qui; (*rel.*) qui; que

whoever qui que; quel que; whoever he is (may be) qui que ce soit; quel qu'il soit

whole tout (*m. pl.* tous)

why pourquoi

wife femme *f.*

willing: I am willing je veux bien

win gagner; remporter

window fenêtre *f.;* vitre *f.*

windowpane vitre *f.*

wine vin *m.*

winter hiver *m.*

wish (pp. 141, 231–232) vouloir (voulant, voulu, je veux, je voulu) (+ *inf.*); désirer (+ *inf.*); souhaiter

with (pp. 246-247) avec; sur; de; chez

without sans; do without se passer de

woman femme *f.;* cleaning woman femme de ménage *f.*

wonder se demander

won't ne pas vouloir (+ *inf.*)

wood bois *m.*

word mot *m.* (*spoken word*) parole *f.*

work (*v.*) travailler; (*n.*) travail *m.;* out of work sans travail

workman ouvrier *m.;* travailleur *m.*

world monde *m.*

worried inquiet (*f.* inquiète)

worry inquiéter; s'inquiéter (*irr. sp.* E)

would (pp. 88–89, 120, 122, 248) vouloir; *as auxiliary verb: (in conditional) conditional of main verb; (= used to) imperfect of main verb*

write écrire (écrivant, écrit, j'écris j'écrivis)

writer écrivain *m.*

wrong faux (*f.* fausse); be wrong avoir tort; do wrong faire du tort

Y

yawn bailler

year (p. 249) an *m.;* année *f.;* Happy New Year Bonne Année, Bonne Nouvelle Année; I was ten years old j'avais dix ans; twice a year deux fois par an; every year tous les ans; youthful years années de jeunesse *f. pl.*

yes (pp. 249–250) oui; si

yesterday hier; yesterday evening hier soir; yesterday morning hier matin

you tu; vous; both of you vous deux

young jeune

young men (p. 250) jeunes gens *m. pl.*

your votre, vos

yours le vôtre, la vôtre, etc.

yourself vous-même

youthful jeune; youthful years années de jeunesse *f. pl.*

Verbs with spelling changes are explained on pp. 302–304.

Index

References are to pages [ex. 157] and, in the *Textes*, to pages and notes [ex. 276 (12)].

Problem words are normally indexed only under their English meaning.